Anthropology and Expei
the Asylum Courts

Although asylum has generated unparalleled levels of public and political concern over the past decade, there has been astonishingly little field research on the topic. *Anthropology and Expertise in the Asylum Courts* is a study of the legal process of claiming asylum from an anthropological perspective, focusing on the role of expert evidence from 'country experts' such as anthropologists. It describes how such evidence is used in assessments of asylum claims by the Home Office and by immigration judges and tribunals hearing asylum appeals. It compares uses of social scientific and medical evidence in legal decision making and analyses anthropologically the legal uses of key concepts from the 1951 Refugee Convention, such as 'race', 'religion', and 'social group'. Material is drawn from field observation of more than 300 appeal hearings in London and Glasgow; from reported case law; and from interviews with immigration judges, tribunal chairs, barristers and solicitors, as well as expert witnesses.

Anthony Good is Professor of Social Anthropology in Practice at Edinburgh University. His current research on asylum arises out of wide experience as an expert witness in asylum cases. His prior research concerned Hinduism, kinship, and rural development in South India and Sri Lanka, where he formerly taught Physical Chemistry at Peradeniya University. Previous books include *Research Practices in the Study of Kinship* (1984; with Alan Barnard), *The Female Bridegroom* (1992), and *The Ceremonial Economy of a Royal South Indian Temple* (2004).

Anthropology and Expertise in the Asylum Courts

Anthony Good

Routledge·Cavendish
Taylor & Francis Group
a GlassHouse book

First published 2007 by Routledge-Cavendish
2 Park Square, Milton Park, Abingdon, Oxon OX14 4RN

Simultaneously published in the USA and Canada
by Routledge-Cavendish
270 Madison Ave, New York, NY 10016

A Glasshouse book

*Routledge-Cavendish is an imprint of the Taylor & Francis Group, an
informa business*

© 2007 Anthony Good

Typeset in Times New Roman by RefineCatch Limited, Bungay,
Suffolk
Printed and bound in Great Britain by
TJ International, Padstow, Cornwall

British Library Cataloguing in Publication Data
A catalogue record for this book is available from the British Library

Library of Congress Cataloging in Publication Data
A catalog record for this book has been requested

ISBN10: 1-904385-55-9 (pbk)
ISBN10: 1-904385-56-7 (hbk)

ISBN13: 978-1-904385-55-4 (pbk)
ISBN13: 978-1-904385-56-1 (hbk)

For Alison

Contents

Foreword

It is a pleasure to acknowledge the contributions of all those whose help and support has helped me carry through the research reported here, and salutary to notice just how numerous they are.

His Honour Judge Hubert Dunn, the then Chief Immigration Adjudicator, gave me access to Taylor House and introductions to key members of the asylum judiciary. Regional Adjudicators Mungo Deans and John Dyson were equally helpful. I benefited greatly from the unmatched institutional memory of John Housden, Deputy Regional Adjudicator at Taylor House, who also helped immeasurably during the early days of my research by introducing me to adjudicators each day. The President of the Immigration Appeal Tribunal, Mr Justice Collins, and Deputy President Mark Ockelton, discussed my research with me on several occasions. Many other tribunal chairs and adjudicators at Taylor House, Hatton Cross, and the Eagle Buildings, behaved with great helpfulness. It is invidious to name names (and my apologies to those not specifically listed here), but I must mention the particular contributions of Spencer Batiste, Nihar Bird, Harriet Coleman, Michael Curzon Lewis, Gordon Denson, Catriona Jarvis, Andrew Jordan, Ilyas Khan, James Latter, Chris Mather, Alistair McGeachy, Frank Pieri, Francis Pinkerton, Michael Rapinet, Jane Reid, Carol Scott-Baker, Hugo Storey, Lance Waumsley, and Rosemary Woodhouse, as well as Presenting Officer John Gulvin. In Glasgow, Hugh Welsh, Marie Cavanagh, and the other ushers, are still as friendly and helpful as ever to the students in my 'Refugees' class, who are required to visit and report on asylum hearings as a coursework exercise.

As all this indicates, I have good reason to be grateful for the openness of this wing of the judicial system, and the seriousness with which the notion of public accessibility to their proceedings is taken. This is in marked contrast, I have to say, to the opaque bureaucracy of the Home Office, into which virtually all my requests for research access disappeared without trace.

I thank Mark Henderson and Mark Symes for their collegiality in supplying unpublished writings and data, and Roger Ballard, Nathalia Berkowitz, Patrick Gilkes, Elizabeth Harris, George Joffé, Gareth Jones, David

McDowall, Werner Menski, Michael Peel, Louise Pirouet, Jonathan Spencer, and Philip Steadman for discussions, or for generously supplying expert reports and other writings. Most acted not only as informants in the research, but as advisors on and consumers of it. That was also particularly true of Sally Verity Smith and Mary Salinsky of the Medical Foundation.

The backdrop to and stimulus for this research was my activity as an expert witness in asylum appeals, and two instructing solicitors in particular became valued informants and advisors in the research. David Burgess was the first ever to instruct me as an expert, and with his colleagues at Winstanley-Burgess, was the source of most such instructions during the early years of my involvement. More recently Tony Paterson took on this mantle; he and I even visited Sri Lanka together on a human rights fact-finding visit, but that is another story . . .

I am grateful to Mark Henderson, David McDowall, Mark Ockelton, and Mary Salinsky for helpful comments on earlier drafts of particular sections, and to the two Glasshouse readers, Robert Thomas and Cynthia Keppley Mahmood, for their constructive and extremely valuable suggestions on the entire manuscript. I thank participants in the Edinburgh, LSE, SOAS, and Oxford anthropology seminars; the seminar of the Refugee Studies Centre, Oxford; the ASA's 2003 decennial conference in Manchester; the international conference on *Women and Migration in Asia* organised by the Developing Countries Research Centre, University of Delhi; the *Expert Evidence* seminar organised by the International Association of Refugee Law Judges and Immigration Law Practitioners' Association; the 2004 Edinburgh conference on *Developing the Anthropology of Law in a Transnational World*; and the 2005 conference of Public Service Interpreters at Heriot-Watt University, for their comments on material from this book. Special thanks to my Edinburgh colleagues for tolerating my incessant rants about my work, and my 'Refugees' students for helping me crystallise my ideas. Of course, the remaining failings are my own.

Fieldwork in 2001/2002 was supported by ESRC Research Grant no. R000223352. I am grateful to Blackwell Publishing Ltd for permission to use material from my papers 'Acting as an expert: anthropologists in asylum appeals', *Anthropology Today* 19(5): 3–7 (2003); and 'Undoubtedly an expert?' Country experts in the UK asylum courts', *Journal of the Royal Anthropological Institute* (NS.) 10: 113–33 (2004); and to Oxford University Press for granting similar permission regarding my article 'Expert evidence in asylum and human rights appeals: an expert's view', *International Journal of Refugee Law* 16: 358–80 (2004).

Anthony Good
February 2006

Abbreviations

ACA	Australian Court of Appeal
AIT	Asylum and Immigration Tribunal
ACPI	Advisory Panel on Country Information
APIs	*Asylum Policy Instructions* (Home Office)
ASA	Association of Social Anthropologists
BIA	Board of Immigration Appeals (United States)
CA	Court of Appeal
CADC	Court of Appeals of the District of Columbia
CG	Country Guidelines case
CIPU	Country Information and Policy Unit (UK Home Office)
CPR	Civil Procedure Rules
CSC	Canadian Supreme Court
CSIH	Court of Session, Inner House (Scotland)
CSOH	Court of Session, Outer House (Scotland)
DIMA	Department of Immigration and Multicultural Affairs (Australia)
ECHR	European Convention on Human Rights
ECtHR	European Court of Human Rights
EIN	Electronic Immigration Network
ELENA	European Legal Network on Asylum
ELR	Exceptional Leave to Remain
FCA	Federal Court of Australia
FCFCA	Full Court of Federal Court of Australia
FGM	Female Genital Mutilation
HC	High Court
HCA	High Court of Australia
HL	House of Lords
HOPO	Home Office Presenting Officer
IAA	Immigration Appellate Authority
IAB	Immigration Appeal Board (Canada)
IAS	Immigration Advisory Service
IAT	Immigration Appeal Tribunal
ICMPD	International Centre for Migration Policy Development

IDP	Internally Displaced Person
IFA	Internal Flight Alternative
ILPA	Immigration Law Practitioners' Association
ILR	Indefinite Leave to Remain
Imm AR	Immigration Appeals (journal)
IND	Immigration and Nationality Directorate
INLR	Immigration and Nationality Law Review (journal)
INS	Immigration and Naturalization Service (United States)
IO	Immigration Officer
IPKF	Indian Peace-Keeping Force
IRB	Immigration and Refugee Board (Canada)
J	Mr Justice
LJ	Lord Justice
LTTE	Liberation Tigers of Tamil Eelam
MEI	Minister of Employment and Immigration (Canada)
MF	Medical Foundation for the Care of Victims of Torture
MIEA	Minister of Immigration and Ethnic Affairs (Australia)
MIMA	Minister of Immigration and Multicultural Affairs (Australia)
NASS	National Asylum Support Service
NGO	Non-Governmental Organisation
NZCA	New Zealand Court of Appeal
Ofpra	Office français de protection des réfugiés et des apatrides
OISC	Office of the Immigration Services Commissioner
PSG	Particular Social Group
RDS	(Home Office) Research Development and Statistics Directorate
RFRL	Reasons For Refusal Letters
RLC	Refugee Legal Centre
RSAA	Refugee Status Appeals Authority (New Zealand)
RWLG	Refugee Women's Legal Group
SEF	Statement of Evidence Forms
SSHD	Secretary of State for the Home Department
UNHCR	(Office of the) United Nations High Commissioner for Refugees
USSC	United States Supreme Court

Table of cases

Table of statutes

Table of statutory instruments

Prologue: Tales of persecution

Ms X, a young Tamil woman from the Jaffna Peninsula in northern Sri Lanka, began helping the Liberation Tigers of Tamil Eelam (LTTE) because of what she saw as oppression by the Sri Lankan army. She was never involved in fighting, but participated in fund raising, cooking, first aid, and making sandbags. As a result her name was listed on an LTTE noticeboard, and when the army recaptured the area she was arrested.

She was interrogated by two soldiers, with a member of a pro-government Tamil militia group as interpreter. She stayed silent about her LTTE links, but the militia man decided she was lying. After he left, the soldiers attacked her with a belt and rifle, then stripped and raped her. Next day the same three people questioned her. She was again stripped and raped by both soldiers, who ordered her not to dress, and interrogated her naked. That evening the soldiers returned in a drunken state; they burned her legs with cigarettes and cigarette lighters, then both raped her again.

One day she was raped by the militia man; on another, the soldiers cut her wrists with a knife. She was forced to perform oral and anal sex with both soldiers. They shaved her pubic hair and burned their initials on her pubic area and inner thigh. On another day she was punched in the mouth and hit with a rifle butt, losing several teeth. She has scars consistent with all these attacks. Finally the camp came under LTTE attack, and in the confusion she escaped. She was helped to leave the country, and claimed asylum in the United Kingdom.

*　　*　　*　　*

While Mr Y, another Jaffna Tamil, was still a child in the 1970s, he was assaulted by police after a riot, and taken unconscious to hospital. Later, after friends involved in a separatist group were shot, he believed the authorities were seeking him too, so he changed his name. He was too frightened to take up his university place; instead he joined an NGO providing housing for Tamils displaced from other parts of Sri Lanka. The organisation's officials were arrested in 1983, then he too was arrested along with a friend who proved to belong to a militant group. Because the friend had an unloaded gun, the police opened fire, hitting Mr Y in the thigh. The bullet could not be removed and the wound became infected. In hospital he was tortured with needles, and his companion was tortured to death.

He was repeatedly tortured and questioned about terrorist links. He denied these but was forced to sign a confession. He was subjected to a mock execution in which he was shot in the hand, arm, and shoulder. In another mock execution, he was shot in the thigh and his leg was broken with a rifle butt. In a third incident he was shot through the head, yet survived. He was forced into a further confession. He could not sign because of his injuries, so marked it with a thumbprint. He escaped, but was caught and his leg was rebroken. Assaults continued after he was transferred to a prison where many Tamils had been murdered by staff and Sinhalese prisoners during the 1983 riots a few weeks earlier. He was later transferred to Batticaloa, suffering assaults en route. Soon afterwards many prisoners escaped, carrying Mr Y with them as he could not walk.

He gradually made his way via Jaffna to India, where he got hospital treatment. With some reluctance he joined P (an anti-government militant group based in India), who required him to design weapons. However, P was riven by internal feuds and murders, so he escaped to another part of Tamil Nadu. He returned to Jaffna after the arrival of the Indian Peace-Keeping Force (IPKF), and helped collect information on human rights violations by the army and LTTE. He fled to India in 1988 to escape the LTTE, but Indian intelligence officials forced him to return and join Q, a pro-IPKF group. He escaped to Jaffna, but was caught and questioned by Q and the IPKF as a suspected LTTE sympathiser. He was tortured and beaten in IPKF custody. After the IPKF withdrew, he fled to India to escape the LTTE. He was rounded up after Rajiv Gandhi's assassination and gave false answers under interrogation, because he was using a false passport. He was beaten, kept in custody for two years, then deported to Sri Lanka.

The security forces questioned him, and he was assaulted until he admitted his true identity. He was handed over to R (a pro-government Tamil militia group) and took part reluctantly in helping them identify LTTE sympathisers. Before the 1994 election he was asked to compile lists of Tamil voters, but fell out with R after publicly stating that these would be used to rig the voting. He tried to flee the country on a false passport, but was handed back to R, who assaulted him and kept him in confinement for two years. Finally he escaped and a friend helped arrange his flight to the UK, where he claimed asylum.

*   *   *   *

Despite their unusually extreme experiences, both Ms X and Mr Y had their initial asylum claims refused by the Immigration and Nationality Directorate (IND) of the British Home Office, and I was instructed by their solicitors to write expert witness reports when these refusals resulted in appeal hearings before adjudicators from the Immigration Appellate Authority (IAA).

Although their accounts of persecution are now in the public domain, having been furnished as evidence in connection with their appeals, I have used pseudonyms and concealed circumstantial details in these summaries, to protect these two individuals from further public exposure. Indeed, it was precisely Ms X's fear of others in the Tamil community learning about her ordeal, because of the shameful consequences of rape for herself and her family, which stopped her from revealing the full, horrendous story at her asylum interview, or even to her first (Tamil) solicitor. The initial refusal of her claim must therefore be understood in light of her not having revealed the sexual assaults by that stage. Consequently, according to the information available to IND at the time, the basis of her claim was that she had been detained for one month and interrogated. As she admitted having assisted the LTTE, such questioning was deemed justifiable in the context of widespread ethnic conflict in Sri Lanka, and not to amount to persecution. Among other things, my report had to account for her earlier reticence by explaining Tamil ideas and practices concerning kinship, sexuality, and purity.

That refusal was therefore far less astounding than Mr Y's 'Reasons for Refusal Letter' from IND, which reduced his story to 'your claim that you had been arrested, detained and *ill-treated*' (my emphasis). Refusal Letters never speak outright of 'torture'; the closest they ever get, even in extreme cases like this, is 'ill-treatment' (Asylum Aid 1999: 55). Legally, there is, in fact, a difference between the two: torture entails the deliberate inflicting of 'severe physical or mental pain or suffering' for a specific purpose, such as information-gathering or intimidation; whereas ill-treatment involves 'intentional exposure to significant mental or physical pain or suffering'. In both cases, it is also necessary that the agents of persecution 'either inflicted this suffering themselves, or else knew or ought to have known about it but did not try to prevent it' (Giffard 2000: ¶3.3.3.1; see §5.2).[1]

Mr Y's treatment was judged not to constitute persecution. The Refusal Letter argued that when last arrested he was released without charge (not mentioning that he was not actually freed, but handed over into R's custody), so the authorities clearly had no further interest in him – and even if they did, he would receive a fair trial. Refusals are often based on such arguments, though in fact detention without charge, especially for long periods, may itself constitute persecution (*Singh*; Asylum Aid 1999: 38).

Most asylum applicants base their claims on less extreme personal suffering than this, whose horror nonetheless goes far beyond normal experience. As the numbers seeking asylum in the United Kingdom have grown, there has been a steady devaluation of the gruesome currency of asylum claims. 'Merely' having a spouse or parent killed before one's eyes – or being raped without a clear political motive – counts for relatively little on the prevailing

---

1 Citations in the form §X.X are cross-references to other sections of this book.

scale of persecution assessment. This book is about the legal treatment of asylum applicants in common law systems such as those of the United Kingdom, United States, Australia, and Canada; about the difficulties which asylum applicants face when required to narrate that persecution in terms intelligible to bureaucrats and judges; and about the role played by 'objective evidence' from anthropologists and doctors in bridging that divide, and thereby helping the courts to decide whether asylum claimants do indeed suffer a 'well-founded fear of persecution'.

Chapter 1

Asylum as a social and political problem

1.1 THE EMERGENCE OF THE REFUGEE

It is by no means self-evident that people's movements should be restricted by the boundaries of nation states (Cohen 1995; Gibney 2004), but as such restrictions do actually exist it is important to assess critically how they are applied, to help ensure that this is done fairly. This book is a study of one aspect of this process, the treatment by British tribunals and courts (and those of other common law countries) of would-be refugees appealing against the refusal of their asylum applications. In particular, it examines the uses made by these legal decision-making processes of expert evidence from doctors, from psychiatrists, and, above all, from 'country experts' such as social anthropologists and political analysts. Consequently, as we shall see, it is concerned also with struggles for hegemony among the rival professional and lay discourses in terms of which these legal struggles are expressed.

Immigration and asylum are major social and political issues, and scarcely a day passed in the late 1990s and early 2000s without them making headlines right across the European Union. The level of public concern is indicated by the unparalleled pace of legislation in the United Kingdom. There have been new, ever more draconian Acts of Parliament in 1993, 1996, 1999, 2002, and 2004, yet still the perceived political 'problem' has not been 'solved'. But what precisely *is* this 'problem'?

The mere existence of the term 'refugee' might delude us into thinking that its meaning is clearly defined, yet it needs to be remembered throughout that the label itself is problematic, and its application to particular persons even more so. In everyday speech 'refugee' is a term conveying broad notions of destitution and escape from natural disaster or warfare, yet the definition furnished by the 1951 Refugee Convention (§4.1) is far narrower and some-what counter-intuitive. This book deals with refugees in that narrow legal sense, but it is important to set it in context by looking briefly at migrants and displaced persons more generally.

A massive increase in human migratory movements, dwarfing anything that happened before, was one of the most significant social processes of the twentieth century and seems certain to accelerate further in the twenty-first, even though the very countries promoting globalisation of capital and commodities have been among the most restrictive where globalisation of labour is concerned. Migration may have many causes – economic betterment; flight from war, oppression, or starvation; reunion with relatives; transnational marriage – and is generally undertaken for a mixture of motives, despite the stereotyped distinction beloved of populist media and politicians between 'genuine refugees' and 'bogus asylum seekers' who are really 'economic migrants'. It is nonetheless true that a growing proportion of migrants reaching Western Europe in recent decades have indeed applied for asylum, and whereas before 1993 asylum applicants were largely subsumed under 'immigrants' in popular and political discourse (Stevens 2004: 69), by 2000 'asylum seekers' had come to stand for 'illegal immigrants' generally. Legally speaking, however, true asylum seekers are persons fleeing persecution, and whether or not they enter a country illegally should have little relevance to the assessment of their asylum claims.

The notion of asylum long precedes that of 'refugee' historically. Even in the nineteenth century the United Kingdom granted asylum, although as there was no actual immigration legislation prior to the 1905 Aliens Act, its significance was, obviously, somewhat different. Hostility to incomers became particularly evident in the hysteria generated by the First World War, when Aliens Restriction Acts were passed in 1914 and 1919. The focus at that time was on immigrants generally rather than those seeking asylum. The latter only came under specifically stricter control after 1971, in response to the xenophobia created by increasing numbers. Asylum has always been at the Home Office's discretion rather than an automatic right. The State can thus portray itself as liberal because it grants asylum to some people (politicians routinely extol the UK's 'proud tradition' in this regard, even as they restrict entry still further), while simultaneously keeping out 'undesirable aliens' such as poor people not obviously able to support themselves (Schuster and Solomos 1999; Schuster 2003: 77–89).

The legal notion of 'refugee' is inextricably bound up with the elaboration of concepts of 'human rights' in the mid-twentieth century. It is obvious why refugees suddenly assumed importance at that time, given the mass displacements in Europe after the Second World War, but underlying this emergency was a process that began earlier – the triumph of ethnic nationalism following the collapse of the multi-ethnic European empires (Malkki 1995: 497; Schuster 2003: 98–9; Gibney 2004: 2). The new ideal of the mono-ethnic nation state inevitably rendered problematic those minority populations not 'belonging' there, or indeed anywhere. In Foucauldian terms, the refugee camps which first appeared in that period were technologies of power – a means of helping destitute persons, certainly, but also a means of controlling, documenting, and screening them – through which 'the modern post-war refugee emerged as a knowable, nameable figure and as an object of social-scientific knowledge' (Malkki 1995: 498).

The most obvious legal consequence of all this was the drafting of the 1951 Refugee Convention, which provided an internationally agreed definition of 'a refugee' (Chapter 4). Another result, more parochially, was the growth of Refugee Studies as a recognised area of academic activity (Black 2001), but this emergent discipline defined 'refugees' more broadly than the purely legal definition furnished by the Convention. It covered mass displacements resulting from natural disasters or wars – as well as people displaced within the borders of their own countries, who are legally not refugees at all, but Internally Displaced Persons (IDPs). This broad focus was entirely understandable, but less so has been the scant attention paid by this new discipline to the study of asylum applicants, especially given the volume of political debate and media coverage directed at them in recent years.

1.2 THE SCALE OF THE 'PROBLEM'

Around 140 million people were forcibly displaced during the twentieth century. A baffling array of statistics is available, but some very basic figures will indicate the current position. The Office of the United Nations High Commissioner for Refugees (UNHCR), the international body responsible for assisting refugees, estimated that the worldwide 'population of concern to UNHCR' was just over 17 million at 1 January 2004. Table 1.1 shows the numbers and locations of refugees, asylum applicants, and IDPs on that date. These totals exclude those returning home within the preceding 12 months, although UNHCR retains an interest in them too.

Table 1.2 lists some of the main Western countries in which asylum was sought during 2002, and the five most common countries of origin of applicants in each case. Many of the striking differences in geographical origin are explicable in terms of historical (for example, colonial) links between host

Table 1.1 Estimated number of refugees worldwide, 1 Jan 2004

Region	Refugees	Asylum Applicants	IDPs
Africa	3,135,800	166,100	571,600
Asia	3,635,700	48,800	1,565,400
Europe	2,207,100	366,500	1,038,500
Latin America/Caribbean	38,300	7,200	1,244,100
North America	585,600	392,500	–
Oceania	69,600	4,400	–
Total	**9,672,100**	**985,500**	**4,419,600**

Source: UNHCR (2004)

Table 1.2 New asylum applications in selected countries, 2003

Country of asylum	Asylum applications	Main countries of origin (descending order)
United Kingdom	61,100	Somalia/Iraq/China/Zimbabwe/Iran
United States	60,700	China/Colombia/Mexico/Haiti/Indonesia
France	59,800	Turkey/China/Dem. Rep. of Congo (DRC)/Russian Fed./Algeria
Germany	50,600	Turkey/Serbia-Montenegro (S-M)/Iraq/Russian Fed./China
Austria	32,400	Russian Fed./Turkey/India/S-M/Afghanistan
Canada	31,900	Pakistan/Mexico/Colombia/China/Costa Rica
Sweden	31,300	S-M/Somalia/Iraq/Bosnia-Herzegovina
Switzerland	20,800	S-M/Turkey/Iraq/Algeria/Georgia
Belgium	16,900	DRC/Russian Fed./S-M/Iran/Cameroon
Norway	16,000	S-M/Afghanistan/Russian Fed./Somalia/Iraq
Netherlands	13,400	Iraq/Iran/Afghanistan/Somalia/Liberia
Czech Republic	11,600	Russian Fed./Ukraine/Slovakia/China/Vietnam
Slovakia	10,400	Russian Fed./India/China/Armenia/Afghanistan

Source: UNHCR (2004)

country and country of origin. Cultural affinity is also significant – above all the presence in the host country of persons of their own ethnicity and cultural background but, failing that, a common language or the opportunity to learn English. Many asylum applicants lack the time or resources to enjoy the luxury of choice, however. They must go wherever their agents take them, and the existence of an effective people-smuggling network may be more crucial than the character of the host country (§3.1).

The annual totals of asylum applications have fluctuated in different ways in different countries. Germany, for example, accounted for over half the entire West European total in the early 1990s, but numbers subsequently declined (UNHCR 2002a: 112–13). In the UK numbers have tended to increase, though not to anything like the extent suggested by some lurid newspaper headlines. In most years, in fact, the total number of asylum applicants arriving in the UK has been smaller than the crowds watching Glasgow Celtic or Manchester United every Saturday.

Table 1.3 gives the total number of asylum applications in the UK annually from 1992 until 2001, and the top five countries of origin in each year. Numbers rise and fall, obviously, according to the prevailing political situation, and one can chart the world's trouble spots, usually with a slight time-lag, from tables such as this. The most consistent appearances were made by Sri Lankans, who figured in the top five in almost every year (in 1996

Table 1.3 Annual asylum applications in the United Kingdom, 1993–2003

| Year | Total Applying | First | Top five countries of origin | | | |
			Second	Third	Fourth	Fifth
1993	22,370	Sri Lanka	Former Yugoslavia	Ghana	Nigeria	Turkey
		1,965	1,830	1,785	1,665	1,480
1994	32,830	Nigeria	Sri Lanka	Turkey	Ghana	India
		4,340	2,350	2,045	2,035	2,030
1995	43,965	Nigeria	Somalia	India	Pakistan	Sri Lanka
		5,825	3,465	3,255	2,915	2,070
1996	29,640	Nigeria	India	Pakistan	Somalia	Turkey
		2,900	2,220	1,915	1,780	1,495
1997	32,500	Somalia	China	FRY (a)	Sri Lanka	Pakistan
		2,730	1,945	1,865	1,830	1,615
1998	46,015	FRY (a)	Somalia	Sri Lanka	Afghanistan	ex-USSR (b)
		7,395	4,685	3,505	2,395	2,260
1999	71,160	FRY (a)	Somalia	Sri Lanka	Afghanistan	Turkey
		11,465	7,495	5,130	3,975	2,850
2000	80,315	Iraq	Sri Lanka	FRY (a)	Iran	Afghanistan
		7,475	6,395	6,070	5,610	5,555
2001	71,025	Afghanistan	Iraq	Somalia	Sri Lanka	Turkey
		8,920	6,680	6,420	5,510	3,695
2002	84,130	Iraq	Zimbabwe	Afghanistan	Somalia	China
		14,570	7,655	7,205	6,540	3,675
2003	49,405	Somalia	Iraq	China	Zimbabwe	Iran
		5,090	4,015	3,450	3,295	2,875

Source: Home Office (2003, 2005). Figures exclude dependants, counted differently from UNHCR.

Notes
(a) Federal Republic of Yugoslavia;
(b) Excluding Ukraine.

and 2002 they came sixth). Turkish Kurds were the next most consistent group over that period. This tellingly demonstrates the persistence of these particular conflicts.

As explained more fully in Chapter 5, initial decisions on asylum claims in the United Kingdom are taken by the Home Office's Immigration and Nationality Directorate (IND), which may recognise claimants as refugees – in which case, they are given Indefinite Leave to Remain in the UK (ILR) – or grant them various forms of temporary, humanitarian status (§5.1). In practice most applications are refused outright, but since 1993 most refused claimants have had rights of appeal at public hearings. At the time of my field research, the first appeal was before an adjudicator from the Immigration Appellate Authority (IAA), an independent judicial body. The losing party generally had a further right of appeal to the Immigration Appeals Tribunal (IAT).[1] Asylum applicants might also apply for judicial review at any point, and a few cases reached the Court of Appeal or House of Lords. Taking all decision-making procedures together, the upshot in 2001, the year in which fieldwork was conducted, was that 42 per cent of applicants were ultimately granted ILR or humanitarian leave. Setting aside countries like Nigeria and India, with numerous applicants but very low success rates (§5.4), that proportion became even greater. Many others did, of course, have arguable claims which they failed to make out in the face of the reluctance of the Home Office to concede as much, and the rigorous standards prevailing in the courts. This was a far cry from the picture being purveyed by sections of the popular press at that time, of a country flooded by 'bogus' claimants.

1.3 BACKGROUND TO THE RESEARCH

In 1993, the Immigration Law Practitioners' Association began producing directories (ILPA 1993, 1997) listing anthropologists and other 'country experts' able to provide background reports on applications for refugee status in the UK. My own entry, for example, indicated that my primary expertise was on Tamil Nadu in south India, involving lengthy fieldwork, shorter visits, and consultancies, from 1972 onwards. My knowledge of Sri Lanka was secondary as far as my direct research went. I have never done actual fieldwork there, though I lived in Kandy for two years in 1970–1972 and have made numerous short visits ever since. Nevertheless, I have frequently been commissioned by solicitors representing Sri Lankan Tamil (and occasionally Muslim or Sinhalese) asylum applicants to write reports assessing the current political and human rights situations in Sri Lanka; the plausibility of their client's account; assertions about Sri Lanka in Home Office documents; and the risks their client might face if forcibly repatriated.

Experts provide only written evidence in the vast majority of cases where they are involved, though it has become slightly more common for them to be asked to give supplementary oral evidence, thereby opening themselves to cross-examination. They rarely meet the asylum applicants concerned – apart possibly from introductions before hearings – nor is this considered necessary as their opinions are meant to reflect general, 'expert' knowledge rather than first-hand familiarity with events in this particular case. The first time I appeared in person there was not even that limited contact, as there had been

---

1   From April 2005 onwards, these two bodies were collapsed into a single Asylum and Immigration Tribunal (AIT). Instead of Adjudicators and Tribunal Chairs there are now Immigration Judges and Senior Immigration Judges. Appeal rights have been significantly curtailed. These structural changes do not, however, affect the core arguments of this book concerning the treatment of expert evidence.

a delay in bringing the applicant from prison, where he was remanded on drug smuggling charges. It was deemed acceptable to question me in his absence, since – reinforcing the point being made here – my evidence was not seen as bearing on the truth of particular incidents in his account.

I am far from the only anthropologist to have produced reports of this kind. In fact, this research arose out of the realisation that most British anthropologists with appropriate regional expertise had received requests to provide written evidence in asylum cases. Many had responded positively on at least a few occasions, but because this involvement had been so sporadic, most knew little about the legal responsibilities of expert witnesses, the judicial processes to which asylum evidence is subject, or the impact and effectiveness of their own reports. So far, indeed, hardly anything has been written from an anthropological perspective about *any* aspect of the process of seeking asylum, no doubt partly because anthropologists have only recently overcome their cultural-relativist suspicions sufficiently to engage with notions of universal human rights (Messer 1993; Turner 1997; Wilson 1997; Wilson and Mitchell 2003). The Royal Anthropological Institute's *Anthropological Index* lists very few articles with 'asylum' (in the sense relevant here) in their title or keyword list, and most of their authors are not unequivocally anthropologists. Not surprisingly, therefore, the discussion of asylum in Malkki's review article on refugees (1995) focuses far more on concept elucidation than on empirical studies.

There is, of course, a growing literature on 'anthropological advocacy', dealing mainly with anthropologists' involvement in legal or political proceedings concerning land rights, cultural artefacts, and anatomical specimens (Paine 1985; Wade 1995; Culhane 1998). Legally speaking, however, 'advocacy' is often an inappropriate term in such contexts, as it is in the present one. Expert witnesses are specifically prohibited in English law from engaging in advocacy (§6.3), and whenever anthropologists act as expert witnesses in formal legal proceedings in Australia or North America, they are under similar legal constraints – although in the Hindmarsh Island Bridge litigation, Australian courts alternated between treating anthropologists as advocates and as experts (Edmond 2004a). Almost invariably, too, the 'advocacy' literature concerns anthropologists mediating between 'indigenous' cultures and hegemonic politico-legal systems; a key issue is whether, or to what extent, the anthropologists are reporting on pristine cultures that exist 'out there', or whether those cultures are actually generated by the interaction between the culture-bearers and the courts – or, for that matter, between their putative adherents and the anthropologists (Weiner 1999: 202). That is not generally the case with asylum claims, where anthropologists are more often cast as pundits on micro-politics than interpreters of cultures. Even when 'culture' becomes relevant – as with the stigma of rape, and its social consequences – asylum courts are not primarily concerned to understand these matters in indigenous cultural terms, as land claims hearings in Australia or North

America might be. Instead they cut directly to the chase: what are the implications of all this 'culture' for the credibility of the applicants' stories, and the well-foundedness of their fear of persecution?

Empirical work on asylum applicants in Europe has been largely interview-based rather than ethnographic (McDowell 1996; Fuglerud 1999), and has not focused on the legal process itself, though it has sometimes addressed its outcomes (Daniel and Thangaraj 1995). One of the few to consider the implications of anthropological involvement in asylum cases is Mahmood, who discusses the ethical issues involved in working with Sikh militants in the US (1996a, b) and has also acted as expert witness in some European cases. Daniel's study of the impact of torture and political violence on Sri Lankan asylum applicants contains ethnographic vignettes from American asylum hearings (1996: 180), but the only detailed account of direct anthropological involvement in providing expert evidence for asylum claims is that by Alvarez and Loucky (1992). It is hard to generalise from this, however, because the anthropologist (Loucky) was in the unusual position of being hired to carry out investigative fieldwork in the applicants' home region.

Clearly, therefore, there exists a major gap in the literature, which needs addressing because of the moral and practical importance of the topic, and to broaden anthropological awareness of yet another area in which their professional skills can be put to rewarding non-academic use. After briefly locating the present research within the broader sphere of the anthropology of law, this book summarises the legal background to asylum claims; describes the decision-making processes to which they are subject; assesses these from an anthropological perspective; and considers how the courts deal with objective evidence from 'country experts', as anthropologists and allied trades are known in this context. As a foil to the consideration of social science experts, the book looks also at the courts' treatment of medical expert evidence, which I initially assumed – wrongly, as will become clear – would be less problematic for administrative and judicial decision makers because of its greater familiarity from other areas of law. At stake ultimately, as we shall see, are conflicting professional standards among social scientists, doctors, and lawyers as to the nature and treatment of evidence, and although I focus here on the differing degrees of reflexivity – in the sense employed by Beck (1994: 6; §11.1) – which lawyers and country experts apply to their professional activities, other aspects of this hegemonic struggle between the judiciary and professional experts have been recurrent themes throughout British legal history (Jones 1994; Redmayne 2001; §6.2). While such momentous disagreements cannot be resolved here, this book does sketch out the terrain over which the preliminary skirmishes in the asylum courts have so far taken place.

In such a fast-changing field of study, it is important for two quite different reasons to specify that the 'ethnographic present' for this book is the period from early 1999 until the end of 2003, although significant changes in law and practice occurring since then are mentioned in footnotes. First, asylum decisions are made notionally in light of circumstances on the day of decision itself, so that as the political, military and human rights contexts in asylum applicants' countries of origin evolve, so too do the arguments and counter-arguments change. Second, the legislative framework within which such decisions are made is itself evolving faster than any other area of British public policy. In that context, this book covers the coming into force of the *Human Rights Act 1998*, and the *Immigration and Asylum Act 1999*, but deals only in passing with the effects of the *Nationality, Immigration and Asylum Act 2002* and scarcely at all with those of the *Asylum and Immigration (Treatment of Claimants, etc.) Act 2004*.

Chapter 2

Anthropologists and lawyers

2.1 THE FALL AND RISE OF THE ANTHROPOLOGY OF LAW

Anthropology and law have always been cognate disciplines, though many of their respective practitioners no longer seem aware of the fact. This section provides a brief perspective on how their relationship flourished, waned, and – arguably – began to prosper again, while the rest of the chapter explains how, despite their closeness, law and anthropology nonetheless display distinct modes of reasoning and attitudes to evidence.

Conley and O'Barr (1990b: 3) define the anthropology of law in terms of its related interests in governance and dispute settlement:

> legal anthropology has focused on two fundamental questions in its examination of other cultures: (1) what are the substantive rules that are the equivalent of law as we define it in our culture? and (2) what are the procedures through which violations of these rules are adjudicated?

I would add two further questions, of more recent pedigree: (3) what are the concepts in terms of which these rules are framed, and by means of which people represent to themselves and each other the meanings of those procedures; and (4) what is distinctive about the legal discourses that employ these concepts, and about how such discourses are used to explain, justify, or excuse the behaviour of certain litigants, and attribute blame or fault to the behaviour of others?

Many early anthropologists were lawyers by profession – Lewis Henry Morgan, Henry Maine, John McLennan – and there is an obvious overlap between law and an anthropological interest in 'custom'. It is conventional to take Maine's *Ancient Law* (1861) as the starting point in explicating this link. In the evolutionary fashion of the time, he distinguished two kinds of law, based respectively on 'status' and 'contract'. In early societies, he argued, personal rights and obligations were acquired by birth, by one's status position in a 'family', defined broadly to include clans and lineages. This system was then gradually replaced by one in which rights and obligations were created by contracts between free individuals. Nuer (African people of south-east Sudan and Ethiopia) are classic examples of people whose society is based on status; in their case, lineage membership. The topic of this book falls well towards the opposite extreme however, in that the rights of asylum applicants are defined by assessing their own, individual circumstances against standards grounded in universalistic notions of 'human rights'.

Moore (1978), surveying the history of legal anthropology up to the 1970s, argues that Maine originated one of its major theoretical strands, predicated upon a diachronic transition from simple to complex societies – or, later, a synchronic contrast between them. In the same camp, she places Durkheim's (1933: 181) distinction between mechanical and organic solidarity, and Gluckman's contrast between multiplex and uniplex relationships (1955: 19). Llewellen and Hoebbel (1941) drew a similar distinction between 'private law' enforceable by kin, and 'public law' enforced by the government; while Gulliver (1963) distinguished 'political' systems, which come to decisions according to the relative strength of the disputing parties, from 'judicial' systems based on the consensual application of shared norms. As we shall see, Conley and O'Barr (1990b: 174) adopt a kind of 'post-modern' version of the same approach, whose focus has moved from the characteristics of the system to the orienting perspectives of the various actors.

The first influential ethnographic study of law was Malinowski's *Crime and Custom in Savage Society*. Not surprisingly, given the centrality of exchange to his view of Trobriand society, he emphasised that law rested on mutual, reciprocally recognised, social obligations. It was 'the specific result of the configuration of obligations, which makes it impossible for the native to shirk his responsibility without suffering for it in the future' (1926: 59). This approach successfully refuted the then-prevalent notion of 'primitive people' as enslaved by custom and tradition, but at the cost of defining law so broadly that it became indistinguishable from normative social relationships generally, making it hard to retain any notion of the anthropology of law as a distinct field of study. Moreover, this can only be part of the picture, because although shared values and norms are important, one cannot ignore the coercive aspect of law, whether manifest in personal retaliation (feud, for instance) or in punishments meted out by the State.

Llewellen and Hoebbel (1941) were the first to study law anthropologically through the medium of *cases*, reconstructed from the memories of elderly Cheyenne informants. The first ethnography based on direct observation of actual cases was Gluckman's study of the Barotse, an African State with a specialised judiciary. He argued that Barotse judges arrived at their decisions by appealing to the concept of the 'Reasonable Man' who 'embraces both sense and uprightness' (1955: 126); this device was used to articulate standard role expectations, and to make explicit social norms and values relevant to the legal problem at issue (1955: 125f; 1965: 20–1). As we shall see, there are contemporary echoes of this in Home Office assertions that asylum applicants' accounts lack plausibility – in effect, that 'no reasonable, 25-year-old, Croydon-based civil servant would have done what you claim you did'.

Gluckman inspired a raft of followers at the Rhodes-Livingstone Institute and the University of Manchester. Indeed, one could argue that the entire corpus of British structural-functionalism impinges upon legal anthropology insofar as it concerns the maintenance of social equilibrium by means of systems of jural rules and norms. Its *pater familias* Radcliffe-Brown argued that law differed from custom only in the existence of 'formal legal sanctions' (1952: 212). Evans-Pritchard's *Witchcraft, Oracles and Magic Among the Azande* (1937), arguably the pinnacle of structural-functionalist writing, is not generally thought of as a contribution to the anthropology of law, yet its principal topic is, after all, the attribution of blame – albeit by consulting a poison oracle rather than appealing to a legal tribunal.

Despite all this – or perhaps *because* of it; in other words, the fading of interest in legal anthropology may have been part and parcel of the decline of structural-functionalism generally – Fuller's subsequent (1994) critical survey pointed out the near-moribund state of the anthropology of law in Britain during the following two decades. He suggested three reasons for this. The first was the ultimately sterile debate between Gluckman and Bohannan over the value of Western legal categories for understanding non-Western practices. This paralleled the formalist-substantivist debate raging in economic anthropology at the same time, with Gluckman in effect taking the formalist position that Western categories are useful analytical tools (1965: 254), and Bohannan, as he did in the economic context too, arguing the substantivist position that one has to work through indigenous concepts (1957: 119–20). The second stultifying factor was the trend towards increasingly formulaic empirical work, which reduced the study of law to the study of processes of dispute settlement, retaining Gluckman's methodology but not his breadth of theoretical vision. This narrow focus on behaviour, Fuller argued, often failed to convey how law was actually conceptualised by parties in these disputes.

The third factor was the rise of *legal pluralism*, studying the coexistence of diverse normative and legal orders. Rouland (1994: 47) traces this notion back to Van Vollenhoven in Indonesia in the early twentieth century, and the Dutch tradition in this field continues (von Benda-Beckmann and Strijbosch 1986), but in Anglophone anthropology it originated with MG Smith's notion that distinct legal systems were associated with different kinds of corporate group (Kuper and Smith 1969), and Pospisil's more analytical portrayal of hierarchies of 'legal levels', such that 'every functioning sub-group in a society has its own legal system' (1971: 107). Pluralist approaches led to a recognition that 'customary' law exists in a dialectical relation with State law. Indeed 'customary law' as such, like so much else about supposedly 'traditional' societies, was made explicit by, and/or in opposition to, the order imposed by colonial masters. As with Malinowski's approach, however, the danger is that precisely because it points out a virtually universal fact – the plurality of legal discourses – legal pluralism risks becoming a 'just so' story which loses explanatory value in particular cases.

To a great extent, fortunately, this danger is avoided by what Merry (1988: 872) terms 'new legal pluralism', a series of studies of the lower tiers of the US legal system as experienced by ordinary members of the public. First, Moore (1973) loosened, without entirely severing, the bond between legal systems and discrete groups, in favour of the more flexible notion of a plurality of 'semi-autonomous social fields', in which 'a certain number of corporate groups are in relation one to another'. Taking the New York garment industry as a contemporary example, she showed that although some of the rules governing this highly volatile social field emanate from the wider social environment – government, the marketplace, relations between different ethnic groups – others are produced 'within the field of action itself', either from 'quasi-legislative' interactions among constituent corporate groups such as contractors' associations and trades unions or, crucially, from the processual interplay between individual actors from different stakeholding groups such as retailers, factors, jobbers, and skilled workers (Moore 1978: 63). Although Moore's work, and that of scholars such as Conley and O'Barr (1990b) and Merry herself (1990), extend the notion of legal pluralism yet further, showing how different understandings of law coexist even within contemporary American society, they do so in ways that pay careful attention to ethnographic specificity. There has been little such work in the UK so far, but its relevance to asylum hearings is immediately obvious, in that applicants often lack even folk knowledge of the principles of British law, and may hold very different ideas regarding justice, legal procedures, and personal rights. The problem is that key participants in court are generally not fully aware of the extent of this incompatibility.

This last point draws attention to the importance of studying law not just as a set of formal processes but as 'a system of thought' (Fuller 1994: 11); to, in other words, the importance of studying legal discourses (Humphreys 1985). Indeed, legal pluralists drew inspiration from anthropological accounts of law as a cultural phenomenon, notably that of Geertz (1983), which could be seen as furnishing, in effect, 'an interpretive view of legal pluralism' (Merry 1988: 886). Predictably, Geertz's approach to law focused on 'the symbols and systems of symbols through whose agency [legal] structures are formed, communicated, imposed, shared, altered, reproduced' (1983: 182; gloss added). Like religious thinking, legal reasoning places events into broader contexts, helping us make sense of the world and suggesting principled courses of action to be undertaken in response.

Certain aspects of Geertz's approach are, however, hard to accept in light of subsequent analyses of differences between legal and anthropological discourses (§2.2). For example, far from 'the cultural contextualization of incident' being 'a critical aspect of legal analysis . . . as it is of . . . sociological analysis' (1983: 181), many have argued that almost the reverse is true; that in formal legal processes the specific contexts within which events took place are downplayed as much as possible in the interests of attaching these events to general principles of law. In asylum hearings the context is often misunderstood if not wholly ignored, and this often threatens to lead legal adjudication astray (Chapter 7). Similarly, in Geertz's claim that law 'makes life's nebulous events tangible and restores their detail' (1983: 182), the second part seems as mistaken as the first part is accurate. If there is one core characteristic which differentiates legal analyses from those of anthropologists, it is that the latter treat ambiguity and complexity as immanent aspects of all real life situations, while the former attempt to prune away what are deemed extraneous details, in order to identify the abstract, general, *de*-contextualised legal principles assumed to lie concealed within (§2.2).

A related question is whether legal discourses represent a distinct, autonomous domain, or whether, or to what degree, they are embedded in the broader discourses and cultures of the societies within which they are located. Rosen, for instance, in his study of *qadi* courts in Morocco, argues for the advantages of viewing law as part of wider culture, as 'a system which, for all its distinctive institutional history and forms, partakes of concepts that extend across many domains of social life' (1989: 5). Further, and here the link with Geertz is clear:

> Though couched as statements of fact, legal decisions are, quite often, really creators of fact. Like religion, law is a kind of metasystem which creates order in a universe that is often experienced in a more disorderly way (1989: 17).

Rosen does recognise, however, that his approach is only partly applicable to Western common law systems since whereas 'law and morality are seen as entirely consonant' in Islamic law, there is in Western law 'a fundamentally problematic aspect to the relation between law and ethics' (1989: 72). A Western judge 'may look beyond the law to the cultural standards or the "conscience of a sovereign people", but for the *qadi*, culture is not outside of the law but integral to it' (1989: 72–3). Moreover, we are back with Malinowski's problem, since Rosen (1989: 5) acknowledges that such a view makes the study of law:

> indistinguishable from a view of how anthropological enquiry in general may be conducted – as a search for the concepts by which a community of human beings categorize and group their experience of an otherwise differentiated universe into packets of meaning, symbolically grasped and manipulated.

So this seems both the strength and weakness of the cultural approach; it embeds law firmly within the broader culture, thereby avoiding unwonted abstraction, but at the cost of largely eliminating those features which distinguish law, *qua* law, from other sets of cultural symbols and arenas of cultural expression. And what are the further limitations of this view if one sees culture as processual and contested? Like Malinowski, Geertz and Rosen can also be criticised for excessive idealism. While it is valid and helpful, up to a point, to see law as a set of symbols, it must never be forgotten that law is 'about repression just as much as imagination' (Fuller 1994: 11). Other discourse-based approaches manage to avoid this criticism, however, such as notions of hegemonic discourse (Gramsci 1971), whereby power lies in the ability to impose one's own definitions onto others. Although this approach has been invoked with rather tiresome frequency of late in many different contexts, it is hard to resist as a model of what goes on in the course of deciding whether someone is, or is not, a 'genuine refugee'.

The study of legal languages did not begin with discourse theorists, however. One of the earliest such studies, taking an ethnomethodologically-inspired approach towards what was then known as 'conversational analysis', and treating law as a specialised example of language use rather than the primary focus in its own right, was Atkinson and Drew's (1979) investigation of patterns of dialogue in British courts and tribunals, and the ways in which legal procedures – most notably, cross-examinations as quite rigid question–answer sequences involving only two of the persons present – require participants to depart from the conventions of ordinary conversation. A significant body of work has since dealt with the practical uses of legal language, and although not all has been conducted by *soi-disant* anthropologists, it has relied greatly upon ethnographic techniques.

In a series of publications on language use in legal processes, for example, John Conley and William O'Barr (Conley, O'Barr and Lind 1978; Conley and O'Barr 1988, 1990a, b, 1998; O'Barr 1982) developed a method which they term 'the ethnography of discourse', based on the assumption that 'careful, qualitative study of legal discourse provides evidence of the goals, strategies, and thought processes of the speakers' (1990b: 35) or, even more succinctly, that 'the details of legal discourse matter' (1998: 129). They apply their method primarily to the kinds of courts most frequented by ordinary members of the public, such as small claims or magistrates' courts in the United States, which hear civil suits involving relatively small sums of money, and in which litigants generally present their own cases rather than hiring lawyers. Because of this relative informality, these courts are ideal sites for studying the legal beliefs and practices of ordinary people, albeit a self-selected group of such people, who not only have problems which they seek to resolve, but have also decided that the most appropriate avenue of resolution is the legal system.

These legal contexts resemble British asylum courts in some respects – for example, their relaxation of strict rules of evidence – but are unlike them in others. Most crucially, far from presenting their own cases, asylum applicants are doubly disempowered before the court, being dependent not only upon lawyers but also upon interpreters to present – or rather, *re-present* – their cases for them. I term these forms of disempowerment because, while legal expertise is essential in steering applicants through the maze of technical law surrounding their goal of refugee status, and an interpreter is vital if there is to be any communication at all, applicants relinquish much of their individual autonomy in their reliance upon these other persons, and are therefore, for good or ill, unable to present their claims in ways they themselves might have chosen. For successful claimants this may seem a price worth paying, but one can imagine unsuccessful applicants retrospectively attributing their failure to this double silencing of their own voice.

Despite this basic difference, Conley and O'Barr's findings remain relevant to asylum hearings in the UK. Their key finding was that the ways in which lay persons analyse issues, and present these to the court, lie along a continuum. At one extreme, some adopt a *rule-oriented* approach, whereby they:

> evaluate their problems in terms of neutral principles whose application transcends differences in personal and social status. In conceiving their cases and presenting them to the court, they emphasize these principles rather than such issues as individual need or social worth (1990b: *ix*).

This is likely to be quite a successful strategy. Because such a perspective chimes with that of legal professionals themselves, there is a good chance that people who present their problems in this way will be fully understood.

At the other extreme, the *relational orientation* is characterised by a 'fuzzier' definition of issues whereby rights and responsibilities are predicated on 'a broad notion of social interdependence rather than on the application of rules' (1990b: 61). For example, the testimony of a typical relational witness emerges as follows (*ibid.*):

> She rarely responds specifically to the issues raised in the judge's questions. Instead, his questions evoke lengthy digressions [which] meander through time and place, drawing her audience ever deeper into her social world, but providing little information about the specific issues that are of interest to the court. Her account contains frequent references to . . . items which are significant to her social situation but are irrelevant to the court's more limited and rule-centered agenda.

It is not that the perspectives of relationally-oriented litigants are illogical or unstructured, though lawyers tend to view them as such; rather, such reasoning conforms to a logic so different from their own as to be largely imperceptible to those steeped in formal legal analysis. Consequently, the courts 'often fail to understand their cases, regardless of their legal merits, and this frequently results in frustration and alienation' (1990b: 61).

Insofar as asylum applicants' cases are put on their behalf by their lawyers, their representations will generally be rule-oriented. Nonetheless, because of their likely unfamiliarity with legal proceedings *per se*, let alone the particularities of law in the UK, it is distinctly likely that applicants themselves will display a more or less pronounced relational orientation in their responses to detailed cross-examination.

Merry, too, was concerned with forms of legal discourse in lower courts in New England, but she approached and analysed these somewhat differently. Of the three types of court covered by her research (1990: 32–3), the small claims courts seem closest to those studied by Conley and O'Barr. They deal with minor civil matters, and once again disputing parties generally represent themselves. Merry introduces the notion of 'legal consciousness', by which she means the 'ways people understand and use law'. This consciousness is (citing Bourdieu 1977) 'embodied in ... practical knowledge' and (citing Comaroff and Comaroff 1987) is expressed 'in the way people act and speak as well as in the content of what they say' (Merry 1990: 5). She thereby combines two perspectives normally kept distinct: law as a strategic process of maximising self-interest in the pursuit of disputes, and law as a struggle between sets of ideological symbols, offering rival interpretations of particular social events (1990: 6). This allows her to avoid the pitfalls identified by Fuller (1994) in that her concern with meaning never loses sight of the underlying coercion. Thus, she sees law as 'an ideology with hegemonic characteristics', a nexus of social and cultural forces which induces consent through its perceived legitimacy, rather than obedience through overt use of force (Merry 1990: 7); however, that hegemonic ideology itself 'contains both elements of domination and the seeds of resistance' (1990: 8).

In fact law's legitimacy derives to a significant extent from the existence of that very possibility, of mounting a successful challenge to its hegemony. Though the institutional odds are stacked against them, significant numbers of asylum applicants do succeed in making good their claims to refugee status, and from time to time the courts even deliver decisions which dismantle parts of the State's apparatus of immigration control. For example, the Court of Appeal ruled in *ex parte JCWI/B* that asylum applicants could qualify for welfare assistance under the *National Assistance Act 1948*. It reasoned that one effect of withdrawing such benefits under the 1993 Act was to diminish applicants' ability to access the appeal process, which was detrimental to the government's stated purpose of assessing genuine claims more effectively. The 1996 Bill, then going through Parliament, was immediately amended to close this loophole. Nothing daunted, the Court later ruled, in *R v. Hammersmith and Fulham*, that Parliament could never have intended those in need to have no recourse, and that local authorities were responsible for providing assistance in kind to asylum applicants meeting relevant criteria

(Harvey 2000: 173). Even when this loophole too was closed by the 1999 Act, which introduced the NASS dispersal system, the High Court decided, and the Court of Appeal confirmed, that support was being wrongly withheld in some instances *('Q')*.

For Merry, 'consciousness' is constructed through a process of interpreting 'cultural messages provided by discourses'; it is thus an aspect of person-hood, whereas 'discourse', like language itself, is a Durkheimian social fact 'rooted in institutional structures' (1990: 9). She identifies three types of legal discourse rather than Conley and O'Barr's bipolar continuum. Her 'moral discourse', being 'a discourse of relationships, of moral obligations ... tagged to definitions of social relationships' (1990: 113), is clearly very similar to their relational orientation, while her 'legal discourse' resembles their rule orientation in being 'a discourse of property, of rights ... of entitlement, of facts and truth' (1990: 112). Her concern is almost entirely with how dis-courses are used by lay litigants rather than legal practitioners. Thus, her legal discourse 'does not refer to particular laws or legal doctrines but to *folk understandings of legal relations and procedures*' (1990: 112–13; italics added). Finally, 'therapeutic discourse' portrays delinquent behaviour as environ-mentally or socially caused, rather than the result of individual fault. This discourse is 'drawn from the helping professions' (1990: 114), but again her focus is on uses of such notions by ordinary litigants rather than profes-sionals. While this discourse partially absolves offenders from blame, it also, by denying their responsibility, credits them with something less than full, autonomous personhood.

Merry devotes more attention to the perspectives of court officials than do Conley and O'Barr, showing how they try to divert 'garbage cases' (1990: 14), such as family disputes, towards mediation programmes rather than allowing them to proceed through normal legal channels. In other words, officials attempt to persuade would-be litigants to redefine their problems in thera-peutic, rather than legal, terms because they are well aware that most such problems are too complex to be reducible to single legal issues. In principle, Merry's notion that these discourses form 'part of an available repertoire to be used from time to time by *all* litigants' as part of their overall presen-tational strategies (1990: 205; italics added), seems more congenial than Conley and O'Barr's rather static association of rule and relational orienta-tions with particular socio-economic classes, genders, or ethnic backgrounds (1990b: 81). Even so, Conley and O'Barr's approach proves more useful below, simply because it applies more directly to the particular circumstances of asylum hearings. The scope for asylum applicants to choose their own styles of discourse, let alone change them strategically according to evolving perceptions of their effectiveness as the case proceeds, is virtually nil, partly because of their lack of even a folk-appreciation of UK law, but mainly because their personal discourses are suppressed by the mediation of inter-preters and legal representatives.

Whatever their differences otherwise, there is at least one characteristic which most recent scholars of the anthropology of law have in common, namely, a focus on 'cases', in the narrow legal sense, as the basic units of analysis, 'from which more abstract principles are generalized' (Conley and O'Barr 1990b: 4). This perspective is frequently shared by litigants themselves, particularly plaintiffs pressing for resolution of their problems through formal, legal processes (Merry 1990: 98). It is worth focusing for a moment on the implications of this approach, which characterises the treatment in this book too.

Even such 'proponents of extreme faithfulness to local cultural ideas' as Bohannan (1957) 'have adopted without comment this unit of analysis which, in the Anglo-American legal tradition, is the basis of the system of precedent' (Conley and O'Barr 1990b: 4). Despite their view that 'the case' is an inadequate and misleading analytical entity (1990b: 29), Conley and O'Barr do not, in practice, depart much from this unit themselves. True, their concern is not merely with formal legal processes but with the overall 'encounter of the litigant with the legal system' (1990b: 8), and they did usually interview protagonists before and after the hearings. But so too do many proponents of the 'case' method, and Conley and O'Barr's 'before and after' data play only a limited role in their analyses, and have a two-dimensional quality that contrasts strikingly with their rich data from the courtroom. They admit in the end that cases are 'sturdy analytic categories' (1990b: 167), and they too repeatedly argue in those terms. This book, too, concerns part of the 'Anglo-American legal tradition' grounded fair and square on notions of case law, so it seems entirely proper to classify the world, at least initially, as informants from within that tradition see it. We expect no less of any ethnographer, however exotic or familiar their location.

While most studies cited so far focus on formal legal proceedings, others stress 'law talk' more generally. Sarat and Felstiner studied conferences between lawyers and clients, paying attention to how 'clients are instructed in the meaning of law' in ways that 'help them relate legal rules and procedures to individual problems' (1990: 135). They identify three types of discourse: *formalism*, whereby law is portrayed as a set of rules governing procedures followed and decisions taken; *equity*, in which rules are seen as adaptable to fit individual circumstances through the legitimate exercise of judicial discretion; and *realism*, in which decisions are seen as reflecting judges' political and cultural backgrounds, with rules serving to justify rather than motivate those decisions (1990: 136–9). The divorce lawyers in their study made overwhelming use of realist discourse, because the wide discretion relating to divorce settlements encourages lawyers to try to bolster their indispensability by stressing their personal insider status rather than their superior legal knowledge (1990: 148). Realist discourse also prepares clients for the possibility of losing, which can then be attributed to the idiosyncrasies of others rather than any failings in legal representation. Insofar as it predicts that decisions in similar cases will vary from judge to judge, realist discourse seems particularly well suited to lawyers preparing their clients for the lottery of the asylum courts. In reality, though, most informal law talk may be expected to consist of some combination of all three idealised strands.

Finally, if we take 'case' in the broader, not only legal, sense of 'case study', then insofar as anthropologists of law operate by generalising from particular cases, they act no differently from all other anthropologists. Despite polemical attempts to question the necessity of generalisation in anthropology (Cohen 1996), the fact remains that, as Conley and O'Barr themselves say, ethnography has always been based on 'careful, detailed observation and inductive analysis' (1990b: *xi*). In short, while Conley and O'Barr usefully make explicit the constraints and limitations of approaching legal topics through a focus on cases, neither their arguments nor their own analytical practices lead to the conclusion that we should – or can – abandon such a method. It is, indeed, the very foundation of the ethnographic approach.

2.2 LEGAL AND ANTHROPOLOGICAL DISCOURSES

Conley and O'Barr note that 'the case' is also 'the primary mechanism of *teaching* law' (1990b: 4; italics added), and this focus in legal education is confirmed by other studies (Mertz 2002). That raises two questions. What is the link, if any, between particular forms of pedagogy and distinctive occupational practices and discourses? More specifically, insofar as distinctive legal discourses or modes of thought can be identified, does it follow that anthropologists of law, too, necessarily adopt legal ways of thinking as a result of their comparable focus on cases as building blocks of their ethnographic studies; or do anthropologists and lawyers, despite this superficial similarity, conceptualise their data through quite distinct, and distinctive, modes of thought? Writers on this issue, including Conley and O'Barr themselves, have concluded that even though both disciplines conceive of their subject matter primarily in terms of 'cases', lawyers and anthropologists of law are nonetheless trained to argue in radically different – and in some respects, directly opposite – ways. Awareness of these differences is important not only for a study like this, but also for the practical reason that it helps anthropologists present their evidence in appropriate ways when acting as experts.

The 'official legal discourse' into which law students are initiated is 'far removed from the language of ordinary people' and 'tends to transform or simply to ignore' the discourses of litigants themselves; moreover, although the purpose of law is to address particular problems faced by individual persons, its professional discourse is 'predominantly about purportedly neutral principles whose application is believed to transcend human variation' (Conley and O'Barr 1990b: 9). Most crucially, law students' primary sources of information are written appellate court decisions (Conley and O'Barr 1988: 468–70; Mertz 2002). Although sequences of preceding events are briefly summarised in such decisions – those initially giving rise to litigation, *and* the preceding litigation in the lower courts – they are divested of specific details, and the contexts within which they occurred are mostly lost. Here, for example, is the start of the leading speech by Lord Hope of Craighead in the House of Lords asylum decision in *Horvath* (see also §4.2.2):

> The appellant is a citizen of the republic of Slovakia. He comes from a village called Palin in the county of Michalovce, where he lived with his wife and child and other members of his family. He and his family are Roma, who are known colloquially as gypsies. The Roma, who are widely distributed across the country, constitute about 10 per cent of the population of Slovakia. They are a small minority in the village to which the appellant belongs. On 15 October 1997 he arrived in the United Kingdom with his wife and child and claimed asylum. He said that he feared persecution in Slovakia by skinheads, against whom the Slovak police were failing to provide protection for Roma. He also said that, along with other Roma, he had been unable to find work, that he had not been afforded the normal public facilities as to his marriage and schooling for his child and that in these respects he was being discriminated against. He maintained that he was afraid that if he and his family were returned to Slovakia they would again be attacked by skinheads as they were Roma, and that they would not get protection from the police.
>
> His application for asylum was refused by the Secretary of State. The [adjudicator] did not find him to be a credible witness and dismissed his appeal. The Immigration Appeal Tribunal found that his assertions of fact were consistent with other evidence which was before them about the position of Roma in Slovakia, so they reversed the [adjudicator's] finding on credibility. But they concluded that, while he had a well-founded fear of violence by skinheads, this did not amount to persecution because he had not shown that he was unable or, through fear of persecution, unwilling to avail himself of the protection of the state. The Court of Appeal (Stuart-Smith, Ward and Hale LLJ) dismissed his appeal against the determination of the tribunal . . .

The appellant's life history leading up to his asylum claim, and the prior litigation in the lower courts, are succinctly set out, one paragraph devoted to each. Such brevity has the practical advantage of restraining the written judgment within manageable proportions, but is also seen as necessary in principle, to 'facilitate the application of the decisive legal principles' (Conley and O'Barr 1990b: 11). Thus:

> the raw material of the case is treated as transparent, transformed into

a window through which the law views the set of constructed meanings it calls 'facts'. . . . What is remarkable is that the process is taken entirely for granted by lawyers and has elicited virtually no scholarly commentary.

Traditional legal theory has focused on rules, rights, and responsibilities, rather than the idiosyncracies of litigants. Most law school teaching is still premised on the formalist belief that law is a set of discoverable principles and its corollary assumption that judges find facts, and then identify and apply the relevant legal principles (1990b: 11).

The dominant schools of legal theory acknowledge that discourse plays a central role in the legal process, because the process of law is an interpretive one, but they see interpretation as the business of judges, who 'decide what the law is by interpreting the practice of other judges deciding what the law is' (Dworkin 1986: 410). In other words, their interests lie in the discourses of professional lawyers, not those of lay litigants. This is clearly a fundamental difference between legal scholars and anthropologists, though even among the former that view is not wholly unchallenged. Writers belonging to the critical legal studies movement (Kennedy 1976, West 1988) question whether legal rules are really neutral, and argue instead that judicial behaviour may be influenced by factors such as class, race, and gender – rather as Conley and O'Barr do in relating rule and relational orientations to the socio-economic status of litigants.

Conley and O'Barr were not the first to note the role of pedagogy in maintaining distinctive professional world views. For example, Paul Atkinson (1977) pointed out the importance of 'clinics' as teaching devices in Edinburgh Medical School. The teacher (a consultant) and a group of students do a round of patient visits in the wards, and a set of Socratic teaching dialogues takes place at each bedside, whereby students elicit patients' complaints through questions and answers, encouraged and commented on by the consultant. At first sight, such training seems to involve immersion in the work of real doctors in the real-life setting of the hospital ward, but things are not quite as they seem. First, the students are not really part of everyday ward activity; if a patient suddenly requires emergency treatment this immediately makes visible what is usually hidden, that their actions are not actually therapeutic. Second, the apparent processes of discovery which students undertake do not yield genuine diagnoses at all, because the 'right answers' are already known to the teacher, who judges students' questions 'relevant' if they seem likely to lead to replication of the initial diagnosis, and their diagnoses 'correct' if they do indeed replicate it. Conversely, if students get off the point, hints are dropped to get the questioning back on course. The prior diagnosis of this patient by qualified medical staff thus defines the 'medical reality' played out during the clinic, and the consultant ensures that this 'reality' emerges in properly systematic fashion.

Patients, too, are implicated in the game. Their medical histories will have been recorded before, yet the fiction is kept up that students are eliciting fresh information. Patients, often well aware of their diagnoses, must conceal these from the students and merely answer their questions. The teacher monitors the flow of information, instructing patients on how much to reveal, or dropping hints to the class. In this way, students go through processes of simulated discovery, leading to outcomes known in advance to the teacher and even the patient. Consequently, students 'discover' what they should discover, and the procedures of clinical enquiry are validated by the orderly appearance of clinical 'facts' (1977: 97).

Bedside teaching is thus a 'working model' of medical reality, designed to affirm the primacy of bedside experience as guaranteeing the medical knowledge of the qualified practitioner. The ultimate effect is to make it appear that symptoms convey an immanent message to those who have learned to see, who have acquired the 'clinical gaze' (Foucault 1973: 109). One 'reads' the symptoms, listens to the replies, and from this, and from one's accumulated experience, one discovers what is really there but previously hidden. Clinics thereby serve as 'training for dogmatism' or 'devices for the reproduction of medical certainty' (Atkinson 1977: 103), through which doctors are taught to see the world in a distinctive way, which henceforth seems to them to be natural and present in reality itself.

This does not mean that medical procedures are ineffective or falsely based. It simply recognises that the models of and for the world inculcated into Western doctors are, inevitably, products of their cultural experiences as medical students. They are also products of the medical profession's hegemony within its own field of expertise. In one of the earliest applications of Foucauldian notions to ethnographic research findings, Atkinson traces the origins of the clinic to the historical struggle between hospital clinicians and laboratory-based medical researchers, a struggle so decisively won by the former that medical researchers are today professionally marginalised. One of the clinicians' key arguments in this struggle for supremacy concerned the privileged knowledge granted them by their accumulated experience and 'clinical gaze'. One result of this triumph of practical knowledge over 'book learning', of artisans over scientists, was that medical education now resembles a form of apprenticeship (1977: 85–6). Training at the bedside, not theories learned in lectures, provides the ultimate validation of the 'authenticity' of medical knowledge, and arguments from experience are commonly used and considered unanswerable. Anthropologists citing their own ethnography occupy similarly privileged positions, since fieldwork is at least as central to their professional status as clinical experience is for doctors; the 'I was there' argument can only be refuted by questioning the ethnographer's honesty or competence.

The Socratic dialogue is a core teaching method in law schools too, as a glance at any Ivy League website will confirm (see also Cicchino 2001). Even so, there are obvious differences between medical and legal training; for instance, even in modern law courses involving mock courtrooms, there are no real litigants replaying their roles as hospital patients do. In that sense, the fictions of legal pedagogy are further removed from the 'realities' they seem to impart. Nonetheless, legal training arguably has similar effects to those of teaching clinics, inculcating a positive evaluation of experience gained through mock praxis. Law students are taught a thought process that involves finding 'facts', selecting appropriate legal rules, and applying these rules to the facts to produce a legally correct result.

Just as teaching clinics make it appear to medical students that diagnoses are arrived at through the 'clinical gaze' of an experienced practitioner, so too the focus in legal training upon the discussion of written judicial decisions implies that this 'apparently straightforward process' is the means whereby specific cases are actually decided. The parallels between doctors applying their 'clinical gaze' and adjudicators reaching asylum decisions using 'judicial knowledge' (Jarvis 2000: 16) seem marked. Consequently, 'the dominant view in both the teaching and practice of law [is] that most cases are decided by a value-neutral process of rule selection and application' (Conley and O'Barr 1990b: 60). Students are required to concentrate on 'the structures of text and authority that give legal opinions power', rather than the 'attendant moral and social contexts' (Mertz 2002). If this is indeed what happens in conventional academic courses, how much more so might it apply to the apprentice-like systems of pupillage, whereby trainee barristers shadow their pupil-masters (Morison and Leith 1992: 21, 159)? Lawyers, like doctors, internalise during their training 'both a way of talking about problems and the logic that lies behind that way of talking' (Conley and O'Barr 1998: 135), and this professional discourse is the means whereby law exerts its coercive and discursive power (Muller-Hoff 2001).

Other scholars agree that there are basic differences between how lawyers and anthropologists think, and although they have all developed their own vocabularies for expressing these, the general implications are strikingly similar in each case. For example, Kandel (1992: 1–4) highlights somewhat schematically six ways in which lawyers and anthropologists think differently.

First, both are concerned with issues of responsibility, but in different ways reflecting their different purposes. Lawyers are concerned with locating liability, with attributing blame or responsibility in order to punish or compensate, whereas anthropologists seek to explain socio-cultural reality in general terms which transcend the faults of particular individuals. Second, acts and their consequences are assessed normatively or even moralistically by lawyers, whereas the prime concern of anthropologists is to describe and explain them as aspects of local culture and practice, while maintaining a stance of pragmatic, if not necessarily ethical or epistemological, relativism (cf. Driessen 1983: 479). One can summarise these first two points by saying that law is *pre*scriptive, while anthropology is *de*scriptive. Alternatively, one might say that lawyers are strongly rule oriented whereas anthropologists are almost bound to be relationally oriented.

Third, lawyers apply abstract principles in order to resolve specific cases, whereas anthropologists study specific cases in order to construct abstract models. Here Kandel is making precisely the same point as Conley and O'Barr when they contrast deductive legal reasoning with the inductive reasoning characteristic of anthropologists. Like her other distinctions, though, this is of course a matter of broad contrasts rather than universal features. Anthropology and law are founded upon these opposed styles of reasoning but not wholly subsumed by them; for example, deductive reasoning is 'central' to legal reasoning but the latter cannot be reduced to the former (MacCormick 1994: ix; see below and §9.1).

The fourth contrast is between discrete and multiple notions of causality. As the Australian High Court noted in *March* v. *Stramare*:

> In philosophy and science, the concept of causation has been developed in the context of explaining phenomena by reference to the relationship between conditions and occurrences. In law, on the other hand, problems of causation arise in the context of ascertaining or apportioning legal responsibility for a given occurrence. . . . Thus, at law, a person may be responsible for damage when his or her wrongful conduct is [only] one of a number of conditions sufficient to produce that damage (gloss added; see Edmond 2004b: 144).

For lawyers, in other words, an event's cause is inseparable from allocation of responsibility for it, and their presentations in court are structured as deductive searches for or denials of blame or responsibility. Every civil injury is presumed to have a human agent as its cause, and the aim is to portray their client's adversary as the agent responsible for the injuries giving rise to litigation. For anthropologists, by contrast, causality is multiple and while actions by individuals may be the immediate causes of particular outcomes, the ultimate causes are seen as systemic. Even applied anthropologists aim to 'change the system' not 'realign the parties' (Kandel 1992: 3).

The fifth difference relates to contrasting notions of 'facts' and 'truth'. Lawyers speak of 'facts' to distinguish them from 'laws' rather than to make claims about their epistemological status. The distinction is procedurally important because matters of law are for judges to decide, whereas juries (if present) decide matters of fact. Legally speaking, therefore, a fact is something which can be decided by a lay person without knowledge of the law, such as the reasonableness of an action or the meaning of an everyday word (*Cozens* v. *Brutus*). For lawyers, moreover, 'truth ultimately lies in the story told by the human witness of the human act', whereas for anthropologists, says Kandel (1992: 3), the equivalent of 'truth' is the replicable analysis of factual data. While there is certainly a valid contrast here, this way of putting it implies a surprisingly scientistic view of anthropology for an article written while post-modernism was in full cry on North American campuses. I do think anthropology is a science, but not in this simple fashion (Good 1996), and for that reason I prefer O'Barr's formulation, that anthropologists are generally not interested in getting to the bottom of what happened in any absolute legal or scientific sense, as in finding out what their informants *think* happened (O'Barr 2001: 321). These issues reappear later in more complex form (§6.1; Chapter 11).

Finally, the two professions are said to display different approaches to temporality. Laws, say Kandel, are atemporal but only sporadically applied to particular events in real time, whereas anthropological fieldwork is centrally concerned with the generation of socio-cultural patterns through the continuous unfolding of events in real time. Again the contrast seems a little stark, and one might question the characterisation of anthropology implied by this form of words since, for example, ethnography clearly involves the study of values – which by definition persist over time – as well as events.

Rigby and Sevareid (1992) take this kind of comparison somewhat further. They start from their experiences as teachers, reporting the different responses evoked when Robert Gardner's celebrated ethnographic film *Dead Birds*, a study of warfare in Papua New Guinea, is shown to groups of law and anthropology students. Law students accept the scenes in the film as 'facts', and use them to illustrate general principles such as the need for codified laws and strong government, whereas anthropology students start by questioning the 'facts' themselves. Is this behaviour truly indigenous or a by-product of colonialism? Is the director imposing Western analytic categories on people in the film? Rigby and Sevareid see this difference as illustrating a general contrast. Lawyers take the notion of 'fact' as philosophically unproblematic, and are concerned with determining which general principles these facts call into play. Anthropologists are more conscious – because of their discipline's focus on fieldwork – of the problems of obtaining and using data, and less inclined to speak of 'facts' without hedging the notion around with qualifications. Clifford (1988: 321) argues, while making similar points, that these characteristics of legal thought are concomitants of the adversarial nature of legal proceedings, which require yes/no answers, not the 'yes but' or 'it depends' equivocations generally favoured by anthropologists.

Furthermore, say Rigby and Sevareid (1992), these contrasts in forms of reasoning go beyond the deductive–inductive dichotomy. Lawyers reason syllogistically whereas anthropologists reason analogically and dialectically. They juxtapose a classic syllogism and an example of legal reasoning, to demonstrate their congruence, but I shall use a different legal example (from MacCormick 1994: 25), which makes my present point more clearly. Suppose a shopkeeper sells a bottle of lemonade; the purchaser drinks it and becomes ill, and it proves to contain carbolic acid. Here, the major premise states the law, the minor premise states the facts found to be true, and the decision is reached by syllogistic reasoning:

	Classical syllogism	Legal syllogism
Major premise (law)	All men are mortal	If goods sold by one person to another have defects unfitting them for their proper use but not visually apparent, then the goods are not of merchantable quality.
Minor premise (fact)	Socrates is a man	In the present case, the goods sold had defects unfitting them for their proper use but not visually apparent.
Conclusion	Socrates is mortal	The goods were not of merchantable quality.

Although their structures are the same there is a crucial difference, namely, that whereas both premises in a classical syllogism are universally valid statements, the minor premises in legal syllogisms are based upon legal 'findings of fact', applicable only at certain times and places. Moreover, decisions reached in one case – in Rigby and Severeid's own example, that a wheelchair is not a cycle within the meaning of the law, but rather the functional equivalent of an able-bodied person's legs, so its use in a public park is not an offence – may become precedents to be cited as factual major premises in other cases. Syllogisms are themselves forms of deductive reasoning. Thus, the generalised form of legal reasoning is: (i) in general, if p then q; (ii) in the present case, p; (iii) therefore, q (MacCormick 1994: 21–32).

By contrast, the analogic reasoning characteristic of anthropologists seeks to explain a phenomenon yet to be understood in terms of phenomena which are already understood (for example, the pervasive analogy that culture is like language). Moreover, anthropologists are entirely used to dealing with situations where different writers take different theoretical perspectives, and to working out their own theoretical approach to particular data by means of dialectical reasoning. Rather than major premise, minor premise, conclusion, anthropological reasoning customarily moves from thesis, to antithesis, to synthesis.

Finally, Driessen points to one further difference between legal and social scientific thinking, broadly consistent with what has been said so far:

> Legal reasoning is nonprobabilistic and is associated with a large tolerance for low-accuracy results. In contrast, social science is inherently probabilistic, and the degree of accuracy is important in distinguishing 'good' from 'bad' social science results (1983: 479).

Above all, through its convention that matters established to the requisite standard of proof become 'facts', most legal decision making 'collapses' probabilities into certainties and thereafter proceeds 'as though uncertainty does not exist' (Fienberg 1989: 78). Arguably, though, this is less true of asylum hearings than of other areas of law (*Karanakaran*; §10.4).

One problem with such stark contrasts between legal and anthropological discourses is that their portrayals of legal modes of thought carry more conviction for anthropological readers than their characterisations of anthropology, all of which seem to require more hedging and glossing than these analyses provide. It would come as no surprise to discover that lawyers felt just the same, but the other way round. For example, although Rigby and Sevareid's contrast is helpful, it may be somewhat overstated. It is certainly true that many before them have portrayed anthropological thought as analogic and dialectical (Tambiah 1973), but lawyers too employ such forms of reasoning. Their analogies are often drawn, characteristically, from within the legal field itself (MacCormick 1994: 155), but this is not always so. One celebrated example of analogic reasoning in British asylum law is Lord Hoffmann's parallel with Nazi Germany in *Islam and Shah*, which led him to conclude that 'women in Pakistan' form a persecuted social group even though not all are in fact persecuted:

> Suppose oneself in Germany in 1935. There is discrimination against Jews in general, but not all Jews are persecuted. Those who conform to the discriminatory laws, wear yellow stars out of doors and so forth can go about their ordinary business. But those who contravene the racial laws are persecuted. Are they being persecuted on grounds of race? In my opinion, they plainly are. It is therefore a fallacy to say that because not all members of a class are being persecuted, it follows that persecution of a few cannot be on grounds of membership of that class. . . . In the case of Mrs Islam, the legal and social conditions which . . . existed in Pakistan and which left her unprotected against violence by men were discriminatory against women. For the purposes of the Convention, this discrimination was the critical element in the persecution. In my opinion, this means that she feared persecution because she was a woman.

It is equally common for judicial decisions to balance rival precedents in what reads suspiciously like a form of dialectic, a tendency which becomes even more evident in the higher courts. For example, Lord Steyn's reasoning in *Islam and Shah* involves detailed examination of international precedents, and the reaching of a conclusion by balancing one against the other:

> There is some authority for this view. The origin of the idea appears to be the decision of the United States Court of Appeals, Ninth Circuit, in *Sanchez-Trujillo* . . . (1986) [but] on circuits other than the Ninth Circuit, a less restrictive interpretation . . . has been adopted. The foundation of

the contrary view is the earlier decision of the Board of Immigration Appeals in *In re Acosta* (1985) . . . It is therefore clear that there are divergent streams of authority in the United States. And it may be right to say that the preponderance of US case law does not support *Sanchez-Trujillo*.

So the differences identified by Kandel, Rigby, and Sevareid seem matters of emphasis rather than absolute contrasts. Moreover, by limiting themselves to discourse they risk presenting idealisations of lawyers and anthropologists, which might or might not be borne out in their actual behaviour. According to Travers a fundamental weakness in the sociology of law is that many sociological accounts 'tell us very little about the content of legal *practice*' (1999: 41, italics added), and there is certainly a need to study the routine, day to day practices of legal practitioners through direct fieldwork, in order to gain a rounded understanding of occupational identity. The simple binary oppositions which characterise comparative analyses of professional discourse are then partly eroded by the realisation that the two professional groups have much in common, such as a concern with the reliability and credibility of informants/witnesses, and the claim to 'an authoritative capacity to sift evidence and derive rational and persuasive conclusions from it' (Jasanoff 1995: 8).

Any such 'checklist' comparisons are bound to involve elements of caricature, however, and the question is whether, despite these reservations, they succeed in identifying valid contrasts which advance understanding. In my opinion there are indeed some valuable points to be retained from these discussions. Above all, it is important to remember that lawyers take matters which have been established to the appropriate standard of proof to be 'facts', and see their subsequent task as deciding how the law should properly be applied to those facts, whereas for anthropologists 'facts' are always products of a particular theoretical approach, and 'truth' is at best provisional and contested.

2.3 ANTHROPOLOGY IN THE COURTS

> Remember not to take what happens here as normal.
>
> (Clifford 1988: 327)

Anthropologists have only rarely appeared as experts in British courts, but there is a much longer tradition of legal engagement in the United States, where even a quarter of a century ago anthropologists had 'appeared in an astonishingly wide range of cases . . . on everything from racial segregation, miscegenation laws, and child custody to the blood types of putative fathers, the nature of religious communities, and the cultural background of criminal defendants' (Rosen 1977: 556).

One explanation for this greater involvement is that anthropology in the United States has always been a far broader church than was true of British social anthropology until very recently. There were also pressing issues on their doorsteps which made it only natural for US courts to encounter the evidence of anthropologists. Their principal role was in cases involving Native Americans, but anthropologists also played key parts in legal battles over segregation in the 1950s and 1960s. Most strikingly, seven years before the landmark 1954 Supreme Court decision in *Brown* v. *Board of Education* that segregated education was inherently unequal, Robert Redfield was called with great success by the NAACP in 1947 as an expert in *Sweatt* v. *Painter*, which challenged the segregated provision of law education in Texas. Redfield was an inspired choice, an experienced educational administrator and trained lawyer, quite apart from his anthropological expertise.

The impact of anthropologists on such cases was arguably limited, in that their evidence was often not a determining factor but merely 'a seemingly objective source of authority to lend legitimacy to decisions reached on other grounds' (Faigman 1999: 120–1). The only occasion when the US Supreme Court acted explicitly on the basis of anthropological information was *Wisconsin* v. *Yoder*, an appeal by members of the Amish community against conviction for failing to send children to school beyond eighth grade. The Court exempted Amish from school attendance, largely on the basis of evidence from anthropologist John Hostetler (whose own Amish background gave grounds for questioning his objectivity; Rosen 1977: 564). This was not an unmixed blessing, however. It led the Court to adopt a less liberal definition of religion, so as not to encourage other claims for exemption (Donovan and Anderson 2003: 101).

Rosen argues that acting as an expert witness should be a two-way street, whereby the impact of anthropologists on the legal process is counterbalanced by the effect of the experience on their own thinking (1977: 567). Even so, it remains relatively uncommon for anthropologists to reflect in print on such matters. Culhane (1998) gives a detailed account of the role of anthropological experts in a Canadian land claims case, but this is based on transcripts rather than direct observation. One rare example of an ethnography based on observation of anthropologists testifying in court is Clifford's account of the 1977 hearing by the Federal District Court in Boston, Massachusetts, of a land claim by the Mashpee Indians of Cape Cod. This occupied a far more exalted place in the legal pantheon than the production line of asylum cases which shuffles in and out of British asylum hearing centres like Taylor House in Islington. Here there were whole teams of lawyers on both sides, headed by high-priced Boston attorneys; the hearing of testimony by the dozens of witnesses lasted 41 days; and each side had arrays of experts, including two anthropologists, a historian, an ethno-historian, a genealogist, a sociologist, and a Native American scholar-activist (1988: 317–18).

Compared to other land claim suits pursued by Native Americans at that time, the Mashpee case was unusual in starting one step further back. Before the question of tribal land could even be raised, the court had to decide whether the Mashpee was in fact an Indian tribe and, if so, whether it was the same tribe that in the nineteenth century lost its land through legislative action (1988: 277). The case was therefore addressed to matters dear to anthropological hearts – typologising and classifying. How does one define 'tribe'? Were and are Mashpee a 'tribe' in terms of that definition? Precisely this question was put to anthropologist Jack Campisi (see Campisi 1991):

> *Campisi*:   I believe they are a tribe.
> *Judge*:   Your belief is one thing. Is it your professional opinion as an anthropologist that they are a tribe?
> *Campisi*:   Yes.

What does a professional anthropologist mean by tribe? Campisi lists five criteria: (1) a group of Indians, members by ascription – that is, by birth, (2) a kinship network, (3) a clear consciousness of kind – 'we' versus 'they', (4) a territory or homeland, and (5) a political leadership (Clifford 1988: 318–19).

This illustrates one of the differences discussed earlier between legal and anthropological discourses (§2.2). Given their pragmatic need to counter the threat posed by uncertainty in adversarial contexts, lawyers seek to 'repackage' anthropological findings by making them appear 'more final, absolute, and certain than they really are' (Donovan and Anderson 2003: 94). While giving evidence, anthropologists themselves may be pressured into unwonted degrees of certainty:

> the need to make a clear case to counterbalance an opposing one, discourages opinions of a 'yes, but', 'it depends on how you look at it' kind. Experts on the stand were required to answer the question: Is there a tribe in Mashpee? Yes or no? (Clifford 1988: 321).

In such circumstances, experts who attempt to remain true to the undogmatic caution positively valued in academia, can easily be made to seem evasive or insufficiently rigorous under forceful cross-examination. Faced with the innate positivism of the courts, it becomes almost impossible to acknowledge the historical and political contingency of anthropology as a discipline:

> On the stand it was difficult to explain that the word *tribe* could mean different things to a scholar discussing a range of aboriginal systems, reservation Indians of the nineteenth century, and legally reorganized groups of the 1930s, or that the term was unlikely to mean the same thing for an author of evolutionist theories writing in the 1950s and an expert

evaluating the aspirations of eastern Indian communities in the 1970s (Clifford 1988: 322).

Courts are, for their part, almost entirely unaware of the moral and methodological dilemmas posed for anthropologists from one culture, especially a hegemonic one, when required to represent or speak for groups of people from another. Such arguments seem particularly applicable to Australia where anthropologists have had equivalent experience of acting as experts, but where the pitfalls of so doing became even more apparent as a result of their involvement in the Hindmarsh Island Bridge controversy. The fact that so much core cultural knowledge was held secretly by particular individuals and groups not only posed very difficult ethical issues in that case, but also raised basic questions about how anthropologists might set about convincing the courts to view cultural values as dynamic responses to contemporary circumstances rather than recognising only those whose historical continuity could be established (Weiner 1999; Kirsch 2001). This last point has arisen in Canadian land claims cases too (Culhane 1998).

Chapter 3

Studying asylum

3.1 PREVIOUS STUDIES OF ASYLUM PROCESSES

Considering its high political profile and the intense public and media concern, remarkably little empirical research has been carried out on asylum processes in the UK. There are innumerable books and articles written by lawyers for lawyers, dealing with legislation (Harvey 2000; Phelan 2001), procedures and guidelines (Henderson 1997, 2003; Berkowitz and Jarvis 2000; Billings 2000; Deans 2000), or case law (Jackson 1999; Symes 2001; Symes and Jorro 2003), but this corpus is based upon legislation and written judgments rather than field observation, and there has been almost no research using critical or deconstructionist methods external to law itself. A number of books set such matters into broader context by dealing with the recent political and legal history of asylum in the UK and Europe (Schuster 2003; Gibney 2004), welfare support (Billings 2002; Robinson *et al.* 2003), human rights (Blake and Husain 2003), or wider policy issues (Pirouet 2001; Stevens 2004). There have also been studies of the treatment of particular categories of asylum applicants, such as women (Spijkerboer 2000; Crawley 2001; see §4.3) and homosexuals (McGhee 2001); or of particular ethnic or national groups such as Czech Roma (O'Nions 1999), Sikhs (Medical Foundation 1999a), Turkish Kurds (Medical Foundation 1999b), or Tamils (Medical Foundation 2000; Good 2003a).

Until recently there was hardly any research into why and how people come to the UK to claim asylum, rather than to some other country. Morrison's (1998) investigation of refugee smuggling into the UK, using case studies and interviews with asylum applicants, found that although personal preferences, based on perceptions of Britain's human rights record, or the presence here of friends or relatives, do play parts in bringing people to this country, many refugees have little say in the matter. For those able to exercise choice, the preferred destination is often Europe in general rather than any specific country. Böcker and Havinga (1999) used similar methods to compare the UK with the Netherlands and Belgium. They identified four principal factors influencing refugees' choices of destination: historical links between the countries of origin and refuge; perceptions as to the general asylum policies of various countries; their relative accessibility; and chance events during the journey. The relative importance of these factors depends partly on circumstances (enforced haste of departure, for example), but the key determinant is usually the first – especially 'the presence of friends, relatives or compatriots in the country of destination' (1999: 51). Bijleveld and Taselaar (2000), also looking at the Netherlands, argue that while the first two factors are important for independent, lone travellers, the destinations of others are generally determined by their *agent's* knowledge about asylum procedures and living circumstances in different European countries.

The Home Office itself only belatedly began commissioning research on this key policy area. Robinson and Segrott (2002), surveying a non-representative sample of 65 asylum applicants, concluded that most persons fleeing persecution are more concerned with escape than with choosing their destinations. The degree of personal choice depends on the extent to which refugees plan their journey rather than being forced to leave at short notice; personal access to travel documents and financial resources; existence of direct transport links; and the extent of their dependence on agents (2002: 4–5). Among those who positively chose to come to the UK, the principal reasons included the presence of relatives or friends here; a belief in the safety and tolerance of the UK towards asylum applicants; historical links between their home country and the UK; and their ability to speak or wish to learn English. However, they found little evidence that asylum applicants had advance knowledge about asylum procedures, welfare benefits, or employment prospects in the UK.

A companion study by Koser and Pinkerton (2002) focused on how social networks – family and friends, community organisations, and intermediaries such as labour recruiters or travel agents – influenced refugees' choices of destination by supplying information, facilitating travel, and assisting them on arrival. Such networks are perceived by refugees as more trustworthy than formal information sources, although in fact network members may pass on only the positive aspects of their experience, and tend eventually to 'lose their intuition' as to the kinds of information prospective refugees might need (2002: 2). Community organisations are particularly effective information channels, being more broadly informed than relatives and friends, yet sufficiently personal to maintain trust. The growing importance of agents has led to them partly supplanting these other networks as sources of information, however.

Equally under-researched – with the important exception of Crawley's (1999) study of interviews conducted by Immigration Officers (§5.1) – is the crucial phase covering the initial making of an asylum claim, its administrative processing by IND, and the initial decision making on the claim. Furthermore, although it is clear how asylum applicants *ought* to be legally represented (Henderson 1997, 2003), there have been few accounts by British practitioners of their actual experiences of representing asylum applicants, along the lines of the case studies by the American lawyer Einolf (2001). The parable by David Burgess (1997), a prominent asylum solicitor, does however illustrate how the structural characteristics of the legal system, coupled with the incompetence, laziness, or downright dishonesty of some practitioners, may signally fail to protect some of the most vulnerable asylum applicants.

It is less surprising to find few accounts by refugees themselves, describing the asylum process from their perspective. After all, most are not fluent in English; a significant proportion come from poor and/or rural backgrounds which offered them little access to education; and many have suffered severe educational and emotional disruption because of the very problems and disturbances which caused them to flee. One striking exception is the book by journalist Victor Lal (1997), tracing the history of his own asylum application following the Fijian coup of 1987. One can only assume that the difficulties, bureaucratic errors, and uncomprehending hostility which he describes – as well as the delays; it took seven years for his claim to be accepted – understate the experiences of most applicants, because they occurred despite his success in mustering numerous influential supporters to his cause, including Oxford professors and the former premier of an Australian State. The overwhelming majority of applicants enjoy no such backing, and one cannot imagine that they fare any better.

There have also been a few medical studies of asylum applicants, particularly torture victims and trauma sufferers (Peel 1998; Forrest 2000; Frey 2002; Iacopino 2002). These call into serious question two crucial 'common sense' assumptions frequently made by IND caseworkers, and sometimes by the courts. The first is that applicants will mention at the earliest opportunity all the serious incidents of persecution which they experienced. The second is that because traumatic events are such important moments in a person's life-history, they will be remembered with especial clarity. Both assumptions are examined critically later in light of medical findings and legal research (§8.2); as we shall see, the reality is more complex.

There have been a few fieldwork-based studies of other sections of the British legal system (McBarnet 1981; Rock 1993), but nothing like the renaissance in legal anthropology evident in the United States. The only previous ethnographic study of British immigration courts was by the sociologist Max Travers, who takes an ethnomethodologically-inspired, comparative approach to the sociology of work and organisations (1999: 4–5). His research embraced immigration generally, not just asylum, and was more directly concerned with the wider political context than my own work. For example, he interviewed politicians, senior civil servants concerned with immigration policy and legislation, and political pressure groups, all of whom fall outside the scope of this book. Conversely, the present research goes beyond Travers in its emphasis on experts and interpreters, neither of whom figure in his account. Such is the pace of change in this field of public policy, moreover, that although my research began within months of Travers' book appearing, the substantive context had already changed in three key respects. First, the *Immigration and Asylum Act 1999* had come into force, though Travers does anticipate its effects to some extent. Second, the 'primary purpose rule', whereby consular officials overseas could refuse entry to husbands or fiancés of British citizens if the 'primary purpose' of the marriage was to gain admission to the UK, had been abandoned to the apparent relief of all parties in the courts. This had especially affected arranged marriages, where prior relationships between spouses were hard to demonstrate in British cultural terms. Third, the *Human Rights Act 1998* had begun to apply to asylum appeals, though its legal consequences remained to be tested. On the other hand, his research, like mine, involved participant observation in hearing centres, and he too 'shadowed' adjudicators and interacted with practitioners, though these were smaller parts of his work and the focus even there was different.

3.2 RESEARCH METHODS

Much of the present research was entirely conventional methodologically, involving as it did more or less formal (that is, pre-arranged rather than pre-structured) interviews with tribunal chairs, adjudicators, barristers, solicitors, country experts and doctors; shadowing the same kinds of people as they carried out their work, or 'hanging out' with them as they drank their coffee; and studying legal archives. Most anthropologists have experience of working in all these ways, which do not require any special description, explanation, or justification.

In addition, however, I spent a great deal of time – far more than initially envisaged, so fascinating did I find it – observing and transcribing actual asylum appeal hearings. The methods and problems involved call for more detailed examination, and it is helpful to compare them with another study of court proceedings already well known in the literature. In his account of the Mashpee case (§2.3), James Clifford describes how he handled a similar situation – though not, crucially from a methodological viewpoint, an identical one:

> I am not fictionalizing or inventing anything, nor am I presenting the whole picture. The reality presented here is the reality of a specific interest and field of vision. I attended most of the trial, and I've used my courtroom notes as a guiding thread. I've read what has been published about the history of Mashpee and the litigation. [He catalogues the relevant bibliography.] And I have consulted the trial record. But I haven't systematically interviewed participants or done first-hand research in the archives or in Mashpee (1988: 289–90; gloss added).

Clifford's sudden recourse to informal mode – 'I've'; 'haven't' – suggests unease as to the adequacy of his methods. If so, there is surely no need. No researcher talks to everyone about everything; it is simply that the structured, bounded context of the law court makes such lacunae more apparent.

The quoted passage reveals some key similarities and differences compared to my own situation and strategy. As a first set of similarities, I too have not invented anything, and it would be vainglorious to pretend that my accounts of hearings present 'the whole picture' or that they are not products of my 'specific interest' and personal 'vision'. I did not interview all participants either, although I did interview some of them and exchanged at least a few words with most others. Unlike Clifford, though, I *have* done archival research, sometimes on the life histories of particular applicants but more often, since most are not public figures, into the general events within which their individual histories unfold. The most fundamental difference, though, is that while I too quote and consult the trial record, that record is not the independent product of functionaries in the court system, but the result of my own note-taking at the time, written up to standards of minimal intelligibility as soon as possible afterwards.

There are no official transcripts of proceedings in asylum appeals. Adjudicators are expected, and were formerly required by rule 43 of the *Asylum Appeals (Procedure) Rules 1996*, to maintain 'records of proceedings' – generally in longhand, though by 2000 a few bold souls were using laptops for this purpose. These are not public documents, though they *are* added to case files and may be considered as evidence by tribunals if there is any dispute over what took place. To tape record hearings was out of the question, but I quickly found that I wanted as full a record as possible of dialogue in court, not merely a précis of the substantive issues. This involved much frantic scribbling, and was only physically possible because of the repeated hiatuses introduced by the need to interpret questions and answers.

Acting as one's own stenographer has obvious disadvantages. As Latour comments of the similar situations which he encountered in the Conseil d'État:

> To the technical character of the files must be added the uncertainties of transcription, the usual oral obscurities, allusions tossed out by people who have known one another for years and, of course, the extreme incomprehension of the observer (2002: 33–4; my translation).

I evolved a style of abbreviated writing from which dialogue could be reconstructed afterwards. Even so, a day in court generally produced at least 20 pages of tightly-packed scribble, and to hasten the writing-up process I used voice-activated software. This cut down on the sheer physical drudgery of typing, but the software was in its infancy, and although it often worked perfectly well, it would sometimes spout streams of consciousness of its own devising. Given careful editing, however, the advantages outweighed the drawbacks.

Even with electronic assistance, writing up these notes often took longer than the original hearing, especially if – as was generally the case – the record needed footnoting with references to cases cited by the representatives, or to the particular Immigration Rules on whose construction key decisions turned. All hearing rooms were equipped with Phelan's (2001) compendium of the relevant legislation and procedural rules, and I carried my own copy around with me too, to render intelligible some of the more abstruse passages of legal argument. This generally had to be done during adjournments or over lunch, however, as it was out of the question to take notes and look up regulations at the same time. Generally, though, as long as relevant paragraph and clause numbers were carefully noted down, all became clear afterwards. A more serious difficulty is that during every hearing the main parties refer regularly to their bundles of documentary evidence, and because they all have these in front of them they generally cite page and paragraph numbers rather than reading out their substantive contents. I did sometimes have limited access to documents beforehand, in that when shadowing particular adjudicators I was generally allowed to glance through evidential bundles prior to the hearings, but in the time available I could do little more than list their contents. While it is far from ideal to be taking notes on matters on which one is not fully informed, there was really little choice.

Court stenographers face similar problems, and it is worth pursuing their situation a little further to gain more insight into the strengths and weaknesses of this kind of transcribed record. Where an official transcript exists it does not, as Clifford points out, 'provide much information on the *effect* of witnesses or events in the courtroom. It omits gestures, hesitations, clothing, tone of voice, laughter, irony . . . the sometimes devastating silences' (1988: 290; italics and ellipsis in original). Transcripts must, by US law, be verbatim records of proceedings, but 'verbatim' itself is not legally defined. The dictionary definition – 'in exactly the same words' or some similar phrase – merely pushes the difficulty one step further back. Is a nod, grunt, or stammer a 'word' in this context? What are the implications of including such 'words', or leaving them out? What about simultaneous speech, or explicitly acknowledged verbal errors or rephrasings? How can court reporters avoid appearing to analyse proceedings while providing a record which is 'correct and authentic'? In coping with such matters, reporters' output must not only abide by the canons of their own profession but also be acceptable in style and content to its primary 'consumers', lawyers and judges (Walker 1990: 212–13).

Although I faced similar difficulties their relative importance was not the same. I felt no pressure to tidy up what was said, preferring to record as faithfully as possible the speech patterns of participants. This was not entirely possible in fact, for purely practical reasons. When one is taking down notes very rapidly, it is actually more time-consuming to record errors and idio-syncrasies than straightforward grammatical utterances, because more information is required in order to reproduce them accurately later. Being free to make my own decisions about what to include in the record, however, I could editorialise by commenting, whenever relevant, on precisely the kinds of non-verbal nuance to which Clifford refers. Further details could be added at the writing-up stage while events were still fresh in my mind – all with the aim of conveying as faithfully as possible the flavour of the reported events. None of this, however, can gainsay the basic and unavoidable prob-lems involved in transforming spoken and acted events into written form (Finnegan 1992: 195–9). Here court reporters are at a marginal advantage over researchers, because only certain kinds of discrepancy in verbatim records are likely to be objected to by lawyers; they may seek to get the record changed when it is a matter of garbled or missing speech, but are most unlikely to object to the 'cleaning up' (or not) of a speaker's grammar, or the omission (or not) of the ums and ahs of normal speech (Walker 1990: 203–4). There is no such consensus when it comes to researchers' priorities in striving for authenticity.

Like Clifford (1988), and Conley and O'Barr (1990b), I often present court proceedings as 'dialogue' rather than paraphrase. Although I had never employed this strategy in previous research, it seemed more appropriate and truer to the ethnographic experience to do so here, though the parentheses around 'dialogue' are meant as a reminder that this is not direct, exact quota-tion. Social scientists 'seldom have the technical competence or the stamina to produce a verbatim transcript' (Atkinson and Drew 1979: 3); here, certainly, despite the work done afterwards to expand my notes, the result is far from verbatim in terms of their stringent requirements. It should therefore be remembered throughout this book that passages of transcribed 'dialogue' are the outcomes of processes designed to retain the feel of the original, and as much as possible – but never all – of its precise content.

Sociolinguists have offered a number of explanations for the power of directly quoted speech (Conley and O'Barr 1990b: 8). One suggestion is that using direct quotations displaces responsibility because the authority of reported speech resides with the attributed source; for example, Parmentier (1986) suggests that when words supposedly emanating from God are directly quoted in the Bible, they carry more weight than when reported in para-phrased form. This seems reasonable, but does not really apply here. A second suggestion is that direct quotations demonstrate that the teller was actually present at the reported event. In some contexts that may enhance the apparent authority of their account, but here again any such demonstration is redundant, since being present is an assumed precondition for doing participant-observation fieldwork. Third, direct quotations may help draw the reader's attention to 'those aspects of an account that the reporter seeks to present as more reliable' (Conley and O'Barr 1990b: 8) – which is precisely why courts generally prohibit, by means of the hearsay rule, the reporting of speech by non-eyewitnesses.

The final suggestion is that direct quotations are more dramatic and involving for the audience (Hymes 1981; Bauman 1984; Briggs 1988), especially when performed, that is, when the reporter 'takes on the persona and/or voice qualities of those whose speech is reported' (Conley and O'Barr 1990b: 196). Performance is not a real possibility in a conventional text such as this, but even so, this explanation seems closest to the mark as far as my intentions in using direct quotation in the present book are concerned.

Bohannan famously said of the corpus of legal anthropology up to that point, that it was 'small and almost all good' (1964: 199). Two decades later, in deliberate antiphrasis, Goldman characterised it as 'large . . . inadequate and almost all bad' (1986: 350). Both positions seem overstated, but Goldman's criticism is relevant here, because it concerned the gulf, as he saw it, between the grand assertions made by anthropologists about legal processes, and the paucity of detailed evidence provided, be it details of court procedure (see Danet 1980: 516) or analysed examples of 'authentic discourse' (Goldman 1986: 350; see Conley and O'Barr 1998: 104). His critique seems less tenable now than it might have been in the 1980s, and use of direct quotation here does at least help to emasculate criticisms of that kind.

To summarise then, there are two particular reasons why direct quotation is a preferred means of presentation in this book. First, to the extent that I succeed in making these quotations true to the spirit of the original speech even if not always in word-for-word conformity to it, they provide a sounder basis for detailed analysis than a paraphrase or summary, since the very act of paraphrasing would introduce a further element of interpretation. Second, their use does, I hope, help convey a greater sense of how it feels to participate in such proceedings than paraphrase ever could. Transcribed records of hearings play an important role at various points in the ensuing discussion. It is important to reiterate, therefore, that these dialogues are not verbatim transcripts, although every effort has been made to make them accurate and intelligible, while not falsifying or misrepresenting the sense of what was said.

Chapter 4

Convention refugees

An anthropological approach

> our explanation of scientific activity should not depend in any significant way on the uncritical use of the very concepts and terminology which feature as part of that activity.
>
> (Latour and Woolgar 1986: 27)

It may seem presumptuous to include here a detailed interpretation of legislation and case law. Is this not better left to the lawyers whose training and daily practice are devoted to precisely that? Yet an ethnography of some distant region which adopted, but never analysed, the most fundamental concepts of its subjects of study would be viewed as grossly inadequate, and as Latour and Woolgar point out, precisely the same should apply to technical terms employed by members of professional groups nearer home. Morison and Leith rightly bemoan the fact that most sociological studies of law merely skirt its periphery because they stop short of addressing its 'substantive' aspects (1992: 155).

It must, however, be remembered throughout this chapter that the approach is that of an anthropologist rather than a lawyer, with all that implies epistemologically (§2.2). My prime concern is to analyse key legal concepts from the external perspective of comparative social science, not to anticipate what a court might or should decide under particular sets of circumstances. Every attempt is made to convey the legal position accurately, but like Jasanoff's important study of science and law in the USA, this book 'is about judicial styles of reasoning and thought' (1995: 22), not a summing up of the state of play under current case law.

4.1 THE REFUGEE CONVENTION IN THE EUROPEAN UNION

The legal notion of a 'refugee' developed out of the burgeoning human rights discourse following the Second World War, and its elaboration reflects the apotheosis of the nation state in the second half of the twentieth century (§1.1; Malkki 1995; Gibney 2004). One of the first international agreements of the post-war order, the *1948 Universal Declaration of Human Rights*, stated at Article 14.1 that 'Everyone has the right to seek and to enjoy in other countries asylum from persecution', and this was later extensively glossed in the *1951 UN Convention Relating to the Status of Refugees*, the key international instrument covering asylum. The Convention's preamble states the need to ensure that refugees enjoy fundamental human rights, recognises that this requires international co-operation, and charges the Office of the UN High Commissioner for Refugees (UNHCR) with co-ordinating measures by signatory States to deal with refugee problems.

The Convention was drafted with post-war Europe particularly in mind, but its initial limitation to persons who became refugees as a result of events before 1 January 1951 was removed under a 1967 Protocol. Article 1A(2) of the 1951 Refugee Convention now defines a 'refugee' as someone who:

> owing to well-founded fear of being persecuted for reasons of race, religion, nationality, membership of a particular social group or political opinion, is outside the country of his nationality and is unable or, owing to such fear, is unwilling to avail himself of the protection of that country.

The Convention must be applied without discriminating among refugees on the basis of race, religion, or country of origin (Art 3). Once admitted as refugees, they become subject to the laws of the country of refuge (Art 12), and should enjoy provisions at least as favourable as those applying to other aliens, regarding their status, property, education, welfare benefits, employment, taxation, freedom of movement, and naturalisation (Arts 7–30, 34).

People initially falling within the Convention definition cease being refugees if – without compelling reasons to the contrary – the circumstances which led to them becoming refugees no longer apply (Art 1C). Until such time, however, refugees present lawfully in a country should not be expelled except for reasons of 'national security or public order', and even then only after due legal process (Art 32). By ratifying the Convention or Protocol, a country commits itself not to 'refoul' anyone having a well-founded fear of persecution for a Convention reason, that is, not to expel or return them 'in any manner whatsoever to the frontiers of territories where his [sic] life or freedom would be threatened on account of his race, religion, nationality, membership of a particular social group or political opinion' (Art 33). Asylum applicants should not be penalised merely because they arrive illegally, provided they come 'directly from a territory where their life or freedom was threatened in the sense of Article 1', approach the authorities 'without delay', and show good cause for their illegal entry. The Convention does not apply, however, to perpetrators of war crimes; crimes against humanity; serious non-political crimes in another country; or actions contrary to UN purposes and principles (Art 1F, the 'exclusion clause'). Perpetrators of acts of 'terrorism' are not necessarily excluded from Convention protection unless these were directed indiscriminately at the public rather than institutions and officials of the hostile state (§4.2.7).

Overall, 126 countries have signed both the 1951 Convention and 1967 Protocol, and eight more signed one or the other. The geographical distribution of signatories is uneven however, not always in the ways one might expect. Participation is widespread throughout Africa and Central America, which even have their own supplementary agreements, the 1969 OAU Convention and 1984 Cartagena Declaration, respectively, whereas Asian participation is scanty. Asian signatories, a highly counter-intuitive bunch, are Azerbaijan, Cambodia, China, Iran, Israel, Japan, Kyrgyzstan, Philippines, Republic of Korea, Tajikistan, Turkey, and Yemen, whereas Bangladesh, India, Pakistan, Nepal, and Sri Lanka have signed neither the Convention nor the Protocol. Like Pakistan, India thought 'refugees' should be defined so as to include the huge numbers displaced by Partition, and 'was not convinced of the need for an international organization whose sole responsibility would be to provide legal protection' (Goodwin-Gill 1996: 264n).

Member States of the European Union have attempted over recent decades to 'harmonise' procedures for coping with would-be Convention refugees, a trend given particular impetus by the extent to which 'tougher' asylum policies became a dominant political imperative right across Europe. Many changes are aimed at expediting the processing of claims, but the effect has also been to weaken refugees' rights and the levels of protection they enjoy.

Although the *1986 Single European Act* created an internal market for goods, services, and capital, it did not provide for free movement of citizens. That was more substantially achieved by the *1990 Schengen Convention*, but the UK was not among the six participating States. Because this also involved strengthening *external* border controls, one alleged consequence was the creation of 'Fortress Europe', just as inaccessible in practice to asylum applicants as to economic migrants, who are both increasingly forced to rely on human traffickers. All 15 Member States agreed the *1990 Dublin Convention*, which aimed to stop applicants moving – or being moved on – from one Member State to another to have their claims assessed. The problem, however, was that national variations in asylum procedures and legal interpretations led to markedly different prospects of success for some applicants, depending on where their claim happened to be processed.

The *1992 Maastricht Treaty*, which formally established the European Union, increased the pressure for inter-governmental co-operation over immigration policies and practices, while the *1992 London Resolutions* defined three key (non-binding) conceptual elements of an EU-wide asylum policy: the notion of 'manifestly unfounded' asylum claims; the idea of 'safe third countries' transited by asylum applicants en route to their destination, in which it is assumed a genuine refugee would have claimed asylum; and the idea that there are countries in which no serious risk of persecution is deemed to exist (see §5.1 on 'white lists'). However, many have argued that these principles are applied inconsistently; that 'safe third countries' do not all hear asylum claims effectively; and that 'white lists' violate the principle that cases be determined on their individual merits.

Further attempts to 'harmonise' policies and practices include a 1995 Resolution setting minimum guarantees for asylum procedures and State obligations, and a 1996 'joint position' on how to interpret the Convention definition of 'refugee'. The *1997 Treaty of Amsterdam* established a five-year timescale, starting in 1999, for developing common immigration and asylum policies. At the *1999 European Council Meeting* in Tampere, EU States reiterated the goal of common guidelines and fair, efficient asylum procedures and reception standards. They asserted their respect for the right to seek asylum, and pledged to apply the 1951 Convention and the principle of non-refoulement to the full, yet critics argue that the measures taken approach the lowest common denominator as regards procedures and standards. This was made explicit by the director of the *Office français de protection des réfugiés et des apatrides* (Ofpra), who explained to a French parliamentary commission in 1996 how the German authorities had 'appliquent exactement notre politique' so as to reduce the success rate of Algerian applicants in Germany to French levels, while France had reduced the success rates of Sri Lankans by adopting German criteria (Decourcelle and Julinet 2000: 144). Even so, and despite the rhetoric of EU 'harmonisation', differences among national asylum regimes remain striking (cf. Schuster 2003).

4.2 UK INTERPRETATIONS OF THE 1951 CONVENTION

As there is no international court wherein refugee claims can be decided, the role of interpreting the 1951 Convention rests with the domestic courts of individual States. The Convention *per se* is not part of British law, but underlies domestic legislation in the sense that the United Kingdom has committed itself not to violate its Convention obligations. In the period covered by this field research, the basic UK legislation was the *Immigration Act 1971*, as amended by the *Asylum and Immigration Appeals Act 1993*, the *Asylum and Immigration Act 1996*, and the *Immigration and Asylum Act 1999*. From October 2000 the *Human Rights Act 1998*, incorporating the *European Convention on Human Rights* (ECHR) into UK law, also began to apply to asylum cases, and during the writing of this book both the *Nationality, Immigration and Asylum Act 2002* and the *Asylum and Immigration (Treatment of Claimants, etc.) Act 2004* passed into law.

Despite this torrent of legislation, much remains for the courts themselves to resolve. The drafters of the Convention left virtually every term undefined, and Article 1A(2) has undergone extensive and evolving legal interpretation ever since. Because the Convention and Protocol have international applicability, this jurisprudence has a strong international dimension, even though asylum decisions everywhere are guided by national legislation and local administrative structures and procedures. British courts regularly cite legal precedents from other countries with common-law traditions such as Canada, Australia, New Zealand, and the USA, as well as decisions by the European Court of Human Rights (ECtHR).

British case law concerning the Convention is very extensive (Jackson 1999; Symes 2001; Symes and Jorro 2003) and is only sketched out below. Key terms in the definition are considered one by one, although of course they cannot be understood in complete isolation from one another. The following sections compare interpretations offered by UNHCR's *Handbook* (1992) with those in the 2002 version of the *Asylum Policy Instructions* (*APIs*), the office manual of the Home Office's Immigration and Nationality Directorate (IND 2002a); they also summarise current UK case law, with special reference to key House of Lords decisions. The logic behind this mode of presentation is that initial Home Office decisions on asylum claims are guided mainly by the *APIs* but also refer to the *Handbook*, which is authoritative even though it does not have the force of law (Symes 2001: 3). These two sources are therefore pivotal for understanding why IND's decisions turn out as they do. When decisions are appealed the courts' interpretations become crucial, however, so case law is dealt with next. These various interpretations may differ at any given moment, but 'feedback' mechanisms keep them more or less aligned over time. IND and the courts are interpreting the self-same legislation, so the scope for wide differences of approach and understanding is restricted. Moreover, whenever significant discrepancies *do* arise, IND is bound eventually to adjust its instructions to fall into line with the courts. After all, it cannot win appeals if it persists in using arguments which those courts have already rejected.

4.2.1 'well-founded fear'

Refugees must have a *well-founded fear* regarding what will happen to them if they are refouled to their country of origin. The existence of such a fear is crucial to a successful asylum claim, so the key task for IND, and subsequently for the courts in the event of appeal, is to decide whether such fears are justified. Clearly, though, there is a potential difficulty over the subjectivity implicit in this phrase. Fear, after all, is an emotion whose genuineness is normally assessed in terms of authenticity rather than factuality, and it is possible to be genuinely afraid for reasons which others think unjustified or irrational. One approach has been to see 'well-founded fear' as comprising an objective element to be assessed on the basis of 'objective evidence' about the applicant's home country, and a subjective element arising from 'fear of the objective conditions' (Harvey 2000: 236–7). The UNHCR *Handbook* sets out this 'two-pronged test' as follows (1992: ¶37, 42–3):

> Since fear is subjective, the definition involves a subjective element in the person applying for recognition as a refugee. Determination of refugee status will therefore primarily require an evaluation of the applicant's statements rather than a judgement on the situation prevailing in his country of origin. . . . A knowledge of conditions in the applicant's country of origin – while not a primary objective – is an important element in assessing the applicant's credibility. In general, the applicant's fear should be considered well-founded if he can establish, to a reasonable degree, that his continued stay in his country of origin has become intolerable to him for the reasons stated in the definition, or would for the same reasons be intolerable if he returned . . . [His] character, his background, his influence, his wealth or his outspokenness, may lead to the conclusion that his fear of persecution is 'well-founded'.

This refers repeatedly to social status, character, and psychology, and the situation in the country of origin is said to be only a secondary factor. UNHCR's approach is not the only one, however. The influential academic authority James Hathaway (1991: 65) strongly rejects any stress on subjectivity, both because of the practical difficulties involved in assessing such matters, and because according to his reading of the Convention the concept of a 'well-founded fear' is 'inherently objective' and has nothing to do with applicants' states of mind.

Hathaway's approach is more in tune with actual practice in assessing claims. For example, the *APIs* approach the issue as follows (IND 2002a: ¶1.2.7):

> In assessing whether an applicant's fear is well-founded, the caseworker must be satisfied both that:
>
> i)   the applicant has a subjective fear of persecution, and
> ii) that objectively there are reasonable grounds for believing that the persecution feared may in fact materialise in the applicant's country of origin. . . .

The *APIs* go on (2002a: ¶1.2.7.1) to caution that caseworkers should not take into account an applicant's nervousness at interview, or panic when faced with removal; they 'should however be sensitive to the gender and cultural norms which may affect an applicant's demeanour'. They are offered no guidance on how to do this, however, and ultimately their decision must reflect 'the objective degree of prejudice' (2002a: ¶1.2.8.4). This process clearly focuses upon 'well-founded' (objective) and dismisses actual manifestations of 'fear' (subjective).

The courts too, while accepting that the test has two elements, interpret these so that the objective element 'trumps' the subjective (Harvey 2000: 238). The leading UK case on the well-founded fear test, *Sivakumaran*, involved six Sri Lankan Tamils whose asylum applications had been refused on the ground that they did not evince a well-founded fear of persecution. In the Court of Appeal Sir John Donaldson argued that the test for this involved two stages: proving that an actual fear existed, and demonstrating why that individual had good reason to possess such a fear. Fear itself was 'clearly an entirely subjective state [and] the adjectival phrase "well-founded" qualifies but cannot transform the subjective nature of the emotion'. The Secretary of State had been wrong to apply a primarily objective test; the subjective aspect could be qualified but not overridden by the objective aspect (2000: 239).

The House of Lords rejected this approach, however. Lord Keith thought that the well-foundedness of the fear should be decided objectively. The Appeal Court's formulation would permit the granting of refugee status merely because a person's fear was genuine, even if unfounded. This absurd outcome would greatly weaken the link between refugee status and human rights violations:

> [T]he general purpose of the Convention is surely to afford protection and fair treatment to those for whom neither is available in their own country, and does not extend to the allaying of fears not objectively justified, however reasonable these fears may appear from the point of view of the individual in question.

Lord Templeman agreed that decisions on refugee status could not be made solely with reference to individual beliefs; Lord Goff added that the Convention was meant to protect those whose fear was 'in reality well-founded'. All reasserted the primacy of the objective aspect of the test, rejecting Sir John Donaldson's stress on subjectivity. Subjective fears felt by asylum applicants therefore play only a small part in assessments of refugee status, compared to the Secretary of State's, and later the courts', appraisals of well-foundedness against the background of objective evidence concerning countries of origin (see Dutton 2003). A further reason for rejecting the subjective element of the UNHCR test has been suggested in several tribunal decisions; taken literally, it would penalise the courageous while rewarding the cowardly (Harvey 2000: 238).[1] We glimpse a Gluckmanian 'reasonable man' argument at work here (§2.1; Symes 2001: 42); the courts put little weight on whether a particular appellant is actually experiencing fear, asking instead whether the objective situation is such that one could reasonably be afraid.

---

1   This does not fully resolve the problem, however. Sikhs, for instance, being socialised not to express fear, may be unwilling to have their asylum claims couched in terms of fear at all (Cynthia Mahmood, pers. comm.).

Political circumstances change, of course. What if someone had a well-founded fear when they fled their country, but the situation has now significantly improved? In his House of Lords speech in *Adan*, Lord Slynn stated that an applicant's:

> well-founded fear must, as I read it, exist at the time his claim for refugee status is to be determined; it is not sufficient . . . that he had such a fear when he left his country but no longer has it . . . The existence of what has been called an historic fear is not sufficient in itself, though it may constitute important evidence to justify a claim of a current well-founded fear.

So assessments of objective conditions should be made with reference to the time when the decision on the asylum claim is made – notionally, the day of the hearing itself. Only a current fear of persecution can be well-founded.

Even this abbreviated account of the case law on well-foundedness illustrates that notions of 'objectivity' are central to the legal analysis of asylum claims. This colours the courts' treatment of expert reports, too, which are routinely characterised as 'objective evidence'. 'Objectivity', like 'fact' and 'truth', is here defined according to legal convention, however, rather than metaphysically. It is important to bear this in mind, because experts are likely to conceptualise factuality, objectivity, and truth rather differently, creating potential for misunderstanding (see also §2.2).

4.2.2 'of being persecuted'

In addition to being well founded, a refugee's fear must be a fear *of persecution*. The Convention does not define persecution, and there is no common international interpretation (Goodwin-Gill 1996: 67). Although the common law requires that it be approached as a normal word in the English language, Rodger Haines QC regards a purely dictionary-based approach as inadequate for a 'principled analysis of the issues' (*Refugee Appeal 71427/99*; Symes and Jorro 2003: 85). The UNHCR *Handbook* says that 'a threat to life or freedom on account of race, religion, nationality, political opinion or membership of a particular social group is always persecution'. Other serious human rights violations would constitute persecution too, if occurring for the same reasons. As with its treatment of 'well-founded fear', UNHCR again stresses the 'subjective character of fear of persecution', stating that because of the psychological differences between individuals, 'interpretations of what amounts to persecution are bound to vary' (1992: ¶51–2).

The main alternative approach again derives from Hathaway, for whom persecution is 'the sustained or systemic violation of basic human rights resulting from a failure of State protection' (1991: 101). Some rights are absolute (such as right to life, and protection from torture); States may derogate from others during emergencies (freedom from arbitrary arrest and detention); and yet others should be achieved progressively (rights to education and work; 1991: 101–12). This interpretation seems stricter than UNHCR's, because the vague 'threat' has become an institutionally precise 'sustained or systemic . . . failure of State protection'. It does, however, as usual in Hathaway's work, make an explicit link between persecution and human rights violations. His analysis was accepted by the House of Lords in *Horvath* (below), but in practice many adjudicators limit 'persecution' to cases of 'danger to life and deprivation of liberty' (Scannell 1999: 76).

Hathaway's wording is also incorporated into IND's working definition. The *APIs* (2002a: ¶1.2.8.1) define persecution as 'continuous or systematic failure of the State to offer protection to someone suffering a threat to life or freedom on account of race, religion, [etc]'. Caseworkers should assess any breach of human rights to see whether it amounts to persecution, and are advised that this 'involves looking at the asylum claim as a whole, taking all relevant circumstances into account'. To qualify as persecution, breaches must be serious enough to constitute a 'basic attack on fundamental human rights', such as, again paraphrasing Hathaway, 'unjustifiable attack on life and limb', as well as 'slavery, torture, cruel inhuman or degrading punishment or treatment'; examples include 'unjustifiable killing, or maiming', and 'physical or psychological torture, rape and other serious sexual violence' (2002a: ¶1.2.8.2). Here, for once, the stark reality of many applicants' experiences punctures the bland bureaucratese.

Actions which *may* constitute persecution include violations of the rights to freedom of thought, conscience and religion; freedom from arbitrary arrest and detention; freedom of expression, assembly and association; right to privacy; access to public employment without discrimination; equal protection of the law; access to food, clothing, housing, medical care, social security, education, and the right to work; or a combination of such measures assessed cumulatively (2002a: ¶1.2.8.3). Government restrictions on such freedoms do not amount to persecution unless applied in discriminatory fashion, however. Moreover, people fleeing prosecution or punishment are not refugees unless the prosecution itself constitutes persecution, or the punishment is cruel, inhuman, degrading, or highly disproportionate. To amount to persecution, such measures:

> must involve *persistent and serious ill treatment without just cause*. They must be of a substantially prejudicial nature and must affect a significant part of the individual's or group's existence to the extent that it would make the individual's life intolerable if they were to return (2002a: ¶1.2.8.3; italics added).

The italicised phrase is taken directly from Lord Justice Staughton's judgment in *Ravichandran*. If such discrimination exists against the applicant's section of the population, the applicant need not have suffered personally, or have been singled out, to have a 'well-founded fear' (*Jeyakumaran*) (Symes 2001: 75).

Normally, the 'agents of persecution' are governments or official bodies, but this need not always be the case. Once again, the *Handbook* and *APIs* differ subtly but crucially in emphasis:

> Persecution ... may also emanate from sections of the population that do not respect the standards established by the laws of the country concerned ... Where serious discriminatory or other offensive acts are committed by the local populace, they can be considered as persecution if they are knowingly tolerated by the authorities, or if the authorities refuse, or prove unable, to offer effective protection (UNHCR 1992: ¶65).[2]

> There will, however, be cases where the agents of persecution are groups or elements within the country of origin other than the authorities. *It is generally accepted that no Government can offer a guarantee of absolute protection* but where seriously discriminatory or other offensive acts are committed by the local populace they may constitute persecution if they are knowingly tolerated by the authorities, or if the authorities refuse, or prove unable, to offer effective protection (IND 2002a: ¶1.2.8.5; italics added).

Both versions accept that persecution may originate from 'sections of the population' rather than the authorities, but UNHCR's version does not explicitly recognise any limits to the State protection a citizen can reasonably expect. The italicised phrase in the *APIs* clearly does, so even if no such help is forthcoming that does not in itself suffice to establish persecution. In this regard the *APIs* are more in line with UK case law, founded on the 2000 House of Lords decision in *Horvath*.

Milan Horvath and his family were Roma who had suffered persecution by skinheads. Their fear was that if returned to Slovakia they would again be attacked, and not be protected effectively by the police. Mr Horvath's asylum application was refused by the Secretary of State, and on appeal the adjudicator did not find him a credible witness. The tribunal later reversed that credibility finding because they found his account consistent with objective evidence on the position of Roma in Slovakia. They also found that his fear of skinheads was well founded, but concluded that this did not amount to persecution because he had not shown himself unable or unwilling to avail himself of State protection (see §4.2.9). His appeal was dismissed by the

2   In his dissenting judgment in *Horvath*, Lord Lloyd queried this final sentence: paragraph 51 of the *Handbook*, on persecution in general, contains no such statement, and the meaning of persecution cannot vary according to whether perpetrated by States or third parties.

Court of Appeal, but in the House of Lords his counsel argued that if his ill-treatment by non-State agents was sufficiently severe to amount to persecution, that in itself was enough, and whether the State could or would offer adequate protection against it was irrelevant (Lambert 2001: 17).

All five Law Lords dismissed Horvath's appeal, but there were some complex differences in reasoning among the three detailed opinions (Lambert 2001). The majority decided, with Lord Lloyd dissenting, that in cases involving non-State agents an essential element of 'persecution' was failure by the home State to make protection available: would-be refugees had to show that their home States were unable or unwilling to provide 'sufficiency of protection' against the feared persecution. But what level of protection could reasonably be expected? Lord Hope felt that the applicable standard was not an ideal one whereby States were expected to guarantee protection from *all* risks, but – recognising that 'we live in an imperfect world' – a practical one equivalent to 'the duty which the State owes to all its own nationals'. Lord Clyde felt that 'sufficiency' or 'effectiveness' were rather imprecise notions, but agreed that absolute guarantees of immunity were 'beyond any realistic practical expectation'. The European Court of Human Rights had recognised that the obligation to protect did not extend to imposing an impossible or disproportionate burden on the authorities (*Osman*). 'Sufficiency of protection' does not, therefore, require elimination of all risk; the basic requirement is that the State has in place a system for protecting its citizens against persecution for Convention reasons, and is willing and able to operate that system, but 'precisely where the line is drawn' depends on 'the circumstances of each case'. Four Law Lords rejected Horvath's appeal on that basis; Lord Lloyd did so for a different reason, that Horvath had failed to show that he was unable to avail himself of the protection of the Slovak State (see §4.2.9).

In his leading speech, Lord Hope considered whether 'persecution' denoted severe ill-treatment in itself, or was restricted to ill-treatment against which the State failed to afford sufficient protection. He concluded, quoting Hathaway (1991: 135), that the Convention was meant to provide 'surrogate' protection in the event of failure of protection by the home State; in other words, 'failure of State protection is central to the whole system'. According to Hathaway's surrogacy principle, the criterion for deciding whether a person is entitled to refugee status by reason of persecution by non-State agents is whether the home State is 'unable or unwilling to discharge its duty to establish and operate a system for the protection against persecution of its own nationals'. Regarding this criterion, Lords Hope and Lloyd adopted the notion proposed by Lord Lloyd himself in *Adan* (below), that both a 'fear test' and a 'protection test' must be satisfied. One could, as indeed the tribunal had found in *Horvath*, have a well-founded fear of persecution but still not qualify as a refugee because one could not show that the State was unable to offer protection.

Lord Clyde found the 'fear/protection' language too emotive, and preferred to divide the Convention definition more neutrally, into its 'first part' and 'second part':

> The first part requires that the person be outside the country of his nationality for a particular reason, namely a well-founded fear of being persecuted for . . . a Convention reason. This part is concerned with the reason why he is outside the country of his nationality. The second part . . . requires . . . that the person be unable, or owing to the well-founded fear already mentioned unwilling, to avail himself of that protection [and] is thus concerned with the possibility of the person returning to his own State.

There was disagreement over Lord Hoffmann's influential treatment of persecution in *Islam and Shah* only the year before, which also concerned non-State agents (§4.2.6). Lord Hoffmann had noted that in order to fall within the Convention, the feared persecution must combine two elements, and adopted the formula in the Refugee Women's Legal Group's *Gender Guidelines* (1998):

$$\text{persecution} = \text{serious harm} + \text{failure of State protection}$$

Lord Clyde quoted this formula approvingly in *Horvath*, but Lord Lloyd noted that it had not been taken up by Lord Steyn in his leading speech in *Islam and Shah*, and to that extent had not received general support. He himself found it unacceptable as it stood, and suggested that a better alternative would be:

$$\text{persecution for a Convention reason} + \text{failure of State protection}$$
$$= \text{refugee status}$$

Whatever the terminology,[3] it was agreed that separating the two tests was merely an analytical convenience because, as Lord Lloyd noted, 'in the end there is only one question', namely, whether an applicant falls within the Convention definition of a refugee.

Moreover, the Lords disagreed over whether the surrogacy principle provided the link between the two tests. Lord Hope thought it did, because even in cases of persecution by non-State agents, the State's failure to provide protection provided 'an essential . . . bridge between persecution by the State and persecution by non-State agents which is necessary in

---

3   No-one has yet applied to the asylum context Judge Wright's formula in *Ethyl*, an American industrial pollution suit: danger = risk × harm (that is, probability × severity) (Jasanoff 1995: 39).

the interests of the consistency of the whole scheme'. Lord Clyde even went as far as suggesting that persecution by non-State agents was ultimately a form of 'constructive persecution' by the State, because it involved State 'encouragement, permission, toleration or helpless acceptance', but Lord Lloyd thought it 'most unlikely' that the framers of the Convention had intended any such notion. He accepted the utility of Hathaway's 'surrogacy principle' in connection with the second half of Article 1A(2) because '[i]f there is a failure of protection by the country of origin, the applicant will be unable to avail himself of that country's protection', but found it unhelpful with regard to persecution, because what turns discrimination into persecution is 'the severity and persistence of the means adopted . . . not the absence of state protection'. He therefore agreed with Horvath's counsel that absence of State protection was not a component of the definition of persecution.

Like other key cases discussed in this chapter, *Horvath* led IND to modify its *APIs*, which triumphantly summarised the outcome as follows (2002a: ¶1.2.8.5):

> Mr Horvath argued that persecution is simply severe ill-treatment for a Convention reason. The Department's argument, accepted by the House of Lords, was that persecution for the purposes of the 1951 Convention involves not only unjustifiable severe ill treatment but also a failure by the State to make protection available. . . .
>
> The Department's view was that it is sufficient that a country has a system of criminal law which makes attacks by non-State agents punishable and that there is a reasonable willingness to enforce the law. The House of Lords agreed that the standard to be applied should not be one that eliminates all risk and would therefore amount to a guarantee of protection in the home State.[4]

There has, however, been vigorous criticism of the Lords decision by a leading authority on asylum law, Rodger Haines of the New Zealand Refugee Status Appeals Authority. He argued (*Refugee Appeal 71427/99*) that their interpretation:

> is at odds with the fundamental obligation of non-refoulement. Article 33(1) is explicit in prohibiting return in any manner to a country where the life or freedom of the refugee would be threatened for a Convention reason. This obligation cannot be avoided by a process of interpretation which measures the sufficiency of State protection not against the absence of a real risk of persecution, but against the availability of a

---

4   The paragraph omitted here is quoted below (§4.2.9).

system for the protection of the citizen and a reasonable willingness by the State to operate that system.

'Non-State agents of persecution' and 'sufficiency of protection' are key issues for others apart from European Roma. Many Sri Lankan Tamil asylum applicants fear the LTTE at least as much as agents of the government. Although it is generally accepted that the LTTE persecutes those who do not support it, especially those seen as traitors, the Home Office position has often been that the LTTE do not constitute 'agents of persecution' because their actions are not 'knowingly tolerated by the authorities', nor are the authorities 'unable, or unwilling, to offer . . . effective protection' (see §4.2.9). Consequently, this issue often has to be addressed in my own expert reports (Good 2003a) – from a social-scientific rather than a legal perspective, of course.

The LTTE has always enjoyed wide support among Tamils, who saw it as defending them against repressive actions by the armed forces and police, yet at the same time it also forfeited sympathy through its ruthless suppression of other separatist groups, and assassinations of democratic Tamil politicians. Moreover, it funded its activities by extorting money from civilians in the guise of taxation, and most families were forced to provide one member to join its ranks. It also pressured expatriates for financial support, using threats against relatives back home as leverage. But, however illegitimate its methods, the LTTE ruled over the 'quasi-State' of Jaffna between 1990 and 1995, fulfilling all the core functions of government (Wilson and Chandrakanthan 1998). It even controlled movements in and out of its territory, issuing 'visas' and travel permits. In short, the Sri Lanka government was clearly unable to offer 'effective protection' to its citizens in the north-east. When the army recaptured Jaffna the LTTE lost its hegemonic position, but even the Home Office's own *Country Assessment* acknowledged that it continued to run 'a parallel administration' in parts of the east (IND 1999: Annex B). It continued to detain and torture 'traitors', and in 1996 alone over 30 'political prisoners' were executed. Tamils travelling to government-controlled areas still had to carry LTTE travel passes, and family members faced punishment if they did not return (IND 1999: ¶5.4.10).

Faced with evidence of this kind, the courts nearly always found that the LTTE *did* qualify as 'agents of persecution' in Convention terms, as they were 'the de facto authority in Jaffna' during that period (*Robinson*). Because it was also easy to show that the LTTE regularly killed alleged 'traitors' and elected representatives in other parts of the country, the courts often accepted, too, that the government remained unable to offer 'effective protection' to such persons even after 1995.

The complications surrounding the case law on persecution do not end here. Two other major issues have been dealt with by higher courts in recent years. The first concerns persecution in civil war contexts. The UNHCR

Handbook (1992: ¶164) notes that people compelled to flee their home country because of armed conflict, 'are not normally considered refugees', though they *are* entitled to protection under the Geneva Conventions of 1949 on the Protection of War Victims and the 1977 Protocol regarding the Protection of Victims of International Armed Conflicts. It lists several exceptions, however, and concludes that every case must be judged on its merits (1992: ¶166). The Home Office position builds upon this, as follows:

> A state of civil war where law and order has broken down (e.g. as between rival clans and sub-clans in Somalia) does not of itself give rise to a well-founded fear of persecution for a Convention reason unless the claimant is at risk of adverse treatment over and above the risk to life and liberty which occurs during civil war (IND 2002a: ¶1.2.6.5).

The mention of Somalia is an allusion to the House of Lords decision in *Adan*. Hassan Hussein Adan fled Somalia because of what was recognised as a well-founded fear of persecution at the hands of the then government. He was granted Exceptional Leave to Remain because government policy was not to return such persons to Somalia under prevailing circumstances, but he nonetheless pursued his refugee claim. The issue was whether, in a clan-based civil war, claimants could suffer a well-founded fear of persecution purely by virtue of their clan and sub-clan membership. In the Court of Appeal, Simon Brown LJ argued that persecution resulting from civil war should be defined fairly broadly, to reflect the Convention's 'broad humanitarian instincts': as civil wars are normally waged for Convention reasons, persons from either side *could* conceivably qualify as refugees. The Lords, however, accepted the Home Office contention that refugees must be able to show 'differential impact'; that is, a greater risk of ill-treatment than other members of their clan. According to Lord Lloyd, 'those engaged in civil war are not, as such, entitled to the protection of the Convention so long as the civil war continues, even if the civil war is being fought on religious or racial grounds'. Afterwards, however, 'the vanquished' may qualify as refugees if 'oppressed or ill-treated by the victors'.

Paragraph 98 of the UNHCR *Handbook* asserts that states of civil war *may* provide grounds for recognition as a refugee. Moreover, the *Adan* decision bucks the trend in recent asylum law by not prioritising the fact that Adan's human rights were arguably threatened in just the same way, whether the war had ended or not (Stevens 2004: 345). The implications for asylum applicants are 'alarming' (Scannell 1999: 77). It is also unclear which forms of disorder qualify as 'civil war'. For example, should *Adan* apply to Sri Lanka, whose ethnic conflict, also commonly called a 'civil war', is not a war of all against all in the same way as segmentary clan warfare in Somalia? In *Rudralingam*, the IAT argued that *Adan* is generally applicable 'to situations of civil war and armed conflict. Sri Lanka is obviously one such situation'.

This is not at all obvious, however. One does not (or *should* not) become a combatant merely by being Tamil or Sinhalese; moreover, one of the warring parties is recognised internationally as the legitimate government of the country. In *Juvenathan*, where the tribunal had cited *Adan* in dismissing the asylum appeal, counsel argued that Sri Lanka was crucially different from Somalia. Otton LJ was 'not persuaded' by this, but as he found the tribunal's decision justifiable on other grounds he did not reach any definite conclusion. The New Zealand RSAA decided, however, that the Convention applied to *any* applicant who faced a specific risk of harm for one of the Convention reasons. As the civil war in Sri Lanka was based on both race and politics, refugee status could not be withheld from a person meeting the 'for reason of' test, if there was 'a real chance of the appellant being persecuted if returned to Sri Lanka' (*71462/99*).

Finally, what if a person has a well-founded fear of persecution in parts of their home country, but there are arguably other parts where they would have no such fear? Seeking refuge elsewhere in the country has been termed the 'Internal Flight Alternative' (IFA), and the UNHCR *Handbook* (1992: ¶91) states that:

> persecution . . . may occur in only one part of the country. In such situations, a person will not be excluded from refugee status merely because he could have sought refuge in another part of the same country, if under all the circumstances it would not have been reasonable to expect him to do so.

This is phrased in inclusive rather than exclusive terms, and was rarely invoked in the 1980s as a ground for refusing asylum (ELENA 2000: 64). Its increasing use to exclude admittedly persecuted persons from Convention protection has coincided with the growth in applications. The Home Office usually claims, for example, that Tamils persecuted in Jaffna can live safely in Colombo, or that Sikhs with a well-founded fear in the Punjab will be safe in other parts of India.

The Court of Appeal decided in *Robinson* that two questions arise in this connection: (i) is there part of their own country where the asylum applicant would not have a well-founded fear of persecution, because the authorities are able and willing to provide sufficient protection there; and (ii) would it be 'unduly harsh' to expect them to live there? Factors affecting 'harshness' include the accessibility of the safe region; the dangers and hardships involved in travelling to or staying there; and whether protection would meet human rights norms (IND 2002a: ¶3.4). For example, an IFA does not exist if one is required to undergo great physical danger or hardship, or hide in an isolated area (Goodwin-Gill 1996: 75), whereas separation from family and friends does not in itself constitute undue harshness (*Gunes*). There was some controversy at tribunal level over the standard of proof to which 'undue harshness' must be determined; was it the 'reasonable likelihood' standard generally employed in asylum decisions (§10.2) or the 'balance of probabilities' as in civil cases? The Court of Appeal decided in *Karanakaran* that there was no need to adhere strictly to any specific standard, because in deciding whether relocation would be 'unduly harsh', cumulative account should be taken of a whole range of disparate factors, however likely or unlikely each was deemed to be (Symes 2001: 259; Storey 1998; §10.4).

It has increasingly been argued internationally that the 'Internal Flight Alternative' label is inappropriate, as the real issues are 'questions of protection, inability, unwillingness and the presence of a well-founded fear for one of the recognized Convention reasons' (*Re S*). The term 'Internal Protection Alternative' is now seen as preferable because it 'helps to reinforce the point . . . that the issue is not one of flight or relocation, but of protection' (*Refugee Appeal 71684/99*; see also Symes 2001: 247; Michigan Guidelines 1999).

4.2.3 'for reasons of race'

One striking feature of Article 1A(2) is its reliance upon several core social science concepts. Thus, a refugee must not only demonstrate a well-founded fear of persecution, but also show that this arises for reasons to do with race, religion, nationality, politics, and social group. However, what asylum lawyers mean by these 'Convention reasons' has arisen cumulatively out of case law, and bears no necessary relation to what contemporary social scientists understand by these terms, or even to social scientific views prevailing when the Convention was drafted. The treatment by the courts worldwide of all five reasons merits a separate study in itself, especially the various legal interpretations of 'particular social group', the most problematic of the five (§4.2.6). The present discussion is, however, limited to comparing, from an anthropological standpoint, the treatment of these five reasons in the UNHCR *Handbook* with the working definitions offered by IND's manual (2002a: ¶1.2.9), followed by a brief survey of the case law. In addition to defining them individually, UNHCR notes that the five reasons overlap in practice, so many refugees fall under more than one. I discuss later (§4.3) the consequences of the fact that the Convention does not explicitly consider gender or sexual orientation.

The UNHCR *Handbook* says that 'race', in this context, should:

> be understood in its widest sense to include all kinds of ethnic groups that are referred to as 'races' in common usage. Frequently it will also entail membership of a specific social group of common descent forming a minority within a larger population. Discrimination for reasons of race has found worldwide condemnation as one of the most striking violations of human rights. Racial discrimination, therefore, represents an important element in determining the existence of persecution (1992: ¶68).

The *APIs* (IND 2002a: ¶1.2.9.1) simply paraphrase the first two sentences of ¶68. In fact, most of IND's discussion of 'Convention reasons' draws directly on the *Handbook* in that way, and caseworkers are referred to it for further details. There is one crucial difference, however, which narrows the scope of all IND's interpretations. UNHCR's discussion of race, for example, concludes at ¶70 as follows:

> The mere fact of belonging to a certain racial group will normally not be enough to substantiate a claim to refugee status. *There may, however, be situations where, due to particular circumstances affecting the group, such membership will in itself be sufficient ground to fear persecution* (italics added).

It adds very similar riders to its discussions of all five Convention reasons. By contrast, IND precedes its discussion of all five with a general disclaimer:

> Merely belonging to a particular race, religion, nationality, or social group, or holding certain political opinions is not enough to substantiate a claim to refugee status, as the applicant must also show a well-founded fear of persecution on account of that reason (2002a: ¶1.2.9).

Although the statements are very similarly worded, the positive phrasing of UNHCR's second sentence invites one to actively consider whether applicants qualify under each provision, whereas the negative presentation in the *APIs* (and the subtle impact of the change from 'normally not' to 'not normally') encourages the presumption that they do not. The fact that the *APIs* do not explicitly recognise the possibility that membership of a particular 'racial group' may of itself suffice to qualify for refugee status, epitomises their general tendency to encourage negative assessments of asylum claims.

The limited case law mostly accords with Hathaway's view that 'race' should be understood as referring to all forms of 'identifiable ethnicity' (1991: 141). In the New Zealand Court of Appeal (Symes 2001: 154) Woodhouse J stated that the term:

> is concerned, not with genetic processes, but with shared characteristics of a socio-political nature such as customs, philosophy and thought, history, traditions, nationality, language or residence without any reference to biological considerations (*King-Ansell*).

Unfortunately, the IAT has sometimes shown itself far less enlightened on this matter. As recently as 2001 one chairman noted (*Sathiyaseelan*; original gloss) that one of the grounds of appeal before him suggested that the appellant:

might have had a well-founded fear of persecution on the basis of his 'ethnicity'. [We shall avoid this mealy-mouthed Americanism in favour of 'race', a term which was good enough for those who framed the Convention] (original gloss).

It is hard to know where to start in cataloguing the errors manifest in that comment. The most trivial is that there is nothing American about 'ethnicity'; 'ethnic group' was first used by eminent British scientists rejecting Nazi racial doctrines (Huxley and Haddon 1936), and the introduction of 'ethnicity' into anthropological usage was primarily a Russian achievement, for reasons all too obvious since the break-up of the Soviet Union (Sokolovskii and Tishkov 1996: 191). Far from being a synonym for 'race', it arose out of an explicit rejection of racism, and was, as Hathaway implies (see also Goodwin-Gill 1996: 43), one of a number of important broadenings of the original definition, taking account of changing circumstances and more enlightened ways of thought.

Whether or not 'race' was 'good enough for those who framed the Convention', it is certainly not good enough now, not least because the vast majority of scholars entirely reject race as an objective basis for classifying persons. The general position is concisely stated by Sanjek (1996: 464):

> there is no line in nature between a 'white' and a 'black' race, or a 'Caucasoid' and a 'Mongoloid' race . . . the many more numerous invisible traits – for example blood factors and enzymes – also vary continuously across populations, and each varies independently, not in parallel with visible racial markers . . . Simplistic racial categories based merely upon a few 'package' traits hardly constitute a scientific approach to human bio-variability.

Gunn argues, though, that greater awareness of the consensus among biologists, geneticists, and anthropologists that 'race is not . . . a scientific category with biological or genetic markers' (2003: 197) would not solve the problems faced by asylum courts in making decisions about racial persecution, because:

> racism exists and . . . people are persecuted because of their perceived racial characteristics . . . What is needed is not an expert definition of 'race', but an understanding of whether an asylum applicant has suffered because of the persecutors' belief that the applicant belongs to a disfavored race (2003: 198).

While the starting premise of this argument accords with Sanjek's view, the conclusion drawn is, in my opinion, mistaken. Gunn takes anthropological definitions to be concerned with characterising 'real' phenomena 'out there' in the world, yet this long ago ceased to be the general approach. Precisely because anthropologists reject 'race' as an objective basis of social differentiation, their definitions all now take explicit account of the fact that such concepts are culturally diverse, contested, and linked only by such 'family resemblances' as a tendency to base social exclusion practices upon external physiological markers. In short, it is precisely the indigenous, emic definitions of race which primarily concern contemporary anthropologists, making their expert definitions directly relevant to those asylum claims which turn upon the question of whether persecutors' actions can indeed be characterised as motivated by beliefs about 'race'. This is all the more necessary because, in my experience, many adjudicators will, if left to themselves, adopt some version of the 'common sense', substantive definition of 'race' now so widely rejected by scholars.

4.2.4 'religion'

Freedom of thought, conscience and religion are affirmed by the Universal Declaration of Human Rights and other international conventions. In the context of Article 1A(2), 'religion' covers communal practices, not just personal faith (*Wang*; Symes and Jorro 2003: 144). Thus, UNHCR's *Handbook* notes that this includes freedom to change one's religion and 'manifest it in public or private, in teaching, practice, worship and observance' (1992: ¶71). Paragraph 72 continues:

> Persecution for 'reasons of religion' may assume various forms, e.g. prohibition of membership of a religious community, of worship in private or in public, of religious instruction, or serious measures of discrimination imposed on persons because they practise their religion or belong to a particular religious community.

Once again the *APIs* contain an almost exact copy of this paragraph. Caseworkers are also told to consider the individual circumstances of each case with reference to country information (2002a: ¶1.2.9.2).

Restrictions on religious activity may or may not be persecutory. Thus, a total ban on practising one's religion would probably be seen as persecution, whereas the existence of laws against proselytisation might not (Symes 2001: 155–7). Persecution resulting from abandoning one's religion or converting to another clearly falls within the Convention, as asylum courts worldwide have recognised. The sincerity of conversion is a factor to be taken into account, but not the only one. Apostasy is seen by some as an offence against Islamic law, so even if the court doubts its genuineness, the question still remains, how is any purported convert from Islam likely to be viewed by the authorities in their home country?

The most common religiously-based claims in recent years have been by

Ahmadis from Pakistan, regarded as heretics by many other Muslims, and by Falun Gong adherents, claiming persecution by the Chinese government.

Over 80 per cent of Pakistan's population are Sunni Muslims, and 15 per cent are Shias. A further 3 per cent are Ahmadis, a sect founded in the nineteenth century by Mirza Ghulam Ahmad, a self-proclaimed prophet aiming to rejuvenate Islam. After Independence, prison sentences were specified for Ahmadis calling themselves Muslims. Penalties for blasphemy were increased until death was the sole penalty. Many Ahmadis have been charged and imprisoned under blasphemy laws. They are prohibited from holding religious gatherings or proselytising, and are targeted by religious extremists. Passport applications pose special problems: Pakistanis must declare their religious affiliation, and if they claim to be Muslims they must sign a declaration saying that Mirza Ghulam Ahmad was an impostor and his followers are non-Muslims.

Under the 1996 Act Pakistan was on a 'White List' of countries for which, in the Secretary of State's view, there was 'in general no serious risk of persecution' (§5.1). Six thousand Pakistani asylum applicants, including many Ahmadis, therefore had their claims certified, meaning that they had no rights of appeal against adverse decisions by adjudicators (§5.2.2). When several unsuccessful applicants sought judicial review of their certification, Turner J upheld their claim on the grounds that Pakistan's inclusion on the White List was invalid. The Secretary of State appealed, but in May 2002 the Court of Appeal, headed by the Master of the Rolls, upheld the decision quashing the certificates (*SSHD* v. *Javed, Ali and Ali*).

One applicant was an Ahmadi. Asif Javed had been expelled from school for explaining his beliefs to other pupils. He was subsequently harassed, attacked, and severely injured by former pupils, but the police were told he had been the aggressor and he was advised to renounce his faith in order to avoid arrest and imprisonment. He was later accused of preaching; the police tried to arrest him, but he escaped. He was then attacked and wounded by a man with a knife. He claimed asylum on grounds of persecution by non-State agents, but IND argued his account was not credible. He had produced a police report naming him as a wanted person, but the Secretary of State claimed – wrongly, it later proved – that no such police station existed.

More to the present point, his claim was refused on the further ground that, although there was some discrimination against Ahmadis, the Pakistan judiciary was independent and there was no systematic persecution of religious minorities. The *Country Assessment* produced by the Home Office's Country Information and Policy Unit (see §9.2) argued that 'Ahmadis are recognised as a minority religious group and rights are safeguarded under the constitution', and Michael Seeney, the official who compiled it, asserted that 'Ahmadis are not persecuted per se', although 'individual Ahmadis may suffer persecution, depending on their particular circumstances'. However, the Court of Appeal preferred the 'bleaker picture' painted by the then IAT

President, Judge David Pearl, an authority on Islamic law. Citing a Canadian Immigration and Refugee Board report that Ahmadis suffered from government-supported discrimination, Pearl J concluded (*Kaleem Ahmed*) that although not all Ahmadis could claim to suffer persecution in Convention terms, the evidence was that they formed 'a religious minority who are likely to meet examples of intolerance, discrimination and sadly at times blatant persecution in their everyday lives'.

The Chinese Falun Gong ('Wheel of Law') sect was founded in 1992 by Li Hongzhi, later exiled in the US. It combines Buddhist ideas of self-cultivation with traditional physical exercises. Many members assert that it is not a religion but a method of self-cultivation; they also deny any political agenda. It was nonetheless banned in 1999, for 'advocating malicious fallacies [which have] put people's life at risk and wreaked havoc on the society', according to the Chinese embassy in Canada (www.chinaembassycanada.org/chn/7697.html). Many followers were detained and forced to make public confessions, and State employees participating in Falun Gong activities were threatened with dismissal or demotion. A Falun Gong demonstration in Beijing in April 1999 ended peacefully, but later demonstrations were prevented, would-be participants detained, and virtually all Falun Gong activities declared illegal. Many followers were sent to labour camps or psychiatric institutions, and the total detained ran to tens of thousands.

Falun Gong appeals tend to be far longer than other hearings – I attended one where examination-in-chief alone lasted an entire day – because legal representatives try to demonstrate the genuineness of their clients' claims by putting them through, in effect, oral theological examinations. They are practical exams too, as appellants are asked to demonstrate their distinctive aerobic exercises. This is a common legal strategy for demonstrating that religious beliefs are genuine (Musalo 2002: 50–2), yet to reduce sincerity to doctrinal understanding is to forget the importance of 'spiritual feelings that come from communion with fellow believers' (Gunn 2003: 201).

Few legal sources have had much to say on what constitutes 'religion' in Convention terms, and 'the term "religion" remains undefined as a matter of international law' (Gunn 2003: 190). According to Hathaway:

> Religion as defined in international law consists of two elements. First, individuals have the right to hold or not to hold any form of theistic, non-theistic, or atheistic belief. ... Second, an individual's right to religion implies the ability to live in accordance with a chosen belief, including participation in or abstention from formal worship and other religious acts, expression of views, and the ordering of personal behaviour (1991: 145–6).

While this has the virtue of generality, it does not specify very precisely what if anything distinguishes religious beliefs from ethical beliefs of other kinds, and as we shall see, defining religion in terms of belief is problematic in any event.

British asylum courts generally treat the matter as self-evident, so the issue has rarely arisen. However, the approach in one key source, the Court of Appeal's judgment in *Omoruyi*, is deeply unsatisfactory from an anthropological perspective. Mr Omoruyi was a Nigerian who claimed to fear death for defying the Ogboni cult. His father was a cult member and wanted him to join as the eldest son, but he refused because it was contrary to Christian teaching. When he refused to allow Ogboni rites at his father's funeral, he was told that he had 'violated the laws of the society and the penalty for this is death'. In his asylum interview he described Ogboni as 'a mafia organisation involving criminal acts', and a 'devil cult' whose rituals involved idol worship, animal sacrifice, and drinking of blood. He later claimed to the Home Office that Ogboni involved 'use of various human organs ... for the preparation of satanic concoctions', and 'ritual killing of innocent people'; cult members were 'determined to see that they kill and destroy me for refusing them the right to perform their cult's rites on the body of my late father'. He alleged that soon after his father's burial, cult members murdered his brother in mistake for him and removed various bodily organs; and that since he had been in the UK his own baby son had been killed and mutilated.

Mrs Scott-Baker, the adjudicator hearing Mr Omoruyi's appeal, accepted his story on the basis of supportive documentary evidence, though it seemed to her 'so incredible'. The tribunal reversed her finding, however, because in its opinion 'the cult as described by the appellant is not credible'. It is unusual for tribunals to overturn adjudicators' credibility findings, and particularly surprising that they did so here because the Home Office's own sources provided partial corroboration.[5] Its *Nigeria Country Assessment* (IND 2002d: ¶6.88–90), citing a reputed anthropologist (Morton Williams 1960) among its sources, confirms that Ogboni is a Yoruba secret society which is officially banned but still powerful throughout Nigeria; that membership is usually acquired patrilineally; that it allegedly engages in 'satanic practices' such as animal sacrifice; and that members are reputedly threatened with death should they break their oaths of secrecy.

Nicholas Blake QC argued in the Court of Appeal that his client's fear arose out of his religion, because his Christian beliefs had prevented him from allowing his father to be buried according to Ogboni custom. Simon Brown LJ preferred the Home Office contention that his problems stemmed not from his Christianity *per se* but from his refusal to comply with Ogboni

---

5 In Canada, the publicity surrounding the similar asylum appeal of Brown Nosakhare spurred the Immigration and Refugee Board to produce a research paper on Nigerian cults (IRB 2000).

demands, so his asylum claim failed for lack of a Convention reason. The Home Office do not seem to have directly questioned Ogboni's status as a religion, but Simon Brown LJ himself did so in his judgment. After citing Hathaway's definition of religion (above), he addressed Mr Blake's argument that Ogboni was a 'religion' for Convention purposes:

> There are, he suggests, clear religious elements to their practices which merit such a characterisation: the worship of idols, sacrifice of animals and the like. This argument I would utterly reject. The notion that a 'devil cult' practising pagan rituals of the sort here described is in any true sense a religion I find deeply offensive . . . It seems to me rather that these rites and rituals of the Ogboni are merely the trappings of what can only realistically be recognised as an intrinsically criminal organisation – akin perhaps to the voodoo element of the Ton-Ton Macoute in Papa Doc Duvalier's Haiti.

Such emotional prejudice does not survive a moment's anthropological scrutiny. The question of how to define religion cross-culturally has of course engaged many anthropologists over the years, though as usual the law shows little or no awareness of this. Four distinct approaches can be identified – a fifth, importantly associated with Max Weber (1963), stresses soteriology and theodicy but eschews definition in favour of minute descriptions and an elaborate typology.[6]

First, *theological definitions* are concerned with religion as a matter of 'faith' or 'belief' in particular doctrines, and represent elaborations upon the Tylorian lowest common denominator, 'belief in spiritual beings' (Tylor 1871: I, 424). This form of words was of course deliberately chosen to avoid the ethnocentrism of defining religion as 'belief in god', which implies monotheism on the Judaeo-Christian model, or even 'belief in gods', which is still too precise in implying the existence of supreme beings. Even so, Tylor's approach remained deistic in its underlying assumption that all religions focus on spiritual or supernatural beings of some kind. This is not universally the case, with Theravada Buddhism an obvious counter-example (Gombrich 1971). The Buddha became extinct when he achieved nirvana, so there is no practical utility in praying to him or expecting him to intervene in worldly events (which is not to say that Buddhists do not occasionally pray to the Buddha as a form of expressive action *in extremis*). Instead, Buddhists worship Hindu gods to solve their practical problems, but insist that these gods 'have nothing to do with religion'.

---

6   Donovan and Anderson (2003: 125–43) give an interesting account of how legal definitions of religion developed in the US, but their discussion of anthropological definitions is idiosyncratic.

More subtle problems arise with the notion of 'belief'. First, religion involves actions too; it prescribes or prohibits certain kinds of behaviour in daily life, as well as requiring activities on its own account, such as rites of worship. Any definition must take that into account, and to be fair, Hathaway's does so. Second, belief – or rather, affirmation of belief – is not always as central a matter as it is for most Christians, Muslims, or Jews.[7] Hinduism, for example, has no creeds to identify and divide its adherents, and displays far less sectarian hostility than Christianity or Islam. It is not belief but behaviour that counts; if one behaves like a Hindu, then for most practical purposes one is seen as a Hindu, as my own experiences in rural South India bear out.

Second, Durkheim (1915: 47) proposed a *sociological definition* whereby a religion is 'a unified system of beliefs and practices relative to sacred things, that is to say, things set apart and forbidden – beliefs and practices which unite into one single moral community called a Church, all those who adhere to them'. This explicitly characterises religions as matters of 'doing', not just 'believing'. Moreover, 'the distinctive trait of religious thought' (1915: 37) is the division of the world into two complementary yet opposed categories of phenomena: sacred and profane. Religions define sacred things differently – and these differences are synecdoches for broader differences, dietary rules being a good example – but access to them is always restricted in some way, and even the priests who approach them on behalf of ordinary worshippers must first undergo purificatory procedures. His term 'Church' must be understood in a broad sense, as recognising that religion is a social affair involving organised collectivities. Rather than assuming that all human groups – or all but one – have deluded themselves, Durkheim explained religious differences sociologically. People rightly sense external powers greater than themselves, constraining their behaviour. Their error lies in conceptualising these as supernatural in character. The only power effective enough to influence everyone's behaviour, yet flexible enough to take different forms in different societies, is society itself, shaping individual behaviour through shared rules, morals, and languages. For Durkheim, society is not the way it is because god willed it so; quite the reverse, our idea of god depends on the nature of the society in which we live.

Third, there are *cultural definitions*, the best known being Clifford Geertz's (1966) famous characterisation of religion as a set of symbols serving as both 'a model of and a model for reality'. Religions, in other words, provide us with models of the ultimate structure and meaning of life in the world, as well as models for how that life should be lived, in the form of ethical precepts and

---

7 Membership of most Christian sects is validated by the affirmation of a creed, but what is primarily at issue is not a person's inner state while reciting it, but their willingness to do so publicly.

moral codes. Religion thereby helps make sense of, and organises, human experience.

Fourth, cross-cutting the differences among the other three approaches, Southwold (1978: 369) advocates a *polythetic definition* of religion. This approach – which would be my own preference – sees 'religion' as a Wittgensteinian 'odd-job' word (Needham 1975: 365) definable only in relation to its signification or use, not with reference to the alleged essence of the 'thing' signified. The advantage of polythetic definitions is their open-ended character, not assuming that all the various manifestations to which the term 'religion' has been or might be applied have one essential attribute in common. Paraphrasing Southwold (1978: 370–1), any phenomenon we might reasonably call religious must have at least some of the following 'family resemblances', and as my glosses show, these incorporate important elements of all the other approaches, without prioritising any of them:

(1) a concern with godlike beings and men's relations with them [cf. Tylor]
(2) a dichotomisation of elements of the world into sacred and profane, and a central concern with the sacred [Durkheim]
(3) an orientation towards salvation rather than worldly existence [Weber]
(4) ritual practices [Durkheim]
(5) beliefs held on the basis of faith [Tylor; Durkheim]
(6) an ethical code, supported by such beliefs [Weber; Geertz]
(7) supernatural sanctions on infringements of that code [all]
(8) a mythology [all]
(9) a body of scriptures, or similarly exalted traditions [all]
(10) a priesthood, or similar specialist religious elite [Durkheim]
(11) association with a moral community, a church [Durkheim]
(12) association with an ethnic or similar group [Durkheim].

In terms of *all* these anthropological standards suggested over the past century and a half, Ogboni is undoubtedly a religion. Whether it is an attractive religion is not for a pragmatic anthropological relativist to say, but neither is that a relevant consideration in legal decisions regarding the existence of a Convention ground. I do not know what Simon Brown LJ's personal religious convictions may be, but they are made relevant – as they surely should not be in a judicial decision – by his sudden descent into ethnocentric prejudice.

Omoruyi has been cited quite often – though fortunately not with reference to this particular conclusion. In *Ahmed*, for example, the Iraqi appellant claimed to have been persecuted by the Islamic Movement of Kurdistan because he sold alcohol (legally) in his shop. The adjudicator who dismissed his appeal assumed that the Convention was concerned only with the actual or imputed religion of the applicant himself, whereas here any persecution was clearly motivated by the religious beliefs of IMIK members. The Home

Office argued that the adjudicator was right, pointing out that UNHCR's *Handbook* (1992: ¶71–3) also focused upon the persecuted individual's own religious beliefs, whereas the appellant's counsel cited another of Simon Brown LJ's arguments in *Omoruyi*, that persecution could arise 'whether the harm is perpetrated by the religious on the non-religious or vice versa'. The tribunal agreed, noting that the Home Office's position, taken to its logical extreme, would grant Convention protection to religious fanatics but withhold it from their victims.

As he does in relation to 'race' (§4.2.3), Gunn argues that consulting the works of social scientists would not solve all judicial problems over defining religion, since in contexts of religious discrimination, 'the scholarly definitions do not describe what religion means to those who are discriminating and persecuting' (2003: 197). Yet again, this seems quite wrong. First, it must be established against some agreed standard that the persecution experienced is indeed 'religious' in character. In that context, awareness of scholarly definitions would at least preclude such judicial philistinisms as those regarding 'ethnicity' (*Sathiyaseelan*; §4.2.3) or the religious character of Ogboni (*Omoruyi*, above). Second, contemporary anthropological definitions of both 'race' and 'religion' are based precisely upon a recognition of their characters as distinctive kinds of socio-cultural values rather than upon their purported substantive, universal essences. An awareness of the culturally-contextualised, contested character of 'religious' beliefs and practices permeates all current anthropological definitions whatever their differences otherwise.

4.2.5 'nationality'

Inclusion of this reason may seem odd – why would a State wish to persecute people for being its own nationals? – but UNHCR's *Handbook* explains that:

> Persecution for reasons of nationality may consist of adverse attitudes and measures directed against a national (ethnic, linguistic) minority and in certain circumstances the fact of belonging to such a minority may in itself give rise to well-founded fear of persecution (1992: ¶74).[8]

It is meant to cover cases where inferior forms of citizenship exist, as under apartheid, or where minorities define their nationalities in ways other than those imposed upon them by the State, as in the USSR (Hathaway 1991: 144). Clearly, therefore, there are many situations in which nationality could form the basis of a valid asylum claim, and on which anthropologists, informed by the theories of Anderson (1991) and others, might be able to shed a great deal

---

8 The *APIs* [2002a: ¶1.2.9.3] simply paraphrase this.

of light.[9] Yet in practice there is so little distinct UK case law on nationality that Symes (2001: 153–5) subsumes his discussion of it under that of 'race', and the searchable case law database of the Electronic Immigration Network (www.ein.org.uk/) does not even include 'nationality' in its index of key words.

This almost total neglect in practice of 'nationality' as a ground upon which to base asylum claims probably has much to do with the degree to which it overlaps with other Convention reasons. Thus, UNHCR's *Handbook* explains that the term is not limited to 'citizenship', but may also overlap with 'race' in the sense that it also covers 'membership of an ethnic or linguistic group'. Moreover, when States contain two or more conflicting national, ethnic, or linguistic groups, it may be hard to distinguish between persecution for reasons of nationality and for reasons of political opinion (UNHCR 1992: ¶75). Both points are exemplified by Sikh asylum claims, which were almost invariably subsumed under religion and/or politics, rather than Punjabi nationality or ethnicity (Cynthia Mahmood, pers. comm.).

4.2.6 'membership of a particular social group'

The phrase 'particular social group' (PSG) was added very late in the drafting of the Convention, with almost no discussion, at the behest of Mr Petren the Swedish delegate. He asserted that 'experience had shown that certain refugees had been persecuted because they belonged to particular social groups. The draft Convention made no provision for such cases, and one designed to cover them should accordingly be included' (UN Doc. A/CONF.2/SR.3, p 14; cf. Grahl-Madsen 1966: 219). Goodwin-Gill (1996: 46n) explains this lack of debate by suggesting that delegates had clearly in mind the former capitalist, mercantile, and middle classes in Soviet Eastern Europe. Others told me that it was meant to cover persecuted homosexuals, though this seems unlikely given the subsequent difficulty in getting sexuality recognised as a ground (§4.3). In any event, courts worldwide have recognised, or have been asked to recognise, a far wider range of PSGs.

Making a virtue out of necessity, legal opinion sometimes implies that the phrase's very indeterminacy is its most desirable feature, allowing courts to cope with the almost limitless range of situations that may arise. In the key Australian case of *Applicant A*, for example, McHugh J commented: 'Not only is it impossible to define the phrase exhaustively, it is pointless to attempt to do so.' On the other hand, this indefinability inevitably generates much debate as to whether the PSG criterion applies in particular circumstances. For example, are couples who resist China's one-child policy, or suffer

9 For example, Sikh asylum claims were almost invariably subsumed under religion and/or politics, rather than Punjabi nationality or ethnicity (Cynthia Mahmood, pers. comm.).

persecution for flouting it, members of a 'particular social group'? No, according to a legal tribunal in *Lin*, because any such group would be constituted by the persecution itself (see *SSHD* v. *Savchenkov*, below). There has also, above all, been much debate about gender (§4.3).

Legal thinking on the PSG issue is based on a set of key judgments in the US, Canada, Australia, and New Zealand (Haines 1998). One common starting point in judicial surveys of international case law is the use by the US Board of Immigration Appeals, in *Matter of Acosta*, of the doctrine of *ejus-dem generis*, a legal 'canon of construction' stating that when interpreting a list of items in a statute, one should read general items in the same spirit as those which *are* specified (Solan 1993: 37–8).[10] Acosta belonged to a taxi-driver co-operative in El Salvador which was targeted by guerrillas for refusing to take part in anti-government strikes. He claimed to have been persecuted because of his membership in a PSG, namely, the co-operative. The Board found against him, however, noting that 'race', 'religion', 'nationality', and 'political opinion' all refer to 'an immutable characteristic . . . that either is beyond the power of an individual to change or is so fundamental to individual identity or conscience that it ought not be required to be changed'. Taxi-drivers were not a 'particular social group' because their occupation was neither immutable nor fundamental to their identity.

An alternative approach is to define the essence of the 'particular social group' itself, following the precedent of *Canada* v. *Ward*. Ward, who belonged to the paramilitary Irish National Liberation Army (INLA) in Northern Ireland, allowed some hostages to escape when he learned they were to be executed. When the INLA 'sentenced' him to death he sought police protection, but was convicted and imprisoned for his INLA activities. The INLA held his family hostage during his trial to ensure that he gave no evidence against them. After serving his sentence he sought asylum in Canada, claiming to fear persecution because of his membership of a PSG, the INLA. Although his application was initially rejected, the Immigration Appeal Board later granted him refugee status.

The Canadian Supreme Court ultimately ruled that although independence was a serious and legitimate political aim, the INLA was *not* a 'particular social group' because being required to give up violent means of achieving that aim would not involve Ward in abdicating his human dignity. Justice LaForest based his leading judgment upon the UNHCR *Handbook* (1992: ¶77):

> A 'particular social group' normally comprises persons of similar background, habits or social status. A claim to fear of persecution under this heading may frequently overlap with a claim to fear of persecution on other grounds, i.e. race, religion or nationality.

10 This is a clear example of analogic legal reasoning (§2.2).

Although this could be read as suggesting a broad interpretation, it was truer to the spirit of the Convention to read it fairly narrowly. *Acosta* provided a 'good working rule', taking proper account of the main themes underlying notions of refugee protection: human rights and anti-discrimination. For Convention purposes, PSGs therefore fell into three possible categories. I have inserted his own later glosses:

(1) groups defined by an innate, unchangeable characteristic [such as gender, linguistic background and sexual orientation];
(2) groups whose members voluntarily associate for reasons so fundamental to their human dignity that they should not be forced to forsake the association [for example, human rights activists]; and
(3) groups associated by a former voluntary status, unalterable due to its historical permanence [one's past is an immutable part of the person].

Influential though this definition has been, it is 'difficult . . . to construct a coherent principle that underlies [these] categories' (Aleinikoff 2003: 271). As this criticism illustrates, and in line with the differences between anthropological and legal thinking discussed earlier (§2.2), legal discourses generally seek to establish monothetic definitions, for practical reasons aimed at facilitating consistent decision making. Even so, where PSGs are concerned the courts have repeatedly – as in *Ward* – adopted the kinds of polythetic definitions favoured by anthropologists (see §4.2.4).

Legal scholars have recently sought to group *Acosta* and *Ward* together, as 'protected characteristics' approaches which define PSGs on the basis of immutable or fundamental aspects of personal identity, in contrast to the 'more sociological' stance (Aleinikoff 2003: 272) taken by the Australian High Court in *Applicant A*, which Aleinikoff terms the 'social perception' approach (2003: 296). Here, faced with applicants fearing forced sterilisation because of non-acceptance of China's 'one child' policy, the Court decided that the 'ordinary meaning' of the phrase 'social group' referred to 'a common attribute and a societal perception that they stand apart' (McHugh J), or 'a certain characteristic or element which unites them and enables them to be set apart from society at large . . . making those who share it a cognisable group within their society' (Dawson J).

For once, the *APIs'* wording on PSGs (2002a: ¶1.2.9.4) departs significantly from the *Handbook*, because the relevant section had to be rewritten following recent decisions in the House of Lords, as we shall now see. Moreover, UNHCR itself (2002c) has updated its advice on how the notion should be understood.

The first significant British PSG case concerned *Savchenkov*, a security guard in a St Petersburg hotel, who claimed persecution by criminals wanting him to be an informer and bodyguard for a mafia boss. He was beaten and threatened, but did not inform the police because he believed they were in league with the mafia. IND argued that victims of violent criminality did not qualify for asylum, and the adjudicator agreed that he was persecuted as a law-abiding person who would not join the mafia, not as a member of a PSG. The tribunal decided, however, that:

> individuals which the mafia seeks to recruit and who refuse do form a social group. They are identified by the approach and refusal . . . So . . . we see the group as identifying and identified by an important recognisable social attribute. Whether or not the group is liable to persecution is then a question of evidence.

In reaching this conclusion the tribunal hinted at, but did not explicitly make, a rather more convincing argument for the *mafia* being a PSG, as the Court of Appeal later pointed out. Nicholas Blake QC argued that his client Savchenkov fell within the second or third of LaForest J's categories, but MacCowan LJ could see no evidence that security guards refusing to join the mafia voluntarily associated with one another, or shared a former voluntary status. In any case, the Convention could not have been intended to cover groups whose existence stemmed solely from fear of persecution, otherwise anyone who had been persecuted 'could automatically claim to be part of the social group and meet the requirements of Article 1'.

Following the Court of Appeal decisions in *Savchenkov* and *Shah* (see below) the *APIs* (1998a: ¶1.2.9.4) came to define PSG in a way that irresistibly recalled past anthropological debates on descent and corporateness:

(a) the group is defined by some innate or unchangeable characteristic of its members analogous to race, religion, nationality or political opinion, for example, their sex, linguistic background, tribe, family or class; *or*
(b) the group is cohesive and homogenous. Its members must be in close voluntary association for reasons fundamental to their rights (e.g. trade union activists). Former members of such a group are also included; *or*
(c) the particular social group was recognised as such by the public.

Whatever the binding factor is, it must be independent of persecution.

Here, (a) and (b) are virtually identical to the *Ward* definition, but (c) differs significantly, reflecting the 'social perception' approach exemplified by *Applicant A*. However, the decision in *Shah* was later reversed by the House of Lords in *Islam and Shah*. This took the PSG issue much further forward in terms of establishing legal precedent, but seems distinctly odd from an anthropological perspective.

Mrs Shahana Sadiq Islam's husband had often been violent towards her. In 1990 she attempted to stop a fight between rival political factions in the school where she taught. One faction made allegations of infidelity to her husband, one of their supporters. He assaulted her and she was twice admitted to hospital. She left her husband, but was unable to stay with her brother as he received threats. She arrived in Britain with her children and claimed asylum for reasons of political opinion and membership of a PSG. The tribunal decided she *had* been persecuted but was not a member of a PSG because women in her situation had no 'innate or unchangeable characteristic' in common, nor were they 'a cohesive homogeneous group whose members are in close voluntary association'.

The Home Office appeal against this decision was heard by the Court of Appeal along with an appeal by Mrs Syeda Khatoon Shah. She had been thrown out of her marital home in Pakistan by her violent husband. She arrived in the UK in 1992, giving birth shortly afterwards. She claimed asylum, citing her fear that her husband might assault her or accuse her of sexual immorality under Sharia law. The adjudicator found her fear of persecution to be well founded, but decided she did not belong to a PSG, the only Convention reason which could conceivably apply. The IAT refused leave to appeal, but she sought judicial review of this decision, and Sedley J directed the IAT to hear her appeal. It was against this decision that the Home Office was appealing.

The Court of Appeal found that Mrs Islam's political opinion claim failed on the facts, so the sole issue was whether either or both women were members of PSGs. Lord Justice Waite could see no common attribute, independent of the feared persecution, which entitled either to claim membership of such a group. Staughton LJ went further, accepting the Home Office argument that PSGs entailed 'cohesiveness, co-operation and interdependence', all clearly lacking in this case. Henry LJ agreed with Waite LJ's reasoning, while holding that 'cohesion' was 'not necessary in every case' – for example, where the group was 'recognised as such by the public'.

Their House of Lords appeals involved the same QCs as *Savchenkov*, David Pannick and Nicholas Blake. On that earlier occasion both had adopted the *ejusdem generis* approach, that 'particular social group' should be interpreted as reflecting a status akin to those denoted by race, religion, nationality, or political opinion. This time, however, Mr Pannick announced that the Secretary of State no longer supported that part of his own submission in *Savchenkov* (Symes 2001: 158). Lord Steyn found this startling change 'understandable' as 'his earlier submission weakens his case on the present appeals', but the implications went far beyond this particular case. IND was, in effect, repudiating paragraph ¶1.2.9.4(a) in the *APIs*, quoted above, the main criterion on which its asylum decisions on PSGs had hitherto been based. A cynic might put this down to the sudden realisation that, if the Law Lords accepted it even tacitly in this case, it potentially embraced too many other applicants (by one reading, *all* women in Pakistan), whereas Staughton's view would allow eligibility to be restricted yet further.

It remained common ground that both women had a well-founded fear of persecution in Pakistan, and that members of a PSG only qualify for

Convention protection if the group in question exists independently of the persecution. The first issue to be decided was whether 'cohesiveness' was a necessary property of a PSG. At the Court of Appeal the Home Office argument that social groups must be homogeneous and cohesive had been accepted by one judge and partly accepted by another, so Lord Steyn examined it carefully. Of the international precedents he preferred the *ejusdem generis* analysis in *Acosta*, which had concluded that persecution on account of membership in a PSG meant:

> persecution that is directed toward an individual who is a member of a group of persons all of whom share a common, immutable characteristic. The shared characteristic might be an innate one such as sex, colour, or kinship ties, or in some circumstances it might be a shared past experience such as former military leadership or land ownership.

Lord Steyn did not, therefore, accept that cohesiveness was an indispensable characteristic of a PSG, a proposition for which there was no English authority save Staughton LJ in the lower court, and Mr Pannick ultimately conceded this. Lord Hoffmann agreed, applying his own *ejusdem generis* logic:

> 'race' and 'nationality' do not imply any idea of co-operation; 'religion' and 'political opinion' might, although it could be minimal. In the context of the Convention it seems to me a contingent rather than essential characteristic of a social group.

The second issue was whether these particular women belonged to PSGs. The broadest view, per Lord Hoffmann, was that 'women in Pakistan', without restriction or qualification, form a PSG 'because they are discriminated against and as a group they are unprotected by the State'. It was no answer to argue that some women were able to avoid the impact of persecution, because that was true even under brutal regimes like Nazi Germany and Stalinist Russia. To accept such an argument 'would drive a juggernaut through the Convention'. 'My Lords,' he concluded, 'there is no satisfactory answer to the argument that the social group is women in Pakistan.' Lord Steyn saw this as 'a logical application' of the reasoning in *Acosta*, which defined 'groups' as people sharing 'a common, immutable characteristic . . . such as sex'.

Mr Blake had also put forward a narrower argument, in case this broader one did not find favour. He submitted that a combination of 'gender, the suspicion of adultery, and their unprotected status in Pakistan' set the applicants apart as members of a separate group. The Court of Appeal had rejected this submission, which it saw as falling foul of the principle that the group must exist independently of the persecution, but Lord Steyn disagreed. 'The unifying characteristics of gender, suspicion of adultery, and lack of protection,' he reasoned, 'do not involve an assertion of persecution.' He cited McHugh J in *Applicant A*, who explained the limits of the principle by saying that 'while persecutory conduct cannot define the social group, the actions of the persecutors may serve to identify or even cause [its] creation', and concluded that on this ground too the appellants could be seen as belonging to a PSG. Lord Hutton, unhappy about the breadth of Lord Hoffmann's argument, *was* able to support the majority decision on these narrower grounds.

There remained the question of the 'causal nexus'. Did the women's fear of persecution arise 'for reasons of' their membership of the group in question? The two sides approached this differently. The appellants asserted that the phrase 'for reasons of' meant that such persons would not face persecution 'but for' them belonging to the PSG, whereas the Secretary of State argued that PSG membership had to be the 'effective cause' of their persecution. Lord Steyn concluded that it made no difference which was adopted,[11] or whether one took the broader or narrower definition of PSG, because in a context of 'State-tolerated and State-sanctioned gender discrimination . . . the argument that the appellants fear persecution not because of membership of a social group but because of the hostility of their husbands is unrealistic'.

Lord Hoffmann's reasoning also focused on the existence of discrimination:

> Within [Pakistan] it seems to me that women form a social group of the kind contemplated by the Convention. Discrimination against women in matters of fundamental human rights on the ground that they are women is plainly in pari materiae with discrimination on grounds of race (gloss added).

Only Lord Millett argued for dismissal, agreeing with the Court of Appeal that the social group was being defined by the persecution. Though women in Pakistan *were* legally discriminated against, these appellants had been persecuted 'because they refuse to conform, not because they are members of the social group'. Even Lord Millett agreed, however, that cohesiveness was not a necessary attribute of a PSG, merely one possible feature of such groups, so IND had to substantially change its instructions to caseworkers. The *APIs* were revised to read as follows:

(i)   Members of a social group have to have in common an immutable characteristic which is either beyond the power of an individual to change, or is so fundamental to their identity and conscience that it ought not to be required to be changed.

---

11 Without deciding between these approaches, the Lords did specify that the 'but for' test should not be applied without reference to context. The Australian High Court noted that its application should take account of policies underlying the Convention as a whole (*Chen*; see also *SSHD* v. *Montoya*).

(ii) Whilst a social group must exist independently of persecution, discrimination against the group could be taken into account in identifying it as a social group, i.e. discrimination against the group could be a factor contributing to the identity of a social group (2002a: ¶1.2.9.4).

Another possible way of looking at the issue would have been in terms of the contrast between a group's internal characteristics, and external perceptions of its supposed members. In the latter case, no cohesion or corporateness is necessary; indeed, whichever theory one subscribes to as to which groups the Convention's drafters had in mind – 'former capitalists of Eastern Europe' (Goodwin-Gill 1996: 360–1), or homosexuals – these were persons who might never have had any group association with one another but who were adversely perceived, as a class, by the State or the majority population. One might have expected this contrast to have arisen in *Islam and Shah*, but it only did so in passing, and indeed – although the decision had far-reaching and, many might think, beneficial humanitarian implications – the reasoning in *Islam and Shah* seems perverse, if not downright nonsensical, in social science terms. 'Women in Pakistan' are not a social *group* because they are not corporate. One can certainly say that they form a recognised social *class* or *category*, but the law does not generally recognise that distinction.

Without pushing parallels too far, one can see recent disagreements over 'social group' in the UK asylum courts as re-enacting theoretical debates in anthropology during the 1960s. Despite their differences over 'complementary filiation', both Fortes (1970) and Leach (1961: 5) assumed the existence of corporate entities called 'descent groups'. But what was meant by *corporateness* in this context? Radcliffe-Brown (1935; 1945; 1950) had used the term in different places to refer to collective participation in rituals; owing allegiance to the same chief; and collective property ownership, but the 'groups' involved were not necessarily of the same kind in each case, so corporateness had several possible meanings.

Crucially, however, it is possible to find descent without corporateness in any of these senses. Scheffler (1966) contrasted *descent groups* as behaviourally observable entities, from *descent categories* as forms of indigenous ideological classification. We must, in other words, distinguish situations where groups are in practice composed of people related by unilineal descent, from situations where people *talk about* their society as though that were so. Both may apply, if not necessarily to the same extent, but one can easily imagine one occurring without the other. For instance, in any agricultural society where sons inherit land from fathers and post-marital residence is patrivirilocal, local communities are bound to *look* like patrilineal descent groups; but there may not be named lineages, and people may not actually think of their society in that way. Conversely, people may think of their society *as if* it is composed of localised patrilineages even when this is not empirically the case. As Evans-Pritchard suggests for Sudan, 'it may be partly just because the agnatic principle is unchallenged in Nuer society that the tracing of descent through women is so prominent and matrilocality so frequent' (1951: 28).

Sahlins (1965) showed that the observed composition of local groups, and the ideology whereby locals discuss such groups, are independent variables. He took a 'raw' genealogy from New Guinea as an anthropologist might record it, and showed how it could be viewed differently in terms of various ideologies, by stressing certain links and downplaying others. Thus, one can portray the self-same genealogy as composed of classic segmentary patrilineages; in terms of an ideology of cognatic descent where each local grouping is built up of links through either parent; as composed of patrilineal clans *not* sharing common residence, and so on. These varied interpretations are possible because genealogies are not timeless biogenetic records, but socio-political constructs, manipulable to suit the dominant ideology or fit individual interests. There may be little or no difference in local group composition between societies with strong descent ideologies (Nuer, Tallensi) and societies lacking such ideologies (Papua New Guinea). Astuti (2000) makes the even more radical point that genealogies may be perceived differently at different stages in the life-cycle. In each case, the difference lies not in the empirical composition of society, but in how people think about it.

The initial Home Office stress on cohesiveness strongly recalls that version of descent theory which argued (or simply assumed) that descent led by definition to formation of corporate groups. In other words, it reflects a structural-functionalist understanding of 'social group', pre-dating Scheffler's crucial distinction between 'groups' and 'categories'. The latter distinction does, however, seem implicit in the Australian 'societal perception' approach of *Applicant A*,[12] although that confused matters through its unfortunate repeated references to 'the social *group category*' and 'the *category* of membership of a particular social *group*' (italics added).

Dr Hugo Storey, in the determination of the legal tribunal in *SSHD* v. *Montoya*, summarised the state of play in English law following *Islam and Shah* by producing a lengthy polythetic definition of his own, reading in part as follows:

(ii)   the PSG ground should not be viewed as a category of last resort; . . .

(v)   If the PSG ground had been intended as an all-embracing category, the five enumerated grounds would have been superfluous; . . .

(vii)   applying the euisdem generis principle to the other four grounds, the PSG category must be concerned with discrimination directed

12 Justice LaForest himself hinted at such a distinction when he later accepted (*Chan*) that persons sharing the characteristic which attracted persecution need not have associated with one another.

against members of the group because of a common immutable characteristic; . . .

(x) in order to avoid tautology, to qualify as a PSG it must be possible to identify the group independently of the persecution;

(xi) however, the discrimination which lies at the heart of every persecutory act can assist in defining the PSG. Previous arguments excluding any identification by reference to such discrimination were misconceived;

(xii) a PSG cannot normally consist in a disparate collection of individuals;

(xiii) for a PSG to exist it is a necessary condition that its members share a common immutable characteristic. Such a characteristic may be innate or non-innate. However, if it is the latter, then the non-innate characteristic will only qualify if it is one which is beyond the power of the individual to change except at the cost of renunciation of core human rights entitlements;

(xiv) it is not necessary . . . for such a group to possess the attributes of cohesiveness, interdependence, organisation or homogeneity; . . .

(xvi) a PSG can be established by reference to discrimination from State agents or non-State agents (actors) of persecution;

(xvii) it is not necessary in order to qualify as a PSG that a person actually has the characteristics of the group in question. It is enough that he will be perceived to be a member of the group (original gloss).

Paragraphs (xi), (xiv), (xvi), and (xvii) show how far the situation has been clarified and made more flexible recently. This approach remains limited in one key respect, however, because paragraphs (vii) and (xiii) confine themselves to 'protected characteristics' and ignore 'social perception' approaches altogether. Even paragraph (xvii), which at first sight seems relevant, deals in fact with the different question of whether group membership is correctly attributed. The social perception stance is still severely under-represented in English case law, which is therefore still far removed from the group/category distinction proposed here. Ironically, since his approach was, in many respects, the narrowest of the Appeal Court judges in *Islam and Shah*, Lord Justice Staughton remains almost alone in having made this distinction, although he came down on the 'cohesive' (corporate) side. A PSG, he stated:

> does to my mind involve a number of people being joined together in a *group* with some degree of cohesiveness, co-operation or interdependence; the members must not be solitary individuals. By contrast a *social category* could be defined in almost any way; if that had been what the framers of the convention intended, they would have said so, although they would thereby (as it seems to me) have undermined the manifest intention to place some limit on the kind of persecution which was needed to make someone a refugee (italics added).

'Social category' is certainly a broader notion than 'social group', but it need not be as all-embracing as Staughton feared, since a *social* category cannot be created by individual whim; its existence depends on social consensus. Thus, the Australian High Court in *Applicant A* did not extend its 'social perception' approach to cover 'statistical groups' sharing common demographic factors but neither recognising themselves as social groups *nor being socially perceived as such*; for example, 'young urban men' in El Salvador (*Sanchez-Trujillo*; Aleinikoff 2003; 277). Individuals facing persecution because they are pigeonholed in some derogatory way by society at large, whether or not they have links with others categorised in the same way, *could* therefore be accommodated by the Convention without broadening its application to a ridiculous extent. This would have the major advantage of resolving many current difficulties in assessing persecution grounded on gender or sexual orientation (§4.3). At present, however, British case law is far from any such (anthropologically-speaking) sensible conclusion.

4.2.7 'political opinion'

Political opinion is probably the most commonly cited ground in refugee claims (Symes 2001: 135) but a successful claim requires more than merely holding political opinions differing from those of the government:

> an applicant must show that he has a fear of persecution for holding such opinions. This presupposes that the applicant holds opinions not tolerated by the authorities [and] that such opinions have come to the notice of the authorities or are attributed by them to the applicant (UNHCR 1992: ¶80).

The *APIs* paraphrase this passage, except that the final reference to 'attributed' political opinion is deferred till much later (2002a: ¶1.2.9.5).

The identification of persecution for reasons of political opinion is not always straightforward. First, how should the courts understand 'political'? Goodwin-Gill defines political opinion as 'any opinion on any matter in which the machinery of State, government, and policy may be engaged' (1996: 49), but this seems rather too focused on institutional politics, and Hathaway (1991: 157) argues that adherence to a broad definition helps maintain the vitality and contemporary applicability of the Convention. Hill J, in the Federal Court of Australia (*Voitenko*), argued that while its use should not be 'limited to party politics [as] understood in a parliamentary democracy', it should remain 'narrower than the usage of the word in connection with the science of politics, where it may extend to almost every aspect of society'.

Recent versions of the *APIs* acknowledge the difficulties in identifying political dimensions of persecution. Asylum applicants themselves may not always claim, or even recognise, that their persecution was politically motivated. Moreover, political acts may include 'less direct actions such as hiding people, passing messages or providing community services, food, clothing and medical care' (IND 2002a: ¶1.2.9.5). Courts in several countries have found that trade union activities, and opposition to corruption, may constitute manifestations of political opinions (Symes 2001: 135–40). Precisely because the opinions concerned are inimical to them, States will tend to portray their countering actions not as political repression but as 'sanctions for alleged criminal acts against the ruling power' (UNHCR 1992: ¶81). Conversely, fearing punishment for what is defined in one's home country as a political offence does not create a valid refugee claim if that punishment conforms to the general law of the country (1992: ¶84, 85). Only 'excessive or arbitrary punishment' amounts to persecution (IND 2002a: ¶1.2.9.5).

Valid asylum claims may also arise out of 'attributed' or 'imputed' political opinion – through belonging to a well-known political family, for example. Moreover, as LaForest J noted in *Ward*, the political opinion leading to persecution 'need not necessarily be correctly attributed to the claimant.' Political opinions attributed by non-State agents like the Algerian GIA or Colombian criminal gangs can also create a well-founded fear (Harvey 2000: 266; Symes 2001: 144–7). However, the courts have tried to set limits to the applicability of the notion of attributed political opinion.

For example, one tribunal argued that 'a Sri Lankan civil servant whose life is endangered by the LTTE is not at risk because of his political opinion: he is simply at risk because he is doing a job which the LTTE would prefer not to be done' (*Kulasegaram*). In my opinion, however, this tribunal misunderstood the paradoxical position of government servants in areas controlled or infiltrated by the LTTE. It suits both sides for civil administration to continue; the government because it allows them to maintain fictive sovereignty over the whole island, the LTTE because it provides them with a civil infrastructure and a means of siphoning off government funds. Civil servants themselves walk a tightrope, however, constantly at risk that either side will construe their behaviour as tilting too far the other way (§5.2).

Conversely, it is possible to have a well-founded fear even if the authorities are as yet unaware of one's political opinion, if it is so strongly held that it 'will sooner or later find expression and . . . the applicant will, as a result, come into conflict with the authorities' (1992: ¶82; cf. IND 2002a: ¶1.2.9.5).

One obvious question is whether, or under what circumstances, one may qualify for refugee status because of a well-founded fear of persecution resulting from political *action* rather than just *opinion*. LaForest J argued that *Ward's* persecution by the INLA for his action in freeing hostages 'stems from his political opinion as manifested by this act'. Tribunals, too, recognise that actions may be manifestations of political opinions, and may need to be equally broadly defined: 'An intellectual might pen a tract or a pamphlet, a cinematographer might make a propaganda film, a political activist might campaign for his or her party in an election, or someone may simply go to fight for a cause in which they believe' (*Orlov*).

That final example raises the question of the boundary between political action and 'non-political crimes' as envisaged by 'exclusion clause' 1F(b). In *'T'* v. *SSHD*, the House of Lords considered whether a member of the Algerian FIS, involved in an airport bombing, was excluded from Convention protection because there were 'serious reasons for considering' that he had committed 'serious non-political crimes'. Lord Lloyd concluded that a crime could be viewed as 'political' in Convention terms 'if, and only if: (1) it is committed for a political purpose . . . (2) there is a sufficiently close and direct link between the crime and the alleged political purpose'.

What, then, of members of other 'terrorist' organisations such as the LTTE? Most applicants with LTTE connections claim just to have undertaken support activities, or to have been combatants in orthodox warfare, and only those who admit direct participation in random acts of terror risk falling foul of Article 1F(b). In *Thayabaran* the tribunal considered this matter in some detail. The appellant had participated in several missions, one of which he knew might have involved a bomb attack, yet the tribunal overturned the adjudicator's decision that he was excluded from protection:

> it is not sufficient to show that the appellant has committed a crime, or even a serious crime. The exclusion clause only applies if there are serious reasons for considering that he has committed a serious non-political crime . . . which did not fall within Lord Lloyd's definition of 'political'.

There are two more reasons for granting asylum on 'political opinion' grounds, both involving actions outside one's home country. First, the very act of claiming asylum may itself constitute manifestation of a political opinion. It may 'disclose the applicant's true state of mind and give rise to fear of persecution', so the decision should rest upon an assessment of the consequences that the applicant would face if returned (UNHCR 1992: ¶83). Second, actions may be undertaken deliberately with asylum in mind. When an Iranian based his claim on having been photographed by officials during anti-government demonstrations outside the London embassy, the Appeal Court ruled that applicants could not rely upon 'unreasonable' activities to support their claim (*'B'*). Later decisions cast doubt on this notion of 'reasonableness', however (*Gilgham*), and in *Danian* the court overturned the IAT's view that the Convention could not apply to those manipulating situations to their advantage. It accepted UNHCR's submission that the question was not whether activities were self-serving, but whether there was a serious risk of being persecuted for a Convention reason on return (Harvey 2000: 267–9; Symes 2001: 128–32).

4.2.8 'outside the country of his nationality'

The Convention defines a refugee as someone who is *outside the country of his nationality*. People fleeing to other areas of their own country are not refugees but Internally Displaced Persons (IDPs). Moreover, one must, save in exceptional circumstances, already be physically, if not legally, in the country where asylum is claimed. Issues such as statelessness and the application of the Dublin Convention (§4.1) are not discussed here.

4.2.9 'unable [or] unwilling'

The question of whether a 'sufficiency of protection' exists in the applicant's own country arises mainly in connection with persecution by non-State agents. Where State agents are involved, as explained by Lord Justice Stuart-Smith in *Horvath*:

> once the applicant establishes that he has a well-founded fear of persecution, generally speaking that will be sufficient to establish that he is both unable and unwilling through fear of the persecution to avail himself of the protection of the State, because the State itself is the persecutor.

Article 1A(2) focuses on the inability or unwillingness of *individual refugees* to avail themselves of the protection of their country of nationality. Moreover, their unwillingness must be attributable to their well-founded fear. Persons unwilling to accept the protection of their home State for other reasons – such as economic betterment – are excluded from Convention protection (Lord Clyde; *Horvath*). Applicants' inability to avail themselves of the protection of the State is not qualified by their fear in the same way, because inability has nothing necessarily to do with any fear of persecution (Stuart-Smith LJ; *Horvath*). In all such cases, the central issue is 'availability of protection against harm' (Symes 2001: 229). According to the surrogacy principle (§4.2.2), external protection only comes into play if national systems of protection are insufficient to prevent a real risk of persecution: individuals are 'required to approach their home State for protection before the responsibility of other States becomes engaged' (LaForest J; *Ward*). There are two issues here: the availability of protection in the applicant's own country; and *their own* inability or unwillingness to avail themselves of that protection. The case law is confused on the second matter, and while the cause of that confusion seems quite simple, its resolution is not, because the legal position is now so convoluted.

For once UNHCR's *Handbook* seems largely responsible for the confusion, because it arbitrarily switches focus from individual to State when it declares that the activities of non-State agents may constitute persecution 'if they are knowingly tolerated by the authorities, or if *the authorities refuse, or prove unable, to offer effective protection*' (1992: ¶65, italics added; see Symes 2001: 236; Symes and Jorro 2003: 195). Because of this inversion, many discussions get sidetracked into seeing things from (arguably) the wrong end, in terms of States offering protection rather than refugees availing themselves of it. In *Aitseguer*, for example, Laws LJ cited ¶65, and referred to 'circumstances where *the State . . . is unwilling or unable . . .* to afford protection' (italics added).

When the *Handbook* considers peoples' *inability* to avail themselves of the protection of their States of nationality, its formulation compounds the problem. Such inability, it says, implies:

> circumstances that are beyond the will of the person concerned. There may, for example, be a state of war, civil war or other grave disturbance, which prevents the country of nationality from extending protection or makes such protection ineffective. Protection by the country of nationality may also have been denied to the applicant. Such denial of protection may confirm or strengthen the applicant's fear of persecution, and may indeed be an element of persecution (1992: ¶98).

Note the transition as the paragraph proceeds. The first sentence adheres to the spirit of Article 1A(2) by addressing the agency (or lack of it) of individual applicants, but sentence two begins the shift in focus towards the agency of the State, carried to its conclusion in sentences three and four. Paragraph 99 is then entirely devoted to *denial* of protection by the State, rather than to individuals' *inability* to avail themselves of such protection. It is true that one cause of such inability may indeed be the State's refusal, but that causal link is far from straightforward (see below).

In ¶100 the *Handbook* reverts to the refugees' perspective, pointing out that unwillingness to avail oneself of the protection of one's home country seems an inevitable concomitant of any claim to be outside that country owing to a well-founded fear of persecution (though, in fact, that need not be so if persecution is by non-State agents). The damage has been done by the two preceding paragraphs, however, which encourage courts to consider the adequacy of State systems of protection – precisely what Haines accuses the Lords of over-emphasising in *Horvath* (§4.2.2) – rather than the well-foundedness of the applicant's fear of persecution *despite* those systems, as Article 1A(2) requires.

Much of the confusion arises because 'inability' and 'unwillingness' have different saliences depending on the perspective taken. Thus, a State's inability to offer protection means of course that asylum applicants are unable to avail themselves of it, but it may also account for their unwillingness to attempt do so, and thereby demonstrate the well-foundedness of their fear in this regard. Precisely the same may be said of unwillingness to offer protection: asylum applicants are clearly unable to avail themselves of protection if the State is unwilling to offer it, and are likely to be unwilling even to try, owing to a fear which in those circumstances may seem quite reasonable. In other words, once the perspectives of individual and State are conflated, as in the *Handbook*, the distinction between inability and unwillingness all but disappears, and so, consequently, does the Convention's clear intention of linking unwillingness, but not inability, to the existence of a well-founded fear. This helps account for the *Horvath* decision regarding sufficiency of protection, and for Haines' trenchant criticism of it, because by switching from an individual's inability or unwillingness to that of the State, one is naturally led to focus on the adequacy of State institutions rather than the likelihood of a real risk of serious harm to individuals.

These are arguments from first principles, however. What matters in practice is the state of play according to case law, and here things remain confused following *Horvath* where, Symes suggests (2001: 236), the Law Lords' views diverged even when they seemed under the impression that they were agreeing with one another.

Lord Lloyd thought that even if Mr Horvath satisfied the 'well-founded fear test', he failed the 'protection test' because he had not shown an inability to avail himself of the protection of the Slovak State. He added:

> the applicant's case . . . is that he regards the local police as ineffective and indifferent . . . But he is not the sole judge of that. The test is objective. The tribunal has found as a fact that the available protection satisfies the Convention standard. There are no special circumstances which would enable the appellant to succeed on the second branch of the protection test [unwilling], having failed on the first [unable] (my glosses).

The final sentence does however indicate that there *could* be special circumstances where precisely this is possible (Symes 2001: 236).

Lord Hope correctly (according to my analysis) focused on individuals rather than States, but concluded that a person's unwillingness to avail himself of the protection of his country of nationality only engaged the Refugee Convention if his fear was of being persecuted 'for availing himself of the State's protection', not if it was a 'fear of persecution by non-State agents despite the State's protection against those agents' activities'. This bizarre distinction may be traced back to Lord Justice Stuart-Smith's leading judgment in the Appeal Court:

> If the State is able to provide sufficient protection, the claim for refugee status will generally fail, unless the applicant can show that he is unwilling to avail himself of that protection, not because he thinks it is

inadequate, but because of fear of the persecution. . . . It may be, for example, that the persecutors have issued true and credible threats against him and his family if he seeks the protection of the State such that he could be said to be unwilling to do so.

The argument, then, is that an unwillingness claim can only succeed if the fear is of the consequences of seeking State protection. But the starting premise is that 'the State is able to provide sufficient protection', and to be truly 'sufficient' it must surely cover these circumstances too. Consequently, this alleged exception seems no exception at all. One is led back to Haines' point; the focus should be on the well-foundedness of the fear, not the adequacy of State protection. Why should protection be granted to persons fearing the consequences of trying to obtain State protection, and denied to those still holding the fear which drove them to leave in the first place, namely, persecution for reasons of (in this case) race or ethnicity? Horvath's family had a fear arising from skinheads' persecutory actions towards them as Roma; he had already tried and failed to obtain police protection, and while it is of course possible that future attempts to do so might provoke the skinheads further, they were clearly predisposed to persecute him in any case.

As we saw (§4.2.2), the Home Office enthusiastically adopted the main points in *Horvath*. The *APIs* take the general meanings of 'unable' and 'unwilling' for granted, but go on to state:

> Mr Horvath argued that under the 1951 Convention a refugee may be a 'person unwilling to avail himself of the protection' of his country of nationality where he fears persecution by non-State agents, notwith-standing the State's protection. The Department argued that the individual must show that protection with which the State is required to provide him [sic] is not available or that he has a well-founded belief that he will be persecuted for availing himself of it. The majority of the House of Lords accepted the Department's argument that the individual's fear can only be well founded if it is a fear of being persecuted for availing himself of the State's protection (IND 2002a: ¶1.2.8.5).

Though binding on British courts, the Lords' decision in *Horvath* is not necessarily accepted elsewhere. Haines' critical commentary (§4.2.2) argues that:

> the purpose of refugee law is to identify those who have a well-founded fear of persecution for a Convention reason. If the net result of a State's 'reasonable willingness' to operate a system for the protection of the citizen is that it is incapable of preventing a real chance of persecution of

a particular individual, refugee status cannot be denied that individual (*Decision 71427/99*).[13]

4.3 GENDER AND SEXUALITY

The omission of gender from Article 1A(2) of the 1951 Convention was a deliberate decision by the drafting conference, not a simple oversight. The Yugoslavian delegate did propose adding the words 'or sex' to the list of Convention reasons, but was opposed by the British delegate on the grounds that 'equality of the sexes was a matter for national legislation'. The UN High Commissioner for Refugees, from the chair, foreclosed further debate by opining that he 'doubted strongly whether there would be any cases of persecution on account of sex' (UN Doc A/CONF.2/SR.5)!

In 1951 it was not yet routine to distinguish 'gender' from 'sex' as social and biological constructs respectively. Although the later observance of such terminological scruples does at least indicate awareness of 'gender' as an issue, it has its own dangers if it bolsters the view that biological differences are somehow more 'real' (Yanagisako and Collier 1987: 15), since in fact 'the "real" differences [are] just as socially constructed as the so called "social" differences' (Spijkerboer 2000: 6). These social constructions of both gender and sex are what concern us here.[14]

Masculine pronouns are used throughout the Convention, though it is meant to be gender-neutral. It has been argued that this 'neutrality' is actually a form of gender-blindness which doubly discriminates against women, because distinctively female experiences tend to be marginalised and because 'procedural and evidential barriers' impinge differentially upon women (Crawley 2001: 5). In symbolic revolt against such bias, several influential texts on asylum law use the feminine voice throughout (Hathaway 1991; Henderson 2003), and feminist critics long assumed that women are effectively discriminated against in asylum decision making, and may not benefit equally from Convention protection (Berkowitz and Jarvis 2000: 1).

It fact, however, women are no less successful than men in their asylum claims – rather the reverse in raw percentage terms (Spijkerboer 2000: 39). This conclusion has been potentially accessible since at least 1990, when the Canadian authorities began publishing gender breakdowns of decisions.

---

13 In November 2004 a tribunal dismissed the Home Office's appeal against the successful human rights appeal of *MH*, coyly described as someone 'already well known in the jurisprudence of refugee law'. It is now Home Office policy not to remove persons who were actually in the UK when their country acceded to the EU, 'unless they pose a threat to public health, public policy or public security'.

14 The vital and complex issue of gender-based persecution is addressed relatively briefly here, because I have discussed it extensively elsewhere (Good 2006a; in press).

Ironically, this was long before they published their pioneering gender guidelines for asylum decision makers (IRB 1993), followed in quick succession by the US (INS 1995), Australia (DIMA 1997), and the UK (Berkowitz and Jarvis 2000). In a further irony, these guidelines all adopt an essentialising approach to 'gender' rather than the relational one which the term seems to require (Crawley 2001: 6), because in practice they deal only with refugee *women*.

The point is not that women are systematically discriminated against, but that 'the social positions of men and women are different in every country and thus the asylum cases of men and women are always different' (Spijkerboer 2000: 5). In other words, the identities of *both male and female refugees* are gendered constructs. The question therefore becomes, what are the differences in the images of male and female asylum applicants held by the immigration officers who interview them initially; their own legal representatives who record their statements; the Home Office caseworkers making decisions on their claims; and the adjudicators who determine their appeals?

Such constructions usually reflect gender stereotypes invoking male activity, rationality, and autonomy, and female passivity, emotionality, and dependence (Spijkerboer 2000: 7). The consequences of imposing values which prioritise male activities in the public sphere are familiar from other contexts, such as the 'invisibility' to development planners of women's productive, reproductive, and community management work (Moser 1993). For example, men's participation in demonstrations or strikes is usually accepted unquestioningly as expressive of their political opinions, whereas women's violation of dress codes or preparation of food for political activists may not be (Crawley 2001: 21–6; Spijkerboer 2000: 4–5). Nor – and this is how Spijkerboer's denial of discrimination can be squared with the feminist critique premised upon marginalisation of distinctively female issues – is it simply a matter of the success or failure of the asylum application. Even successful applicants undergo this gendered 'reduction of the refugee as Other' (Barsky 1994: 239).

It comes as no surprise (following Said 1991) that Muslim asylum claimants are particularly subject to fantastic constructions on the part of occidental decision makers (Crawley 2001: 9). Above all, Muslim women making asylum claims face a Western received view of Islam as socially backward and monolithic in its absolute denial of any public voice to women (Spijkerboer 2000: 7). Consequently, their claims can succeed only if they appear to repudiate Islam entirely, rather than arguing from their opposition *as Muslims* to the version of Islam imposed upon them by their State of origin (Akram 2000). Even if their claim succeeds, escape from persecution in the name of one hegemonic interpretation of Islam, has been achieved at the cost of being compulsorily redefined in the name of another.

Despite the abrupt dismissal of sex-based persecution at the founding conference, it is astonishing that the words 'sex', 'gender', and 'rape', never appeared in the core texts – the Convention itself and UNHCR's *Handbook*. Later UNHCR documents (2002b, for example) have of course addressed such issues, and the *APIs* accept that 'rape and other serious sexual violence' may constitute persecution if committed for a Convention reason (IND 2002a: ¶1.2.8.2; see Hathaway 1991: 112n). The circumstances under which rape *does* constitute persecution for a Convention reason remain controversial however, and although cases are rarely dismissed because rapes are not deemed sufficiently serious forms of violence, they are commonly found not to give rise to claims under the Convention (Spijkerboer 2000: 109).

Even when detainees are raped by agents of the State, the Home Office usually argues – in Sri Lankan cases anyway – that this did not constitute torture, or even persecution, because it was an individual act not condoned by the authorities. The courts sometimes agree. For example, in a judicial review application from a Muslim man who had been raped while detained by the Sri Lankan army Mr Justice Ognall agreed that these were criminal acts rather than torture. The adjudicator had found that:

> this was violent conduct by two persons in positions of authority, that undoubtedly it was perpetrated upon the applicant . . . while he was in their custody, but that no material had been placed before him which served to demonstrate that that brutal conduct was the product of persecution. It was merely, to use an inappropriate phrase, these two soldiers on a 'frolic of their own' . . . [P]ersons in positions of authority not infrequently abuse their position to violate in whatever way captives [sic]. That is regrettably a fact of life. It is another to demonstrate that violation by soldiers is to be viewed as the product of a policy of persecution to the captive in question. [D]eplorable though that conduct was . . . they were assaulting him in this way to gratify their own licentiousness (*Roomy*).

'Frolic' is legalese for acts undertaken for personal gratification rather than carrying out orders or policy; even so, the insensitivity of its use here is breathtaking. As this example also illustrates, many decisions reflect misperceptions of rape as an act of sexual gratification rather than of violence (Crawley 2001: 35), and of sexual intercourse as an 'inherently private' activity (2001: 95; Muller-Hoff 2001). This particular decision pre-dated the Medical Foundation's report on sexual abuse of male detainees in Sri Lanka (Peel *et al.* 2000), which confirms that the most likely motive is 'demonstration of complete control over the victim', and that the perpetrators 'do not perceive themselves or their acts as homosexual'.

Such reasoning is, of course, even more likely when the victim is female. Spijkerboer, analysing the Dutch authorities' treatment of the rape of a Tamil woman from Jaffna, points out (2000: 52) that both her interview report and the decision refusing her asylum application ignore the political context:

The version of the facts presented in the decision lacks any reference whatsoever to political issues. Even the fact that the son was suspected of being an informer immediately prior to his execution, which is mentioned in the interview, is overlooked. What is not overlooked, however, is the fact that the LTTE men were drunk. The decision thus presents alcohol as the cause of Anne's first rape.[15]

One finds similar examples in British courts. In *SSHD* v. *'D'*,[16] the Home Office appealed against the granting of asylum to a Tamil woman. The adjudicator had not believed that the appellant's political activities would attract adverse interest from the Sri Lankan authorities, but granted asylum because she had twice been raped by soldiers. The tribunal chairman, poetically reducing the rape to a matter of the soldiers 'having their way with her', denied in principle that rape under such circumstances constituted persecution for a Convention reason:

> These were not systematic rapes to humiliate a prisoner in custody; but escapades by lecherous soldiers on frolics (to use the old-fashioned term) of their own. No doubt they thought they could get away with raping a Tamil girl; and possibly any family association with the Tamil Tigers reinforced that impression. Clearly rapes by security forces do occur . . . as is unfortunately often the case where troops of any power are occupying an area with a population they see as different from themselves. It is not easy for the authorities to deter this sort of activity on the part of their more brutal and licentious soldiery; but there is evidence that those in Sri Lanka have taken firm action where they could, in one case resulting in death sentences against members of the security forces.[17] It cannot be said that there is a general risk of rape, with no effective protection against it, for Tamil girls in the north and east. [Her barrister] was equally unable to explain . . . why being raped twice in these circumstances should put this asylum-seeker at any greater risk of it on return. [While] 'systematic rapes to humiliate a prisoner in custody' might well amount to torture, what is said to have happened in this case could not be so described, as a matter of ordinary English.

Just as Spijkerboer and Crawley suggest, such decisions downplay the political context, and assume that sexual desire is the primary motive. Compare

15 He uses Western pseudonyms to remind us that refugee identities are legal constructs (2000: 45).
16 This and the following cases are in the public domain, but I omit appellants' names to avoid gratuitous publicity.
17 [In fact that case involved the rape *and murder* of a Tamil schoolgirl; no soldier has stood trial on rape charges alone during the ethnic conflict, still less has been found guilty.]

the granting of asylum by this same chairman, when still an adjudicator, to 'N', an 'attractive young Tamil girl', with his comment in refusing the appeal of 'M', a Tamil woman aged 50: 'Without wishing to appear unchivalrous, we have to say that there can be no significant risk of rape at her age.' While not the sole criterion in these decisions, because the situation in Sri Lanka had changed in the interim, the sexual desirability of the victim was clearly seen as a crucial factor.

Such decisions reflect cultural assumptions that male sexuality is 'an innate, independent and quasi-biological drive which . . . can suddenly overwhelm a man' (Crawley 2001: 96). Its violent expression can then be dismissed as aberrant but only to be expected, so even when the rapist is a soldier or policeman who is actually on duty, he is perceived as acting from personal lust rather than engaging in behaviour condoned or encouraged by the State (2001: 35). It seems, though, that such arguments are ethnically determined, for while rapes of Tamil women are commonly viewed as offences by delinquent individuals, rapes of Bosnian women tend to be interpreted as politically motivated ethnic cleansing (Spijkerboer 2000: 101). But why this concern with motivation in the first place? The argument that violence by a State agent is a private act, not politically motivated, seems largely restricted to sexual violence (2000: 113, 128).

Another consequence of the Convention's 'gender-neutrality' is a lack of clarity as to the Convention reason under which claims of gender-based persecution are most appropriately formulated. The choice may sometimes be dictated by the particular circumstances of the case, but when faced with gendered persecution based upon (male) notions of family honour; Female Genital Mutilation (FGM); domestic violence; or violations of reproductive rights, lawyers often have to make strategic decisions over whether to present the claim in terms of their client's membership of a particular social group, or on grounds of political opinion. The potential of both strategies is illustrated in the case of FGM, an enormously controversial issue in US asylum law. In *Matter of Kasinga*, an appellant from Togo was deemed to belong to a social group 'defined by the immutable or fundamental characteristics of gender, ethnicity, opposition to the practice, and the fact of having "intact genitalia" ' (Musalo and Knight 2001: 54), whereas in *Matter of MK* a woman from Sierra Leone was granted asylum partly because of the political opinions which led her to reject this aspect of her society's cultural practice (Crawley 2001: 140).

As it happens, however, there have been no high-profile FGM cases in British asylum jurisprudence. Instead, the key precedent case as regards issues of gender and sexuality, *Islam and Shah*, was concerned with domestic violence. As we saw (§4.2.6), it opened up the possibility that even rather broad categories of women might constitute 'particular social groups'. It also compelled the Home Office to recognise the possibility that persons defined by sexual orientation, too, might under certain circumstances constitute a PSG. The *APIs* were accordingly amended to read:

groups who share an immutable characteristic (including women and homosexuals or other persons defined by sexual orientation) may constitute a social group if they are subject to persecution in their society by reason of their being members of that group (2002a: ¶1.2.9.4).

Under current UK law, therefore, the temptation for lawyers representing female applicants who have experienced domestic violence or sexual abuse, must be to couch their arguments in social group terms, citing *Islam and Shah*.[18]

Yet the *APIs* also recognise the possibility that political opinion and action may be gender-specific:

A woman who opposes institutionalised discrimination against women or expresses views of independence from the social or cultural norms of society may sustain or fear harm because of her actual political opinion or a political opinion that has been imputed to her. She is perceived within the established political/social structure as expressing politically antagonistic views through her actions or failure to act. *If a woman resists gender oppression, her resistance is political* (2002a: ¶1.2.9.5; italics added).

What is more, the IAA's own guidelines recognise that 'an asylum applicant may be persecuted in a gender specific manner for reasons unrelated to gender (e.g. raped because of her membership in a political party)' (Berkowitz and Jarvis 2000: 3). It follows that in the UK too, under certain circumstances, political opinion may be a more appropriate ground under which to argue gender-based asylum claims.

4.4 UNHCR AND IND: AN OVERVIEW

It is worth reiterating that the purpose of this long survey has been ethnographic, not jurisprudential. I have tried to convey as accurately as possible the ideas and practices of those under study, but the case law *qua* law is summarised more authoritatively by others (Jackson 1999; Henderson 2003; Symes and Jorro 2003). The aim here was to analyse asylum law anthropologically as a distinctive 'mode of thought', and seen in that light, what is striking is the extent to which it occupies a solipsistic parallel universe, its interpretations largely unaffected by thinking and research in social science.

---

18 In *Matter of R-A-*, by contrast, the US Board of Immigration Appeals relegated *Islam and Shah* to a footnote, ruling that no Convention reason was engaged by domestic violence in Guatemala.

To an extent this is inevitable because the purposes of the two professions are incompatible (Gunn 2003), but greater anthropological awareness could – and in cases like *Sathiyaseelan* (§4.2.3) and *Omoruyi* (§4.2.4) certainly would – guard against judicial descent into prejudice masquerading as 'common sense'.

The 1951 Convention requires a very great deal of interpretation, as is by now only too clear. The above discussion strongly suggests that Home Office interpretations in the *Asylum Policy Instructions* are consistently narrower than those of UNHCR's *Handbook*. The most obvious explanation is political; the charge is made that, far from taking 'a creative view of the grounds for persecution . . . in the light of modern developments and approaches', the UK takes a 'restrictive approach' which tends to treat the Convention as 'a checklist for exclusion' (Justice *et al.* 1997: 21). This may well be so, but it is important to recognise other, more subtle reasons for this narrowness of approach.

Although the *Handbook* and *APIs* both contain advice for decision makers, they differ in both their status and their relationship to British case law. In accord with UNHCR's global remit, the *Handbook* presents a set of timeless universal principles, aiming to advise all countries on the proper approach to take. The *APIs*, by contrast, instruct British civil servants on the present state of domestic law, to maximise the chances that administrative decisions to grant or withhold refugee status will be upheld in the event of appeal. Their purpose is not to influence the law but to conform to it, and one cannot expect them to contain statements of principle, however restrictive or liberal, which stand little chance of endorsement in British courts. To that extent, if the approach in the *APIs* is indeed restrictive, ultimate responsibility for that lies with Parliament and the courts.

Yet it is all too easy to incorporate subtle linguistic cues, steering readers towards more or less charitable interpretations. On that count, the overall effect of the *APIs* is likely to be to encourage IND staff to err on the uncharitable side within the grey area between an asylum decision obviously in accord with the law and one clearly at variance with it. And once the scales of justice are tipped, however slightly, in one direction, the weight of evidence required to tilt them back in the opposite direction has inevitably increased.

Chapter 5

Claiming asylum

5.1 PROCESSING AND ASSESSING APPLICATIONS

Initial decisions on asylum claims are made by the Immigration and Nationality Directorate of the Home Office (IND). Its procedures change frequently and my knowledge of them is largely second-hand, so this section merely summarises procedures set out in the *Asylum Policy Instructions* (IND 2002a), adding evidence – where I have it – of how things worked out in practice during 2000–2002.

Applications are categorised according to when they are made. Those who make *port applications* when entering the country are interviewed first by Immigration Officers (IOs). Most are granted temporary entry while their application is dealt with, but some may be detained if there are 'good grounds for believing' they will not keep in touch voluntarily (IND 2002a: ¶1.1.4.1). *In time/in country applications* are those made by people already legitimately present in the UK, including refugees *sur place*, that is, people whose fear of persecution arose after arrival because of events back home. *Out of time/in country applications* are those made by people who had been in the UK legitimately but whose leave to remain has expired. Finally there are *applications from illegal entrants* who entered clandestinely. IND expects 'genuine' applicants to declare themselves on entry. This may be unrealistic, given the fear many refugees feel towards officials and the circumstances under which they have travelled. They may be wholly unfamiliar with the UK – indeed, may not even know it *is* the UK – and are often exhausted and terrified, yet any delay in claiming asylum is seized on by the Home Office as undermining their credibility.

Crawley (1999) found marked differences in the conduct of initial interviews by IOs at different ports, partly because of widespread confusion over their purpose. The White Paper (Home Office 1998) and *Asylum Directorate Instructions* (IND 1998a) portrayed them as purely fact-finding exercises, enabling applicants to explain in their own words why they feared persecution in their home countries, but most IOs saw them as tests of credibility (Crawley 1999: 50). Given such misapprehensions among interviewers, it was hardly surprising that interviewees too were unclear about their purpose, and did not realise this was their main, if not only, chance to explain the basis of their claim (1999: 13). Some had no idea what the interviews were for; others understood them to be just information gathering; while yet others thought the interview was the actual decision-making process (1999: 50). Confusions were worsened by the lack of legal representation (1999: 38), and by a curious deficiency in the information given to interviewees. Leaflets for in-country applicants contained assurances of confidentiality, and explained why it was important to reveal even 'painful and embarrassing' matters. These were entirely missing from leaflets given to port applicants, which were, moreover, available only in English (1999: 47–8).

For their part, IOs viewed many asylum claims as ruses to circumvent immigration procedures (Crawley 1999: 23). They also held preconceptions about 'genuine' refugees, which significantly affected the conduct of interviews; for example, their judgment was influenced by whether asylum was claimed spontaneously, or only after refusal of entry. IOs viewed sceptically anyone arriving with false documents or no documents at all (1999: 25), even though the tightening of visa regimes and introduction of carrier penalties means that most applicants have no legal way of entering the UK. As long ago as 1987, Lord Bridge commented:

> I find it strange that such an important interview as this should be entrusted to an immigration officer at the port of entry with no knowledge of conditions in the country of origin of a claimant for asylum (*Bugdaycay*).

In fact, judgments were influenced by rules of thumb concerning appellants' nationality, gender, class, age, and demeanour (see Coussey 2003: ¶17–18). Young single men were 'often assumed to be economic migrants'; women were 'assumed to have no political identity or fear of persecution . . . independent of spouses and other male relatives'; and 'If they are immaculately dressed you think, well, are they fleeing for their life or not?' The claims of some nationalities were taken more seriously than others: 'The obviously genuine ones tend to be Arabs' (1999: 26). Many IOs were convinced they could recognise true refugees; it 'shines out like a beacon' (Crawley 1999: 27).

At the time of my research, most applicants were given self-completion Statement of Evidence Forms (SEF) on which to set out the basis of their claims. These had to be returned within ten working days or asylum would be refused on 'non-compliance' grounds. They also had to attend subsequent asylum interviews. IND then began omitting the self-completion stage, dealing with claims by asylum interview alone. All applicants are interviewed before any decision is taken,[1] unless they are being refused on non-compliance grounds or there is already enough information to warrant refugee status (2002a: ¶1.1.2.2).

Because of IND reorganisation, Crawley could not pay comparable attention to these asylum interviews by IND caseworkers (1999: 1). The rules governing their conduct at that time were published in the *Asylum Directorate Instructions* (IND 1998a: ¶16.3). These interviews were generally quite long (114 minutes on average; *Mapah*), and legal representatives were on balance more satisfied with them. They occurred long after arrival, so were unaffected by any exhaustion or disorientation caused by the journey. Moreover, IND staff were better informed than IOs about countries of origin, and explained the purpose of the interview better.

Interviews are transcribed by hand as they proceed, so questions are often in note form, although answers should be recorded verbatim. These may be the only written accounts of appellants' stories, because many less conscientious solicitors do not take witness statements themselves. When one remembers the likely state of mind of the applicant, the involvement of an interpreter (§7.2), and the interviewer's limited knowledge of politics or culture in the applicant's home country, there is clearly considerable scope for mutual misunderstanding and errors of omission and recording. This is even more likely if interviews are not conducted properly, and Crawley reported allegations that transcripts were often not read back, while some applicants claimed to have been threatened with instant deportation if they did not sign the transcript (Asylum Aid 1999). Many applicants complained that they were never asked about matters they wanted to raise, while others were too afraid to speak freely (Asylum Aid 1999: 59ff; Crawley 1999: 59). This applied especially to women – whose reticence might be associated with cultural restraints – and those of both sexes who had suffered sexual assault. Transcripts seen in my role as expert often revealed applicants being explicitly discouraged from raising matters that interviewers deemed irrelevant, or being cut short when their replies seemed idiosyncratic or too lengthy.[2]

Such abuses and procedural defects were possible because no lawyers or advisors were present at most immigration interviews, while even at IND interviews they were merely observers, who could comment afterwards on the conduct of the interview but might be asked to leave if they intervened in the process. IND saw their presence as a 'concession' and created obstacles to their participation. At Lunar House in Croydon, for example, the practice

---

1 The *APIs* formerly contained the unfortunately phrased statement: 'Applicants should always be interviewed before their application is refused' (IND 1998a: ¶1.1.2.5).

2 Following the Court of Appeal decision in *Dirshe* (2005), IND has had to tape-record asylum interviews whenever asylum applicants cannot afford their own interpreters or legal representatives. See www.ind.homeoffice.gov.uk/ind/en/home/laws_policy/policy_instructions/apis/interviewing.html? (consulted 20 November 2005).

during 2000 was that representatives were allowed in only if they arrived with their clients. If an eager applicant showed up early at reception, their representative might be refused permission to join them later. Asylum interviews thus exemplify 'the power asymmetry that characterizes encounters between asylum applicants and the State' (Blommaert 2001: 444). When the 1996 Act was debated ministers gave assurances that the asylum interview was not the be-all and end-all and that applicants would be able to give further details later on (Crawley 1999: 12), yet IND routinely picks on omissions and minor discrepancies in these interviews so as to attack credibility.

Commenting on Crawley's findings, the then President of the IAT, Judge David Pearl, accepted that 'the quality of information gathering leaves a great deal to be desired [and] improving this essential aspect of asylum status determination is a prerequisite for full compliance of [sic] our obligations under the Geneva Convention' (Crawley 1999: *vii*). Since Crawley's research, moreover, the requirement to read statements back to appellants has been dropped, in response to pressure to speed up the processing of claims. Although the courts decided this was not actually unlawful, they called it 'an unwarranted change in practice which . . . opened the door to further complaint of misinterpretation, misunderstanding or misrecording' (*Bilbil*), and noted that reverting to the prior system would 'enhance confidence in the impartiality of the procedure' (*Mapah*; see §7.2).

On the basis of interview transcripts, SEFs, and any medical reports or other documentation applicants may have, IND then decides whether to grant refugee status (Indefinite Leave to Remain; ILR) or a temporary, humanitarian status with fewer rights.[3] As explained later (§8.3), these grants are heavily dependent upon decisions as to appellants' credibility. Yet at the same time, although the UNHCR *Handbook* stresses that claims should be considered on their individual merits, not by blanket assessments of the general situation in countries of origin (1992: ¶37), decision making based on nationality has been written into British policies at certain periods. Under the 1996 Act there was a 'White List' of countries – Bulgaria, Cyprus, Ghana, India, Pakistan, Poland, and Romania – where there was deemed to be *no* general risk of persecution (Trost and Billings 1998). Their nationals were dealt with by 'fast track' procedures with distinct elements of self-fulfilling prophecy. Because information about such people was collected in different ways, the likelihood of their claim being recognised was reduced (Crawley 1999: 25). The White List was abolished by the 1999 Act, but a variant was reintroduced under the 2002 Act, initially involving prospective new EU

---

3   The status termed Exceptional Leave to Remain (ELR), prevailing at the time of my research, was replaced on 1 April 2003 by Humanitarian Protection, a less generous provision, and by Discretionary Leave granted, for example, to unaccompanied children for whom there were no adequate reception arrangements in their country of origin.

Member States, but extended in 2003 to involve other countries including, astonishingly, Sri Lanka.

IND's procedures (2002a: ¶17.3) acknowledge the special role of the Medical Foundation for the Care of Victims of Torture (MF) in providing treatment, counselling and therapy to torture victims, and the time allowed for submitting supporting evidence is often extended if there is written confirmation that MF is examining the applicant and producing a report. IND's policy in 2002 was that people with well-founded fears of torture should be recognised as refugees if there was a Convention reason; otherwise they should be granted ELR. However, staff were told that while medical evidence could not be dismissed out of hand, they need not accept all MF reports as prima facie evidence of torture, especially if they thought the report departed from MF's own guidelines. They were said to reject such evidence in nearly one third of cases (Asylum Aid 1999: 17), or might decide that although torture had occurred, it would not happen in future because in-country conditions had improved (IND 2002a: ¶3.2.4.2).

In the past, delays were considerable. It could be two years before IND even acknowledged receipt of an application, and by 1998 there were 10,000 applications on which no decision had been taken after five years or more (Home Office 1998: 16). From 2000 onwards, however, the average time taken for initial decisions was greatly reduced. This is good in principle, because delays increase applicants' worry and expense, while others can use appeals as devices to prolong their stay. Unfortunately, however, the quality of Home Office decisions is by no means always satisfactory. This is shown, first, by the fact that appeal success rates tended to rise over time (Home Office 2002: Table 1.1; see §5.4). Second, the Independent Race Monitor reported in 2002 that 14 per cent of asylum decisions in her sample 'seemed harsh'; she was troubled by rejections purely on grounds of credibility, and felt that 'in some cases, the burden of proof applied was beyond the standard of reasonable doubt' (Coussey 2003: ¶29–31).[4] However, IND rejected her suggestion (2003: ¶39) that rejections based solely on credibility should be double-checked. Her most recent (2004–2005) report continues to reflect concerns that some asylum refusals are based upon ethnocentric assumptions or cynicism (Coussey 2005: ¶3.21–3.24). Finally, a survey of decision making by the National Audit Office reported 'weaknesses' in decision-making processes, including 'basic errors of fact and unclear language' (2004: ¶23).

The outcomes of these decision-making processes showed startling variations over time. Prior to the 1993 Act, 76 per cent of *all* applicants – not just all successful ones – were granted ELR. That figure fell to 22 per cent immediately after the Act came into force, and then to below 9 per cent. The

---

4   This confuses *burden* with *standard* of proof, and reasonable doubt is the wrong standard (§10.2).

Home Office claimed that many people were earlier given ELR purely because of the size of the decision-making backlog (Scannell 1999: 74, 80–1), but the suspicion remained that standards had shifted in response to increasing numbers of claims. ELR was normally only granted after an asylum application had been refused, or if no initial decision had been taken after seven years. It could be given because return might expose an applicant to cruel, inhuman or degrading treatment; cause an unjustifiable break-up of family life; reduce life expectancy; cause acute physical or mental suffering; or for other special compassionate grounds. At times it has been policy to grant ELR to all nationals of particular countries, on humanitarian grounds (IND 1998a: ¶5.1.2.1).

Most applicants are refused refugee or humanitarian status, however, and receive Reasons For Refusal Letters (RFRLs) explaining why. RFRLs consist largely of generic statements varying little from letter to letter. Caseworkers are encouraged to rely on standard paragraphs in the interests of consistency, and the *APIs* (2002a: ¶11.1), contain model paragraphs on general issues, into which can be inserted details of individual applicants and countries of origin.[5] If the applicant's problems are not considered serious enough to constitute persecution, the standard paragraph reads (retaining the original format):

> You have alleged that, if you were to return to [ ]: [LIST HARM WHICH APPLICANT CLAIMS S/HE WOULD SUFFER, INCLUDING MEASURES OF DISCRIMINATION][6] However, the Secretary of State does not consider that this harm would constitute persecution as described in the UN Handbook or as interpreted by the courts.

There are standard paragraphs for use in cases where it is concluded that the fear is of prosecution rather than persecution, or that the claim is not based upon a Convention reason. If the claimed source of persecution is not the government, the RFRL will assert that 'such individuals cannot be regarded as "agents of persecution" within the terms of the 1951 United Nations Convention'. Even if persecution clearly originates from persons in positions of authority, the letter may nonetheless say – as in many RFRLs for Sri Lankan Tamils – that:

> In order to bring yourself within the scope of the Convention, you would have to show that these incidents were not simply the random actions of individuals but were a sustained pattern or campaign of persecution

---

5 RFRLs also use country-specific standard paragraphs, often from CIPU *Country Reports* (§9.2).
6 Footnote in original: [e.g. 'you would be arrested and detained by the police'].

directed at you which was controlled, sanctioned or condoned by the authorities, or that the authorities were unable, or unwilling, to offer you effective protection.

Applicants travelling with the help of agents often reach the UK by complex routes involving stopovers in places like the Gulf or Moscow. This is commonly used to cast doubt on credibility:

> The Secretary of State noted that immediately prior to your arrival in the United Kingdom you spent [TIME] in [COUNTRY], a signatory of the 1951 United Nations Convention relating to the Status of Refugees. The Secretary of State considers that you had opportunity to claim asylum in [COUNTRY] and that your failure to do so casts doubt on the credibility of your claim to be in genuine need of international protection.

This is still said in virtually every RFRL, although the courts have made it abundantly clear that it is not an appropriate consideration when assessing asylum claims. This was robustly restated by Mr Justice Collins in early 2003:

> where someone wants to get to the United Kingdom, understandably because members of the family are here already, and arranges to do that in the back of a lorry travelling across Europe, the fact that she does not claim in one of the countries through which the lorry travels en route cannot conceivably by itself throw doubt on whether she is indeed a genuine asylum seeker. That is a thoroughly bad point (*Degirmenci*).

RFRLs also set out applicants' appeal rights. Section 69 of the 1999 Act lists five possible appealable decisions; for example, section 69(1) covers rights of appeal in 'port' cases, triggered by refusal of leave to enter the country as a refugee. These are all appeals against immigration decisions rather than against refusal of asylum *per se*, so the ground of appeal is that 'a requirement to leave the UK as a result of the decision would be contrary to the UK's obligations under the UN Convention' (IND 2002a: ¶13.1.2).

5.2 APPEAL HEARINGS

First appeals against IND decisions are heard by adjudicators from the Immigration Appellate Authority (IAA), and second appeals, with leave, by the Immigration Appeals Tribunal (IAT; see §5.3). Subsequent appeals are possible, with leave, to the Court of Appeal or Court of Session, and there is always the possibility of judicial review (Thomas 2003). The 1999 Act introduced a streamlined process designed to prevent appellants prolonging their stay by mounting a series of appeals (IND 2002a: ¶13.1.1.1).

The *Human Rights Act 1998* began to apply to immigration matters from 2 October 2000, so that applicants' human rights appeals are now routinely heard along with their asylum appeals. Article 2 (right to life) and Article 8 (respect for private and family life) are often cited, but by far the most common is Article 3: 'No one shall be subjected to torture or to inhuman or degrading treatment or punishment'. The situation of appellants already refused asylum prior to this date was a matter of controversy during the early stages of my fieldwork, but their right to make separate human rights appeals, if their asylum appeals had failed, was settled in *Pardeepan*.

Asylum appeals are adversarial public hearings. There are many hearing centres around the country, and the number of adjudicators rose sharply during the drive to speed up the decision-making process, so that by 2001 there were 366 part-time and 32 full-time adjudicators. There was a Chief Adjudicator (His Honour Judge Dunn, followed by His Honour Judge Henry Hodge) based at Taylor House in Islington; a Deputy Chief Adjudicator; and six Regional Adjudicators. My research took place mainly at Taylor House and the Eagle Building in Glasgow, which handles all Scottish appeals. Taylor House has around 25 courts, and Glasgow has seven.

Adjudicators and tribunal chairs are appointed by the Lord Chancellor and must have seven years approved experience of legal practice, or other legal experience fitting them for appointment – the latter proviso is most often invoked to appoint academic lawyers. Some are County Court judges or recorders; others are solicitors in other fields; some even practise as immigration solicitors themselves, though they do not sit in centres where they may represent clients, nor hear cases involving representatives from their own firms. There have been recent attempts to recruit more women and members of ethnic minorities into these positions, but at lunchtime the 'mess' – as some do insist on calling it – at Taylor House still resembles a rather spartan gentleman's club.

Asylum applicants are generally represented at appeal hearings by counsel in England and solicitors (occasionally advocates) in Scotland, although it is of course always solicitors who actually assemble and submit their evidence. The Immigration Advisory Service (IAS) and Refugee Legal Centre (RLC) provide legal representation at asylum appeals (IND 2002a: ¶17.2), and acted for a large proportion of applicants in the past, but since the upsurge in numbers most applicants now have representatives from the private sector. Most operate under the regulatory umbrella of the Law Society and Bar Council in England and Wales, or the Law Society of Scotland and Faculty of Advocates in Scotland; other providers in the for-profit sector must register with the Office of the Immigration Services Commissioner (OISC), a regulatory body set up under the 1999 Act, while advisors in the not-for-profit sector require OISC certificates of exemption. The Secretary of State is occasionally represented by counsel, but usually by a Home Office Presenting Officer (HOPO), a civil servant often with no formal legal qualifications. For many young barristers immigration work is a stepping stone to more lucrative kinds of brief, while HOPOs may hope for promotion to tribunal level, or other areas of Home Office activity.[7]

Male adjudicators wear dark business suits (no wigs or gowns here), and although there is greater variation among female adjudicators, their dress is also businesslike. Counsel dress even more formally. Dark pinstripes are de rigueur for men, although one or two emerge thus attired like butterflies out of the chrysalises of their motorcycle leathers each morning. Most female barristers – of whom there are many, perhaps a majority, in this jurisdiction – wear trouser suits, with 'power-dressing' accoutrements of careful make-up and rather high heels. HOPOs are similarly though less expensively dressed; a dark suit, but less of a fetish for pinstripe. The most outrageous pinstripes are sported by Scots advocates, who can easily be identified across a crowded hearing centre.

As the support received by asylum applicants is below the level of basic welfare payments, most qualify financially for legal aid. In addition, however, their cases must have a good chance of succeeding, be of significant wider public interest, or raise vital human rights issues. Law firms awarded franchises by the Legal Services Commission can apply for contracts to provide legal assistance in asylum cases, but many asylum applicants find it hard to gain access to specialised asylum lawyers, a problem exacerbated by the dispersal scheme which distributes applicants around the country. At the time of my research, financial support was available for legal representatives to attend asylum interviews as well as actual appeal hearings, but this is no longer so following subsequent restrictions on legal aid.[8]

Appeal dates are fixed weeks in advance, but communicated only to those directly involved. Summary details appear on the IAA website the night before, but only on the morning of the appeal, in the hearing centre itself, are full case listings available, as in the fictitious example shown in Figure 5.1. Most lists contain only asylum appeals, but for purposes of illustration I include several other types of case. If the respondent is the Secretary of State for the Home Department, it is probably an asylum or human rights appeal, or a combination of the two. More information can be gleaned from the appeal code. An HX or AS prefix indicates an asylum appeal; CC means the same, but indicates that the Home Office has certified it (below). In bail hearings (prefix GW in Scotland), the respondent is an Immigration Officer.

---

7   In 2001 many HOPOs were seeking transfers into 'removals', though these were administrative posts unlikely to involve man-handling deportees onto planes or breaking down mosque doors.

8   The Immigration Services Commissioner, who had not been consulted about these changes, told the Parliamentary Select Committee on Constitutional Affairs (21 October 2003) that it would be virtually impossible for representatives to meet minimum professional standards within the time allowed.

IMMIGRATION APPEALS – ADJUDICATOR'S HEARING
GLASGOW (EAGLE BUILDING)
31 February 2003

HEARING ROOM: Court 2 am		Substantive list
ADJUDICATOR: Mr J Jones		
USHER: Ms A Smith		
10:00 AM	**CC/12345/2001**	
	MR X Y v. Secretary of State	Respondent's rep:...............
	Smith & Co. Solicitors	Interpreter: Mandarin
10:00 AM	**GW/0999**	
	MR B v. Immigration Officer	Respondent's rep:...............
	Bloggs & Soap, Solicitors	Interpreter: Urdu
10:00 AM	**HX/22222/2001**	
	MRS S I v. Secretary of State	Respondent's rep:...............
	Immigration Counsellors Ltd	Interpreter: Arabic
10:00 AM	**HR/33333/1999**	
	MR MX v. Secretary of State	Respondent's rep:...............
	A Patel, Solicitors	Interpreter: Arabic
10:00 AM	**TH/11111/2002**	
	MR H R v. Entry Clearance Officer (Dhaka)	Respondent's rep:...............
	Mr A Bangali	Interpreter:

Figure 5.1 A listings notice.

Cases with a TH or IM prefix where the respondents are Entry Clearance Officers, may be family reunions or applications to visit relatives in the UK. A local sponsor may be listed rather than a legal representative. Visitors' appeals, with VV prefixes, are for those refused visitor visas, in respect of family visits, for example.

5.2.1 The hearing process

Appeals are all given the same nominal starting time and there is no guarantee that they will be heard in list order, so all parties must be present at the start of the day. The period between 9.30 and 10.00 each morning is hectic, as appellants, counsel, solicitors, and HOPOs arrive in droves, swarming round the ushers' desk or scrutinising the lists. Counsel walk through the foyer calling out the names of their clients, whom they may have met only once, if at all. Other counsel may be seeking out their HOPO, to ascertain the Home Office approach on certain matters.

Just before 10.00 these crowds disperse into the hearing rooms. These are designed to be less intimidating than normal courts. The adjudicator has a raised desk with the royal coat of arms on the wall behind. The appellant sits at a table directly facing the adjudicator, with the interpreter to the appellant's right. The square is completed by desks for the representatives, to left and right. Tribunal hearing rooms are a touch larger and grander. When all are present and correct, an usher leads the adjudicator into court by a separate door, knocking loudly and calling out 'All rise' as they enter. The adjudicator, usually burdened with more bundles than can conveniently be carried, plonks these down on the desk, wishes everyone good morning, and then invites them to be seated.

Documents should be submitted seven days in advance but in practice are often accepted even if handed in at the hearing itself, especially if they are well-known items such as Home Office *Country Assessments*. Sometimes one party has to be allowed time to read a new document of which they were previously unaware; this may require the adjudicator to rise briefly, especially if it is the HOPO who needs the time, but more usually the case is simply put to the bottom of the list. Even if submitted on time, documents may not actually get to those involved. All IAA files are held at Loughborough, and given the numbers of appeals and hearing centres it is perhaps not surprising that they often fail to reach adjudicators until the morning of the hearing, if at all. The Home Office is even more prone to mislaying documents. Sometimes this is easily remedied, but occasionally cases have to be adjourned because entire Home Office files are missing.

A typical day for an adjudicator involves three or four substantive cases. They start by checking that all parties are present, and legal representatives submit forms confirming that they are qualified to appear. The adjudicator deals with any preliminary issues like adjournment applications or missing files, then decides which case will be heard first. Representatives and appellants in other appeals are given projected start times, and nearly always go out of the hearing room until their case is due. Indeed, representatives may have been banking on this interlude to confer with their clients. Alternatively, they can at least check into chambers on their mobile phones and deal with other business.

Adjudicators are sovereign in their own courts, as one said to me, and have a lot of freedom as to how hearings are run. Their personal styles range from formal to informal, friendly to pompous. For example, they vary in what they tell appellants before the hearing starts. As a minimum, they confirm that the appellant and interpreter understand one another. Some then tell appellants what will happen during the hearing, and explain their own independent status. They may require witnesses to take oaths, although I almost never saw this done. Quite apart from the practical difficulty of identifying appropriate oaths for persons of such diverse backgrounds, there is general scepticism over the value of oath-taking: 'I tend to think', said one experienced adjudicator, 'that if people are going to tell me the truth, they will do so whether they have taken an oath or not.' A few adjudicators in Glasgow require witnesses to affirm, but this is for 'ritual' reasons (their word), to emphasise the importance of the occasion, not because of any enhanced truth value.

The hearing proper begins with the examination-in-chief. The appellant's representative first confirms their client's name, address, nationality, and date of birth. For most appellants there will be a SEF form, an asylum interview transcript and, if they have decent solicitors (far from always the case), a witness statement. In England, Counsel 'establishes' each in turn, asking the appellant whether they were read back to them in their own language, whether their contents are true, and whether they are happy to submit them as evidence. Appellants sometimes point out errors, especially in interview transcripts, and these are clarified. Once these documents have been established, the representative may ask a few questions, but often none at all.

Hearings in Glasgow are a little different, however, reflecting differences between English and Scots law. Although immigration is a reserved Westminster matter, any judicial reviews of Glasgow cases are heard by the Court of Session rather than the High Court. Scots law gives less weight to witness statements, so examinations-in-chief tend to be more thorough and last longer in Glasgow (Mungo Deans, pers. comm.), a matter not to the liking of the appellate authorities, under intense political pressure during the fieldwork to 'clear the backlog' of undecided appeals before the looming election. It does mean, however, that Glasgow hearings have less of a 'production line' feel than those in Taylor House.

There may also be medical reports in the evidence. Many Sri Lankan cases hinge on issues of scarring, but oddly, the main issue in 2001–2002 was not how scars were caused but how visible they were, although if it was accepted that they were indeed caused by torture that helped establish past persecution. The security forces sometimes deliberately mark detainees' bodies with cigarette burns, and occasionally even brand them, to make it immediately apparent that they have been detained before. There was also some evidence that returning failed asylum applicants were examined for visible scars, although evidence of strip-searching at the airport was more tenuous. The key issue in many appeals, therefore, was how these scars were likely to be perceived by the Sri Lankan authorities if the person was returned; did they *look* like results of torture or combat, irrespective of how they were really caused? Such cases therefore occupied a kind of ontological never-never land, whereby the key issue was to get inside the mind of their potential persecutor, the 'Reasonable Man' in the Sri Lankan security forces, rather than to decide whether appellants' stories were true.

Because of this, representatives usually ask adjudicators to view scars directly. Their responses vary greatly. Some adjudicators refuse point-blank to look at any scars, others will look at scars on the face and limbs 'but not on the trunk', and yet others send HOPO, counsel and appellant off for a 'private viewing' in an interview room, in the vain hope that they will reach agreement as to their severity and significance. Adjudicators who refused to view scars generally justified their stance to me by saying it was demeaning for appellants to display these in open court. Appellants themselves seem generally to prefer this temporary indignity if it lessens the possibility of them being sent back. Indeed, some are positively eager to display scars and have to be restrained from undressing entirely. The following incident (appeal HX/59717/2000) involved a male Tamil asylum applicant, counsel, interpreter and adjudicator, and a female HOPO. His counsel was not claiming scarring as a major issue – the scars were relatively unspectacular according to the debased currency of such cases – merely that their existence aggravated the risks stemming from his record of past detention and association with the LTTE:

Counsel:	I understand you have scars on your body?
Appellant:	Yes.[9]
Counsel:	Can you explain where?
Appellant:	On arm, near elbow.
Adjudicator:	Just a second, just a second . . . Which arm?
Interpreter:	Right.
Appellant:	Also left arm just above elbow. Also right thigh. Also right ankle.
Adjudicator:	Do we have photos?
Counsel:	No sir.
Adjudicator:	Oh dear, we'd better have a look at them then. No medical report?
Counsel:	No.

The appellant went to the adjudicator's bench and displayed his elbows and ankle. The adjudicator invited the HOPO to look. She did so, cursorily.

---

9   Throughout this book words are put directly into appellants' mouths whenever interpreters are translating, but attributed to interpreters when they speak on their own behalf.

Without prompting, the appellant pulled down his trousers to reveal the scar on his thigh, underpants hanging loosely down. The HOPO and interpreter studiously looked elsewhere. The appellant pulled up his trousers and returned to his seat.

Adjudicator:	Let me read what I have noted down. 'Patch of pink scarring on right elbow; single scar on left elbow; scar on right ankle; very faint, barely visible scar on thigh.'
Counsel:	Can you briefly explain how each scar arose?
Appellant:	At V—— camp, scar on right elbow due to being hit with butt of gun. Scar on thigh at same time. Scar on right ankle and left elbow, when held at police station during torture.
Counsel:	Which police station?
Appellant:	M——.
Adjudicator:	The others were from the army?
Appellant:	Earlier ones by army.

Cross-examination generally takes up most of the hearing, lasting typically between 20 minutes and an hour. This is partly because many HOPOs are not very skilled, but they do deliberately re-traverse ground in the hope of eliciting minor inconsistencies which can be used to cast doubt on the appellant's credibility. Adjudicators may ask clarifying questions, but without 'entering the arena' or advancing either side's case. Appellants' representatives then have the chance to re-examine. Adjudicators sometimes spell out matters they would like counsel to try to resolve, but they are in any case well advised to tackle head-on any apparent discrepancies revealed by cross-examination; if not, adverse conclusions may be drawn. For counsel this represents a leap into the abyss, as – unlike examination-in-chief, when there may have been some rehearsal – they have no way of knowing what their client is going to say.

The distinctive language employed by legal representatives serves, like all such sub-cultural dialects, to demarcate them from lay people present (Mellinkoff 1963). Its most immediately obvious aspect is the use of what may be termed 'courtly' forms of language. Though less elaborate than in higher courts, these lend asylum hearings a character which would be strangely appealing if one were not constantly reminded of the horrors seething beneath the quaint veneer. Adjudicators are addressed as 'sir', 'madam', or 'ma'am', even if they are County Court judges who would be 'Your Honour' in their usual habitat. The rival representative is 'my friend', as opposed to 'my learned friend', though barristers unfamiliar with immigration work occasionally lapse into the grander form.

Far more importantly, this professional discourse is couched in shorthand legal jargon which is almost certainly unintelligible to the asylum applicant, and only partly comprehensible to other lay persons present, including most crucially – given its likely consequences – the interpreter (Chapter 7). Indeed, according to the critical legal studies movement, this is a key means whereby law maintains its hegemony. Some would go further, and say that it is not so much the hegemony of *law* as some abstract set of determinate legal principles transcending the context and the identity of the persons to whom they are applied, but rather that this specialised language privileges the interests of powerful *men*, who are likely to be well versed in compatible discourses through their professional and occupational activities (Kennedy 1976; Boyle 1985; West 1988). Thus, 'rule-orientation could be characterized as an acquired skill which is the property of the literate and educated business and legal class' (Conley and O'Barr 1990b: 80).

Just as some have argued that poor people, uneducated people, and many women are systematically disadvantaged by professional legal discourse practices, so too, suggest Conley and O'Barr (1990b: 80) the 'factor of race may operate in a similar manner because it is still the case that disproportionate numbers of blacks in America are poor, under-educated, and relegated to occupations on the peripheries of economic and political power'. In the context of asylum, persons of different national and cultural backgrounds, who do not speak even the everyday English of the native under-privileged, are likely to be doubly disadvantaged by the predominance of legal discourse at their appeal hearings – indeed, this probably applies throughout the entire asylum process. Even asylum applicants coming from professional backgrounds themselves (very much the minority) are likely to find that the skills which served them well enough back home are of little value in orienting them towards the very different principles of British law.

Law is also, as we saw (§2.2), characterised by distinctive modes of reasoning, at odds with that of many ordinary people, especially those lacking the professional and occupational experiences of the powerful elite. Most fundamentally, whereas everyday reasoning is typically inductive, legal reasoning is fundamentally deductive (Conley and O'Barr 1990b: 48). Almost as important is the over-arching legal stress on rule-oriented reasoning, in terms of which asylum hearings fall somewhere between formal courts, on the one hand, and the informal courts studied by Conley and O'Barr, on the other. Asylum applicants are mostly people for whom the law's orientation toward a specific set of rules is quite alien, and who are likely, for instance, to attach far more importance to social obligations than to contractual ones. Most are unaware that it improves their chances of success to present their cases in rule-oriented terms, eschewing 'extraneous' factors such as personal feelings. Fortunately for them, however, their relational orientations are partly suppressed thanks to the interposing of their legal representatives between themselves and judicial decision makers.

The representatives set out their arguments fully in their final submissions. HOPOs generally start by relying on the Home Office RFRL, but this may be so poorly worded, argued, or compiled that they have to dissociate themselves from certain paragraphs which are obviously about another case – sometimes even referring to the wrong country of origin – or have been left blank apart from the words 'insert standard para here'. They draw attention to particular passages in their objective evidence – generally confined to the CIPU *Country Assessment* (§9.2) – which are said to support the Home Office position. They may also cite previous tribunal determinations, especially 'starred' decisions (§5.3), arguing that these should be followed as precedents.

HOPOs generally attack appellants' credibility by listing alleged discrepancies in their accounts. They sometimes also employ *a priori* 'Reasonable Man' arguments. Many are young and inexperienced, however, and it is often evident during hearings that the HOPO is unable to comprehend that inherent cultural differences, and the stark realities of life in conflict situations, may generate ideas about 'reasonable' behaviour which are markedly different from those current in Greater London. For example, one Tamil appellant (HX/08903/2001) claimed to have been a Grama Sevaka (village officer) in an area not under full government control, and to have been forced to pass government funds to the LTTE. Cross-examination repeatedly illustrated the HOPO's bafflement over the dilemmas which the appellant had faced, and matters came to a head during his final submissions:

Adjudicator:	Credibility is going to be important. Do you accept he was a Grama Sevaka, I think that is going to be the basis of his claim?
HOPO:	It is not challenged in the refusal letter, but with regard to him being a Grama Sevaka, he has given us details of what his roles and responsibilities were. I do challenge this document.
Adjudicator:	Why? It is just a general reference document, are you saying it is false? Do you have to say it is false if you are saying he is not a Grama Sevaka?
HOPO:	I cannot assert that it is.
Adjudicator:	Well, the burden of proof is on the respondent.
Counsel:	And at a higher standard!
Adjudicator:	Well, even at the lower standard, the respondent has not sought to claim it was untrue. The appellant has told me he obtained it because he was thinking of leaving the country. I think, on its face, it is hard to say it is not genuine.
HOPO:	Yes, but the circumstances he has described – about all Grama Sevakas being involved in dealings with the LTTE, and the army knowing that – it seems implausible that the army allowed this to happen.
Adjudicator:	The situation has to be, these are areas of come and

	go, people have to live there and have to be governed. The appellant's account is, he just went one step too far, if his account is credible.
HOPO:	He also stated that he was giving them government money.
Adjudicator:	And *that's* the step too far!
HOPO:	That leads to it being corruption. Rather than persecution, he would face prosecution.
Adjudicator:	But prosecution becomes persecution because of the way it operates; we might accept that difference in the UK, but there it might not even get to trial. If we accept his account, as I think we have to –
Counsel (archly):	This is one of those rare cases where it would have been useful to have an anthropological expert.
Adjudicator:	And we have one sitting here; do you know Dr Good?
Counsel:	Yes ma'am. As I interpret my friend, his point is on implausibility not credibility. If it is a matter of plausibility, we have to be careful to change our mindset; I ask you to appreciate the local landscape.
Adjudicator: (exasperated)	On behalf of the Secretary of State, *do* you accept he was a Grama Sevaka?
HOPO:	As far as I can see, the Secretary of State has accepted he was a Grama Sevaka, but with regard to his dealings . . .
Adjudicator:	And that you don't accept . . . because my interpretation is, that's how things are . . . but you are saying it is implausible and you don't accept my suggestion that he just went one step too far. So if it is implausible, you would like me to find him not credible?

Barristers often submit 'skellies' (written skeleton arguments) beforehand, and sometimes also chronologies of key events in the appellant's account. Such documents are appreciated by adjudicators as ways of steering them through the masses of documentation; the chronology may also help neutralise Home Office attempts to question credibility because of alleged discrepancies over dates, by providing a supposedly definitive version. Counsels' ability to provide these depends largely on when they are instructed, however. As basic good practice, they should attend a 'con' with the instructing solicitors and appellant well before the appeal date, to explore matters at first hand. In reality, many counsel are not instructed until the night before the hearing. They may be able to get around this to some extent by having a basic template of their skeleton, to which particular details can be quickly added or removed, but production of a chronology demands time to master the material, so as not to muddy the credibility waters by introducing yet more apparent 'discrepancies'.

In their closing submissions, they begin by answering any credibility points raised in the RFRL or by the HOPO, before advancing arguments based on rival interpretations of the objective evidence, both that supplied by the Home Office and their own – which is generally more extensive and variable, and may include reports by medical or country experts. They too are likely to cite previous tribunal determinations which should be followed. It is by no means unknown, in fact, for both sides to cite the same determinations, drawing attention to different paragraphs or urging different interpretations of the same key passages. If the asylum appeal is also an appeal under the *Human Rights Act 1998*, both sides end their submissions with arguments about the applicability of the European Convention on Human Rights to the appellant's circumstances.

There is a chronic shortage of HOPOs, so the Home Secretary is often unrepresented at appeals and must rely on documents submitted beforehand, a situation which attracts disapproving comment from tribunals.[10] Adjudicators face special problems when no HOPO appears, because it is hard to make findings of fact and credibility in the absence of cross-examination, and they cannot ask probing questions themselves without running the risk of compromising their perceived independence. I have seen the most suave of adjudicators stomp up and down his office swearing when informed by his clerk that there would be no HOPO that day.

Because decisions made under such circumstances were so often appealed on the ground that adjudicators' questioning went beyond acceptable bounds, the IAT issued guidelines on how adjudicators should behave in the absence of a HOPO – these were termed the '*Surendran* guidelines' after the appeal in which they were first set out, but were subsequently reproduced and endorsed by the President in *MNM*. They state that Home Office non-appearance should not be taken as an indication that its decision has been withdrawn, and the appeal should proceed on the basis of the written material it has submitted. If RFRLs question credibility, or adjudicators have their own doubts about that or other matters, they should ask appellants' representatives to deal with these in examinations-in-chief or concluding submissions. While at liberty to seek clarification, as usual, they themselves should not adopt inquisitorial roles or 'raise matters which

---

10 'we applaud the adjudicator's vigorous efforts to grapple with the issues, despite the absence of any presenting officer (a species so far as we can see unknown in England north of Leeds). . . . We hope a presenting officer will be present [at the remitted hearing, and] we should not blame the fresh adjudicator . . . for refusing to proceed unless one were present' (*Sarmoor*).

a Presenting Officer might have raised in cross-examination had he been present'.

Adjudicators almost always reserve their decisions rather than announcing them at the hearing. In any case, they have to produce a written determination, giving decisions on the asylum appeal and, if relevant, the human rights appeal too. Whatever the decision, the losing party is generally able to submit grounds of appeal within a specified brief period after promulgation.

IND caseworkers are told that when decisions go against them they should accept 'with good grace' unless there are strong grounds for thinking that the adjudicator made a legal error or that the decision is 'Wednesbury unreasonable' ('so outrageous in its defiance of logic or of accepted moral standards that no sensible person . . . could have arrived at it'; 2002a: ¶14.1, Annex A). A proper determination should decide the substantive issues; give sustainable reasons for those decisions; and include correct references to the law, standard of proof, and any precedents or other material considered in reaching the decisions. It must include findings of fact on the main episodes in the asylum applicants' story, a credibility finding, and an indication of how much weight was attached to each significant piece of objective evidence (see §10.5). Findings for which there is no evidence, and gross errors of fact, are considered good grounds for appeal, as are instances where the reasoning linking evidence to conclusion is unclear, or where adjudicators consider evidence not available to other parties, such as their personal experience. Tribunals rarely overturn adjudicators' findings on credibility, so IND tells its caseworkers to accept them unless the conclusion is 'outrageous . . . or relevant evidence has been ignored', or it is 'obviously irrational or contradictory' (2002a: ¶14.1, Annex A). It does seem clear, however, that, no doubt as a result of growing political pressure, the Home Office has become increasingly prone to appeal in recent years.

5.2.2 Certification

Under the 1999 Act, if an asylum claim was 'certified' under paragraph 9 of Schedule 4 (IND 2002a: ¶5.2), an accelerated appeal procedure was followed which might rule out any IAT appeal against an adjudicator's decision. Some grounds for certification were procedural: claims could be certified if claimants arrived without passports, presented false documents, or destroyed their documents, allegedly either to disguise their true identity or to conceal the fact that they had valid passports. All were seen as detracting from the credibility of claims to persecution, though UNHCR note that 'possession of a valid national passport is no bar to refugee status' (1992: ¶48). IND recognised that some applicants needed false papers to leave their home country, but argued that they should inform Immigration Officers 'at the earliest opportunity' (2002a: ¶5.2). Yet courts did not always accept that this was a reasonable expectation of someone who has suffered persecution (*Matinkima; Adimi*; Dutton 2003).[11]

Applicants often asserted that their documents were retained by their agents, but IND viewed such claims as unreasonable attempts to frustrate immigration controls (2002a: ¶5.2). In *Sivaharan* counsel conceded, for some reason, that giving back one's passport like this was not a reasonable excuse, but in *Naguleswaran*, where the applicant was only 16 years old, Mr Justice Elias found that the adjudicator had been wrong to uphold certification of the claim:

> If the traveller is unsophisticated, bemused, or otherwise very much in the hands of his agent or travelling companion, it may be perfectly understandable that he will hand his documents to such a person . . . They may, at least to some extent, be in a position of trust towards the asylum seeker. *A fortiori* that may be the case where the traveller is still a minor.

More substantively, claims might be certified if they did not engage any of the five Convention reasons or were judged 'manifestly unfounded' – so obviously untrue that 'on a reasonably quick appraisal, [they] can be seen to be plainly and obviously without foundation' (*Vallaj*). Claims were also certifiable if they were fraudulent, frivolous, vexatious, or if the evidence was so manifestly false that 'credibility is totally undermined' (2002a: ¶5.2). The reason for certification which adjudicators saw as most detrimental to credibility, however, was that the claim had only been made after removal proceedings had been instigated (Jarvis 2000: 17).

For adjudicators to uphold certificates, they had to agree with every reason given by the Secretary of State, so although some claims arguably met several criteria, caseworkers were urged to certify them only on the ground which seemed 'most straightforward to establish and the least open to challenge' (IND 2002a: ¶5.2). Claims should not be certified merely because they were implausible or some evidence was false, provided the main claim had supporting evidence. Above all, they should not be certified if there was a reasonable likelihood that the applicant had been tortured. If an appeal was certified because claimed torture was not considered likely, the RFRL had to explain why IND had come to this view.

If an adjudicator dismissed a certified appeal but overturned the certification, the appellant could apply for leave to appeal in the usual way; but if an adjudicator dismissed the appeal *and* upheld the certificate, the appellant had

---

11 This precise form of certification was repealed by the 2002 Act. Appeals against the certification of applications as 'manifestly unfounded' (see below) became 'non-suspensive', so that appellants could still be removed even while such appeals were pending.

no further appeal rights. But what if, as is now normally the case, an appeal involved both asylum and human rights claims? Appeal rights in certified asylum claims were set out in Schedule 4 of the 1999 Act, but it was common ground among all parties in the courts that this had been appallingly drafted. Paragraph 9(2) read:

> If, on an appeal to which this paragraph applies, the adjudicator agrees that the claim is one to which this paragraph applies, paragraph 22 does not confer on the appellant any right to appeal to the Immigration Appeal Tribunal.

As written this stated fatuously that appeal rights were lost if the adjudicator merely agreed that the claim *had* been certified! The real intention of course, as the Home Office accepted before the Court of Appeal (*Zenovics*), was that appeal rights were lost only if the adjudicator agreed it had been *correctly* certified. Even when reworded accordingly, the paragraph made it appear that both appeal rights were lost even if only the asylum claim was certified. The tribunal in *Zenovics* read it that way, decided this was unfair, and requested the Secretary of State to adopt a policy of certifying both claims or certifying neither. The Court of Appeal could not believe Parliament had meant to rule out human rights appeals in cases where asylum claims were certified, so it ruled, despite Home Office reluctance, that paragraph 9(2) should be understood as follows:

> If, on an appeal to which this paragraph applies, *the adjudicator agrees with the opinion expressed in the Secretary of State's certificate* paragraph 22 does not confer on the appellant any right of appeal to the Immigration Appeal Tribunal *in respect of that claim* (italics added).

In other words, even if an adjudicator upheld the certification of an asylum claim, the claimant might still, subject to leave being granted, appeal to the IAT in connection with their human rights claim.

5.3 TRIBUNAL HEARINGS

At the time of my research, the Immigration Appeal Tribunal (IAT) consisted of the President, Mr Justice Collins; Deputy President, Mr Mark Ockelton; 10 Vice-Presidents, 26 chairs, and 38 lay members (Leggatt 2001). Most tribunal panels have three members, but two-member panels are fairly common – if a booked member suddenly becomes unavailable, for example. For appeals raising general issues of law or procedure, all three members may be IAT Vice-Presidents in their own right. Generally, however, the 'wing members' – less charitably, 'bookends', according to the more cynical, weather-beaten barristers and HOPOs – are lay assessors, appointed by the Lord Chancellor through a process which seems predominantly to select socially concerned members of upper-class British society, albeit with a strong leavening of Justices of the Peace and representatives of 'ethnic minorities'.

From the back of the court, one cannot fail to notice that at most hearings the lay tribunal members never utter a word. The most obvious reason is that leave to appeal is granted on the basis of arguable errors of law or procedure, not in order to revisit adjudicators' assessments of the facts. Although it is hard to separate the two – and tribunals often stray into factual areas in practice, not least because they have jurisdiction to consider appeals on the ground that adjudicators' findings of fact are unsustainable (*Assah*; Symes and Jorro 2003: 800) – this raises the issue of what role lay members can really be expected to play. Discussions at hearings usually focus on particular clauses in Asylum Acts and Immigration Rules, and entail detailed analyses of rival case law, so it is unsurprising that lay members rarely intervene. Their passivity gave me the clear impression that they could play little effective part in decision making, insofar as this involved assessing the *legal* safety of decisions. The Deputy President assured me that I was mistaken, citing a well-known case in which lay members' views had prevailed over his own. I am simply in no position to judge for myself.

Whatever role they may or may not play in tribunal decisions, a more useful place for lay assessors, it seemed, would have been at first level appeals where those very experiences as men and women of the world, which presumably made them suitable appointees in the first place, could be brought to bear on the oral testimonies of actual appellants. John Housden, Deputy Regional Adjudicator in Taylor House and possessor of one of the IAA's longest institutional memories, explained the position of lay members as an historical residue. Under the 1969 and 1971 Acts adjudicators were appointed by the Home Secretary and seen as having administrative rather than judicial functions. At that time the IAT had been the lowest level of judicial decision making, so it made sense for lay members to be located there. In 1987, however, it was decided that adjudicators' roles were judicial rather than administrative, and responsibility for them was transferred accordingly to the Lord Chancellor's Department (Harvey 2000: 156), leaving lay IAT members high and dry.

Mr Housden thought this oddity was so long-lasting that it would cause too much embarrassment to seek to remedy it after all that time. However, it was seized on by the Leggatt review of tribunals as 'a significant structural anomaly which . . . brings in the expert contribution of non-lawyers too late in the process, and creates serious problems for the IAA and for the courts' (Leggatt 2001: II, 21). Leggatt identified three such problems, all traceable to this historical shift in the status of adjudicators. First, tribunals continued in practice to address issues of fact as well as of law, so the breadth of possible grounds of appeal offered too much scope for challenge by judicial review whenever leave to appeal was refused. Second, there was 'considerable uncertainty' over the role of lay members. Third, the 'culture of pervasive challenge of IAA decisions ... has a deleterious effect on the perceived authority of the IAA as a whole' (2001: II, 22).

Leggatt therefore recommended creation of a first tier appeal tribunal with lay members who would 'bring relevant experience and skills to the decisions to be taken, such as knowledge of conditions in particular countries, or of refugees' (2001: II, 23). This would be the sole judge of issues of fact, with a second tier right of appeal to a tribunal consisting of a lawyer sitting alone, which would hear only matters of law. Judging by his reference to lay members' 'expert contribution' to IAT deliberations, however, Leggatt had misunderstood the basis on which they were recruited; although some certainly had wide general experience, they were *not* appointed because of their expertise on refugees or countries of origin. In any case, the 2004 Act took more draconian steps, including a reduction in rights to scrutiny by higher courts.[12]

Tribunal hearings tend to be much shorter and less predictable in form than those before adjudicators. Appellants often do not even attend, and when present are nearly always silent, uncomprehending spectators. It is quite rare even for court interpreters to be booked for tribunal hearings – which meant that on one occasion I briefly took on the interpreter's role myself at the President's request, to explain to a bemused Tamil family that the hearing (which I was attending as a researcher) was being delayed because of the non-appearance of their barrister, following a dispute over fees between his chambers and their solicitor.

Tribunal chairs often cut a swathe through prepared submissions or attempts at extended oratory, by arriving in court with specific questions to which both sides are asked to respond. Tribunal appeals usually involve more experienced counsel and senior HOPOs, better able to deal with legal abstractions, and the discussions are allusive rather than declamatory, so a listener without access to the documents can barely follow the argument. As already noted, IAT appeals tend to revolve around the legal safety of the adjudicator's determination rather than reconsideration of the factual evidence. If it becomes clear, nonetheless, that factual evidence *does* need to be reassessed, the tribunal generally 'remits' the appeal to be heard *de novo* by a different adjudicator. Tribunals, too, generally reserve their decisions, though the President's own practice was to announce them immediately where possible, composing his determination into a dictaphone in open court.

The IAT attempted to consolidate its position as a court of record by instituting 'starred' determinations whose findings on key issues of law were said to be binding on adjudicators. In 2003, it also began to distinguish

---

12 The new system had yet to come into effect when this book was completed.

between 'reported' determinations, which are actually published, and the unreported majority which can only be cited by counsel subject to stringent restrictions. The IAT itself decides which decisions will be reported however, so although the outcomes of reported cases are similar to those for decisions as a whole (Yeo 2005a: 7), many barristers perceive a bias towards reporting decisions favouring the Home Office.

The IAT moved during my research from Taylor House in Islington to Field House off Chancery Lane. Its occasional peripatetic sittings gave way to hearings via video links, with the appellant's representative and HOPO in Glasgow, Manchester, Leeds, or Birmingham. There had been apprehension among legal representatives in Glasgow over the likely effects of this change. Most opposed the idea at first, though many were won over after a Glasgow Users' Group meeting which the President actually chaired from London, by video. No-one seemed to have a clear answer when I first asked about public access; would it be at just one location and, if so, which? Later, the President told me all three locations would be public, though I have not tested this in practice. When I attended such a hearing in Glasgow, the immediacy of communication was perceptibly diminished by the small video monitor (Field House has more advanced technology), although my opinion may have been coloured by a series of enforced adjournments triggered by a faulty fire alarm in Field House.

5.4 OUTCOMES

Although the figures in Table 1.3 (page 9) provided a clue right at the start, it is important to underline the sheer scale of the administrative and judicial decision-making processes described in this chapter. This section looks successively at initial decision making by the Home Office, and judicial decisions by adjudicators, the IAT, and the High Court. Figures do not refer to single cohorts of applicants because these decision-making processes are generally spread over several calendar years.

In the year 2000 80,315 persons applied for asylum in the UK, excluding an estimated 18,500 dependants (Home Office 2001). That same year, there were 10,375 decisions under a back-log clearance exercise, granting settlement in the UK to persons who had applied for asylum before July 1993 and were still awaiting initial decisions; and 97,545 decisions were made under normal procedures, whereby 10,375 applicants (11 per cent) were granted refugee status (ILR), 11,495 (12 per cent) received ELR, and 75,680 (78 per cent) were refused. These averages conceal great variations according to country of origin, however. For example, of 11,250 Somalis whose applications received initial decisions during 2000, 5,310 (47 per cent) were granted refugee status, a further 3,575 (32 per cent) were granted ELR, and only 2,365 (21 per cent) were refused. Of 8,060 Sri Lankans, by contrast, 900 (11 per cent) were granted refugee status, a mere 285 (4 per cent) received ELR, and 6,875 (85 per cent) were refused. These contrasting outcomes (far from the widest national differences) belie the fact that both countries were considered by the courts to be experiencing 'civil war' (§4.2.2).

In 2001 applications fell slightly to 71,365 (92,000 including dependants), but the Home Office reached decisions on 119,015 applicants under normal procedures – the highest total ever, and the result of very strong political pressure to reduce waiting lists and shorten decision times. Overall, 11,180 (9 per cent) were granted ILR, 19,845 (17 per cent) were granted ELR, and 87,990 (74 per cent) were refused. Outcomes again varied widely according to nationality; for example 61 per cent of Afghan applicants were granted ELR. In that year, 35 per cent (2,845) of Somalis received ILR at first decision, as against 14 per cent (1,415) of Sri Lankans, while 24 per cent (1,960) of Somalis and only 5 per cent (525) of Sri Lankans were granted ELR (Home Office 2002).

In 2002 applications rose by 18 per cent to 84,130 (103,080 including dependants), with Zimbabweans and East Europeans accounting for most of the increase. The number of initial decisions fell by 21 per cent, to 83,540. Of these, 8,270 (10 per cent) were granted ILR, 20,135 (24 per cent) received ELR, and 55,130 (66 per cent) were refused. In that year, 37 per cent (2,515) of Somalis received ILR at first decision, and 21 per cent (1,405) were granted ELR. Sri Lankans were appreciably less successful than before, with only 8 per cent (340) gaining refugee status and 6 per cent (275) being granted ELR, though the number of Sri Lankan applications was significantly down on previous years (Home Office 2003).

As for adjudicator appeals, the annual totals since the present system was created, and their outcomes, are given in Table 5.1. The overall increase is

Table 5.1 Annual totals of asylum appeals to the IAA

Year	Appeals Determined	Allowed		Dismissed	
		Total	%	Total	%
1994	2,440	95	4	1,970	86
1995	7,035	230	3	5,565	82
1996	13,790	515	4	10,785	79
1997	21,090	1,180	6	18,145	86
1998	25,320	2,355	9	21,195	84
1999	19,460	5,280	27	11,135	57
2000	19,395	3,340	17	15,580	80
2001	43,415	8,155	19	34,440	79
2002	64,405	13,875	22	48,845	76
2003	81,725	16,070	20	63,810	78
2004	55,975	10,845	19	43,760	78

Source: Home Office (2005: Table 7.1). Because of withdrawn appeals and rounding-up, figures in each row may not add up. The 2004 figures are provisional.

very striking. The corresponding totals for IAT appeals, given in Table 5.2, also showed a pronounced increase, but it was less dramatic where actual decisions were concerned because of the filtering effect of the need to apply for leave.

The increasing numbers, exacerbated by the complexity of asylum matters, help explain why the system suffered such severe delays, but the Home Office blamed the procedures themselves. A consultation document prior to the 1999 Act identified several causes of delay:

(i)   the multi-tier character of the process;
(ii) the fact that tribunals remitted over half the appeals to adjudicators for fresh hearings rather than deciding them themselves;
(iii) the need for adjudicators to produce written determinations in every case;
(iv) the failure of the IAT to produce an authoritative body of case law, which meant that many legal issues remained unresolved and helped explain why so many appellants ultimately sought judicial review (Lord Chancellor's Department 1998).

Others suggested that the Home Office's own delays and inefficiencies played a more significant part. It might seek anything up to six adjournments (Asylum Aid 1999: 8), and the *Guardian* reported in March 1999 that computerisation and an office move had caused chaos 'with 9,000 items of unopened post, hundreds of applicants queuing for hours in the open, and thousands of files inaccessible, stored in a car park basement that staff cannot enter because of fumes'. It is certainly true that the emphasis – and resources – in UK asylum determination procedures during the 1990s fell

Table 5.2 Annual totals of asylum appeals to the IAT

Year	Leave Applications Decided	Appeals Determined	Allowed	Dismissed	Remitted
1994	1,385	270	10	65	190
1995	3,000	390	20	105	240
1996	5,345	900	55	285	550
1997	8,130	1,375	–	–	–
1998	10,315	1,090	–	–	–
1999	9,575	1,790	–	–	–
2000	5,490	2,635	815	1,385	215
2001	13,540	3,190	475	1,140	1,430
2002	22,825	5,565	620	2,015	2,700
2003	32,180	9,450	1,490	3,230	4,220
2004	30,520	8,785	1,060	2,965	3,915

Source: Home Office (2005: Table 7.2). Because of withdrawn appeals and rounding-up, figures in each row may not add up. The 2004 figures are provisional.

increasingly on the appeal stages, whereas Canada and the United States put their resources into initial administrative decision making (Billings 2000: 258).

Looking at recent figures in more detail, the IAA determined 19,395 appeals by refused asylum applicants in 2000. Of these, 17 per cent were allowed and 80 per cent dismissed, the remainder being withdrawn or abandoned. That same year, the IAT determined 2,635 appeals, of which 31 per cent were allowed, 53 per cent dismissed, and 8 per cent remitted to adjudicators to be reheard *de novo*. There were 2,095 decisions on Judicial Review applications, of which 555 (26 per cent) were granted. Of the 760 Judicial Reviews determined, 365 (48 per cent) were allowed and 300 (40 per cent) dismissed (Home Office 2001).

In 2001, the IAA determined 43,415 asylum appeals, well over double the number in the previous year, and a reflection of the great expansion in the appellate apparatus. Of these, 19 per cent were allowed and 79 per cent were dismissed. There were 15,540 applications for leave to appeal to the IAT during 2001, although about two-thirds were refused. The IAT actually determined 3,190 appeals, a much more modest increase, of which 15 per cent were allowed, 36 per cent dismissed, and 45 per cent remitted – a shift of such magnitude that one can only assume it reflected deliberate IAT policy. Leave was granted in only 290 (13 per cent) of the 2,300 Judicial Review applications considered, and such a marked tightening up must again, one assumes, reflect a change of judicial policy. Of 380 Judicial Review applications determined, however, 260 (68 per cent) were allowed and only 60 (16 per cent) dismissed (Home Office 2002). In other words, although leave was granted far less often than in previous years, there was a far higher success rate among those whose applications were in fact heard.

In 2002, IAA determinations showed another huge increase, to 64,405; the number of appeal decisions had thus tripled in just two years. Interestingly, the proportion of successful appeals also rose noticeably, to 22 per cent. Applications for leave to appeal to the IAT rose massively to 25,600, and the number of second appeals determined rose almost exactly in proportion, to 5,565. Of these only 11 per cent were allowed, 36 per cent (as in the previous year) were dismissed, and remittals rose still further, to 49 per cent. Leave was granted in only 260 (9 per cent) of the 2,980 Judicial Review applications, a further marked decrease from the previous year. Only 90 hearings actually took place, and the success rate plummeted: only 25 (30 per cent) were allowed whereas 60 (67 per cent) were dismissed (Home Office 2003). In short, the number of dismissals was exactly the same as in 2001, but the number allowed was less than a tenth of the earlier figure. This dramatic change appears less astonishing, however, once one realises that it was due largely to the settlement of many Judicial Review applications by the Home Office (Robert Thomas, pers. comm.).

The marked fall in successful appeals needs further disaggregation, though the following figures (which the Home Office derives from the Presenting Officers Unit and are only available for the three most recent years) are not directly comparable with those in preceding paragraphs because they exclude remittals. Thus, of 2,060 non-remitted appeals by asylum applicants in 2000, 650 (32 per cent) were allowed and 1,225 (59 per cent) dismissed, whereas 170 (46 per cent) of the 370 appeals by the Secretary of State were allowed and 165 (45 per cent) dismissed. In 2001, of 1,460 appeals by asylum applicants, 315 (22 per cent) were allowed and 1,020 (70 per cent) dismissed; the Secretary of State was the appellant in 305 determined appeals, of which the IAT allowed 160 (52 per cent) and dismissed 120 (39 per cent). In 2002, only 410 (16 per cent) of the 2,500 appeals by asylum applicants were allowed and 1,880 (75 per cent) were dismissed, while of the Secretary of State's 360 determined appeals, the IAT allowed 215 (60 per cent) and dismissed just 130 (36 per cent). The trend is obvious; the overall drop in appeal success rates is caused by a halving in the proportion of successes by actual asylum applicants whereas, in sharp contrast, the Home Office success rate rose by one-third over the same period. Once again, in the absence of any obvious reason for thinking that asylum applicants suddenly became appreciably more 'bogus' over this short period, one can only put this down to policy and political pressure.

Breakdowns of appeal success rates by nationality have been hard to come by until recently. A House of Lords written answer on 5 March 2001 showed that whereas only 9 per cent of 25,230 appeals to the IAA were successful in 1998, the success rate was 18 per cent for Somalis (admittedly from a tiny sample of 30 appeals), while of 1,040 appeals by Sri Lankans a staggering 495 (48 per cent) were allowed.[13] Still more would later have succeeded before the IAT of course, but no countrywide figures were available on this. Even so, adjudicators had decided, in half the cases going to appeal, that the Home Office's refusal of asylum to Sri Lankans had been wrong!

For the very first time, the *2001 Asylum Statistics* (Home Office 2002) gave breakdowns by nationality of adjudicators' decisions, which showed that in percentage terms the most successful appellants in 2001 were those from the Horn of Africa: Sudanese (43 per cent), Ethiopians (42 per cent), and Eritreans (40 per cent). Next came Iranians (38 per cent) and Sri Lankans (37 per cent). Only 20 per cent of Somalis and 18 per cent of Afghans were successful at this level, but it must be remembered that very large proportions had succeeded at the level of first decision. The least successful appellants before the IAA were Nigerians (1 per cent), Jamaicans (2 per cent), and Poles, Ghanaians, and Indians (all 3 per cent). These groups were generally unsuccessful at first decision too: in 2001, the Home Office granted ILR to only 45

---

13 www.parliament.the-stationery-office.co.uk/pa/ld200001/ldhansrd/vo010305/text/10305w01. htm

Ghanaians (as against 45 grants of ELR and 315 refusals), 25 Nigerians (130; 1,100), 15 Indians (45; 2,845), 5 Jamaicans (15; 460), and fewer than 5 Poles (10; 790) (Home Office 2002).

These trends were largely maintained in 2002. Success rates for Sudanese (46 per cent), Eritrean (39 per cent), Iranian (38 per cent), and Ethiopian (37 per cent) applicants remained high. They were joined by Zimbabweans (38 per cent) and Somalis (35 per cent), whereas Sri Lankan successes declined (23 per cent), no doubt largely because of judicial perceptions regarding the impact of the ceasefire which came into force early in that year. The least successful nationalities were much as before, though the actual rates rose somewhat for Jamaicans (9 per cent), Ghanaians and Nigerians (both 6 per cent) and Poles (4 per cent), leaving Indians (still 3 per cent) bottom of the success league (Home Office 2003).

While these nationality profiles were generally steady, or changed for reasons explicable in terms of perceived political developments 'back home', the figures reported earlier in this section reveal striking shifts in outcome over a very short period – albeit, it must be remembered, a period during which significant changes in asylum and immigration legislation came into force, as well as the Human Rights Act. It is also striking that whereas IAT and High Court decisions, in congruence with increasingly oppressive and intolerant government statements, targets, and policy changes, got per- ceptibly tougher over this period, decisions by adjudicators did not. Indeed, they bucked the trend in 2002 by actually giving a higher proportion of positive decisions than before.

It is tempting to relate this contrast to differences in the organisation and geographical distribution of these various judicial groupings, and the differ- ing opportunities these provide for managerial oversight and the develop- ment of corporate cultures of decision making. Because there are so many adjudicators from such relatively diverse backgrounds (§5.2), because so many are quite new appointees, and because they sit all over the country, often in isolation from their peers, consistent decision making is, one may surmise, rather difficult to achieve through either the influence of Regional Adjudicators or simple peer group pressure. Even in a large centre like Taylor House, where full-time adjudicators can and do discuss tricky interpretations over lunch, there are part-timers who sit only occasionally and whose exposure to such internal self-calibration is far less.

By contrast, tribunal members are all concentrated in one place, no longer even occasionally peripatetic as they were before video-linked hearings were introduced. Many of them meet professionally and socially almost every day. Not only is it their explicit task to repair any tendency for adjudicators to depart too far from the norm in their decisions (§10.5), but they will also find it potentially far easier to achieve convergence themselves, either in response to guidance or monitoring by the President and senior Vice-Presidents seated in their adjoining offices, or simply through the development of a common 'house culture'. I cannot speak from first-hand knowledge of the High Court, but presumably collegiality is evident there too, if not perhaps to the extent manifest by tribunal chairs.

The limited quantitative evidence above suggests – but does not, of course, prove – that tribunal chairs and High Court judges are more responsive than adjudicators to changes in government policy. If so, one may hypothesise that such responses are facilitated by the socially and geographically centralised structures within which these particular judicial decision makers operate.

Chapter 6

Expert evidence

6.1 'OBJECTIVE EVIDENCE'

This chapter examines how the special status of expert witness evolved in Anglo-American common law traditions, and then describes how expert evidence is used in asylum appeal hearings. First, however, it is necessary to explain the importance of 'objective evidence' to the asylum process, and the idiosyncratic legal notion of 'objectivity' which that term embodies. A 1987 dictum by Lord Bridge in *Bugdaycay* is frequently cited by lawyers representing asylum applicants, to remind the court that the outcome of a wrong decision may be extremely serious:

> The most fundamental of all human rights is the individual's right to life and when an administrative decision . . . may put the applicant's life at risk, the basis of the decision must surely call for the most anxious scrutiny.

This notion of 'most anxious scrutiny' carried particular force in 1987 because there was then no appeals procedure for refused asylum claimants, whose only legal remedy was judicial review. The appeals process was actually introduced as an attempt to avoid delays created by judicial reviews, and to pre-empt an anticipated adverse European Court ruling in *Vilvarajah* (Thomas 2003: 488).

Since the *Asylum and Immigration Appeals Act 1993* came into force there has been a statutory right of appeal for nearly all asylum claimants, but the potential consequences of being disbelieved and sent back remain just as drastic. Applicants face a major difficulty, however. For obvious reasons most cannot produce documentary corroboration of their ill-treatment, much less call as witnesses those who have persecuted them. Decisions on asylum claims are therefore heavily dependent upon assessments of claimants' credibility, and the plausibility of their stories in relation to background information on the situation in their countries of origin, generally referred to as 'objective evidence'. As the original tribunal in *Horvath* pointed out:

one cannot assess a claim without placing that claim into the context of the background information of the country of origin. In other words, the probative value of the evidence must be evaluated in the light of what is known about the conditions in the claimant's country of origin (see Dutton 2003).

Many discussions of expert witnesses start from the premise that experts themselves take more literally than judges the 'objective' character of their knowledge, and fail to recognise its contextual, contingent character (Jasanoff 1995; Wynne 1996). For social scientists, at least, this seems the wrong way round. Most anthropologists are likely to feel somewhat squeamish about having their evidence labelled in this fashion, because many of the most important things they have to say arise out of the hermeneutic interpretation of intersubjective understandings communicated to them by individual informants (cf. Jasanoff 1996: 110). Whereas Jasanoff stresses the courts' role in exposing the myth of scientific consensus on environmental issues (1995: 91), my focus, as with Clifford (1988) and Jones (1994), is on how adversarial proceedings pressurise experts to profess *greater* certainty than they really feel.

There is a more fundamental issue here, however. For anthropologists, 'objective' and 'subjective' simply mean external and internal to the observer, respectively, whereas for lawyers 'objective' evokes, as it were, the subjectivity of Gluckman's (1955: 126) Reasonable Man:

> when a jury is told to apply a 'subjective' test it means to apply the test of what the person on trial thinks – the 'outsider' standard. By contrast, when a jury is told to apply an 'objective' test, it means the jury should apply the standard that the jury thinks the community or average person subscribes to – an 'insider' standard (Kandel 1992: 3).

The absence of juries in asylum appeals does not affect Kandel's argument, because one would expect legal standards to be more consistently applied by the judiciary than by a lay jury. Legal notions of 'objectivity' are not as static as Kandel's contrast might imply, however. The shift detected by Porter (1995) in the public legitimation of expertise, from *disciplinary* to *mechanical objectivity*, seems clearly manifest in changing standards of reliability and admissibility applied to expert evidence, particularly in the US (Edmond and Mercer 2004a: 8; see §6.4).

Given, however, the distinctive legal notion of 'fact' discussed earlier (§2.2), and bearing in mind that the standard of proof in asylum cases is for there to be a reasonable degree of likelihood of persecution on return (§10.2), it seems clear that an expert's task is to assess matters as any reasonable person sharing their expertise would assess them, rather than to provide an account that is 'true' in any absolute metaphysical sense. As the US Supreme Court commented in *Daubert* (§6.4): 'Rules of Evidence [are] designed not for the exhaustive search for cosmic understanding but for the particularized resolution of legal dispute.'

6.2 A BRIEF HISTORY OF EXPERT WITNESSES

There are sharply contrasting views on the standing of expert witnesses in legal processes. A recent manual for experts begins 'The history of the expert in court is a long and honourable one' (Hall and Smith 2001: 1), whereas a textbook on evidence, co-authored, as it happens, by the now Deputy President of the IAT, refers to a general feeling that 'expert witnesses are . . . close to being professional liars' (Heydon and Ockelton 1996: 384). Such polarised views come as no surprise, because throughout its history the English judiciary has striven to maintain its hegemony over the scientific and technical professions from which experts are drawn.

The present discussion focuses upon two nicely complementary recent studies by Jones, who sees the present status of expert witnesses in English law as the historical outcome of 'competing professional bids for power in social decision making' (1994: 11); and Redmayne, whose starting point is the challenge posed for legal systems by 'the need to defer to, yet exert a degree of control over, the experts' (2001: 1). Both draw on science studies literature to explore McBarnet's insight that legal cases are 'constructed' before coming to court, through discretionary processes of selecting and organising salient 'facts' (1981: 3; Jones 1994: 5; Redmayne 2001: 7). Underlying this important similarity is a basic difference in approach, however. Jones adopts the external, critical perspective of an historical sociologist, while Redmayne stays firmly within the legal paradigm. Jones pushes McBarnet's insights further than Redmayne by examining science and law in terms of the 'strong programme of constructionism' developed in science studies (1994: 2; Bloor 1976). Redmayne is sceptical of constructionist claims where physical sciences are concerned, however, and is not prepared to follow sociologists like Latour and Woolgar (1986) who see reality itself as 'created by the process of fabrication that occurs in the laboratory' (Redmayne 2001: 7). Beyond a certain point, he feels, this 'begins to resemble the scepticism of flat-earthers' (2001: 12). He finds the approach more convincing where psychology and psychiatry are concerned, however, because such expertise concerns 'interactive' rather than 'natural kinds' (2001: 9; Hacking 1999: 32).[1] Elementary particles are natural kinds which either exist or do not, although our ideas about them, like their actual names, are constructed by physicists. Mental illnesses, on the other hand, are 'interactive kinds'. Because people are aware

---

1   Serendipitously, Hacking's own example of an interactive kind is 'woman refugee'.

of how they or others are classified in these terms, and what that classification means, they interact with the medical categories in a variety of ways (1999: 104). Social sciences (and law, though Redmayne does not stress the point) concern interactive kinds almost by definition.

Redmayne accepts the notion of *building* a case – that the police routinely exercise discretion in deciding what lines of enquiry to pursue, what evidence to include in the file, and how to describe that evidence (2001: 7). He accepts also that such constructed cases may be difficult to challenge, because these discretionary processes are well hidden; because witnesses may come to believe the police interpretation of events; or because defendants lack the resources to do so effectively (2001: 10). He is, however, reluctant to go so far as to say that cases are *fabricated* – the legal equivalent of the strong constructionist model in science studies – because where events examined in court are concerned, it is not very persuasive to maintain that 'there is no fact of the matter against which to measure the authenticity of police case constructions' (2001: 11; gloss added).

There is some force to Redmayne's criticism that Jones' version of case construction is so thoroughgoing that the social interests of actors seem to predominate, almost unconstrained by facts and evidence (2001: 17). What is more, his distinctions between 'building' and 'fabrication' in case construction, and between 'motivational' and 'cognitive biases' in expert evidence (§9.4), are more precise and refined than the analytical categories employed by Jones. On the other hand, there is greater sociological nuance in Jones' accounts of both scientific and legal facts as 'negotiated constructs', and of law and science themselves as contestable social processes, even though lawyers and scientists alike routinely conceal this fact in their presentation of evidence (1994: 273–4). Moreover, even if, as Redmayne suspects, scientists' choices among competing interpretations 'are usually rationally justified' (2001: 12n), this in itself is no argument against 'strong constructionism', since to say that an interpretation is 'constructed' in no way implies that it is *irrational*. In what follows, I try to take the best of both approaches, focusing on those aspects of their arguments which seem most relevant to the position of anthropological and other experts in asylum courts.

The distinctions between jurors and witnesses, and lay witnesses and experts, emerged gradually in English law during early modern times. Jurors were initially made up of both witnesses and investigators; ordinary persons who knew the parties and the background to the dispute, and experts who would investigate particular circumstances and report back to the court (Jones 1994: 24–5). Specialist jurors might be used in criminal matters too; for example, medical evidence came to be used in cases of rape (1994: 26). Sometimes entire specialist juries were appointed. Gradually, however, jurors changed from being persons appointed precisely because of their knowledge of the particular facts of the case, or their specialised expertise, to persons whose initial ignorance of those facts and specialisms was the best guarantee of their impartiality (1994: 31, 33; Thayer 1969). This new understanding, fixed by *Bushell's Case* in 1670, served to diminish the power of juries vis-à-vis the judiciary. Whereas jurors had previously been better informed than judges about the facts at issue, both were now dependent upon witnesses called to give evidence as to those facts; the judge, however, held the upper hand through his superior knowledge of the law. But now that jurors themselves were neither well informed on local background, nor specialists on technical matters, they required information from witnesses of another kind, experts who could explain the significance of certain specialised types of fact. Ironically, therefore, one side effect of this 'judicial strategy to obtain greater control over trial outcomes' was that the decision-making power of the specialist juror was transmuted into that of the specialist expert witness (Jones 1994: 33).

In *Folkes* v. *Chadd* (1782), an engineer named Mr Smeaton gave evidence on why a harbour had silted up, and Lord Mansfield could not believe that 'when the question is whether a defect arises from a natural or artificial cause, the opinions of men of science are not to be received'. This is usually cited as the precedent case for the acceptance of expert opinion in English courts, though Jones argues that the practice was actually decades older. While it did establish that experts were no ordinary witnesses, it also confirmed the loss of their former quasi-judicial status, to say nothing of the independence they had enjoyed even earlier as specialist jurors. As witnesses, they 'fell squarely within the ambit of judicial control' (Jones 1994: 59).

This was not, however, a unilineal progression from one form to another. If one surveys the whole range of legal activity, including the Admiralty and Patent Courts where the judiciary are still 'highly dependent upon scientific expertise' (Jones 1994: 38), one finds specialist jurors, court experts, and expert witnesses all coexisting in the contemporary UK. Throughout the nineteenth and twentieth centuries, therefore, the House of Lords repeatedly had to reassert, in the face of a perceived trend towards judges simply following the advice of expert assessors, that a judge 'is bound in duty to exercise his own judgment, and it would be an abandonment of his duty if he delegated that duty to the person who assisted him' (1994: 45); and that it would be 'intolerable if appeals were treated as being not from one judge to another but from one assessor to another' (1994: 43).

In practice, the version of science required by the law is actually closer to 'scientism', an empiricist, value-free caricature of real science (Jones 1994: 5). Where adversarial proceedings are concerned, the aim is not so much to deconstruct the opposing case as to demolish it. One way of achieving this is to attack the credibility of the other side's expert evidence. To forestall this as much as possible, lawyers 'routinely require their scientific witnesses to mask the contingent nature of their conclusions and their methodologies' (Jones 1994: 14; see Clifford 1988: 321). 'Judicial verdicts and their scientific underpinnings are essentially contestable,' says Jones (1994: 274). 'In the means they use to construct their cases lawyers and scientists routinely conceal this.' This helps explain why legal debate starts from the premise that the 'best explanation for dissenting experts [is] that they must be suffering from partisanship' (Jones 1994: 97). The 'strong constructionist' model in science studies points to numerous other possibilities, of course: in fact, 'disagreement among scientists is normal and natural' (1994: 99). Nonetheless that premise, stemming from a simplistic notion of scientific activity and epistemology (albeit one in which scientists themselves, *especially when testifying in courts of law*, are often complicit when they accept that questions put to them are susceptible of yes/no answers; see §11.2) forms the basis of a widespread legal view, beautifully exemplified by the comment about 'professional liars' with which this section began, that experts are persons of low integrity. This in turn can serve to rationalise their progressive exclusion from processes of judicial decision making (1994: 99).

One form taken by this exclusion was the elaboration of the 'ultimate issue' rule, which continues to affect the acceptability of expert reports in asylum appeals even though the rule itself was actually abolished in civil cases by the *Civil Evidence Act 1968* (Jones 1994: 124; Henderson 2003: 218). No witness may give their direct opinion on the main issue at stake, such as (in criminal courts) the guilt or innocence of the accused. The generally cited legal precedent for prohibiting experts from commenting on the ultimate issue is the 1821 case of *R* v. *Wright*, but judges continued to voice concern during the nineteenth and twentieth centuries over the need 'to prevent trial by jury from becoming trial by expert' (Jones 1994: 104).

The equivalent in asylum cases is the principle that experts should not offer opinions as to whether a particular appellant falls within the ambit of the 1951 Convention; as to their credibility; or even – though this is contested by some medical experts (§8.5) – as to the causes of scars on their bodies.

Experts seen as transgressing these rules risk having their evidence devalued or even ignored altogether. In a typical example, the tribunal hearing the appeal of a Colombian law student (*Gomez*) who had tried to help a farmer facing extortion demands from FARC guerrillas, criticised aspects of an expert report by Professor Jenny Pearce. She had offered the opinion that the students involved:

> tried to investigate this case, encouraged by their tutor. Partly they hoped to do well in their law studies, but partly they probably felt they were simply carrying out their duty to make the legal system work. . . . I would disagree therefore with the Home Office's statement that your client cannot be a victim of persecution if she is targeted by non-State armed groups.

Though it recognised Pearce's expertise and relied upon her accounts of how Colombian political and judicial systems operated, and the influence of guerrillas, the tribunal saw these comments as detracting from the value of her report:

> the Tribunal . . . is not assisted by her efforts to apply this knowledge to the circumstances of this particular appellant in the form of speculation about an appellant's motives. . . . An expert is not a judicial decision maker. A country expert's function is to set out the general facts in the light of the objective evidence. Insofar as he or she has reason to comment on an individual case, his or her remarks should normally be confined to assessing whether what is said to have happened to a particular individual or individuals correlates or not with the general evidence about persons similarly situated.

That is the position regularly taken by tribunals, and underlines the importance of experts receiving proper advice from their instructing solicitors. Experts may legitimately comment on the probability of the evidence given the hypothesis, but not upon the probability of the hypothesis given the evidence. That is because confusing the two 'may significantly distort the value of the evidence. . . . This confusion is sometimes called the prosecutor's fallacy' (Redmayne 2001: 47). For example, if DNA found at a crime scene matches that of the defendant to an extent found among only one person in three million, it does not follow at all that there is only one chance in three million that it is not his DNA (2001: 58).

Even in the heyday of the ultimate issue rule there were ways of circumventing it, most obviously through use of hypothetical questions, which are in any case a standard strategy for disempowering experts and compelling them to engage on the lawyers' terms rather than their own. Such questions give the appearance of eliciting comment on abstract matters of scientific principle, rather than improperly asking the expert to express a direct opinion on a disputed fact:

> Suppose, assume, and if are the operative words of the magic formula. Rather like a spell, the question would not work unless the proper words were uttered. The question and answer would technically become improper and inadmissible unless uttered in the correct form (Jones 1994: 114).

Crucially, although the hypothetical facts may correspond almost exactly to those at issue, their actual framing was in the hands of the examining lawyer. Rather than reporting on the facts of the actual case as they themselves saw them, experts were manoeuvred into commenting on a version of those facts constructed by the examiner. Through this legal artifice, lawyers gained 'extensive control over the form of an expert's testimony and consequently reduced the degree to which experts controlled their own evidence'

(Jones 1994: 114). Once experts have been constrained in this way, their views may be rendered irrelevant under cross-examination, if the other side can show that any of the hypotheses upon which they are based do not apply to the matter at hand.

While the ultimate issue rule was being elaborated, the hearsay rule was perforce being relaxed. Although technically 'hearsay' when an expert offers opinions based on 'the collected wisdom of his discipline' (Jones 1994: 106), such opinions became increasingly difficult to exclude as the sciences engaged in the systematic accumulation and dissemination of knowledge, 'providing a storehouse upon which professional experts may draw, and within the confines of which they are generally educated' (1994: 107). It consequently became less a matter of the admissibility of such evidence, than of its 'weight and probative value' (1994: 108; see Chapter 9).

Fostered by this greater systematisation of scientific knowledge, simplistic notions of scientific objectivity tend to be taken for granted by all parties in the adversarial context of the law courts – an unfortunate misapprehension when decisions governing livelihood, life, liberty, and death are generally at stake, but an understandable one given that experts themselves collude in its maintenance. Expert reports achieve an aura of authority thanks to the same linguistic and stylistic devices as characterise scientific papers (Jones 1994: 183; Good 2006b). They convey the same sense of impartial appraisal, of standardised, routinised methodologies allowing little or no scope for personal idiosyncrasy (Jones 1994: 183–4). Consequently, constructed facts appear *un*constructed and readers 'are convinced that they have not been convinced' (Latour and Woolgar 1986: 240); rather, it seems that 'the facts have spoken for themselves' (Jones 1994: 184). Such views – widely held among scientists themselves, and reinforced by the naive scientism characterising legal views of scientific evidence – encourage the further legal belief that miscarriages of justice can only be 'due to bad science and bad scientists' (1994: 223), rather than legal processes themselves. Thus, one basis for the legal denigration of experts is the belief that they are 'hired guns' prepared to argue whatever they are paid to argue.

6.3 THE DUTIES OF EXPERT WITNESSES

What, then, are the duties and responsibilities of expert witnesses under current English law? Many barristers favoured the 'balanced' (Speaight 1996) statement by Mr Justice Garland (*Polivitte*), which saw the expert's role as twofold:

first, to advance the case of the party calling him, so far as it can properly be advanced on the basis of information available to the expert in the professional exercise of his skill and experience; and, secondly, to assist the Court, which does not possess the relevant skill and experience, in determining where the truth lies.

Unsurprisingly, however, judges have preferred an alternative position which elevates the expert's duty to the court into first place. The most cited statement of an expert witness's duties in civil courts, set down by Mr Justice Cresswell in the *Ikarian Reefer* case,[2] reads as follows:

(1) Expert evidence presented to the Court should be, and should be seen to be, the independent product of the expert uninfluenced as to form or content by the exigencies of litigation. . . .

(2) An expert witness should provide independent assistance to the Court by way of objective unbiased opinion in relation to matters within his expertise. . . . An expert witness . . . should never assume the role of an advocate.

(3) An expert witness should state the facts or assumption upon which his opinion is based. He should not omit to consider material facts which could detract from his concluded opinion. . . .

(4) An expert witness should make it clear when a particular question or issue falls outside his expertise.

(5) If an expert's opinion is not properly researched because he considers that insufficient data is available, then this must be stated with an indication that the opinion is no more than a provisional one. . . .

(6) If, after exchange of reports, an expert witness changes his view on a material matter having read the other side's expert's report or for any other reason, such change of view should be communicated (through legal representatives) to the other side without delay and when appropriate to the Court.

(7) Where expert evidence refers to photographs, plans, calculations, analyses, measurements, survey reports or other similar documents, these must be provided to the opposite party at the same time as the exchange of reports.

While the broad principles are thus very clear, their practical implementation is inevitably less straightforward. For example, the 'form' and 'content' of expert evidence are bound to be influenced to some degree by 'exigencies of litigation'. Solicitors themselves limit the matters on which they wish experts to comment, because there are only certain kinds of issue on which expert evidence is admissible, which may differ markedly from those meriting inclusion in academic publications; and because experts should only comment on matters arising in the proceedings. It would be wrong to get experts

2   This was the name of a ship, allegedly set on fire in pursuit of an insurance claim.

to modify or delete comments on core issues, but it is perfectly proper to ask them to delete sections on issues not actually raised (Speaight 1996). Moreover, however unbiased their evidence, and however rigorous their eschewing of advocacy, experts are clearly not providing 'independent assistance to the court' insofar as they are engaged and paid by one of the litigating parties. This is addressed in the Civil Procedure Rules (below) by a preference for experts being appointed by the court rather than by the contending parties. Further, does the expert's duty to consider all material facts apply only to questions actually put, or extend to omissions generally? Here again one can imagine barristers wishing to interpret this rather more narrowly than judges. Most barristers would certainly argue that, given the adversarial nature of legal process, experts are not obliged to mention matters they were not asked about; and a report that does so can legitimately be edited by counsel before submission to the court.

The Court of Appeal endorsed all seven principles, but on the fourth it offered 'one word of caution', feeling that the lower court had been too stringent regarding the legitimate expertise of the experts involved. In Lord Justice Stuart-Smith's words, 'when he is assessing the significance of certain evidence, [an expert] must be entitled to weigh the probabilities and this may involve making use of the skills of other experts or drawing on his general . . . knowledge.' The bounds of disciplinary competence (§6.4) are always matters of some vagueness and ambiguity, even more so for anthropologists than, say, medical experts whose competence is more precisely regulated and codified, in law and by their professional body, and (I had initially assumed) more widely understood by lawyers.

An associate who regularly gives expert evidence in criminal cases notes that whereas he always tells 'the truth' and 'nothing but the truth', 'the whole truth' is a different matter altogether (Neil Montgomery, pers. comm.; see Jasanoff 1995: 48). Doctors have similar concerns. At a meeting I attended under Chatham House rules, an eminent Professor of Forensic Medicine expressed his perennial unease at being required to take the oath in this form, but was reassured by a senior Scottish Law Lord that he need not understand it quite so literally. Staughton LJ's judgment in *Derby* v. *Weldon*, cited by Cresswell J in support of his fifth principle, does indeed qualify the requirement somewhat:

> I do not think that an expert witness, or any other witness, obliges himself to volunteer his views on every issue in the whole case when he takes an oath to tell the whole truth. What he does oblige himself to do is to tell the whole truth about those matters which he is asked about.

Even this is problematic, however, as it continues to take the notion of 'the whole truth' for granted. Whether anthropology deals in 'truth' at all is open to debate, but no anthropologist would ever claim access to the *whole* truth where the presentation, let alone the interpretation, of ethnographic evidence is concerned. Reports should not be put before the court unless they still broadly reflect the expert's current opinions – which is one of the problems with 'recycling' expert reports in asylum appeals (§9.5) – but it would be unreasonable to imagine that any report constitutes the author's final views on the matter. Here again there was a difference in emphasis between the two courts in the *Ikarian Reefer* case. Whereas Mr Justice Cresswell had expressed concern because one expert changed some of his views during the hearing, Lord Justice Stuart-Smith saw such 'flexibility' as 'common' and 'inevitable' (see Edmond 2000: 222–3).

During Lord Woolf's consultative review of English civil law, the role of expert witnesses was a topic of particular concern. It was widely argued that their 'inappropriate' use caused excessive expense and delay, and made cases unnecessarily complex. There was also concern over experts' alleged 'failure to maintain their independence from the party by whom they had been instructed' (Woolf 1996: ¶23.1). The resulting Civil Procedure Rules (CPR; Lord Chancellor's Department, no date) now apply to most civil cases in English county courts, the High Court, and Court of Appeal. Section 35.3 of those Rules specifies that:

(1) It is the duty of an expert to help the court on the matters within his expertise.
(2) This duty overrides any obligation to the person from whom he has received instructions or by whom he is paid.

In the interests of making legal processes quicker and cheaper, expert evidence is normally given as a written report (¶35.5), but the other party can put clarifying questions to the expert once it has been submitted; this never happens in asylum appeals in my experience, except in those rare instances where experts attend in person to be cross-examined. If these are not answered, the court may rule that the party instructing the expert cannot rely on that evidence (¶35.6). Finally, ¶35.10 addresses the contents of the report as follows:

(1) An expert's report must comply with the requirements set out in the relevant practice direction.
(2) At the end of an expert's report there must be a statement that –
  (a) the expert understands his duty to the court; and
  (b) he has complied with that duty.
(3) The expert's report must state the substance of all material instructions, whether written or oral, on the basis of which the report was written.

Paragraph 1.1 of the Practice Direction summarises Rule 35.3 as given above, while the rest of Section 1 elaborates on this in terms largely derived from the *Ikarian Reefer* judgment. Section 2 deals with the structure of expert reports, and subsequent sections discuss the sharing of information between contending parties; the circumstances under which experts may be cross-examined about the contents of their instructions; and procedures for putting questions to experts.

The CPR's most radical innovation was to give the court itself power to appoint a single joint expert, taking instructions from both parties (¶35.7, ¶35.8). This measure rests, however, upon the highly questionable assumption that 'science' is inherently consensual, and that ensuring experts' neutrality vis-à-vis the litigating parties will automatically increase the reliability of their evidence. It also, with consequences still not entirely clear, introduces an inquisitorial element into otherwise adversarial legal proceedings (Edmond 2000: 242–9). Finally, it invests court experts with a level of authority such that it might be harder for judges to disregard their opinions (Edmond 2004b: 139). Presumably this option now exists in asylum cases, at least in higher courts, although – perhaps not surprisingly, as the Home Office almost never calls experts of its own anyway – I know of no instances of its use. Consequently, despite its obvious importance for civil law more broadly, I shall not pursue the issue here.

6.4 RELIABILITY AND ADMISSIBILITY OF EXPERT EVIDENCE

British and American approaches to expert evidence have tended to be out of phase with one another. In the late nineteenth century, just as the English judiciary was trying to diminish the influence of experts by restricting the roles of assessors, courts in the US were doing precisely the reverse. Court experts 'enjoyed an immense but brief popularity in the United States at a time between 1880 and 1920 when America was generally more receptive to all things scientific' (Jones 1994: 49). This enthusiasm waned, however, when it transpired that 'scientists disagreed among themselves even where they were not paid hirelings', and that the disagreements did not apply merely to interpretations of facts but to the very facts themselves. There was no guarantee, therefore, that even the court's assessor 'represented the impartial and accepted view of the profession as a whole' (1994: 50).

In reality, the judiciary might not have been entirely displeased by this discovery: 'If the promise of the new science was fulfilled, law could expect to be demoted to second place. What a relief, then, when it was discovered that men of science disagreed so frequently' (Jones 1994: 70). Consequently, American courts began reverting to the use of expert witnesses in recent decades, but these were not presumed to be impartial, and were treated with a scepticism that extended to attacks on their professional status and credibility (1994: 51; Jasanoff 1995: 32).

Whereas the status of expert has to be achieved in the US, it tends to be ascribed in the UK, where 'English courts never developed the more sceptical view of scientistic claims' (Jones 1994: 55; see Edmond 2000: 234). This helps explain the markedly different stances of the almost exactly contemporary studies by Jones, who focuses on the extent to which experts in UK courts are pushed into unwonted certainty by the adversarial character of legal processes (1994: 186); and Jasanoff, who stresses the 'commodification' of expertise in the US, and the effectiveness of cross-examination in deconstructing experts' claims (1995: 45, 53). Jones' approach is more appropriate for British asylum hearings, where there is almost never a 'rival' expert on the 'other side', and where experts are in any case less clearly distinguished from other witnesses (*Kapela*; Good 2004a: 119).

Moreover, the Federal Rules of Evidence in the US are potentially more limiting as regards experts' roles (see www.house.gov/judiciary/evid00.pdf). They contrast ordinary witnesses, who are strictly limited in the degree to which they can legitimately express 'opinions or inferences' (Rule 701), with expert witnesses who *may* express opinions providing these are based on facts or data obtained using reliable methods reliably applied (Rule 702). Rule 703 further specifies that opinions given by experts must relate to data 'of a type reasonably relied upon by experts in the particular field in forming opinions or inferences upon the subject'. Rule 704 then deals with the ultimate issue rule, stating that opinion evidence which would otherwise be admissible cannot be objected to merely because it addresses the ultimate issue, with the one exception that experts may not testify as to the link between a defendant's 'mental state or condition' and the crime they are charged with.

Admissibility rules governing expert evidence are legal rather than factual matters, and hence subject to the discretion of the judge (Edmond 2004b: 140). In 1923, for example, the US Supreme Court held in *Frye* that expert evidence based on a primitive lie detector test was inadmissible, because the technique was not sufficiently well established or widely accepted. Thereafter, the admissibility of evidence depended upon the status of the scientific technique producing it. Any newly invented or discovered technique would first pass through an 'experimental stage' during which it was tested rigorously, and only after the scientific community had agreed that it was valid or 'demonstrable', would evidence produced thereby be admissible in court (Giannelli 1980). The focus was thus on disciplinary consensus, although because the borderline between experimental and demonstrable is usually hazy in practice, judges retained considerable discretion as gatekeepers for expert evidence (Jasanoff 1995: 62; Redmayne 2001: 103).

The *Frye* test was the dominant admissibility rule for expert evidence until the 1993 decision in *Daubert*, wherein the Supreme Court found that the Federal Rules of Evidence superseded the *Frye* test, and delineated a new test based on Popperian notions of falsifiability, as well as general acceptance. The Court stated:

(1) Ordinarily, a key question to be answered in determining whether a theory or technique is scientific knowledge that will assist the trier of fact will be whether it can be (and has been) tested [citing Popper 1989: 37].

(2) Another pertinent question is whether the theory or technique has been subjected to peer review and publication. Publication . . . is not a *sine qua non* of admissibility; it does not necessarily correlate with reliability . . . [citing Jasanoff 1990: 61–76].

(3) Additionally, in the case of a particular scientific technique, the court ordinarily should consider the known or potential rate of error . . .

(4) Finally, 'general acceptance' can yet have a bearing on the enquiry.

Though Popper's views were already seen as old-fashioned by science studies specialists, the Court seems to have felt that he provided a rigorous yet simple standard which legitimated a general raising of admissibility standards. *Daubert* managed to incorporate Jasanoff's constructionist theories too, however, exemplifying how common law prefers pragmatic 'muddling through' to philosophical coherence (Jasanoff 1995: 63; see Edmond and Mercer 2004a: 20).

The *Daubert* test gained increasing acceptance, and underwent further elaboration. In *Kumho Tire Co.*, for example, the Supreme Court clarified that it applied to 'technical' as well as 'scientific' expertise, but also emphasised that it must be applied flexibly (Roberts 1999). Even so, falsifiability remains arguably too demanding yet too broad a criterion for demarcating science from non-science; for example, astrological predictions are more straightforwardly falsifiable than many existential statements at the core of physics. Redmayne (2001: 115) argues against an over-literal reading, however; in his view, 'the word "science" is only playing the role of a proxy for "reliable", because what *Daubert* is really trying to do is lay down standards for deciding when evidence is reliable enough to be admitted'.

To some extent, one can see the contrast between *Frye* and *Daubert* as exemplifying the broader trend detected by Porter (1995), namely, the shift from a *disciplinary* approach to objectivity, grounded in 'tacit learning, experience, social relations and trust, insight, and the need to link solutions to their specific contexts', to a *mechanical* approach, relying on 'quantification, formal rules and a fixation with methodological review' (Edmond and Mercer 2004a: 8) in an attempt to limit the acceptability of individual (read idiosyncratic, unreliable) opinions. Despite their differences, however, both *Frye* and *Daubert* do define reliability in terms of techniques for obtaining or analysing data, rather than the content of the data themselves (Edmond 2004a, b). At first sight, this seems more advantageous for anthropological experts. If it were primarily a question of subject matter, then even within the relatively constrained scope of British social anthropology, let alone its far more diverse North American counterpart, anthropologists themselves would be hard put to agree where precisely their intellectual frontiers with other disciplines lie. But because the focus is on methods, Kandel (1992) suggests, neither test need cause many problems in practice, given that field-work involves generally accepted techniques for collecting observational, oral, documentary, and historical data. It certainly seems that the *Frye* criterion can be met, given the degree of acceptance within anthropology of the basic methodology of participant-observation (Donovan and Anderson 2003: 102). Where *Daubert* is concerned, however, Kandel seems over-optimistic (see also Thuen 2004: 266). Which, if any, anthropological techniques meet *Daubert*'s falsifiability criterion however flexibly applied? And whereas *Frye* allowed disciplinary consensus to decide methodological reliability, *Daubert* makes the court itself the final arbiter (2003: 103; Peterson and Conley 2001: 213).[3]

Such problems are not peculiar to anthropologists, of course. Some writers argue that expert opinions in all 'soft' sciences, where strict measurements may be lacking, can and should receive judicial scrutiny for reliability or general acceptance before being admitted in evidence, and that it would be strange indeed if expert testimony in, say, psychology or economics, were more easily admissible than testimony in the 'hard' sciences, purely because their principles were *less* amenable to objective testing. 'The very fact that the soft sciences generally allow more room for subjective interpretation . . . would seem to argue for more stringent evidentiary criteria, not less' (Murphy and Cuccias 1997).

But should the reliability tests be the same as for 'hard' sciences? Jasanoff highlights the particular problems posed by ethnography in this regard, because of its 'intersubjectivity' and the 'interpenetration of multiple subjective viewpoints' (1996: 110); and because of the uncertain 'cognitive status' of the field notes upon which it is based, and their problematic relationship with the final analytical product (1996: 111). MacCrimmon (1998) suggests a way around this, however: the expertise of social scientists should not be equated with that of physicists, but with 'the specialized knowledge of . . . the fire inspector who testifies about the cause of a fire' (see also Renaker 1996). Their expertise should, in other words, be assessed against the extent and appropriateness of their personal experience rather than the falsifiability of their disciplinary techniques. For country experts in British asylum courts that does indeed seem to be largely what happens (Good 2004a: 119), although in the US, practical experience does *not* necessarily make one an expert (Jasanoff 1995: 60).

Although English law is far less precise in specifying reliability criteria for expert evidence, the behaviour of English courts towards experts is broadly

---

3   In similar vein, Crown lawyers in a Canadian First Nation land case sought to have anthropological evidence excluded as 'unscientific' (Culhane 1998: 132). The judge admitted it, while reserving the option to attach little weight to it in his final decision.

consistent with the more explicit US principles, according to Hodgkinson (1990: 138), writing pre-*Daubert*. Evidence may be excluded if purported experts are found to lack expertise on the topic on which they are giving evidence, or if part of their evidence goes beyond the bounds of their legitimate expertise, but there is no clear-cut way of deciding this. *R* v. *Silverlock* considered whether a solicitor was qualified to give expert evidence on handwriting, seeing that its study was not part of his actual profession. The court decided that while expert witnesses must of course be skilled, the means of acquiring that skill was not a determining factor; the evidence of a skilled and experienced person should not be excluded merely because that experience was not gained by way of their business or profession. Redmayne notes the potential circularity of making expertise itself the test for being recognised as an expert, but concludes that the variety of potential experts is so great that, pragmatically, no more precise statement is possible (2001: 95–7).

Any raising of admissibility standards for expert evidence inevitably makes it harder for litigants relying upon such evidence to succeed (Edmond and Mercer 2004a: 5). In practice, though, the degree of rigour required of particular experts depends upon broader judicial judgments as to the relative reliability of entire disciplinary professions. For example, whereas evidence from an allopathic medical practitioner tends to be accepted at face value in asylum hearings, subject only to the doctor's CV indicating appropriate training and experience, psychiatrists and psychologists are not accorded such generalised recognition. Courts commonly expect them to set out the factual bases of their opinions, and the tests and criteria whereby this opinion was derived from those facts (see §8.5).

For psychiatric experts, moreover, there is always the risk of the court ruling that the facts they rely on 'fall within the common stock of knowledge of a lay jury' (Jones 1994: 109). In *R* v. *Turner*, for example (Redmayne 2001: 145), Lawton LJ stated that expert evidence might be needed on the nature of a mental disorder, but 'Jurors do not need psychiatrists to tell them how ordinary folk who are not suffering from any mental illness are likely to react to the stresses and strains of life.' He added:

> The fact that an expert witness has impressive scientific qualifications does not by that fact alone make his opinion on matters of human nature and behaviour *within the limits of normality* any more helpful than that of the jurors themselves; but there is a danger that they may think it does. . . . The jury in this case did not need, and should not have been offered the evidence of a psychiatrist to help them decide whether the appellant's evidence was truthful (emphasis added).

As with the ultimate issue and hearsay rules (§6.3), this 'common stock of knowledge' criterion is more strictly applied when decisions rest with a lay jury. Where decisions are made by judges themselves, as in asylum hearings, there is less emphasis on exclusionary rules (Redmayne 2001: 3) as judges are assumed to be better able to weigh all forms of evidence and less likely to be inordinately impressed by the smoke and mirrors of expert testimony. The absence of juries probably helps explain why the reliability of expert evidence has been so little debated in the asylum courts. Paradoxically, adjudicators and tribunals often address the qualifications of medical experts while weighing their evidence, but have paid far less attention to those of country experts. One might expect the position of anthropologists to be even less secure than that of psychiatrists, partly because there are so few precedents for them appearing as experts in British courts, and partly because their knowledge, too, risks being deemed part of the 'common stock'.[4]

Few British anthropologists have experience of acting as experts across a range of jurisdictions. Roger Ballard (pers. comm.), who has acted not only in asylum and immigration matters, but also in family law cases and criminal matters affecting British Punjabis, finds striking contrasts between different branches of law, which seem – bearing out Jones' and Redmayne's contentions – closely linked to the presence or absence of a jury. Civil courts are prepared to receive ethnographic evidence about context, and his evidence has never been ruled inadmissible; indeed judges sometimes question him at length on issues such as honour, shame, and Islamic law. Criminal courts are far more restrictive. The evidence in R v. *Jameel Akhtar*, a heroin smuggling case, included a conversation in Urdu, taped by Customs officers. Though literally accurate, the transcripts naturally omitted the tone and style of the speakers. Listening to the tapes, it seemed to Ballard that Mark, the Customs informer, was leading the conversation, and that many apparently 'incriminating' statements by the accused were polite grunts and agreements such as Punjabis normally make when harangued by political or economic superiors. He wrote a report to this effect, but the trial judge ruled that this was not evidence of fact, but a commentary on matters which were the sole responsibility of the jury. This decision was confirmed by the Court of Appeal. It noted that defence counsel:

has stressed the different cultural background of the jurors in this case and those concerned in events in Pakistan. That is true, but juries in this country often find themselves trying cases of this sort, and with assistance from the judge . . . they are able to do that perfectly fairly. None of the issues in this case are unusual. [I]nsofar as Dr Ballard's evidence was going to be relied upon by the defence to seek to elucidate the truth or

4 Some recent IAT decisions *have* raised questions about particular witnesses, albeit inconsistently. The expertise of Mr Brian Allen, who holds a Diploma in Anthropology and has lengthy East African experience but has never been to Somalia, was questioned in *SSHD* v. *AA [Somalia]*, yet his evidence was decisive for another tribunal deliberating over the same period (*KS [Somalia]*).

plausibility of what Mr Akhtar gave as the explanation of his various conversations with Mark, we consider it was inadmissible in any event. It was or would be evidence seeking to support the credibility or truth of another witness. . . . It was evidence of cultural background which, in our judgment, would not be admissible in any event when the issue in the case was whether when they met on those occasions Mark and Akhtar had been discussing heroin or herbal remedies: a matter in our judgment not illuminated at all by any expert in any discipline whatsoever.

Although the conversation was partly in a language they did not speak or understand, the Worcestershire jurors were deemed capable of assessing its significance for themselves. The unusual feature was that this decision was left to the judge: in Ballard's experience, barristers themselves usually filter this evidence pre-emptively before such a stage is reached.

Another anthropologist, Stephanie Schwandner-Sievers (2005), has not only acted as an expert in asylum appeals and criminal cases, but has also been approached by police seeking 'cultural background' to aid their investigations into violent crimes involving Albanians. Like the Mashpee land claim (§2.3), this raises the practical and ethical difficulties associated with 'communicating "culture" (and its social consequences) without reproducing essentialist rep-resentations'; in this context, the risk lies in portraying exotic cultural features like 'blood-feuds' as 'causes' of delinquent behaviour (see §7.4).

6.5 INSTRUCTING 'COUNTRY EXPERTS'

'In these very offices,' an adjudicator told me during a seminar in the prem-ises of a leading firm of commercial lawyers, 'you'll often find three or four barristers holding meetings just to draw up the terms of reference for instruct-ing expert witnesses.' Compared to that, the engaging and instructing of experts in the asylum courts is a rudimentary business, with none of the sophisticated strategies employed in expensive, protracted civil litigation, such as 'onion-peeling', the pursuit of scientific evidence just as deeply as, but no deeper than, necessary to support the case to the greatest extent; and 'cherry-picking', the selection of experts, or of questions to put to those experts, to produce the desired answer (Peterson and Conley 2001: 220–7).

Medical expert evidence, based on psychiatric or physical examination, is submitted in many appeals, not least because of the special significance of torture in asylum claims. In a minority of instances, too, solicitors decide to supplement the general country evidence (§9.2) by commissioning case-specific (occasionally, generic) reports by country experts. They may decide that such a report is needed if the appeal involves an unusual issue on which existing documentation is silent, or to obtain an independent assessment of the plausibility of particular sequences of events. The presence or absence of expert reports cannot always be so rationally explained, however. Some solicitors – particularly the better ones – use experts almost routinely, and this is really an expression of their greater conscientiousness, reflected in their assembling of better thought-out bundles of evidence generally. Most, however, do not. Cost is not generally the issue here, as reasonable fees can usually be met from legal aid; rather, many solicitors are disorganised and overloaded, and never get around to it (Mark Henderson, pers. comm.).

Both practitioners and decision makers accept that doctors must be contacted long in advance when medical reports are required. During 2001, for example, the premier specialists, the Medical Foundation, had a waiting list of around six months, and it is by no means unknown for hearings to be adjourned for this reason. No such latitude is granted for country experts, however, and to make matters worse, they are commonly not even contacted by solicitors until just before the appeal hearing. Deadlines are therefore ridiculously tight, often for no apparent reason except that, to some extent, such brinkmanship is intrinsic to legal culture:

> Lawyers themselves frequently read case papers only the night before trial [and] court organization itself tends towards last-minute changes of court time-tabling of cases . . . In such circumstances, lawyers need an expert who . . . requires little in the way of pre-trial consultation' (Jones 1994: 143).

In general, neither the specificity of the instructions nor the time allowed to reply to them, are sufficient to allow experts to do themselves, or asylum claimants, justice. Experts should be given specific questions to address in their reports, but in the asylum field this by no means always happens. Country experts' experiences do not bear out Jones' contention that lawyers deliberately 'give the expert limited space in which to do damage [by] giving him . . . highly specific instructions' (Jones 1994: 167). Quite the contrary, the 'instructions' provided by many solicitors, often the very ones with the tightest deadlines, consist merely of a request to prepare a report, with no indication of what issues to cover. Most experts complain that they often have no proper instructions at all. This is all the more serious because, as several prolific experts noted, they *never* receive guidance from solicitors on what is or is not permissible on their part. Most have never received formal training, either; the professional bodies providing training and accreditation for expert witnesses, such as the Academy of Experts, Society of Expert Witnesses, and Expert Witness Institute, are geared towards those deriving significant incomes from high-fee civil litigation. For most country experts, their income from writing reports would barely pay the membership fees of such bodies.

It is good practice for solicitors to send experts the entire 'bundle' of evidence on which the appellant intends to rely, including the SEF form, asylum interview transcript, the Home Office RFRL, the grounds of appeal, correspondence between solicitors and Home Office, medical reports, news items, photographs, and so on. The appearance of such a huge bundle as little as 48 hours before the deadline for submitting the report further limits experts' ability to gain a detailed grasp of the case, and virtually rules out opportunities for reflection. Operating in such haste, and often in ignorance of the legal status of their own evidence, experts can easily expose themselves to criticism – and more importantly, have their reports devalued, jeopardising the asylum applicant's case – by making factual errors or unwittingly commenting on matters beyond their competence.

Up to a point, it is permissible to edit expert reports (Jones 1994: 180–2). According to the Law Society (no date) changes may be requested 'for the sake of accuracy, completeness, clarity or consistency'. Solicitors can also ask for irrelevant matters to be removed, but should not seek the removal of material where this would skew the opinion expressed. I have indeed occasionally been asked to omit or reword particular passages, and have found the boundary between permissible and improper requests not always clear. Solicitors can, of course, withhold reports altogether if the implications for their clients are too negative.

Finally, it is not at all easy for experts to learn from their mistakes. As in other areas of law, country experts 'rarely receive any feedback. As bit players they are expected to have no compelling interest in the outcome of a case' (Jones 1994: 144). Even when one specifically requests a copy of the adjudicator's determination, this seldom materialises. For lawyers perpetually scrambling round the asylum treadmill, the focus is on not being excessively late in submitting the next set of documents, rather than revisiting cases from two or three months back. Generally speaking, experts' only clue as to whether their work was considered effective and was well received by the court 'comes from being hired again' (1994: 144).

6.6 EXPERT REPORTS

Experts used in asylum appeals are almost never given guidance by solicitors on the form their reports should take nor, generally, are they aware of the existence of the Civil Procedure Rules (§6.3). As a result, their reports differ widely in form. Some are even written in the form of letters to the instructing solicitors rather than being addressed to the court, which immediately conveys a sense of amateurism.

My own format gradually took shape as my experience grew. It begins with a brief CV stressing my familiarity with Sri Lanka. Subsequent paragraphs indicate my experience as an expert witness, citing appeals in which my reports drew favourable comment. I explain that I have never met the appellant (see §9.3) and am assessing their case on the basis of documents supplied by their solicitors, which are listed. I then summarise the appellant's statement (if any) and interview transcript. It is important that this summary is accurate; HOPOs will seize on any errors as damaging to the appellant's (and the expert's) credibility. My earliest reports also summarised the history of ethnic conflict in Sri Lanka, but my research revealed that adjudicators knew all this because they heard so many Sri Lankan cases. I now limit myself to the current human rights situation, and evidence regarding torture of detainees.

Occasionally appellants are well-enough known for there to be independent corroboration of their stories; for example, I have reported on two MPs and a human rights lawyer. In any case, expert evidence may serve to confirm that a story is culturally plausible, and consistent with events in the appellant's home country over the relevant period. However, a fine line must be drawn here. It is not necessary for accounts to be independently corroborated, and Henderson (2003: 192) warns legal representatives to challenge any suggestion that this is the purpose of the expert evidence. The tribunal has clearly stated that it is a misdirection:

> to imply that corroboration is necessary. It is in the same category as the statement, so frequently found in the Home Office reasons for refusal of a claim 'That there is no evidence to support' such and such a fact. There is usually evidence in the form of the appellant's statement. That is evidence. Whether it is accepted and what weight is attached to it are different matters (*Kasolo*).

In any case, these introductory matters merely set the context for answering the solicitor's questions, which are best quoted verbatim. There is much overlap between cases in the questions experts are asked, not only because similar issues keep arising, but also because refusal letters are highly formulaic, with standardised paragraphs used over and over again (§5.1). While this reflects the poverty of IND's decision making, it does have the advantage, given the looming deadline, that research done in connection with one case often proves relevant to others. However, experts' views depend, at least in part, on the specific circumstances of each appellant, so even standard questions may require special research.

Common questions in Sri Lankan appeals include: Does the appellant's release from detention without charge or through bribery, indicate that they are of no further interest to the authorities? Are records kept of such detentions, and would these be accessible to immigration officers if the appellant was returned? What is the likelihood that persons of this background will be detained on return? If they have scars, will these increase the risk of detention? If detained, are they likely to face torture or 'inhuman and degrading treatment' Are they at risk from the LTTE and/or pro-government Tamil militias? Have the ceasefire and peace talks affected the risk faced by such persons, if returned? These are topics about which anthropologists have considerable knowledge because of their general familiarity with the country, and they certainly fall within the scope of political anthropology as broadly defined, but answers generally require assessments of broad national trends rather than micro-ethnography. More conventional anthropological matters do sometimes arise, however. I have had to deal with caste, purity, marriage patterns, and domestic relations, in order to answer questions on Tamil attitudes to rape, or the social status of single girls and widows.

A certain 'added value' may be gained from expert reassessment of material in CIPU *Country Reports* (§9.2) or other standard documentary sources, but expert reports are most useful when they provide information from first-hand experience or less accessible sources. As court decisions are notionally based on the situation on the day of the hearing, up-to-date information is at a premium. Consequently, experts cannot rely on conventional academic sources, and the internet becomes a primary source of news and information. Although this provides a vast database of information and opinion (Mason 2001a, b; ICMPD 2002), there is also much crass propaganda and unsubstantiated assertion. Just as the courts do later (Chapter 9), experts must be seen to weigh information according to the reliability of its source.[5] Partly for this reason, they need to cite sources wherever possible. If answers are based on personal experience, that should also be stated, and the extent of the expert's first-hand knowledge explained. As required by the CPR, a report should conclude with a 'statement of truth', including an affirmation that the expert has discharged their primary duty to the court. My own statement of truth does not follow the CPR wording, but addresses the same issues, and has been recommended in a best practice text for immigration lawyers (Henderson 2003: 218).

The purpose of country experts' reports is to provide authoritative comment on issues 'outside the knowledge or experience of the fact finding tribunal', especially in cross-cultural situations where experiences 'do not appear to make logical sense' (Henderson 2003: 204). In an article much quoted in legal literature on asylum, Lord Bingham (1985: 14; quoted in *Kasolo*) denounced judicial application of 'reasonable man' tests to persons of different cultural backgrounds:

> No judge worth his salt could possibly assume that men of different nationalities, educations, trades, experience, creeds and temperaments would act . . . in accordance with his concept of what a reasonable man would have done.

Even so, many RFRLs assert that asylum claims lack credibility because applicants' accounts of their own behaviour, or that of the authorities in their

---

5   For my own strategy regarding Sri Lankan sources, see Good (2003b).

home countries, appear implausible to immigration officers or IND caseworkers, in whose view 'the sensible persecutor or sensible victim would have done things differently' (Henderson 1997: 48). It is common, therefore, for experts to be asked to comment from this angle on particular statements in an RFRL.

In addition to general assertions about the Convention or the legal definition of persecution – which are beyond the remit of country experts, who address them at their peril – RFRLs also contain country-specific standard paragraphs, making assertions about government policy regarding human rights breaches; the safety of other parts of the country; or the implausibility of the applicant's account of how they managed to flee undetected. Such assertions are hard for appellants to counter purely through their own testimony, which may be attacked as self-serving. Moreover, if their representatives argue such matters with reference to Amnesty or State Department reports, HOPOs almost invariably respond that those are general documents making no specific reference to this particular case.

One role of an expert report, therefore, is to link this general material to the appellant's personal circumstances, by showing how human rights abuses detailed in that general material have impacted, or might in future impact, on persons such as the appellant. Expert evidence that a government has not taken proper steps to combat human rights abuses by its security forces, or that its attempts to do so have failed, may support the claim of a well-founded fear. Similarly, expert evidence may demonstrate how easily asylum applicants can leave the country by using false documents, bribing officials, or hiring agents. Elsewhere (Good 2003a) I have examined country-specific standard paragraphs commonly used in RFRLs to Sri Lankans during 2001, and the kinds of evidence which can be deployed in expert reports when – as is frequently the case – such paragraphs contain tendentious or irrelevant assertions. At that time, for example, many RFRL compilers seemed unaware that Tamils and Tamil-speaking Muslims were distinct groups affected quite differently by the ethnic conflict. Since then the issues have changed, but Refusal Letters are as prone as ever to overstatement and simplification.

It is an expert's duty to assess evidence in balanced fashion, based on their general knowledge of the countries and contexts concerned, and to draw attention to any other evidence that might support the applicant's account (or not), or call into question (or not) assertions in the RFRL or prior appeal determination. In doing so, however, experts often tread a fine line between assessing evidence and engaging in advocacy. When appraising claimants' accounts they are meant to assess coherence, consistency, and plausibility rather than credibility or truth, though that distinction is often clearer in principle than in practice (see §8.4). Although experts rarely have to defend their conclusions in open court, they are well advised to limit themselves to opinions they would feel confident of being able to justify – in terms of legal, not academic criteria – under cross-examination (§9.5).

Chapter 7

Interpretation

> But doesn't the adversary system for producing recordable facts and durable judgments assume a mediating culture surrounding its theatrical confrontations? [W]hat if this shared culture and its common sense assumptions are precisely what is at issue in the proceedings?
>
> (Clifford 1988: 329)

Asylum hearings nearly always straddle cultural and linguistic divides in precisely the way envisaged by Clifford. Yet even though anthropologists are, according to one very influential view, first and foremost interpreters of cultures (Geertz 1973), the instructions they receive are usually concerned more with exploring the histories and polities of applicants' countries of origin than with eliciting insights into their particular cultural backgrounds. By contrast, virtually every asylum hearing requires interpretation in a narrower and more literal sense, via the participating expertise of a court interpreter. Their role, too, should be seen as fitting within the scope of this book; in the US, indeed, Federal Rule of Evidence No. 604 specifies that interpreters are subject to precisely the same qualifying rules as experts. This chapter therefore looks at the lacunae which the need for linguistic and cultural interpretation inserts into the asylum process. It examines both the translation of oral statements from one language to another during interviews and hearings, and the broader kinds of cultural interpretation which asylum claims often require but all too rarely receive.

7.1 INTERPRETERS IN THE ASYLUM PROCESS

Section 192 (iv) of the UNHCR *Handbook* (1992) states that asylum applicants 'should be given the ... services of a competent interpreter', and indeed, most asylum applicants are utterly dependent upon the skills of interpreters, as they undergo screening interviews with Immigration Officers and lengthy substantive interviews with IND caseworkers; meet their solicitors to fill out SEF questionnaires and provide written statements; undergo examinations by doctors or psychiatrists; have pre-hearing conferences with their barristers; and are examined and cross-examined at the hearing itself.

The interpreter's role is complex and demanding, as we shall see, and entails far more than 'mere' translation. Whereas the US, Canada, and Australia introduced formal accreditation procedures for court interpreters from the 1970s onwards (Mikkelson 1998; no date, b), their role receives astonishingly little acknowledgment in British courts. There is even less in the way of legislation or formal rules governing their conduct. Despite the increasingly multilingual character of the population of England and Wales, the Civil Procedure Rules, introduced as recently as 1999, mention interpreters only in the context of Welsh language (Lord Chancellor's Department, no date), and until recently, police and courts were merely encouraged but not legally required to use interpreters from the National Register of Public Service Interpreters or similar lists (Colin and Morris 1996: 78). What is more, the IAA's otherwise comprehensive *Notes for Adjudicators* (Deans 2000) say nothing about dealing with interpreters, though it is by no means unknown for their competence to be questioned.

The IAA hires official interpreters for asylum hearings directly on a self-employed piecework basis. They must be British nationals or entitled to work in the UK. They are paid by the hour, and the adjudicator signs a form at the end of the hearing, confirming its duration. The IAA (2002) asserts that its interpreters are interviewed, briefed, trained, and assessed through role plays and simultaneous translation tests, before actually being used in court. It uses agency interpreters too, however, and here requirements may be less stringent. In any case, because asylum claimants speak an astonishing range of languages and dialects, there may be only a tiny field of potential interpreters to choose from. Consequently, many interpreters have little training and speak strongly idiomatic or disjointed English. Things rarely seem as bad as in the American instance described by Daniel (1996: 180–1), but there is ample scope for applicants to be severely disadvantaged.

The IAA's initial attempt to produce guidelines for interpreters, in 1993, was heavily criticised: it 'deals in detail with late arrival by interpreters, failure to appear and working hours [but there] is no reference to any attempt to screen interpreters on the grounds of political or other bias and the document is silent on the subject of interpreting skills and experience' (Colin and Morris 1996: 65–6). Its subsequent handbook for interpreters (IAA 2003), too, deals mainly with conditions of employment rather than legal processes, but does at least specify that interpreters must 'be impartial to all parties' and 'not have links with any government, political party or organisation that could affect the fairness of the Court Service' (IAA 2002). However they can, and often do, work in Home Office asylum interviews too (§7.2).

At appeal hearings, if no interpreter was requested beforehand or the appellant earlier expressed a wish to give evidence in English, adjudicators are entitled to judge for themselves whether interpretation is needed in the interests of justice (*Cavasoglu*). That apart, it is entirely a matter for appellants and their representatives whether oral evidence is given through an interpreter. That same IAT decision recognises that even appellants with good conversational English may prefer the security of an interpreter in the pressurised setting of a courtroom; adjudicators should not express views on the matter nor, by implication, should adverse inferences be drawn. In practice, virtually every asylum appeal does involve an interpreter.[1]

Interpreters in Canadian immigration courts take oaths requiring them to interpret or translate accurately (Barsky 1994: 60). There is a printed form of words in many British hearing rooms, too, for interpreters to use if required to affirm, but most adjudicators seemed unaware even of its existence. It would be odd, of course, if interpreters were put under oath when asylum applicants themselves are not (§5.2.1).

Interpretation at Home Office interviews and in IAA courts overwhelmingly involves 'consecutive' rather than 'simultaneous' interpretation. Interpreters translate questions and comments directed at asylum applicants, and translate back their replies. They should first listen to the question in full, and translate it, then listen to the answer in full, and translate back. Interpreters may not be equally proficient at translating in both directions, but even if they are, these are demanding and complex processes, all the more so because they must be performed off-the-cuff, with no opportunity for editing or second thoughts. There are, however, aspects of such stylised dialogues which slightly ease their task, and even provide them with a degree of, generally unacknowledged, power to control the course of proceedings.

In ordinary conversations, 'allocational rules minimise gaps and overlaps' and 'repair sequences' exist for dealing with ' "breakdowns" in the "one at a time" system' (Atkinson and Drew 1979: 41). It cannot be predicted who will talk next, and although ideally people speak one at a time, this is not always the case. Interviews and court hearings are structured to avoid such problems, however. Above all, conversation is restricted to two parties, for whom '*turn order is fixed*, as is the *type of turn* which each speaker's talk constitutes' (1979: 61; original italics). The interviewer or HOPO utters a question to which the witness supplies an answer, leading to another question, and so on; these sequences are not 'locally-managed' like normal conversations, but 'provided for by courtroom procedures' (1979: 65). Cross-examination seeks

---

1 This right is not unlimited, however. When a group of Thai-speakers demanded to be interviewed in Pali, the ancient religious language of Buddhism, the New Zealand courts decided that claimants could not refuse to proceed with interviews in their own first languages, nor even in languages in which they were 'sufficiently proficient', where the latter was the only practical option (*Refugee Appeal 72752/01*).

to 'build up the facts *progressively*' and 'get the witness's agreement to those facts', the ultimate aim being 'to challenge or blame the witness' (1979: 105, 106; original italics). In a monolingual court, questions and answers are moulded by expectations over what the interlocutor will say next. For example, counsel expects that any accusation will be followed by a denial, and tries to turn that expectation to advantage: 'the accusation may be constructed so that a simple "flat denial" can be seen to be unsuccessful' (1979: 114). One crucial element is counsel's '*selection of descriptions*' (1979: 106; original italics) so as to create contexts in which witnesses are ensnared merely by responding, whatever the factual contents of those responses. Witnesses themselves, however, may anticipate where this is leading, and give 'qualified' answers designed to nullify the next accusation (1979: 116). These include 'hedging' when making potentially damaging admissions (Berk-Seligson 2002: 179; Danet 1980: 525); thus, the illocutionary force of a simple 'yes' answer may be mitigated by responding 'well, I suppose so'.

Such hegemonic forms of discourse are harder to sustain when basic communication requires the use of an interpreter. This disrupts normal turn-taking processes in both gross and subtle ways. It removes some of the 'controlling power' normally held by the examining lawyer (Berk-Seligson 2002: 145), and gives limited power to interpreters themselves, through the practical control they exert over turn-taking.

On the other hand, interpreters are generally compelled to act complicitly as regards the 'silent actors' present at every hearing, namely, 'the legal concepts that govern the allocation of refugee status'. In general, an applicant 'simply has no idea of the legal significance attributed to her answers and, therefore, she cannot properly represent herself'. The interpreter, debarred from explaining this context, is left uncomfortably placed as ' "piggy in the middle" in a linguistic exchange where interviewers mean more than what they say, and the applicant digs her own hole by answering literally to questions whose larger contextual meaning she is ignorant about' (quotations from Rycroft 2005). Concerning internal relocation (§4.2.2), for example:

> the ubiquitous question is: 'Have you tried to move to a different part of Romania?' Many applicants say 'No, there would have been no point.' And the discussion on relocation ends right there. The fact that applicants did not attempt to relocate will count against them, although, had they known where the question was aiming, they may have explained that in Romania the police keep centralized records, and that in order to move away one has to request a residence visa from the police. Therefore, someone fleeing the police can hardly be expected to approach them for a visa. [The] gap in comprehension is played out in relevant questions that go unasked and explanations that are not proffered (Rycroft 2005).

As previously noted, interpreters are always expert witnesses of a kind,[2] whose collective influence on asylum processes far exceeds that of acknowledged experts. Occasionally, though, interpreters figure more explicitly as experts. They may be asked about the level of mutual comprehension between speakers of different dialects, or to assess whether a particular appellant is really of the claimed nationality. It is especially common (so IND allege) for Kenyans to masquerade as Somalis. In *Hydir*, the HOPO sought a brief adjournment to allow him to call a Somali speaker as an expert witness. When the hearing resumed there was a second interpreter, Mr Abas Hatimy, also provided by the Court Service but as a Home Office witness. The HOPO asked the appellant to render a few simple phrases in Somali, then asked Mr Hatimy whether in his opinion Mr Hydir was from Somalia. Astonishingly, none of this was objected to by Hydir's counsel, but Mr Hatimy himself questioned whether it was appropriate for him to answer, as an employee of the Court Service. On being assured by the adjudicator that it was, he said that he thought Mr Hydir came from Kenya. In his final submission, counsel argued that Mr Hatimy should not be regarded as an expert witness, and the tribunal agreed, noting that 'the Home Office should come to a hearing with the expert witnesses it wishes to call. . . . It is not appropriate to rely on Court Service interpreters to give experts' opinions.'

7.2 INTERPRETATION PROBLEMS

Applicants face considerable difficulties when it comes to substantiating problems with interpretation during asylum interviews. Much the same applies to appeal hearings, where even complaints made at the time may be rejected.

The procedure at Home Office asylum interviews, until recently, was for the interpreter to read out the transcript at the end, back-translating the questions and answers for the benefit of the applicant. The applicant would then sign the transcript to confirm its accuracy, and the interpreter would sign to confirm that this process had been followed. In practice, however, transcripts were not always read back, and applicants sometimes signed out of acquiescence to perceived authority rather than acceptance of their accuracy. As there is usually no independent check on the quality of interpretation at asylum interviews, it is very hard for applicants to prove that errors occurred. Legal representatives sometimes take along independent interpreters to monitor the process (Henderson 2003: 133), but for financial reasons that generally does not happen, and in any case, because IND sees the

---

2   'an interpreter can be the most dangerous of expert witnesses' (Judge Adrian Head; www.expertsearch.co.uk/head.html, consulted 19 February 2002).

presence of representatives and interpreters at these interviews as a 'concession', and creates obstacles to their participation (§5.1), applicants are greatly restricted in their ability to draw attention to problems. Interviewing officers always stipulate that any such objections must, like solicitors' comments, be left until the end – even though, as two experienced interpreters point out, inaccurate or incomplete interpretation casts doubt on the entire interview (Colin and Morris 1996: 64). From late 2002 onwards, IND staff were no longer required even to read transcripts back, so many representatives now advise clients not to sign them.

At the time of my research, the written transcript was the only record which existed, as interviews were not tape-recorded. Solicitors acting for *Mapah*, a French-speaking Cameroonian, had sought judicial review when their request to tape his asylum interview was refused as contrary to Home Office policy (though it emerged that the Home Office themselves had been trying this out in a pilot study). The Home Office argued that applicants had opportunities to challenge the written record through their solicitors; that the training of interviewing officers, and the protocols they followed, ensured that they acted fairly; that IND staff and adjudicators were duty bound to consider complaints; and that any failings would be corrected by higher courts. The court found that IND was acting lawfully in prohibiting applicants from recording their own interviews, and that sufficient safeguards existed to ensure that the process was fair. In 2005, however, following the introduction of restrictions on legal aid, the Court of Appeal declared it unlawful for IND to prohibit the taping of asylum interviews, whenever applicants could not afford the presence of their own interpreters or legal representatives (*Dirshe*; see §5.1).

Whenever asylum applicants are required to tell their harrowing stories, it is important to create a sympathetic atmosphere (Fox 2001). If they feel they are not being understood, this hardly inspires confidence. Nor is it just a matter of technical competence; Home Office interpreters may use familiar rather than polite modes of address in asylum interviews, belittling asylum applicants and disadvantaging them in ways to which the interviewer and even their own solicitor are oblivious (Colin and Morris 1996: 61). Even competent, well-intentioned interpreters may be unable to overcome the suspicions harboured by applicants, however. Paradoxically, the closer their own background to that of the applicant, the more they may be suspected of being informers for the authorities back home, or purveyors of unwelcome gossip.

In court, too, effective interpretation is crucial to the achieving of a fair outcome, yet unless things go obviously wrong, courts tend to view interpreters as mere translation machines who do not exist as distinct participants in their own right during judicial proceedings (Berk-Seligson 1990: 156; 2002: 54). Other aspects of proceedings compound the difficulties inherent in interpretation. For example, interpreters' textbooks stress advance preparation and use of reference books (Colin and Morris 1996: 18), but in asylum courts, as things stand, this would be impossible to put into practice. When interpreters arrive at hearing centres they know nothing about the cases in which they will be acting, or any special issues involved. They receive no advance briefing and almost never see copies of any documents, such as statements or country reports, referred to in cross-examination. It is important to remember, too, that interpreters are translating a highly specialised form of speech, distinctive not only in its technical vocabulary but also its dialogic structure. They are often required to translate discussions about matters remote from their personal life experience, or couched in professional jargon. Quite apart from linguistic fluency, interpreters should ideally be conversant with legal terminology in both countries. Even then it seems unlikely that such niceties as the differences between being 'detained', 'arrested', and 'charged' are directly translatable from one legal system to another, though the seemingly interchangeable ways in which these particular words are used in asylum hearings may reflect appellants', rather than interpreters', lack of understanding of legal terms.

All these factors seriously inhibit the interpreter's ability to translate clearly and accurately, but they by no means exhaust possible problems. 'Consecutive' interpretation, to work well, makes demands on the principal interlocutors too. One very basic point is that examination and cross-examination should be addressed to the appellant in the first person, not to the interpreter. Similarly, the interpreter should be the appellant's mouthpiece, speaking their words directly in the first rather than third person. That is, questions should begin 'Did you . . .?' rather than 'Did he or she . . .?', and answers should be in the form 'I . . .' rather than 'he or she says that . . .' (Berg-Seligson 2002: 60–1). Barristers are generally much more skilled at this than HOPOs, but they do suffer lapses, and even adjudicators sometimes nod. As in American courts (2002: 63), such lapses are most common when some hitch arises which seems attributable to a non-English speaker's failure to understand.

Moreover, representatives' questions should be concise and clearly structured. Once again barristers are generally far better at this than HOPOs, some of whom seem incapable of formulating questions without complex strings of conditional clauses. These may be particularly problematic; for example, English-speaking Tamils (including interpreters) typically use the words 'would', 'could' and 'should' differently from speakers of standard English. Problems often arise with 'who, where, why' questions, too, because many appellants initially respond with yes/no answers rather than substantive responses (Berk-Seligson 2002: 63); and with passive tenses, which may 'result in the misassigning of agents to verbs' (2002: 137).

Problems seem even more likely in connection with appellants' responses. Some of the same issues arise; for example, appellants nearly always address replies to interpreters rather than the court, through inexperience. They are less likely to use technical jargon, but passive constructions do often play a crucial role because in many languages, as in English, they are used as blame avoidance mechanisms. For example, 'I was detained' is less likely to provoke further questions about the detainers than 'They detained me' (cf. Berk-Seligson 2002: 105), but who is to tell whether this effect was produced (or negated) by the interpreter's choice of how to render the response into English? Such subliminal matters may seem trivial in themselves, but the cumulative effect could be crucial. To guard against this, interpreters need to give, as closely as possible, 'the same impression' as the speaker would have produced had there been no language barrier, including stumbles, false starts, moods and demeanour (Colin and Morris 1996: 91). Problems tend to be magnified by the fact that answers usually have to be longer than the questions which provoke them, yet appellants may be under pressure – depending on the strictness of the adjudicator – to reply sentence-by-sentence rather than in continuous narrative.

However skilled the interpreter, appellants are never fully aware of what is happening in court. Interpreters should supposedly 'provide simultaneous whispered interpretation' while a discussion is taking place, as well as consecutive interpreting of questions and answers (IAA 2002), but in fact this never happened fully in any hearing I attended. The normal situation (Colin and Morris 1996: 65), is that appellants only receive translations of direct questions to them, not of discussions on procedure or evidence. Even closing submissions are generally not translated. Some interpreters do this of their own volition, but I have even heard adjudicators ask them to stop, presumably because it is distracting. It is very much the exception rather than the rule for adjudicators to specifically request simultaneous translation, though even that falls short of the principles established for criminal cases by *R* v. *Lee Kun* (1996: 65). The first time I saw an adjudicator do this, I was so struck by its positive impact that I commented on it afterwards. She said she was following a recent practice direction, and that adjudicators had often avoided doing so previously because of the time taken and the difficulties caused for interpreters.[3]

Despite all these potential problems, appeals based upon interpretation problems still stand little chance of success, especially if no concerns were expressed at the time. In *Iqbal* it was claimed that the cumulative effect of interpretation faults when the case was before the adjudicator amounted to 'material prejudice'. The subsequent tribunal therefore considered what had happened in some detail. Although the initial complainant had been a relative of the appellant with no interpreting qualifications, the adjudicator had taken it seriously. He had directed the appellant's representative to prepare an affidavit of complaints which he considered next day with a different

---

3   Good practice requires that interpreters receive a ten-minute break when asked to switch modes (Colin and Morris 1996: 98), but I have never heard this requested or awarded in asylum hearings.

interpreter. The most serious complaint was particularly revealing of how court procedure may impact adversely on appellants. The interpreter was accused of having 'missed out altogether the Appellant's allegation that he was "stripped, hung upside down and beaten until he was unconscious" '. What had happened, however, was that after the appellant spoke these words, the adjudicator stopped him and asked him to repeat his answer in shorter passages so it could be properly translated. When repeating his account he did not mention this incident, so it was not translated. The adjudicator decided, reasonably enough, that the interpreter could not be blamed for this.

The tribunal concluded that the adjudicator had been right to continue with the hearing, and that his conclusions should stand. 'Interpretation,' they said, 'is not an exact science and different people will translate the same comment in different ways.' There was 'no discernible error' on the adjudicator's part, and it could not be right that 'the mere fact of a complaint about an interpreter must per se lead to a hearing being aborted'. Yet this potentially crucial omission would never have come to light had the complaint not been made. It is also noteworthy that adjudicator and tribunal turned a complaint about failings in the *process* of interpretation resulting from court procedure, into one about the adequacy of the *interpreter*, who was exonerated. While the adjudicator was doubtless justified in proceeding once the problem had been identified, the fact remains that its direct cause was his insistence on shorter replies. Interpreters themselves stress the importance of translating complete uninterrupted answers whenever possible, since 'If an interpreter asks a witness to proceed sentence by sentence, then the interpreter is potentially interfering with the evidence' (Colin and Morris 1996: 91); yet sentence-by-sentence translation is stipulated in the IAA Guidelines and, as here, often insisted on by adjudicators. Experienced tribunal chairs, one may surmise, tend to take that for granted, having made many similar interventions themselves in the past, yet these pragmatic aspects of procedure are unfair if they allow vital evidence to slip away. After all, the appellant *had* described his torture and was almost certainly unaware that this had never been translated.

If such complaints are not made until after the event, they generally receive even shorter shrift. As one tribunal remarked:

> it ill-behoves the Appellant . . . to raise an issue as fundamental as that of the language used in interpreting both his replies to questions at interview and at the hearing before the Adjudicator. Ample opportunity existed for such objections to be raised during the interview, during the two year period that elapsed between the interview and the hearing, and at the hearing itself (*Zohouli*).

Moges, an Ethiopian case, illustrates just how much evidence is needed to overturn a decision on grounds of questionable interpretation. Several doubts were raised by counsel during the hearing, based on signals from the appellant's brothers, but the adjudicator asked clarifying questions and satisfied himself as to what the appellant meant to say. He also established that the interpreter was very experienced. He announced that he would tolerate no further signals from the back of the court and would clear the room if they continued. However, he then made a negative credibility finding in his determination, because he had found the appellant's answers evasive. At the tribunal hearing, counsel produced a list of instances of misinterpretation taken from her own notes at the hearing, and statements from four others present in court, including several solicitors and barristers. The tribunal expressed sympathy for the adjudicator's dilemma, but said he ought to have adjourned the hearing rather than risk an obvious appeal by pressing on (see the Lithuanian case below).

In *Davidhi*, a Kosovan appellant claimed to have had problems understanding the interpreters (both Albanian nationals) at his asylum interview and appeal hearing. The IAA sought clarification from an expert at Salford University, who responded that: 'The Albanian language spoken in Kosovo can be readily understood by any native Albanian, and vice versa: any native of Kosovo can readily understand Albanian.' Faced with this, counsel had no option but to withdraw this ground of appeal. For good measure, the tribunal added an 'unanswerable' argument from personal experience, akin to the 'clinical gaze' stance discussed earlier (§2.2):

> The two of us have a good many years' experience between us of oral hearings before adjudicators, with evidence taken through interpreters. Our experience suggests that, if there is any real problem with interpretation, that all too rapidly becomes obvious to everyone present. It is clear that . . . this was not the case here.

Despite this received wisdom it is actually quite common for Kosovan Albanians to claim such difficulties, and interpreters occasionally agree.[4] The most prolonged problem I observed (HX/61700/2000) began with a hiatus, awaiting the arrival of an interpreter from Swan Street, a 'satellite court' specialising in Kosovan cases. The usher then arrived with Interpreter 1; he was not the person originally booked, but the usher had found him in the building, his scheduled case having finished early. The adjudicator checked that he and the appellant understood one another, and the hearing began. Almost immediately, however, the usher reappeared with Interpreter 2, the woman originally booked for this hearing. The adjudicator excused

---

4   Left to themselves, however, many interpreters soldier on regardless. Admitting to problems may seem to reflect adversely on their competence, and impacts on their fee, as they are paid by the hour.

Interpreter 1, with profuse apologies, and checked that Interpreter 2 and the appellant understood one another. During examination-in-chief, however, problems become apparent:

Counsel:	At any time, were you a member of the LDK?
Appellant:	I took part in demonstrations, and my father was member.
Counsel:	The grounds of appeal say you were a 'full and active member', correct?
Appellant:	That is correct, maybe I didn't clarify.
Adjudicator:	Where is this, page 40?
Counsel:	This was a solicitor's error; the appellant is confirming he was not a full and active member. He says this is incorrect –
HOPO:	He is saying it is *correct* now!
Counsel:	Can you confirm whether you were a member or just a supporter? Does he understand the question?
Interpreter 2:	I don't think so, may I clarify? (Repeats the question.)
Appellant:	I have been a member, but mostly participated in demonstrations.
Counsel:	Your earlier statement suggests that your father was a member, but you were not.
Appellant:	That is correct.
Counsel:	*What* is correct?
Adjudicator:	Perhaps the problem is, what does he mean by 'being a member'?
Counsel:	This is becoming more confusing; were you ever a card-carrying activist for the LDK?
Appellant:	I have been but not that much, but my father was a member.
Counsel:	Were you a member or supporter of the KLA?
Appellant:	Haven't been member; have been a supporter, and was followed by police, up to point that couldn't support any more. (Pause)
Interpreter 2:	He wants another interpreter if possible, as he doesn't understand. I am Albanian Albanian, and he is Kosovan; is difficult for me too.

Interpreter 2 was permitted to leave. She went out saying that she knew of another interpreter in the building. As everyone waited, counsel confirmed to the adjudicator that he was happy to accept the formal part of proceedings thus far, but would want to revisit the membership issue. The adjudicator and HOPO discussed ways of reorganising the day's list, as the adjudicator had to finish early to attend the Chief Adjudicator's farewell dinner. Counsel in a later case looked in to say that Interpreter 3 had already left the building for lunch, so the adjudicator adjourned.

When he returned, Interpreter 3 was present and the membership issue was immediately clarified. The appellant explained that he himself was only a supporter of the LDK and KLA, but his father was an actual member of the LDK. Thereafter the hearing proceeded with no evident problems. It is ironic that of the three interpreters used, problems arose only with the one officially booked for the hearing.

By contrast another Kosovan specifically *requested* an Albanian interpreter, because he wished to give evidence that he had collaborated with the Serbs (*'AT'*). He was ashamed to admit this before a fellow Kosovan, and frightened lest it became widely known. The interpreter at the hearing proved to be Kosovan after all, through administrative error, and when the adjudicator refused an adjournment request, AT refused to give evidence. On this ground, among others, the adjudicator found him not credible. The tribunal decided that the adjudicator had been wrong to refuse an adjournment, as the interpretation request had been made properly, well in advance.

As here, problems may stem from regional dialects or accents. For example, there are often difficulties when Egyptian interpreters are used in appeals by North Africans, though both ostensibly speak Arabic. The authorities also often provide Urdu speakers when Punjabi was requested, or vice versa. Even if interpreter and appellant speak the same dialect, comprehension problems may arise because of differences in generation, social status, or gender. Interpreters have generally been in the UK for some time and may be out of touch with political events or current slang back 'home'. For example, many Tamil interpreters are middle-aged men or women who arrived in the UK in the 1970s or earlier, before the ethnic conflict got underway. The stories told by the traumatised young people for whom they interpret, played out against a backdrop of ruined buildings, military checkpoints, torture, and death, must seem utterly remote from the cultured, cosmopolitan Jaffna of their own childhood. I once heard an appellant try to describe a visit received while in detention, but the interpreter could not understand the words he used; it transpired that he had been using the Tamil phrase for 'International Committee of the Red Cross'.

Adjudicators' decisions to proceed or adjourn when interpretation problems arise are regarded as 'procedural issues' because they may affect natural justice (*Gashi*), yet in practice it is almost impossible for adjudicators to assess the quality of interpretation. The interpreter concerned is hardly an unbiased witness, and there is generally no-one else in court able to judge. The position is particularly difficult when objections come only from one side. Adjudicators must take into account the stage in the proceedings when they are made, and the reliability and expertise of the objectors (*Raza*). If the impugned interpreter has to be questioned directly, this should be done in the presence of both sides (*Kutukcu*).

Solicitors sometimes provide their own interpreters at hearings, so counsel can confer with appellants beforehand. Sometimes these interpreters sit in court and very occasionally they alert counsel to problems with interpretation. One dramatic example arose in the appeal of a young Lithuanian woman who claimed to have been threatened, to persuade her to give false evidence in a trial (HX/61706/2000). There was quite a crowd at the hearing. The appellant was accompanied by a friend, and – most unusually – by the solicitor who had prepared the appeal. She told me it was her first asylum case and she wanted to witness it. In view of later events, this may have been somewhat disingenuous.

A bearded man (Mr K) was sitting next to counsel (Ms A), who interrupted cross-examination several times following stage whispers by Mr K. For example, the official interpreter (Mrs S) referred to 'a case' against the appellant, which Ms A claimed was not accurate. After several such interruptions, the adjudicator complained about the noise Mr K was making, and became still more annoyed when Mr K interrupted him to claim that Mrs S was asking additional questions:

Adjudicator:	(To Mrs S) Please translate very carefully without putting supplementary questions, even if it doesn't make sense. (To Mr K) And you, sir, please keep quiet, and if any problems arise pass a note to Ms A. (To Mrs S) Please ask the appellant if she is happy with the interpreter.
Appellant:	Yes.
Adjudicator:	(to Counsel) Just who is this gentleman?

Mr K risked further anger by butting in to reveal that he was a teacher from the Institute of Linguists, who also sometimes acted as court interpreter. Furthermore, he had examined Mrs S when she qualified three years earlier! The HOPO resumed questioning. Counsel soon claimed another fault in interpretation; the appellant had said a warehouse was 'broken into', not 'burgled' as Mrs S rendered it. She almost immediately intervened again to say that the HOPO's next question was confusing; it could be construed as referring to the appellant's unfair dismissal case rather than the earlier hearing. 'She is not confusing *me*!' retorted the adjudicator. 'The Presenting Officer has not mentioned the unfair dismissal case yet.'

Counsel interrupted again; the appellant had not said that she 'was taken' to the Ministry, she had said that she 'went'. The adjudicator was getting exasperated, and cautioned Mrs S: 'Be careful, you can see what is happening here!' Mrs S sought and received the adjudicator's permission to ask the appellant to speak more loudly and clearly. It emerged that the appellant first came to the UK for three days on a package tour, but did not claim asylum. She then returned two months later. While this was being established there was continual whispering and exchanging of notes between Mr K and counsel.

Finally the HOPO challenged her directly: 'Is my friend happy with the interpreter? There is no point going ahead if she is just setting things up for an appeal on grounds of interpretation.' Counsel asked to take instructions from her client, and the adjudicator rose for five minutes. Counsel went outside with the appellant. When they returned, counsel mouthed silently to the HOPO, 'She's not happy.' When the adjudicator returned, counsel requested a brief discussion, so he cleared the court apart from counsel and the HOPO. We all stood about outside. Mr K led Mrs S off to an empty hearing room, a 'paternal' arm around her shoulder. She looked tearful on return. Mr K justified himself to me; the only reason more solicitors did not do this, he claimed, was the cost; they had to pay an independent interpreter the full daily rate of £134. We were called back to hear the adjudicator announce that he was abandoning the hearing in the interests of justice. It would be listed again with a different interpreter – 'and not Mr K either!', he added.

There seems little doubt this was a premeditated 'ambush' by counsel, in order to secure an adjournment. Whether the interpretation really *was* significantly inadequate is impossible to say, but clearly the adjudicator had little choice. It would have been pointless to continue because, as the HOPO pointed out, had he gone ahead with the hearing and found against the appellant, an appeal on grounds of faulty interpretation would have been inevitable. If a tribunal later found that interpretation had indeed been unsatisfactory, the evidence would have to be taken again, so even if the initial adjudicator had found the appellant credible the case would have been remitted to be heard *de novo* by a fresh adjudicator, in case there were material facts which the appellant had been unable to put across (*Mustafa*).

Whatever counsel's motives here, it is clearly vital that genuine problems are brought to official attention, because inadequate interpretation can drastically affect an applicant's apparent credibility. This is best done at the hearing itself and as early as possible. The IAT has, however, recognised that representatives may occasionally only become aware of problems afterwards, perhaps through someone present in court who had no right of audience there (*Kaygun*). In *Raza*, an appeal did succeed on the basis of a complaint not made until after the hearing, and by a relative of the appellant to boot, but circumstances were unusual as the complainant was a British policeman!

7.3 THE IMPACT OF INTERPRETERS ON ASYLUM HEARINGS

The expectation in British and North American law is that court interpreters will give verbatim translations of whatever is said by each speaker (Berk-Seligson 2002: 65). Indeed, courts tend to apply rule-of-thumb distinctions between 'translation', seen as 'an acceptable word-for-word activity', and the 'interpretation' of what is said, which is the prerogative of lawyers (Colin and Morris 1996: 17). Mikkelson (no date a) describes this as 'a pervasive myth within the judiciary', and it is frequently pointed out by interpreters themselves that whereas courts tend to assume that literal translations are also accurate ones, in fact verbatim translation, strictly adhered to, produces 'distorted communication' (Colin and Morris 1996: 17). Although some courts now give interpreters scope to employ 'functional equivalence and meaning-based translation' (Mikkelson, no date a), interpreters still commonly feel that the constraints placed on their role by legal processes limit their ability to facilitate communication. For example, Morris concludes that:

> Legal practitioners, whose own performance, like that of translators and interpreters, relies on the effective use and manipulation of language, were found to deny interpreters the same latitude in understanding and expressing concepts that they themselves enjoy (1995: 26).

That does not mean that interpreters wish to stray beyond their primary role of facilitating communication. All respondents in a survey of court interpreters in New Zealand 'understood their role to be strictly that of interpreting and were adamant about keeping it this way' (Fenton, no date). They rejected Barsky's plea for interpreters to be 'legally recognized as active intermediaries between the claimant and the adjudicating body' (1996: 46), who could help compensate for asylum applicants' unfamiliarity with legal process by actively advising them and eliciting more information. This proposal was described as 'dangerous and unsafe', and a potential 'violation of their professional ethics'. The key dilemma therefore, from the court interpreters' perspective, is how to achieve high standards of communication without professionally and legally inappropriate lapses into the role of advocate.

Interpreters are not witnesses either, so should not volunteer clarifications or be asked to give evidence. This is a tricky matter, though, because they can sometimes nip confusion in the bud by transgressing these limits. The following extreme example arose in an Iranian case (HX/05528/2001). The adjudicator was unusually tolerant, perhaps because he realised that counsel was very badly briefed (he had complained to me beforehand about the incompetence of his instructing solicitors):

Counsel:	What was your occupation in Iran in the 1970s?
Interpreter:	Before the revolution?
Counsel:	Yes.
Appellant:	I was the deputy head of the gendarmerie.
Counsel:	Is that the police or army?
Interpreter:	No, was police force. There was the army, and the gendarmerie were the police.
Counsel:	And that was in the 1970s . . .?

Interpreter: Sorry, did I mention name of town, K–?
Adjudicator: Is it in the statement?
Counsel: So just before the revolution, what was your position?
Appellant: I was in charge of communications, but at same time deputy to Commander X's division of the gendarmerie.
Counsel: I would like you to clarify, because in your statement you mentioned you were in the army as a major?
Appellant: Was the gendarmerie.
Counsel: What was your rank?
Appellant: Major.
Counsel: We all know there was a revolution in the middle of 1978; what happened to you?
Interpreter: Sorry, revolution was 1979; your question was, what happened to him afterwards?
Counsel: Yes.
Appellant: Because I was in charge of the forces opposing revolutionary demonstrations and activities, and when Khomeini came to Iran a few months before date of revolution, most officers went to local mullahs, local clergy.
Adjudicator: What?
Interpreter: Clergy.

(Counsel's mobile phone went off, to his intense embarrassment.)

Appellant: They declared their allegiance to Ayatollah Khomeini.
Interpreter: Changed sides.
Appellant: I was the only one who didn't do that.

A further issue was that this particular appellant kept bursting out with answers in English, before questions could be translated. This should not happen: if someone elects to use an interpreter, they are expected to do so throughout, not jump to and fro between languages. The reasons become obvious when one witnesses the disruption caused, particularly when the appellant's comprehension is poorer than they think. Here again, the interpreter sometimes usefully exceeded his brief:

Counsel: Were you arrested?
Appellant: Yes.
Counsel: What happened?
Appellant: Imprisoned for three months, then sentenced.
Counsel: What was the sentence?
Appellant: Originally sentenced to death by revolutionary judge.
Counsel: Clearly this was not carried out on you, were there others?
Appellant (in English): A Major was persecuted.
Interpreter: Sorry, he was using bad English; he means 'executed'.

Inevitably, though, the interventions of such a proactive interpreter are not always helpful. After the re-examination, there was some technical discussion between counsel and adjudicator before the HOPO began her final submission:

> *Interpreter* (interrupting):   Want me to translate verbatim or give him the gist?
>
> *Adjudicator*:   Well that's up to you, as long as it doesn't interfere with the flow.
>
> *Interpreter*:   Shall I tell him no decision today?

The interpreter was jumping the gun, because adjudicators normally do not state until right at the end whether they are reserving their decisions. However, his untimely intervention led the adjudicator, as if by reflex action, to launch quite prematurely and inappropriately into his standard homily about the decision-making process, which should of course come after he has heard closing submissions, not before. What is more, the irrepressible appellant then announced that he wanted to listen to the English himself without translation!

This hearing raised major questions over the interpreter's role. He clearly exceeded his remit by giving his own evidence and challenging particular facts or forms of words in questions. At one point he was asked to translate a document where the Home Office translation was in dispute; this in itself is somewhat irregular, and I am even less sure that it was proper for him to translate the document 'privately' to counsel, as he proceeded to do, before doing so to the court at large. Most adjudicators would have slapped all this down from the start. He did certainly prevent potential confusion on several occasions, over dates (below), the status of the gendarmerie, and so on, yet one felt he had his own 'take' on the issues – where did he stand politically? Was he an exiled dissident himself? – and it was impossible not to wonder whether he was doing more than just translate.

This was the most extreme instance of interpreter intervention that I observed. Because he interfered so openly with the form and content of questions and answers, and even the course of the hearing itself, the interpreter's potential for influencing the outcome became very clear. Moreover, I was aware only of the most obvious instances; I cannot say how his instantaneous choices of words in Farsi and English influenced the appellant's understanding of and responses to questions, and the court's reactions to those responses. This example provides a salutary reminder that although interpreters are usually treated by judges and lawyers as 'noise-free' channels of communication, in reality they exert powerful and usually unknowable influences on proceedings, and – perhaps – on the decisions reached.

7.4 CULTURAL (MIS)TRANSLATION

For claims under the 1951 Convention to be fairly evaluated, applicants' stories must be placed within their cultural, socio-economic, and historical contexts (UNHCR 1992: ¶42; Barsky 2000: 58). Standard documentary sources and expert evidence both play parts in establishing such contexts, and country experts too often find themselves in the position of having to explain, or explain away, culturally-specific differences in behaviour. This is an area where one might expect anthropologists to come fully into their own, though their role is normally limited to commenting on any such matters manifest in the documents in front of them when writing their reports. Even if they attend hearings to give oral evidence, the exigencies of procedure may prevent them from addressing fully, if at all, any cultural misunderstandings arising during the hearing itself.

Yet such misunderstandings are quite common (Kalin 1986). Some revolve around straightforward factual matters, capable of definitive resolution if the court has the necessary information, but they are important if allowed to stand because HOPOs seize on any apparent inconsistencies so as to call credibility into question. To illustrate how easily potentially damaging confusion may arise, consider the following discussion during evidence-in-chief in a Tamil appeal (HX/07085/2001):

> *Counsel*:   You described at your interview and in your statement that you were arrested a second time in Colombo. We have a document at pages 15–16 of the appellant's bundle, do you have the original of that with you in court today?
>
> *HOPO*:   Sorry, what page?
>
> *Counsel*:   15–16; and do you have the Tamil version which appears at pages 17–20?
>
> *Interpreter*: That is not Tamil . . . Sinhala!
>
> *Counsel*:   Right. This name which appears as number four, who is that person?
>
> *Appellant*:   That is me.
>
> *Adjudicator*: Can you explain why it is written Chelvan with a 'Ch'?
>
> *Interpreter*: Chelvan can be spelled either 'Che' or 'Se'; translator has used that.
>
> *Adjudicator*: I'm just checking what *he* said, not what you're saying!
>
> *Counsel*:   In your statement you have spelled your name 'Selvan'; is that the correct spelling?
>
> *Appellant*:   Yes.
>
> *Adjudicator*: Can I just . . . this page 15 relates to . . . which page is it a translation of; is it page 14 or have I lost the plot? I would like while we have the interpreter here, for you to tell me whether the name is the same as on the document, but you

don't do Sinhala do you? Is the name in the statement in
English and the name in Sinhala the same?

Interpreter: It would be 'Che–'.

The doubt over whether the person mentioned in the document was the
person now applying for asylum arose because of the need to transliterate,
not merely translate, when converting written Sinhala into written English
(and there had possibly been an initial transliteration from Tamil to Sinhala
by the official writing the document). The adjudicator sensibly – but probably
wrongly in terms of strict procedure – sought the advice of the interpreter,
who correctly pointed out that both spellings were variants of a single word
in Tamil and Sinhala.[5] One can well imagine, however, that doubts might have
been sown in the mind of a less pragmatic, more rule-bound adjudicator if
this seeming discrepancy had remained unaddressed.

The most common inconsistencies arising at asylum hearings concern
dates. Any vagueness on the appellant's part as to when particular events
took place – and even more so, any discrepancies between precise dates given
at interview, in their statement, to the doctor, in cross-examination, and so on
– is certain to be seized upon by the Home Office as damaging the credibility
of their account as a whole. The plausibility of such arguments varies; it *may*,
for example, be thought incredible for an appellant not to know the date of
birth of a close relative, the date of their own alleged marriage, or the date
they finally left their own country. Whether they can reasonably be expected
to remember the exact dates on which they were arrested or tortured, especially if this happened several times or long ago, is however a matter calling
for highly subjective judgments by the adjudicator. Introspection suggests
that exact dates are by no means always essential parts of our memories of
particular events that are otherwise recalled in some detail. There is also a
double bind element; too great a fluency with dates may well indicate memor-
isation rather than actual memory, suggesting that the applicant is telling a
learned (though not necessarily untrue) story, rather than actively remembering events during the hearing itself.

This is, moreover, a problem exacerbated by cultural differences. One com-
plication which courts rarely take into account – because few representatives
are well-enough informed to ask them to do so – is that many asylum applicants come from countries which do not follow the Gregorian calendar. Discrepancies over dates may therefore arise from inaccurate conversions of
dates into a calendar with which appellants may be unfamiliar. This was
perfectly exemplified in the appeal of a Tamil man (HX/11102/2001) heard
immediately before the Iranian appeal discussed above (§7.3), by the same

---

5 'Celvan' or 'Selvan' is a precise transliteration, while 'Chelvan' indicates normal
   pronunciation.

adjudicator and with the same HOPO. In fact, it was the chance juxtaposition of these two hearings that first raised in my mind many of the questions addressed in this chapter. Consider the following exchange during cross-examination:

HOPO: When did you arrive in Colombo?

Appellant: 21st September 99.

HOPO: In your interview, page A4, you say you went to Colombo in August 99?

Appellant: I went in August.

HOPO: Remember the date in August?

Appellant: 21st.

HOPO: So, 21st August 99?

(Untranslated dialogue between appellant and interpreter, involving use of the names of various Tamil months.)

Appellant: I went on 21st September 99.

HOPO: You've just said you went in August?

Appellant: I went in September.

HOPO: So can you explain why in your interview you said you went in August?

Appellant: Must have forgotten.

Adjudicator: There are language difficulties sometimes; can we ask if he is sure, we have had two conflicting dates?

HOPO: Are you sure?

Appellant: I left Colombo on 23rd September, so must have gone there on 21st September.

HOPO: I find it implausible that when you applied for asylum and had your interview a short time after arrival, you got the date wrong and said August?

Appellant: When I arrived here I was frightened.

HOPO: But only a week earlier you were in Colombo?

Appellant: I stayed in Colombo only one day.

HOPO: No, what I'm saying, you arrived in the UK in September when you claimed asylum?

Appellant: Yes.

HOPO: You are saying you arrived in Colombo on the 21st, but you were interviewed only eight days prior [sic] to your arrival in Colombo, surely you wouldn't make that mistake?

Appellant: Always had fear.

HOPO: Surely you wouldn't have made a mistake about an event only one week previously?

Appellant: Was frightened for my life, so must have given wrong date.

HOPO:	So how long did you stay in Colombo before leaving?
Adjudicator:	He has just answered that . . . approximately one day.
HOPO:	So you left next day?
Appellant:	23rd September morning, only one full day stayed in Colombo.

There is a very simple explanation for what happened here. Months in the Tamil luni-solar calendar are out of phase with those in the Gregorian calendar. Thus, the Tamil month of *Avani* begins in mid-August and ends in mid-September, although the exact Western dates differ each year. It only takes the Home Office interpreter to render *Avani* as 'August' at the asylum interview, and the court interpreter to translate it as 'September' during the hearing, and the HOPO can triumphantly provide the court with a credibility-damaging 'discrepancy', though there may have been no inconsistency whatever on the part of the hapless appellant.[6] In this instance, fortunately, the interpreter did some clarifying of his own with the appellant, though again he was technically exceeding his duties.

Confusion sometimes arises because of misunderstandings between appellant and interpreter at the hearing itself. Incorrect mental conversion of dates by the interpreter led to the following exchange during examination-in-chief of a Tamil woman (HX/60385/2000); all dates are written exactly as spoken in court. Counsel was attempting to 'establish' the asylum interview transcript:

Counsel:	Do you accept that it contains a truthful and accurate account of your claim to asylum?
Appellant:	They have written dates wrong.
Counsel:	What dates?
Appellant:	I came to Vavuniya on 10–8–99, but they have recorded 10–9–97.
Counsel:	And your interview states – at A6, sir – that your husband was arrested on 15–9–97; is that correct?
Appellant:	Actual date was 15–8–99.
Counsel:	And what date were *you* arrested?
Appellant:	20–9–99.
Adjudicator:	What date?
Interpreter:	20–9–99.
Adjudicator:	There must be some mistake, because you came here on 10–9–99?

---

6 His confusion could only have been deepened by the HOPO's mistaken use of 'prior' at one point, but I did not notice whether the interpreter translated the mistake, or corrected for it.

Interpreter: Yes, she was arrested on 20–8–99 and came here on 20–9–99.

Adjudicator: I don't think she did. It was 10–9?

Interpreter: Sorry sir.

During closing submissions, the HOPO conceded that there were errors in the interview transcript. That apparent confusion from long ago was, however, compounded by the interpreter at the hearing, who translated the Tamil month as '9' (September) rather than '8' (August). However, the discrepancy was obvious, and the adjudicator intervened. The interpreter attempted to stick by it but was rebuffed by the adjudicator. In correcting himself, he got the date of her arrival in the UK wrong, and again the adjudicator picked this up. Because the adjudicator was on the ball, because the appellant herself first drew attention to the problem, and because the dates she now gave made more sense in relation to her overall testimony than those initially provided by either interpreter, the HOPO did not seek to draw adverse conclusions, yet similar events before a less alert adjudicator could easily have led to an apparently convincing credibility challenge.

I was at a loss to understand why such problems were never raised in mitigation at asylum hearings. Conversations with barristers suggested that even those with most experience of Tamil appeals were unaware that Tamils had their own calendrical system. Astonishingly, they have never been alerted to such a potentially helpful issue by those instructing them, even though many appellants have Tamil-speaking solicitors. During appeal HX/11102/2001 the Tamil solicitor was actually present, yet although the problem was apparent to me, neither he nor the interpreter gave any sign of having registered it. Solicitors and interpreters tend to come from those cosmopolitan strands of Jaffna Tamil society where both English and Tamil are spoken from birth, sometimes even in a single sentence. My hypothesis is that code-switchings to and fro are such second nature to them that they do not appreciate intuitively that the appellant and adjudicator each possess only half the clues to the puzzle – and different halves at that. The adjudicator was clearly open to the idea that there had been a misunderstanding, but no-one was ready or able to explain it to him.[7] It remained unclear, therefore, whether the appellant would receive the benefit of the doubt, especially as, near the end of submissions, the following exchange took place:

Counsel: Sir, in my submission, Sri Lanka is not safe for this appellant; he would be at risk and the objective evidence shows the human rights situation is deplorable, and my friend hasn't taken issue on credibility this morning.

---

7   It was out of the question for me to intervene, or even explain the problem afterwards to the adjudicator, whom I was 'shadowing' that day.

Adjudicator:	Oh, I don't know about that! There was quite a lot of cross-examination on dates, et cetera.
Counsel:	Sir, I submit that the dates were simply a mistake, and I am arguing that they are not relevant.
Adjudicator:	Yes. I will weigh it obviously.

Tamils are not the only appellants having rival calendars to contend with in presenting stories free from 'discrepancies'. During the appeal of Mr A, a Nepali (HX/40348/2001), problems arose when the appellant's solicitor (Mr M) was dealing in his examination-in-chief with a purported arrest warrant:

Solicitor:	Turning to the second document, it states at the top right-hand corner in English, 'Police Bulletin'; can you tell the court the date of that document?
Appellant:	Saturday 1st *Asoj*, 2056.
Solicitor (to adjudicator):	Sir, this document is in bulletin format, I just want to make sure you have – er – page three of this bulletin. (To appellant) The section which has been pencilled here, what is that about; what does that section say?
Appellant:	'A has been involved with Marxists for last four years.'
Adjudicator:	What's the headline again?
Appellant:	'The police are searching for A.'
Solicitor:	What else does the article say?

(The appellant began reading at length, but the adjudicator stopped him.)

Interpreter:	I'll need to ask him to shorten it.
Appellant:	'For the last four years in Nepal the Marxist people have been creating a public fight, and it has been acknowledged that involvement with the particular party – in the full activities with the party – Chitwan district and Kathmandu Valley Development Community, the resident A the police are searching for. The mentioned person has been away from home and has been hiding in different places, and the police are searching for him.'
Interpreter (aware she was incoherent):	Can I say, sir, it is a very long sentence.
Adjudicator:	Does it give the year?
Interpreter:	No year, sir.
Adjudicator:	Where does *Bhadau* 25th come with regard to *Asoj* 1st?
Appellant (in English):	A month difference.
Adjudicator:	A month between?
Appellant (in English):	Yes.
Adjudicator:	What is the month?

Appellant (in English):   *Bhadau* is first, then *Asoj* is second, the next month.

Adjudicator: How many days in *Bhadau*?

Appellant (in English):   In some of months in Nepali calendar can be 32 days.

Adjudicator: And are you telling me *Asoj* comes immediately after *Bhadau*?

Appellant (in English):   Yes it does.

Adjudicator: So this can only be seven days after it?

Appellant (in English):   This is seven days before this paper was printed.

Adjudicator: Then why did you say a month between them, 25 days?

Appellant (in English):   What I tried to say was, change of month, from one month to another, is 30 to 32 days between them.

Adjudicator (who had repeatedly warned Mr A of the dangers of intervening in English):   Mr A, this is a good example of what I was talking about, being confused and creating confusion. Please be careful! Mr M?

Solicitor: Yes sir. This document here that is number three on the list, the inventory, what is that?

Appellant: This is a letter from – from Chitwan paraput – it's an arrest warrant.

Solicitor: What else does it say?

Interpreter: This letter is issued to arrest A, son of X, because they came to know he was involved with different activities with Maoists – different kind of criminal activities.

Solicitor: What is the date on that document?

Interpreter: 2056, and number two which is *Jestha*, and the date is the 9th.

Adjudicator: And that's the second month? Mr M, I know I'm interfering in a shameless manner; what is your birth date in the Nepali calendar?

Appellant (in English):   Nepalese calendar? I cannot remember Nepalese calendar because I got used to using English calendar now. According to English calendar my date of birth is 26/9/74.

Adjudicator: What is your date of birth *in Nepalese*?

Appellant (in English):   There is no such thing as birthday in Nepalese so I need to convert it into Nepalese calendar.

Adjudicator: Are you telling me you don't know what your Nepalese birthday is?

Appellant (in English):   I cannot remember just now.

Adjudicator: That's fine if that's what your answer is!

Appellant (in English):   I have got used to English calendar just now.

Adjudicator: That's fine. Mr M?

Mr M, one of the most experienced immigration specialists in Scotland, had told me beforehand that there were problems over Nepali dates in this case, but the adjudicator seemed well prepared for them, and had already questioned the interpreter about date conversions earlier in the hearing. Problems here were exacerbated because the interpreter was a timid young woman, hard to hear and very unassertive, while the appellant, westernised in dress and manner, insisted on interpolating English answers throughout, despite repeated warnings that he was doing himself no good.

It is hard to know what impact this particular exchange would have had upon the adjudicator. It certainly creates the impression of an appellant who is confused over his story; on the other hand, it is hard to see what adverse conclusions the Home Office could draw from his claim not to know his own birthday in the Nepali calendar, because their case did not involve calling his nationality or identity into question. It is not even clear why the adjudicator asked that question in the first place. Presumably the Bulletin gave the date of birth of the wanted person and the adjudicator was seeking to confirm that it was indeed the appellant.

Many representatives and adjudicators *are* aware that Iranians – though not, in my experience, other nationalities – do not use the Gregorian calendar, and it has become widely recognised that this may cause problems. In the Iranian case quoted above, I had noticed when looking through the appellant's bundle beforehand that it included a dates conversion table for the Iranian and Gregorian calendars, with explanatory notes, prepared for general use by an immigration advisor who was himself Iranian. That proved no guarantee that confusion would be avoided, however:

HOPO:	You say you were arrested and held by the Revolutionary Committee; how can you be sure of the date of this?
Interpreter:	When was that, I can put the question but –?
HOPO:	When were you arrested by the Revolutionary Committee?
Appellant:	About four or five days before New Year 1358, which would be 21st March 1979.
Interpreter:	He says about 15 days after actual revolution, which is same thing.
HOPO:	Now you say that on 11th February 1978 you were told to join the newly-formed government?
Interpreter:	Can I say something? There is 621 year gap, but between 1st January and 21st March the gap is 622, and they always get mixed up. So your question was?[8]
HOPO:	I am trying to clarify; which year were you asked to join the newly-formed government?

8   The interpreter is referring to the numerical 'gap' between the Iranian and Gregorian eras.

Appellant:	We are taking into account I was in prison for 15 months – it would be two years after revolution.
HOPO:	No, you were saying all other officers switched allegiance; when was this?
Appellant:	This was exactly one day after arrival of . . .

(Appellant interrupted interpreter.)

Adjudicator:	What did he say?
Interpreter:	Well, he *had* said one day after Khomeini, but he now says one day after the revolution, so he says 23rd B-, which would be 12th February 1979.
HOPO:	1979?
Interpreter:	Yes.
HOPO:	(visibly confused): Thank you.

Again the interpreter had sought pre-emptively to clarify possible sources of misunderstanding. He was thwarted by the appellant suddenly changing his story – confused either by the interpretation, or his own limited English – and by the fact that the HOPO was manifestly unable to get her head around the notion of an alternative calendrical system.

Variations in kin relationship terminology can also create problems. In the Kosovan Albanian case involving three interpreters (§7.2), the following dialogue occurred soon after the hearing got finally and definitively under way:

Counsel:	What happened to your home in Kosovo?
Appellant:	House burned down and my family is staying with my cousin.
Interpreter 3:	May I ask him, we only have one word for relative and cousin?
Adjudicator:	Certainly.
Appellant:	My father's uncle's son.
Adjudicator:	Cousin once removed!
Appellant:	But we are very close.

Here, uniquely in my experience, the interpreter made explicit the fact that Albanian terms are differently *structured* from the English terms, so the court was alerted to the fact that there was scope for innocent misunderstanding.

On other occasions adjudicators possessed the requisite cultural knowledge themselves. As well as asylum cases, they often hear family reunion appeals where, for example, girls of South Asian ethnicity, although British citizens born and brought up in the UK, enter into arranged marriages with relatives on visits to South Asia and then apply for their husbands to join them. In this case, the couple had married in Bangladesh in September 1997, after which the wife returned to the UK in May 1998. Although an interpreter had been requested, the wife declined to use her and gave evidence in fluent estuarine English. The HOPO attempted to use discrepancies between her evidence and what her husband had said at his interview in Dhaka to argue that this was not a genuine, subsisting marriage at all, but a ruse to get him into the country. She, on the other hand, maintained that the marriage accorded entirely with customary practice. The HOPO took her through the process of arranging and celebrating the marriage. He asked how she and her husband met. She said they fell in love during her visit to Bangladesh, and as they were related appropriately her grandfather had suggested that they marry. The HOPO pounced:

HOPO: *He* says that *his* grandfather suggested the marriage!
Wife: My grandfather did, yes.
HOPO (eagerly):   His or yours?
Adjudicator (wearily):   Mr M, they are cousins; they have the same
                 grandfather.

The HOPO looked utterly baffled, but got the message that for reasons unclear to him the adjudicator was not impressed by this major 'discrepancy' he had unearthed. One can well imagine how a similar situation, involving an interpreter and a less well-informed adjudicator, could have led to misunderstanding.

Not surprisingly, I most often became aware of such misunderstandings in Tamil cases where I could follow the dialogue as far as frantic note-taking and linguistic rustiness allowed. In one instance (HX/55562/2000), the HOPO was dealing during his cross-examination with matters raised in the Refusal Letter as casting doubt on the appellant's credibility:

HOPO: Your elder brother is in Sri Lanka?
Appellant: Yes.
HOPO: Is he safe?
Appellant: No, still facing problems; still being captured and released.
              He has a wife.
HOPO: Your elder brother is not involved with the LTTE because he
              has a family?
Appellant: Yes.
HOPO: But on pages A5 and 6 you say your elder brother was a
              member of the LTTE; why do you say that?
Appellant: I meant my cousin-brother. He is my mother's younger sis-
              ter's son, who grew up with us and is considered to be like
              my brother.
HOPO: Why not mention him among your family members?
Appellant: I was asked about my own brothers and sisters.

> *HOPO*:   But you consider him a brother?
> *Appellant*: I was asked to list my own siblings.

English-speaking Tamils routinely use 'cousin-brother' for those relatives whom anthropologists label 'male parallel cousins'. Interestingly, in light of my earlier hypothesis, this appellant's counsel – who did not intervene to sort out this apparent confusion – was an 'old-school', highly westernised Tamil. It would have been so self-evident to him what his client meant, that he presumably thought it was not worth bothering with. Fortunately, the adjudicator was equally aware. Unlike her colleague in the previous example, she did not make this evident at the time, but she commented to me afterwards that the HOPO was relatively new and must not yet have come across this Tamil idiom of the 'cousin-brother'.

Confusion may, however, arise for reasons about which adjudicators are quite understandably ignorant. Cross-examination of another Tamil man (HX/58388/2000) proceeded as follows:

> *HOPO*:   You have one brother in the Tigers?
> *Appellant*: Two brothers.
> *HOPO*:   What are their names?
> *Appellant*: K and R.
> *HOPO*:   K joined the Tigers in 1990, when did your second brother join?
> *Appellant*: 1996.
> *HOPO*:   Why did you not mention in interview that R joined?
> *Appellant*: I *did* say.

Later, the HOPO began his closing submission as follows:

> I rely on the Secretary of State's RFRL. There is good reason to doubt that he was arrested and detained as claimed. He says his brothers were in the Tigers, but at interview he only mentioned his younger brother. (Counsel rose to dispute this.) Anyway, there is a discrepancy.

This was another instance where I seemed the only person in court to be aware of the likely reason for this 'discrepancy'. Everyday Tamil has no composite term for 'brother', only the terms *annan* ('elder brother', 'senior parallel cousin'), and *tampi* ('younger brother', 'junior parallel cousin'). At the hearing, the interpreter scrupulously asked the appellant whether he had 'an *annan* or a *tampi*' in the LTTE, to which the appellant replied that it was one *annan* and one *tampi*. The interpreter then translated this as 'Two brothers'. I do not of course know what had happened at the asylum interview, but it is easy to imagine that an initial reference to his *tampi* would have been translated as 'one brother', and that the characteristic eagerness of the caseworker to press on would not have allowed him to amplify this by mentioning his *annan*. All supposition on my part, but the point is that neither the representatives nor the adjudicator were aware that Tamils differentiate elder and younger siblings in this way. In an appeal where everything hung on the adjudicator's decision about credibility, this could have been the last straw.

Relationship terminologies are, of course, not the only examples of indigenous classifications which do not map neatly onto those in English. Similar ambiguities regarding different parts of the body may be crucial when comparing an appellant's evidence of how they were tortured with the placing of scars on their bodies, as reported by medical examiners or observed on the spot by adjudicators. The following example arose when I was asked to write a supplementary report on a Tamil appellant. My first report had been for his adjudicator appeal (HX/38524/2001); he had lost, and was now appealing to the IAT against that decision.

In his determination the adjudicator mentioned an ambiguity during cross-examination regarding the location of bayonet wounds on the appellant's body. His adverse credibility finding was not based explicitly on this, but the effect of such discrepancies is likely to be cumulative. Yet this 'discrepancy' could have been simply an artefact of translation choices made by different interpreters on separate occasions. Thus, the basic Tamil word for foot and leg is the same (*kal*). This does not of course mean that Tamils cannot distinguish feet from legs, but they do so using composite terms; ankle is *kanukkal*, heel is *kutikal*, and knee is *mulankal*. In everyday speech, however, people often use *kal* in all these senses, specifying more precisely only when necessary. It is impossible to know, after the event, how precise each statement by the appellant had been, and whether the interpreters had taken account of any composite prefix he might have used, when rendering his descriptions into English; it is, however, easy to see the scope for confusion.

These examples have concerned fairly straightforward aspects of cultural difference, which could mostly have been fully explained had the requisite information been available. Far more complex and hard to resolve, however, are suggestions that certain acts, which appear odd to British eyes, are explicable simply in terms of appellants or others following the 'traditions' or 'culture' of their society. Legal practitioners routinely conceal the contested nature of cultural practices (McKinley 1997; Akram 2000), which they see as fatally weakening asylum claims dependent upon persecution resulting from such practices. This legal resort to cultural essentialism may place anthropologists in something of a quandary, as Schwandner-Sievers (2005) points out. Faced with police and courts seeking to explain crimes or acts of persecution in terms of 'Albanian traditions of violence', does she grit her teeth and accept the premise (criticised by Kuper 2001: *xi*) that culture itself is the explanation for strange or questionable behaviour, thereby contributing to 'the reification of these contexts by articulating them within the constraints of . . . legalism' (Hepner 2003), or try to explain the fluid and processual character of culture, and thereby risk raising doubts as to the validity of the appellant's motives?

7.5 TRANSLATION AND PERFORMANCE

When witnesses testify in court their performances, including their general demeanour, may in practice be as important as the content of what they have to say when it comes to influencing the court's opinions as to their credibility (§8.3). Quite apart from emotional reticence induced by torture or rape (§8.2), however, their freedom to perform is greatly inhibited by legal rules of procedure and evidence (Atkinson and Drew 1979: 8). Although the partial relaxation of such rules at asylum hearings mitigates this problem, it is made worse again by the need to conduct proceedings through the mediation of an interpreter.

The most straightforward difficulty is that appellants are constantly being pressured to divide their answers into 'bite-sized chunks' punctuated by long pauses. The disruptive effect may be considerable, as my own experiences of testifying as an expert witness brought home to me. While experts are not subject to the vagaries of translation, they must nonetheless pace and structure their replies so that adjudicators can write them down more or less verbatim. This adversely affects one's ability to provide coherent, structured answers on complex issues. Even more striking, I find, is its effect upon my own degree of conviction. During enforced pauses all kinds of qualifications and reservations flood into my mind, with the result that when the next sentence can finally be uttered, I have already hedged it around mentally with provisos, and it no longer sounds fully authentic even to me. It would be astonishing if many asylum appellants did not experience similar feelings of inauthenticity, for these and other reasons. At their hearings they must recount highly traumatic life experiences, possibly forced to the back of their mind until then – their own torture or rape; the violent death of a close relative – yet they are required to do so in a form which is the very antithesis of a cathartic confessional. The persuasiveness of their account is almost bound to be adversely affected.

The interposition of an interpreter may have more subtle consequences too. Even 'the notion of a life story itself . . . is the product of a particular culture' (Linde 1993: 220), and within such stories, where they do exist, coherence is partly 'imposed by the structure of narrative itself' (Rosaldo 1976), which immediately raises the possibility that this happens differently in different languages. Thus, English life story narratives involve sequences of past-tense clauses, 'whose order is taken to reflect the actual order of the events reported' (1976), whereas Tamil narratives involve strings of past participles, and extensive use of reported speech employing the gerund *enru* ('saying'), which also means 'expecting, thinking, imagining, supposing, pretending, or desiring' (Winslow 1981: 184). Many Tamils, including interpreters, carry over some of these idioms into English, so even in translation it may be unclear, to ears accustomed to British linguistic conventions, whether events really happened or are hypothetical.

Hearings proceed differently when appellants' English is fluent enough even for the esoteric context of legal proceedings. The advantages of dispensing with an interpreter were vividly illustrated in the appeal of Mr O, a Nigerian Christian who had been an oil company executive (CC/12083/2001). His story went as follows. He was transferred to a Muslim region, leaving behind his wife, a civil servant. The first time she visited him, he was attacked by fundamentalist Muslims for interacting with her in public. He was sentenced to death in a Sharia Court and imprisoned prior to his execution. He managed to escape and returned to his native village, but was asked to take over from his dead uncle as chief priest of a local cult. He refused, and incurred further cult hostility by refusing to allow his stepsisters to undergo circumcision. He fled to Lagos and took refuge in a church. A 'humanitarian organisation' provided him with a Swaziland passport (he had spent most of his early childhood there), so he flew to the UK and claimed asylum.

His counsel was the inexperienced Ms L, and the HOPO was Mr M, whose manner often suggests personal animosity towards appellants. The experienced and punctilious adjudicator insisted on taking things down verbatim, which is harder when no interpreter is involved because there are none of the translation delays which normally allow him to keep up. Partly as a result, but also partly because of counsel's incompetence and the aggressiveness of Mr M, questions and answers often had to be repeated or rephrased. This generated a lot of background 'noise', but for practical reasons the answers I recorded were the tidied-up ones given at dictation speed.

The fact that Mr O answered directly rather than through an interpreter had several obvious effects. First, his answers tended to be longer than is usual. Second, he was able to comment on court proceedings to a degree far beyond most asylum applicants. The following extract from cross-examination shows how both points worked to his advantage:

HOPO:	When did your uncle die, who was chief priest previously?
Appellant:	He was already dead when I got back. He was in the mortuary, not yet buried.
HOPO:	When did he die?
Appellant:	I don't know.
HOPO:	I shall just read a short extract from the asylum interview record – sir, page A11 – word for word; '*on getting to my native village, a month after my father's brother, uncle died was buried*'. As I read that, your father's brother died a month after your arrival.

Appellant: That is not what I said.

HOPO: Are you saying the record is not accurate?

Appellant: I was compelled to sign because the interviewer was in a hurry to leave. If you look at my signatures, you will see they are not regular; if I take time to sign, it will be regular. I requested that the document be handed over so I had time to examine it, but she compelled me to sign because she was in a hurry.

HOPO: This interview was conducted in March; why are you at this point saying there were inaccuracies in the recording?

Appellant: The report was not handed back to me. I was meant to see it by my lawyer, but because I was detained in Oakington, they took me away; I never had contact with anybody. They took me to Stockton-on-Tees. When I was bailed I saw my lawyer and I pointed out to him there were a lot of mistakes, it wasn't correct, but at that time he had already filed for the appeal.

HOPO: If there were a lot of mistakes, why adopt it at the start of the hearing?

Appellant: I never said that.

HOPO: Your counsel, here to represent you, said she was going to adopt it.

Appellant: I never heard her say that. Took my time yesterday to read it, and if she said was adopting it, I didn't hear.

HOPO: Sorry, back to the village; how long had you been in the village before the elders appointed you to become chief priest?

Appellant: My Lord,[9] I cannot remember the number of period days after I arrived in the village because at that time my mind was not at rest.

HOPO: Are we talking days, weeks, months?

Appellant: I can't really place it.

Counsel (who had been in a torpor, seemed suddenly to switch back on): In light of what has been said about adopting the statement, can I have a brief consultation with my client as I am professionally embarrassed and may have to withdraw from the case?

Adjudicator: Actually you did not.

Counsel: I did.

Adjudicator: No, you *said* you were going to, but you never actually put it to him. As it was never put to the appellant I don't think

---

9 The appellant repeatedly used this incorrect form of address to the adjudicator.

you were embarrassed. But if you want a short consultation I will allow it.

Ms L left with her client, and returned shortly afterwards, indicating that
Mr O was happy for her to continue representing him.

Because Mr O could follow exchanges between court personnel, not normally translated by interpreters, he was able to defend himself vigorously
when necessary:

HOPO: Is it not the case, anyway, that Sharia Law does not apply
                 to non-Muslims?
Appellant: Not true, because they impose law on anybody, because
                 they have already declared the State a Muslim State.
HOPO (to adjudicator):   I have information before me, sir – I refer to
                 the CIPU report – that Sharia Law does not apply to
                 non-Muslims.
Appellant: Not true, my Lord.

While Mr O's English was excellent on the whole, it betrayed idiosyncrasies
which might have led in some circumstances to attacks on credibility. On the
other hand, they allowed his personality to come across in an appealing way,
which simply does not happen in renditions by interpreters. Here Mr O was
being examined about his wife's arrival in the north, and the claimed attack
by 'Muslim fanatics', angered because he was associating with her in a public
place:

Counsel: Where were your wife and child at this point?
Appellant: Were already in the car, in taxi.
Counsel: And what happened then?
Appellant: They started beating me, gave me wounds all over my body.
Counsel: How were they beating you?
Appellant: They used metals and a knife; I sustained injuries all over my
                 body.
Counsel: And then what happened?
Appellant: While they were still beating me, I told my wife in our local
                 dialect to ask the driver to escape, to zoom from the
                 environment.
Counsel: And did that happen?
Appellant: Yes.

Most important of all, the very fact that questions were being put directly
to Mr O, and that he was speaking for himself, directly to the court, in
response, had an enormous impact on the perlocutionary force of his replies.
In many cultures, including English-speaking ones, the persuasive impact of

a narrative is much enhanced when the narrator achieves what folklorists call 'the breakthrough into performance', by shifting from third-person reportage to enacting the story by speaking the parts of the characters rather than merely reporting what they said (Bauman 1984; Hymes 1981; Conley and O'Barr 1990b: 40). Most asylum applicants are unable to achieve any such 'breakthrough' because of the depersonalising effects of the interpretation process. The main lesson of Mr O's case concerns the greatly enhanced quality of the verbal interaction he enjoyed with court personnel, irrespective of the legal or anthropological credibility of his account.

Chapter 8

Assessing credibility

The potential risks to asylum applicants are so serious, including risk to life itself, that asylum claims should, as we saw (§6.1), receive 'most anxious scrutiny' – a phrase brandished talismanically at some point in virtually every appeal hearing. According to the Canadian Immigration and Refugee Board (IRB), there are three stages involved in scrutinising and deciding asylum appeals: determining the credibility of the evidence;[1] weighing that evidence to assess its probative value; and, on that basis, determining whether the burden of proof has been met (IRB 1999b: ¶4.1). The next three chapters address these processes, and although it is not possible to separate them completely in practice, the distinctions are at least heuristically useful. The focus is on expert evidence, but this must be set into the context of the treatment of evidence generally, especially that from applicants themselves.

8.1 PRINCIPLES OF CREDIBILITY ASSESSMENT

Because corroborative evidence is so often lacking in asylum claims, credibility assessments based on the internal coherence of the account, its external consistency with 'objective evidence', and its 'inherent implausibility' (Weston 1998: 88), are employed throughout the decision-making process to filter out supposedly 'bogus' claimants.[2] These may all too easily fall prey to prejudice or lack of understanding, however, when the person whose credibility is being assessed comes from a cultural and political background very different from the assessor (§6.6; Bingham 1985: 14; Ruppel 1991: 5). Yet as Catriona Jarvis, herself an adjudicator, points out (2000: 6),

---

1 Even if credible, evidence may still be rejected as not relevant, i.e. 'not of assistance in coming to a logical conclusion regarding the issues to be determined' (IRB 1999a: ¶11.5).
2 Similarly, Thomas (forthcoming) notes that claims may be found incredible because of internal inconsistencies in the applicant's account; inconsistencies between that account and the available country evidence; or because the account is deemed to lack plausibility or truthfulness.

credibility findings 'go to the heart of the identity' of asylum applicants, and 'to get it wrong is to add insult to injury . . . to inflict yet further damage upon a human being who has already undergone experiences incomprehensible to most of us'.

Muller-Hoff (2001) sees parallels between the widespread view that many rape cases are based upon false allegations (see Adler 1987: 15; Brown *et al.* 1993: 17), and the presumption that many asylum claims are 'bogus'. Both frequently depend upon uncorroborated evidence, and although it is established law that corroboration is not required in asylum cases (Deans 2000: 124; Henderson 2003: 192; Symes and Jorro 2003: 56), Home Office caseworkers nearly always, and the courts sometimes, behave as though it is. When asylum claims are themselves based upon accounts of rape, such 'common sense' scepticism may be raised to the power two (§8.2). Moreover, Muller-Hoff (2001) notes that credibility decisions may provide scope for judicial decision makers to:

> make normative statements outside the scope of law, to set morality standards and to enforce policy decisions and to give them the authority of legal 'knowledge', thus, disguising their subjectivity and challengability [sic].

Credibility assessments are decisions as to whether an appellant's own testimony should be accepted as evidence contributing towards meeting the requisite burden of proof (Kagan 2003). They are clearly crucial in most instances (but not decisive overall, since even appellants who are disbelieved may merit refugee status because of their circumstances or conditions in their home country). Such decisions are generally made by the adjudicator who first hears the evidence, and in the UK, as elsewhere, higher appeal bodies rarely subject their decisions to more than 'very light scrutiny' (*ibid.*), even though many seem to depend upon subjective impressions rather than the application of clearly stated principles. Indeed, no such principles exist within the British asylum system.

Since the time of my field research, the issue of credibility has been addressed in sec. 8 of the *Asylum & Immigration (Treatment of Claimants, etc.) Act* of 2004. This stipulates that credibility assessments should take into account any behaviour which seems designed to mislead, to conceal information, or to obstruct the decision-making process (Thomas, forthcoming). Examples given include failing to produce a passport; producing a false passport; destroying a passport or travel documents; failing to claim in a safe third country; and failing to claim until after being arrested under immigration provisions. In other words, the approach taken still strongly recalls earlier legislation concerning certification (§5.2.2), in focusing upon appellants' behaviour on arrival in the UK. It remains the case, therefore, that British adjudicators and immigration judges have no official guidelines on the most crucial matter of all, namely, how to assess the credibility of the substantive basis of an appellant's claim. Small wonder, then, that credibility decisions seem influenced, to some degree, by stereotypes rather than a claimant's own particularities (see Kagan 2003). 'I love Colombian appeals,' one senior adjudicator said to me, 'they're always so delightfully implausible.' Less anecdotally, more than twice as many women as men (15 per cent as against 6.5 per cent) are judged credible by British adjudicators (Harvey 1998: 191; Jarvis 2000: 8).

In some other jurisdictions, rather more progress has been made in this regard. A useful general survey of the issues involved in assessing whether evidence is indeed 'credible or trustworthy' is again provided by the Immigration and Refugee Board of Canada (IRB 1998: ¶1.1). It notes that such assessments are made more difficult by the fact that many rules of evidence used in other courts do not apply, which is broadly true of British asylum hearings too (Brooke LJ, *Karanakaran*). According to the IRB (1998: ¶1.2), testimony must be evaluated in the light of:

> conditions and laws in the claimant's country of origin, as well as the experiences of similarly situated persons in that country. The Federal Court has cautioned, however, that '[t]here can be no consistency on findings of credibility'. Credibility cannot be prejudged, and is an issue to be determined ... in each case based on the circumstances of the individual claimant and the evidence.

The IRB's guidelines note that credibility findings, especially when adverse to appellants, must be founded properly in the evidence and in reasonable inferences drawn therefrom (1998: ¶1.6). They should take account of 'the integrity and intelligence of the witness and the overall accuracy of the statements', as well as the witness's 'powers of observation and capacity for remembering'. They involve assessments of demeanour, although these should not be given excessive weight and should focus on such considerations as whether witnesses appear 'frank and sincere or biased, reticent and evasive' (¶1.7), rather than on physical appearance (¶2.3.5). They should also take into account whether the witness is an involved 'actor' or 'mere bystander', and whether they have an interest in the outcome (¶1.7), though credibility should not be doubted merely because evidence is self-serving (¶2.4.6). They should consider all the evidence, not just portions of it, and it should be considered all together, not bit by bit (¶2.1); this involves more than just seeking out inconsistencies, because even if particular pieces of evidence are found to lack credibility – in which case 'clear reasons must be given' (¶2.2.1) – the claim must still be assessed on the basis of whatever evidence *has* been found credible (¶2.1.2). Moreover, applicants should have opportunities – through cross-examination for example – to clarify matters where credibility is in question (¶2.5.1).

8.2 TELLING THEIR STORIES

For most asylum applicants the principal evidence as to the persecution they have experienced resides in their personal narratives of suffering, which is why decisions on credibility are such important preliminaries to the determination process. A detailed study of asylum interviews remains to be carried out (§5.1), and even less is known about how asylum lawyers structure their clients' statements to maximise their acceptability as evidence; but it seems reasonable to expect, at least, that such accounts will be converted from relational into rule-oriented mode (§2.1). McKinley (1997) describes just such a restructuring for a Zimbabwean applicant in the US, fleeing from an abusive forced marriage.

With that proviso, the asylum interview, statement-taking by their own solicitor, and the appeal hearing itself, all provide opportunities for asylum applicants to narrate their stories of persecution. For some applicants, though, the very incidents most helpful to their claims have to be coaxed out of them (if they ever emerge at all) by sympathetic and trusted interlocutors. What is more, these stories often come out differently on different occasions, giving rise to the 'discrepancies' for which hawk-eyed Home Office staff are always on the *qui vive*.

No doubt many applicants do want to tell their stories to as wide an audience as possible – as a therapeutic catharsis; to 'bear witness' to atrocities inflicted on their family or community; or to obtain official validation of the seriousness of their persecution (see, in a different context, Conley and O'Barr 1990b: 130). During my research, one Nepalese appellant, on being informed what I was doing there, came up and thanked me profusely for listening to his story; it was clearly important to him that people came to hear of his problems. Whether applicants are prepared to open up straight after arrival, to complete strangers in a strange country, is another matter, yet one 'common sense' Home Office assumption is that genuine applicants will mention all serious incidents of persecution at the earliest possible opportunity. When the truth is finally coaxed out of them by doctors or solicitors, the Home Office invariably attacks their credibility on the grounds that 'you would have mentioned when first interviewed something so central to your asylum claim'. The following comment in a Refusal Letter to a Sri Lankan Tamil woman, in an appeal where I acted as expert, is typical:

> When the immigration officer asked you whether you had any other reasons or events that caused you to seek asylum, you did not add anything further. Even bearing in mind your apprehension as expressed in your additional statement, he considered that your failure to mention anything about the alleged rape in 1987 undermined your credibility in raising it later.

Yet that interview had been conducted by a male Immigration Officer in the presence of a male Tamil solicitor previously unknown to the applicant. Both circumstances were bound to inhibit disclosure. Shame before men generally, and a fear that information may percolate out to local members of their community, severely inhibit many women's willingness to disclose sexual assault (Berkowitz and Jarvis 2000: 48). Many have not even told their immediate family what happened.

Adjudicators and tribunals pay rather more attention than the Home Office to cultural and circumstantial reasons why women may not divulge sexual assaults on such occasions, but they too do not always accept this as a sufficient explanation for silence, as in this tribunal appeal by 'S', a Turkish Kurd:

> In our considered opinion, while her excuse was that she was ashamed and embarrassed to reveal that matter to male Immigration Officers, that excuse does not stand up when it is considered that she had been in constant touch with her solicitors, some of whom must have been female, when she could have brought such matters to light, but had failed to do so.

The argument about contact with female solicitors appears purely speculative. What is more, it is well known that many rape victims fail to report such attacks; this has been termed the 'silent reaction to rape' syndrome, and attributed to the 'tremendous psychological burden' felt by victims (Burgess and Holmstrom 1974).[3] Because of the extra pressures they face, one might expect this to be at least as true for refugees, even at the cost of weakening their legal cases. It applies to men too. Medical Foundation doctors report that male asylum applicants from Sri Lanka who suffered sexual abuse during detention are even more likely to remain silent until a relationship of trust has been established than are female rape victims (Peel *et al.* 2000; Peel 2002).

Clearly, therefore, it would be quite wrong to base a negative credibility finding on initial reticence alone; explanations for late disclosure should be taken very seriously. That does not of course mean that every applicant who ultimately claims to have been raped is telling the truth. Adjudicators must decide on credibility 'in the round', and there was, for instance, no medical or psychiatric report supporting S's claim to have been raped; such a report might have lent significant weight to her case.

Another 'common sense' supposition is that traumatic events will be remembered and recounted with preternatural clarity and vividness. This goes hand in hand with a general assumption that variations and inconsistencies

3 This American study does not consider cultural variations, however, and there are problems with such 'scientising' of social issues (Dobbin and Gatowski 1998).

between different tellings of an event, even months or years apart, are damaging to general credibility – hence the significance attached by the Home Office, and to some degree the courts, to apparent inconsistencies in different versions of applicants' stories. On both counts, however, anthropological and medical evidence point in the opposite direction.

The first issue is the incommunicability of pain. Certain pains (toothache, for example) are socialised by being labelled in everyday speech. Sufferers can map their own private experiences onto these public labels and 'from there sympathy and empathy take over, making the pain in question more or less shareable' (Daniel 1996: 142).[4] The physical pain of torture, however, 'does not simply resist language but actively destroys it, bringing about an immediate reversion to ... the sounds and cries a human being makes before language is learned' (Scarry 1985: 4). What is more, even if it has an interrogational purpose (which is not always the case), all torture is also terroristic (Daniel 1996: 137); its 'ability to shatter relationships [and] destroy trust' (Turner 1995: 58) is so great that victims often refuse to believe that their own comrades were indeed tortured, even when they themselves witnessed it (Daniel 1996: 143, 150). Not surprisingly, torture victims find it almost unbearably hard to discuss such doubly desocialising experiences. Telling one's story of persecution involves transforming private experience into public meaning, and thereby constitutes a triumph of 'agency in the face of disempowerment' (Hastrup 2003: 314, citing Arendt 1958 and Jackson 2002). Small wonder that torture victims find such agency beyond them at first, and that even when they achieve it, often with therapeutic or legal help, their accounts are not in vivid technicolor, but mere sketches from which 'all the emotional edges have been eliminated' (Scarry 1985: 32). In court, their 'listlessness', their 'passionless listings of atrocities committed by the torturer', appears unconvincing (Daniel 1996: 143). The very inexpressibility of the pain of torture renders its expression unbelievable.

Second, a recent medical study examined variations in the recounting of traumatic events by Kosovan and Bosnian asylum applicants (Herlihy, Scragg and Turner 2002; cf. Cohen 2001). The discrepancy rate was as high as 30 per cent for descriptions of central elements for both traumatic and non-traumatic events; however, credibility is best judged with regard to peripheral memory, and here there were more discrepancies for traumatic events. Moreover, the longer the delay between interviews, the higher the discrepancy rate for those with Post-Traumatic Stress Disorder. I attended a seminar in which Turner summarised these findings, prior to publication, to an audience of adjudicators. Several were dismayed to discover that one cannot base

---

4   Skultans (1974) notes that spiritualists in South Wales treat pain as an emotion rather than a sensation, thereby turning it into an experience which can be communicated to and shared with others.

credibility judgments on the consistency of accounts with previous versions, and admitted that they generally did so in coming to their decisions. They gained scant reassurance. Turner confirmed that trauma memories are fragmented, so it is *not* the case that people remember very clearly the details of particularly important events. Discrepancies in recounting past experiences are quite high under any circumstances, but higher for traumatic events; so such discrepancies have no necessary connection with overall credibility.

Scholars working on oral histories and life stories would be far less surprised than these adjudicators by such findings. The sociolinguist Linde, for example, argues that life stories are generally judged on the basis of coherence rather than factuality, coherence being both 'a social demand and an internal, psychological demand' (1993: 220). Whereas psychiatrists like Turner focus on the latter aspect, linguists and social scientists are of course interested primarily in the former. They overlap to some degree however, because ultimately the narration of autobiography is both a cultural artefact and a manifestation of culturally specific views on the nature of personhood (Langness and Frank 1981: 101). For example, by Western convention autobiography is expected to express motivations, emotions, and other elements of the 'inner self', whereas in other cultures it may serve as a vehicle for affirming the public self. In both cases, but especially the latter, its content therefore depends on the social relationship between teller and listener (Rosaldo 1976).

The causal chain in such narratives must also be 'adequate'; that is, the sequence of events narrated must be accounted for in ways acceptable to the listener (Linde 1993: 221). When speakers feel causality to be inadequate, they may present the next step as an accident or 'socially recognized discontinuity' (1993: 221). From a legal standpoint, moreover, it is sometimes necessary to proceed sequentially in order to demonstrate that the witness has the requisite first-hand knowledge of the evidence to be introduced – what lawyers call 'laying a proper foundation'. Such sequencing is, however, related to Western cultural understandings of causality, whereby only events that occur prior in time can cause subsequent events (Conley and O'Barr 1990b: 41). Ultimately, the 'most pervasive and invisible coherence system is common sense – the set of beliefs and relations between beliefs that speakers may assume are known and shared by all competent members of the culture' (Linde 1993: 222). Where asylum narratives are concerned, however, the cultural and experiential differences between teller and listener may be too great for common sense assumptions to be shared to anything like this degree. That is why witness statements are so crucial. They allow asylum applicants' legal representatives to structure their accounts according to the expectations of British culture, and legal culture in particular. Causal adequacy can thereby be assured prior to the hearing, although it may of course begin to unravel once cross-examination starts.

Because *performance* is an intrinsic component of oral expression, the full meanings of narratives emerge only during their telling. This emergence of meaning is, however, greatly inhibited by the exclusionary rules of evidence prevailing in courts of law. These rules are intended to circumvent 'identifiable practical problems posed by ordinary discourse' (Atkinson and Drew 1979: 8), but one consequence is that 'the rhetorical force of the account' is significantly diminished, making it less involving for the speaker, less dramatic and interesting for the listener, and – often, as a result – less credible for the decision maker (Conley and O'Barr 1990b: 40). Because of the less stringent evidential rules in asylum courts these prohibitions do not all apply to the same extent; on the other hand, the interpolation of interpreters may have similar dampening effects upon the performative force of appellants' utterances (§7.5).

The meaning of a narrative is related to 'the interaction with . . . the audience and its expectations' (Finnegan 1992: 93). In other words, such stories do not lurk in monolithic, immutable form in some subconscious limbo, ready to be regurgitated whole on each appropriate occasion; rather, they are 'realised through performances carried out and mediated by people' (1992: 93–4). For legal anthropologists, therefore, it is a commonplace that accounts by litigants will:

> vary considerably and in relation to the environment and point in the process where they are given. . . . A 'story' does not exist fully developed on its own, but only emerges through a collaboration between the teller and a particular audience . . . a research interviewer asking questions, a judge presiding in an informal court, a lawyer talking with a client (Conley and O'Barr 1990b: 171).

The usual caveat applies of course; some discrepancies and elaborations may indeed indicate untruthfulness, but that decision has to be based on overall credibility, not purely on the discrepancies themselves. Clearly, however, such findings call into question some prevalent 'common sense' assumptions made by asylum decision makers, and exacerbate the difficulties in reaching fair decisions.

8.3 JUDICIAL ASSESSMENTS OF CREDIBILITY

Although the burden of proof in asylum cases lies with applicants (§10.2), the fact that many find it impossible to produce supporting evidence led UNHCR to specify in its *Handbook* (1992: ¶196) that even in the absence of such evidence, applicants whose accounts seem credible should receive the benefit of any doubt. According to UNHCR, credibility means, largely, that their statements are 'coherent and plausible', and do not 'run counter to generally known facts' (¶204).

The Home Office approach to credibility is markedly less generous. Evidence considered by IND in assessing credibility includes applicants' statements, interview records, and other documents, judged against 'an objective assessment of the conditions in the prospective country of return at the time of decision' (IND 2002a: ¶1.2.10; see also §10.2). The fact that applicants may also have economic motives for coming to the UK should not affect their credibility provided they satisfy Convention criteria. Caseworkers are also told not to draw hasty conclusions when families have remained behind; women and children may be less at risk, or the applicant may have been unable to afford to bring them. They are even advised, provided there is evidence of a well-founded fear of persecution, to give applicants the initial benefit of the doubt over falsehoods, discrepancies and exaggerations, as these may reflect a real fear of being returned (2002a: ¶1.2.11). It is impossible to know how all this advice influences their working practices, but in any case it does not apply if 'the account lacks coherence' or 'general credibility is doubtful' (¶1.2.10), and in practice caseworkers nearly always *do* cast doubt on credibility. In the opinion of many asylum lawyers, IND starts from the presumption that applications are 'bogus'.[5]

First appeals are especially crucial where credibility is concerned, because unless adjudicators' assessments are clearly wrong or utterly counterintuitive, tribunals, in their stock phrase, 'will not lightly overturn' their findings on credibility – and with good reason, for adjudicators do after all hear appellants giving oral evidence and undergoing cross-examination. Adjudicators are told to make their own credibility assessments uninfluenced by the Home Office view, indicating, with reasons, which evidence they accept (§10.5). They are advised that demeanour is an unreliable guide except in extreme cases, but that inconsistencies in appellants' evidence, or between their words and deeds, may be significant (Deans 2000: 120–3, citing *Amin, Karanakaran*, and *Chugtai*).[6]

An analysis of asylum decision making in Canada, by a multidisciplinary research team noted that Immigration and Refugee Board members tended to reach credibility assessments by applying their own 'assumptions of a universal Canadian cultural "logic"' (Rousseau *et al.* 2002: 62). For the researchers, however, the Board's assumption that there existed a single frame of reference in refugee hearings, shared by decision maker and applicant,

---

5 Embarrassingly, the 1998 White Paper illustrated 'asylum abuse' by citing an applicant who told a 'series of lies' to support his claim and gain income support (Home Office 1998: 10). He was later granted refugee status by the House of Lords (*Salem*), and awarded back-dated benefits in full.

6 See also *MM*, where the tribunal agreed that assessments of appellants' oral evidence and their manner in giving it could be valuable for explaining particular credibility findings, but warned that this was 'an area for real caution' lest they slip over into judgments based on appellants' 'demeanour'.

seemed highly problematic (see also Clifford 1988: 329). While recognising the legal and procedural difficulty of the decision makers' task, they also noted the 'capricious' treatment by Board members of evidence from experts such as doctors and psychologists (Rousseau *et al.* 2002: 55).

Canadian hearings are tape-recorded and transcribed,[7] and study of such tapes revealed not only the effect of psychological trauma on applicants' testimony, as might be expected, but also the extent to which repeated exposure to narratives of torture and rape produced 'massive' avoidance reactions among decision makers themselves, who displayed a high incidence of 'emotional distress', expressed prejudice, and considerable cynicism (Rousseau *et al.* 2002: 64). The report concludes that such behaviour shows 'a very strong emotional reaction, a lack of empathy, and an association of the victim with the aggressor, all symptoms of an inability to cope with the emotional stress created by the hearing' (2002: 59–60). It includes examples of Board members denigrating, discounting, or not even reading psychological reports; discounting cigarette burns on an applicant's body because 'she herself was a smoker'; giving little consideration to objective evidence; and using judicial knowledge in inappropriate ways. In one case, 'the chairwoman stated repeatedly that she did not want to hear a description of the torture suffered by the claimant, and that reading the PIF [Personal Information Form] was sufficient proof regarding that issue. . . . The claim was rejected for lack of credibility' (2002: 58; gloss added). At another hearing, 'a Board Member, showing clearly that he did not believe the story, angrily asked the claimant how he could have asked for help from their torturers; five minutes later, and still angry, he asked how the claimant could have left his companion in the hands of their torturers' (2002: 59).

Such procedural irregularities and combative behaviour would appear quite outrageous in a British hearing, and I never witnessed anything as extreme. However, while I am not qualified to diagnose avoidance or distress, I can certainly say that some adjudicators and tribunal chairs display cynicism about applicants generally, or prejudices in the form of stereotyped views about particular nationalities. It seems common for professionals in stressful occupations to distance themselves from the traumas to which they are repeatedly exposed, through denial, avoidance, minimising the seriousness of situations, and emotive reactions such as anger, lack of empathy, or cynicism (such as gallows humour in operating theatres; Katz 1981), but there are clearly adverse consequences for claimants if such reactions are 'impacting negatively' upon judicial evaluations of their credibility (Rousseau *et al.* 2002: 43).

The most systematic research into how British adjudicators reach credibility decisions was carried out by Jarvis, herself an adjudicator, using

---

7   See Barsky (1994) for a critique of this process.

questionnaires and follow-up interviews. Adjudicators were asked to rank 27 factors pertaining to credibility in order of importance, distinguishing appeals in which applicants gave oral evidence from those in which, for whatever reason, they did not. Some were factors common to all judicial assessments, such as consistency or a failure to answer questions put, while others were more peculiar to asylum appeals, such as late disclosure of torture or the narrowly procedural matters emphasised by the Immigration Rules (Jarvis 2000: 10). Replies indicated considerable variation in *stated* practice, and showed that many credibility decisions rested on adjudicators' 'gut feelings', their application of common sense (possibly another way of saying the same thing), or recourse to personal experience (2000: 16).

To that extent, as one respondent bluntly put it, the process is 'a lottery' in which the decision depends above all on which adjudicator happens to hear the appeal (Jarvis 2000: 19). Some general conclusions do however emerge, for good or ill, from Jarvis's findings. Thus, appellants have less chance of winning if they choose not to attend, or attend without giving oral evidence. Many judges see oral evidence as essential for establishing credibility, because they cannot see how 'compliance with fundamental justice could be achieved by a tribunal making significant findings of credibility solely on the basis of written submissions' (Bertha Wilson J, in *Federation of Canadian Sikh Societies*). Others, like Lord Justice Sedley (*Yousaf and Jamil*), are 'less sanguine about the revelatory character of oral evidence, especially where it has to be mediated by an interpreter'. He cautions that:

> Nothing in the experience of our ordinary courts encourages one to think that in the witness box the truth will necessarily out and liars be exposed. If anything, it tends to be documentary material which demonstrates that the unconvincing witness has been telling the truth or the convincing one been deluded or lying.

If this is so when strict rules of evidence apply, there must be even more doubt under the relaxed rules found in asylum appeals, and when witnesses may be traumatised. Nonetheless, adjudicators' responses showed that, in general, the identified factors 'will weigh more heavily against you if you don't attend and give oral evidence than if you do' (Jarvis 2000: 20). Although it is an error of law to make a negative credibility finding on this basis, the fact that it so obviously still happens is perhaps not surprising when one considers that there is generally no other evidence (apart from standard objective sources) bar the appellant's own.

On the other hand, most Home Office reasons for certifying claims (§5.2.2), such as applicants' lack of identity documents or failure to claim asylum in transit, cut little ice with most adjudicators, the one exception being when no claim was made until after removal proceedings were instigated (Jarvis 2000: 17). Similarly, adverse credibility findings are more likely when a claim is lodged only after that of a family member has been dismissed, though this may disadvantage wives who adhered to cultural norms of dependence, and initially allowed their claims to be subsumed under their husbands' (2000: 21).

Numerous studies show that demeanour is an unreliable guide to credibility in any area of law (Jarvis 2000: 40, and sources therein). This is especially so in asylum courts, given appellants' diverse cultural backgrounds and expectations regarding interpersonal behaviour. One recent tribunal cautioned that 'judging demeanour across cultural divides is fraught with danger' (*'B' [DRC]*), yet it figures importantly in the assessments of many adjudicators (Jarvis 2000: 23, 40). Like other legal decision makers, adjudicators are more inclined to believe appellants who are physically attractive, unless they seem to trade on their attractiveness in a manipulative way (2000: 40–1). Such prejudices may be particularly pernicious when allied to misconceptions about rape as an expression of sexual attraction, as they encourage the propensity to believe that the fears of attractive young ladies are well founded but those of older women are not (§4.3).

Although they are crucial starting points in almost every appeal, credibility assessments are not conclusive: 'an applicant's story may not be credible in the light of the objective circumstances but still the case is established' (*Nimets*). Decisions should be grounded on the existence of future risk, 'as to which the credibility of an account of past events is clearly often highly relevant but not necessarily determinative' (Symes and Jorro 2003: 466). The ultimate issue is the existence of a 'well-founded fear of persecution', evaluated primarily on the basis of 'objective evidence' about the situation in the applicant's home country, so in practice the outcomes of most appeals depend on adjudicators deciding which version of the objective evidence they prefer as regards risk on return. But as the veteran tribunal chair Mr Care pointed out, 'background information is crucial to most findings of plausibility and frequently credibility as well' (*Kanagasundram*). The evidence of country and medical experts may therefore be important for credibility assessments too, yet these experts themselves cannot easily address such matters directly, as we shall now see.

8.4 COUNTRY EXPERTS AND CREDIBILITY ASSESSMENTS

To say that credible statements must be 'coherent and plausible' and not 'run counter to generally known facts' (UNHCR 1992: ¶204), begs the questions of how to assess plausibility, and which facts are generally known. These are the very issues addressed by country experts such as anthropologists, who are generally asked to comment on whether applicants' stories are plausible, consistent with local history, and in accord with the known behaviour of key individuals and groups. The semantic terrain between 'plausibility' and 'credibility' is, however, a labyrinth for lawyers, and a veritable minefield for expert witnesses.

Because country experts provide and assess key parts of the objective evidence, and are often asked to comment on the plausibility of asylum applicants' accounts, it is hardly surprising if they are also tempted to take what must appear the small further step of commenting on the implications of their assessments for applicants' credibility. Naturally enough, they take for granted their competence to assess the kinds of arguments and evidence with which they deal professionally; for example, anthropologists are fully accustomed to evaluating and interpreting informants' statements. But whereas in academic contexts 'plausibility' and 'credibility' may seem virtually interchangeable terms, in legal circles 'credibility' is a term of art, a judgment which only the court is entitled to make. Whether 'plausibility' enjoys the same status has been a matter for debate.

Thus, Dutton (2003) argues strongly that when assessing credibility, decision makers should not give the Immigration Rules (the kinds of procedural matters leading to 'certification'; §5.2.2) equal weight to the objective evidence. He himself favours the approach adopted by Lee J in the Federal Court of Australia (*W148/00A*), which 'allows the use of common sense but minimises the uncertainty shaped by personal prejudices and sentiments inherent in the subjective approach'. This appeal concerned a Syrian, imprisoned by the intelligence authorities for refusing to go to Iran as a spy. His claim had been rejected by the Australian Refugee Review Tribunal, but Lee J stated that they could not exclude his account from consideration simply by asserting that it was 'implausible'; to qualify for such a description, events must be 'beyond human experience of possible occurrence, that is to say, inherently unlikely'. Dutton sees four advantages in this approach. First, it recognises that an asylum applicant, of all people, is a 'candidate for the unusual', as Schiemann LJ stated in the Court of Appeal (*Adam*). Second, it uses as objective a definition of common sense as possible, based on generalised human experience rather than personal opinions. Third, it 'provides for certainty in that it is a clear method and makes no allowance for individual preconceptions', but, fourth, it also 'enables common sense to reject the most incredulous [sic] and fanciful of accounts' (Dutton 2003).

The tribunal in *MM [DRC]*, chaired by the President, criticised this approach, however, preferring to define 'plausibility' as 'apparent reasonableness or truthfulness'; its assessment might involve judgments 'as to the likelihood of something having happened based on evidence and or inferences'. Background (objective) evidence was often crucial in 'revealing the likelihood of part or the whole of what was said to have happened actually having happened', but plausibility was by no means always conclusive in assessments of credibility:

A story may be implausible and yet may properly be taken as credible; it may be plausible and yet properly not believed. . . . there is a danger of 'plausibility' becoming a term of art, yet with no clear definition or consistent usage. It is simply that the inherent likelihood or apparent reasonableness of a claim, is an aspect of its credibility, and an aspect which may well be related to background material, which assists in judging it. This danger is reflected in the comment of Lee J which, with respect, we do not find helpful to us. We do not regard 'implausible' or 'inherently unlikely' as meaning 'beyond human experience or possible occurrence', nor do we regard that latter phrase as the relevant benchmark for an adverse conclusion as to plausibility or credibility.

There is, therefore, an important difference between expressing the view that an account is plausible, or consistent with objective evidence; and judging it to be 'credible'. Many experts, ill-advised by their instructing solicitors, simply do not realise that the first two opinions are permissible, even helpful to the court, but the third is not. Conversely, the courts, unaware that this legal nicety is not apparent to others, may devalue reports which they see as attempting to usurp their authority.

The situation is complex, however, because the higher courts have not always entirely ruled out the possibility of decision makers being assisted by expert views on credibility. In his High Court decision in *Ez Eldin*, for example, Mr Justice Blofeld had rejected the argument that a tribunal should have taken account of the views on an Egyptian appellant's credibility expressed in an expert report by George Joffé, then Deputy Director of the Royal Institute of International Affairs. He noted that:

difficulties arise if an expert . . . attempts himself to assess the credibility of an applicant, and to extrapolate from that his opinions as to what is likely to happen to him. . . . I doubt if an expert's opinion of an applicant's credibility is, in itself, admissible. Credibility is essentially a matter solely for the court or Tribunal that hears the case.

For the subsequent Court of Appeal hearing, Joffé was asked by Ez Eldin's solicitors to comment on Blofeld J's judgment. He responded as follows:[8]

I, of course, agree that the credibility of the evidence provided by a claimant is solely a matter for the court . . . I must, however, within the context of my expertise, indicate whether or not such statements are consonant with what I know of the objective circumstances [and] I must also comment upon the consequences that would follow if such

---

8   I am grateful to George Joffé for supplying copies of reports and correspondence.

statements were to be correct – but that . . . is not to determine or comment on their accuracy or veracity. By definition, an expert witness is obliged to provide the court with sufficient information of the objective circumstances of the case in order to aid the court in determining the credibility of the claimant.

As this indicates, Mr Justice Blofeld had perhaps lumped two rather different things together. For an expert to purport to assess an applicant's overall credibility is one thing; to express 'opinions as to what is likely to happen to him' if his story is true is another. These opinions are precisely what solicitors hope to elicit when they commission expert reports. For example, my instructions from a leading firm of asylum solicitors included the query: 'Is Mr M likely to be on police records, and would this, combined with his scarring, put him at significant risk of serious mistreatment, if he is obliged to return to Sri Lanka?' In such situations, one first assesses whether the asylum applicant's story is consistent with the objective evidence, 'consistency' being a matter on which experts *are* permitted to comment. On the assumption that the story will be found to be true, one then assesses the objective evidence on how persons of that background are treated. This seems the kind of 'extrapolation' which Blofeld J criticises, but if they cannot draw such conditional inferences it is hard to see the point of experts reporting to the court at all.

Certainly the Court of Appeal seemed sympathetic to Joffé's argument, and Lord Justice Brooke in his leading judgment commented:

> Mr Joffé had set down a number of detailed matters relating to his knowledge of the Egyptian State's concern about . . . Islamic fundamentalism . . . It must be extremely difficult for . . . adjudicators to form their view of credibility in relation to somebody who comes from a culture different from theirs . . . In those circumstances [an] adjudicator always needs all the help that can be given by those who know more about such matters

This exemplifies a long-running difference of opinion (see also *Karanakaran*; §9.6), whereby the Court of Appeal consistently argues for a greater degree of deference towards uncontested expert evidence than the IAT – motivated partly, no doubt, by a desire to maintain its hegemony (§6.2) – seems willing to grant. True to form, some tribunals entered caveats regarding Brooke LJ's comments, but in so doing they sometimes, arguably, exaggerated their own cultural awareness and general expertise on 'humanity' (see also §9.7):

> while it is not on the whole the daily business of Her Majesty's judges in the superior courts to assess and make the appropriate allowances for cultural differences, that is exactly what adjudicators have to be doing every day of their working lives. Some of them are better at it than

others: all can use help, so long as it is help, properly presented. While those comments are a useful reminder that there are differences between different peoples, modern thinking suggests our common humanity is more important (*Zarour*).

Consequently, despite the occasional sympathy of the higher courts, experts should think twice before bandying about their opinions on credibility. To some extent, though, the position depends upon the stage at which the report is sought. Prior to an adjudicator hearing, credibility is still an open question. IND may well have reached adverse conclusions on the matter, but these are mere assertions by one party in an adversarial process, made with far less professional authority than that underlying the opinions of the expert, who can legitimately disagree with their premises. By the time of tribunal appeals, however, adjudicators have already made credibility findings, so experts may have to allow for the fact that aspects of an appellant's account have already been deemed not credible. When an adjudicator reaches such conclusions for what the expert considers unsustainable factual reasons, the situation is quite delicate. This is another area where improperly instructed experts may get into difficulty. As the legal decision itself is unassailable by them, they must find some way of calling the adjudicator's deployment of objective evidence into question without trespassing onto legal decision making.

In *Nishanthan*, for example, two aspects of the adjudicator's reasoning seemed culturally misguided. First, the appellant's father, a recognised refugee, had been in the UK since 1989. The appellant had said at the hearing that he did not know the details of his father's persecution, which led the adjudicator to conclude: 'That the Appellant does not know what troubles his father faced and that he has not asked him or been told by his mother lacks credibility.' Quite apart from the illogicality of this argument – as his father's legal presence in the UK was not in dispute, what reason could there be for the appellant to *falsely* deny knowing about his father's 'troubles'? – it ignores the patterns of deference which inhibit young Tamil men from interrogating their fathers. Second, the appellant said that his mother paid a bribe to secure his release from army detention, but he had not asked her how much she paid. The adjudicator cast doubt on this too, stating: 'That the Appellant did not ask his mother these details lacks credibility.' This argument too depends upon assumptions about normal behaviour within families which do not take cultural context into account, assumptions all the more questionable concerning secret, shameful matters like paying bribes. In my report I concluded:

It is not for me, obviously, to address the adjudicator's legal finding on credibility. However, what I do say is that, from my alternative professional standpoint as an anthropologist, if a Tamil research informant were to tell me either of these things, premised as they both are upon the cultural inappropriateness of children interrogating their parents, I would find nothing at all anthropologically unbelievable about either circumstance.

Leave to appeal was granted specifically on the credibility issue, and although I was present to give oral testimony I was not in fact called upon because it was clear as soon as the tribunal arrived in court that they intended to remit the appeal for rehearing. Their written determination stated:

> We do not find it surprising or incredible that the appellant did not know about his father's experiences. His father left Sri Lanka when the appellant was 11 years old. We do not find it surprising or incredible that the appellant did not question his mother about the bribes or know how much was paid and to whom. Dr Good's expert report confirms that the appellant's lack of knowledge about his father and failure to question his mother is consistent with his age and cultural background.

8.5 MEDICAL EXPERTS AND CREDIBILITY

Medical evidence is important in many asylum claims, particularly those allegedly involving torture, because torture occupies a special status in relation to the 1951 Convention and the European Convention of Human Rights. For example, where there is prima facie evidence of torture, asylum claims should not be certified. According to the 1984 UN Convention Against Torture, torture is any act whereby 'severe pain or suffering, whether physical or mental, is intentionally inflicted on a person' for whatever reason, provided that 'such pain or suffering is inflicted by or . . . with the consent or acquiescence of a . . . person acting in an official capacity'. IND also accepts that forcible abortion, sterilisation, and genital mutilation 'probably' count as torture if officially sanctioned (2002a: ¶3.2.2.1).

The decision to cover medical as well as social scientific evidence in this research was based on the assumption that doctors would provide a control group whose legitimate expertise would already be familiar to lawyers, whereas anthropologists would be an unknown quantity, the status of whose evidence might create doubt and misapprehension. Whatever the truth of the second part of this hypothesis, my presumptions about medical evidence were rapidly proved false. When adjudicators learned what I was researching, they often launched into complaints about doctors who 'purported to decide cases for them' by stating that appellants' stories were true.

Criticisms of the kind made by Blofeld J in *Ez Eldin* are, indeed, far more commonly levelled against doctors than country experts. For example, HOPOs often object that doctors' opinions are based only on what applicants tell them:

Mr Ridge, in his submissions, pointed out that the medical report only formed part of the general evidence and was, in any event, based upon the story that the appellant had told the doctor and he pointed out that the adjudicator had found the appellant to be lacking in credibility, and therefore the findings of the doctor with regard to his medical condition were based on information which was incorrect (*Yurdakurban*).

Such arguments are even occasionally accepted by adjudicators. Thus, according to the tribunal in *Rajivan*: 'The adjudicator considered the medical report. She concluded that it did not assist the appellant's case because it was based on what the doctor had been told by the appellant.' Adjudicators have even gone so far as to decide that doctors have been hoodwinked. One tribunal (*Gimedhin*) strongly criticised an adjudicator who, in rejecting a report by Dr Gail Hinshelwood, one of the Medical Foundation's most senior psychiatrists, had said:

> the examiner appears *understandably* (emphasis added by tribunal) to have relied rather more on the appellant's emotional responses to examination which she claims were 'definitely those of an abused woman' . . . It is my view that the appellant's emotional response to the doctor was calculated and false.

However, the tribunal found that the adjudicator 'was so dismissive of the potential weight of the report that it amounts to an error of law to say that it provided no independent support to her claim and that the rape claim was a fabrication'.

Another adjudicator (*Salami*) attracted tribunal criticism by seeming to privilege his own assessment over that of the medical expert:

> we were unhappy about the approach of the adjudicator to medical evidence . . . The adjudicator dismissed the consistency of the medical evidence and its support for other evidence in stating that . . . the author had not had 'the same opportunity of assessing the appellant' as the adjudicator had. [W]e have some doubts as to whether an adjudicator is better able to assess an appellant in the artificiality of the hearing room than a psychologist, particularly where, as here, the psychologist apparently saw the appellant regularly over a period of time.

Such criticisms by HOPOs and adjudicators forget that taking patients' histories is normal medical practice prior to diagnosis, not something doctors wilfully indulge in only when writing reports on asylum applicants. They are at least as experienced as judges in assessing such information, and it is absurd to assume that they merely believe what they are told. This is made explicit in the Medical Foundation's guidelines for examining torture victims (see also Peel 1998: 156), which IND (2002a: ¶17.3) has explicitly stated are 'fair' :

> Consistency and credibility are continuously assessed as the interview and examination proceed. In coming to a conclusion, the doctor must make a series of judgments, assessing the subject's demeanour as well as the history and physical signs (Forrest 2000: 41).

A more sophisticated and tenable version of this critique can therefore be grounded upon whether or not the history was assessed objectively in accordance with the kinds of accepted medical procedures referred to by Dr Forrest, as the following tribunal comments (emphases added) exemplify:

> the opinion expressed by the doctor is clearly wholly dependent upon information provided to him by the Appellant as to his mental state and *there is nothing to indicate that this has in any way been assessed in accordance with internationally recognised standards* or amounts to any more than a summary of what the Appellant said to him (*Arumugam*).

> Whilst plainly this report relies largely on the husband's subjective account of his past experiences, *it does describe with care what materials he took into account in reaching his medical assessment.* We are impressed by its objective quality (*Hooshya*).

Another common objection is that doctors should say no more than the medical evidence is *consistent with* the applicant's account. In *Sutharshan* the President commented as follows on a report by psychiatrist Dr Philip Steadman, 'someone whose reports are regularly put before the Immigration Appeal Authorities':[9]

> this particular report is one which contains Dr Steadman's views upon the credibility of the appellant. We wish to make it as clear as we can that no medical expert has any business to give opinions on credibility. What he is there to do is to describe the injuries, if any, that he observes and the mental condition, if that be material, and he can of course indicate what might have caused any particular injury . . . [W]e would like to give a clear warning that opinions of those who appear to enter the arena, and to give opinions which a doctor has no business to give, are less likely to carry weight, the reason being that the Tribunal and the adjudicators will regard them as advocating the cause of the individual appellant rather than giving a proper objective view.

---

9   Discussions with adjudicators revealed a degree of 'expert fatigue', whereby experts were criticised less for the quality of their reports, than simply because they wrote so many of them.

That limitation is far from universally accepted by doctors themselves, however. Forrest sees credibility assessments as central to medical examinations:

> All participants in the asylum process inevitably need to make some estimate of the applicant's credibility. The examining doctor is not excluded from this process of assessment and should have credibility in mind throughout the history-taking and examination and have made some personal assessment of it by the end (2000: 48).

He does, however, distinguish between accepting an account of torture as credible, and going on from that to infer the credibility of the entire story:

> It is no part of the doctor's function to give an opinion as to overall credibility of the case, though it is quite in order to express an opinion as to whether the medical evidence supports the allegation of torture (2000: 50).

Doctors are, however, sometimes taken to task for doing precisely that, for arguably violating the ultimate issue rule (§6.2) by saying not merely that scarring is consistent with the explanation given, but how likely it is that the scars were caused as described. In *Nsubuga*, Dr Michael Peel, an experienced Medical Foundation doctor, had concluded his report by saying: 'Therefore, in my expert opinion . . . there is a reasonable degree of likelihood that the scars were caused in the way that [the appellant] describes.' The tribunal criticised this conclusion in the following terms:

> While it is certainly within Dr Peel's expertise to say that scars are consistent . . . with a given history, nothing in any medical expertise he may have entitles him to make the step from that to saying that the history was reasonably likely to be true. That was the adjudicator's business, and no-one else's. . . . When he took it on himself to go further . . . he was going outside the area of his expertise, and doing no service to justice, the appellant, or his own professional reputation. It was for the adjudicator, in the light of the evidence as a whole, including . . . Dr Peel's, to consider whether the history was reasonably likely to be true.

Another tribunal, to whom he used virtually the same words, complained that Dr Peel seemed 'to be trying to do what is the Adjudicator's job in reaching a conclusion about the Appellant's evidence' (*Vethanayagam*). Dr Peel is unrepentant, however (pers. comm.). He feels it is legitimate to state a professional opinion on the likelihood of scars being caused in the manner claimed, and some tribunals are more sympathetic, as in this response to a report by one of his colleagues:

In no way are we bound by the doctor's conclusion that the Appellant's account is likely to be true. At the same time it would be quite wrong for us to ignore and attach no weight to the uncontested evidence of an expert in this field. In the experience of the Tribunal the reports of the Medical Foundation are generally of high quality ... We do attach weight to what is said by Dr Horder and we are grateful to her for her assistance (*Njehia*).

Just as medical reports supporting torture claims are especially important, so, conversely, an absence of such evidence may undermine credibility, particularly when time has been allowed to obtain such a report. If that report proves unfavourable, the applicant's representatives will not submit it of course, but caseworkers are told that in such cases they may draw negative conclusions regarding the applicant's credibility, unless the account of torture has already been found credible for other reasons (IND 2002a: ¶17.3). On the other hand, medical evidence submitted following an initial refusal can be reviewed even before an appeal is heard, and if it proves convincing, asylum or ELR can be granted without the appeal going ahead; if not, applicants are told in writing why the decision was not reversed (¶3.2.4.3). Asylum Aid (1999: 67) imply, however, that it is rare for decisions to be changed in this way.

Medical experts are in a stronger position than country experts in some ways, however, because up to a point their evidence is immune from direct attack by lay HOPOs, or total rejection by adjudicators lacking medical qualifications. This principle has been reaffirmed repeatedly, and the following examples could be replicated many times over – although that very fact shows that Home Office staff and adjudicators have often not heeded the advice:

It is not appropriate for a civil servant without medical expertise to reach a conclusion contrary to that reached by a psychiatrist simply by drawing on his own native wit (*Khaira*).

Any medical report or psychiatric report deserves careful and specific consideration ... it is incumbent upon an adjudicator to indicate in the determination that careful attention has been given to each and every aspect of medical reports, particularly given that these are matters of expert evidence which cannot be dismissed out of hand (*Mohamed*).

Mr Martin ... is not a doctor. With great respect to him, faced with a report such as that of Dr Peel he had simply no justification for rejecting it (*Guney*).

The stances taken by Drs Forrest and Peel go further, however, reflecting the Medical Foundation's view that whenever expert medical evidence 'is consistent with the testimony of torture [it] should be accepted as achieving the standard of proof required in asylum cases' unless challenged by 'a medical expert of equal standing' (Medical Foundation 2000: 79). Not surprisingly, there is little sign of such arguments finding favour among tribunals and adjudicators. From their perspective, as the *Sutharshan* determination makes clear, there are nearly always alternative explanations for appellants' injuries, whose likelihood can only be assessed in light of *judicial* findings as to their overall credibility. What is more, as a recent tribunal (*HE [DRC]*) noted, the adjudicator 'will have often more material than the doctor, and will have heard the evidence tested'.[10] In short, this disagreement provides a perfect example of the kind of hegemonic struggle between disciplines which forms a central theme of this book.

The Medical Foundation sees itself as having an 'educative function' vis-à-vis the Home Office and the IAA, not only as regards what medical evidence can and cannot show but, even more importantly, how medical evidence should be evaluated in deciding a claim. Examples cited elsewhere (§4.2.3; §4.2.4; §9.3–9.7) suggest a need for country experts to provide decision makers with similar guidance, though the lack of any obvious institutional framework equivalent to the Medical Foundation presents a serious practical difficulty. Moreover, even the Foundation – well organised, highly respected, and morally unassailable though it may be – has all too evidently had limited success in its self-imposed mission to 'educate' Home Office staff and the courts on how to approach medical findings.

8.6 EXPERTS AND JUDICIAL HEGEMONY

As shown in Chapter 6, immigration courts are arenas for clashes between different, sometimes incompatible codes of professional and ethical behaviour. The difficulties in getting diverse professionals to take seriously one another's viewpoints even where they stand on equal footing have often been pointed out – in the context of multidisciplinary international development consultancy teams, for example (Chambers 1983: 22–3) – and should not be underestimated. Here, moreover, they are most certainly not equal. Although anthropologists and doctors may regard themselves as supreme arbiters of fact and opinion – even credibility – within their own professional spheres, the courts are not their home turf and the struggle for authority between experts and judiciary will have only one winner.

Yet that victory may sometimes be achieved at some cost to the securing of justice. The hegemony of the judiciary in their own courts would give no cause for concern if decisions were always clearly based upon a proper

10 In light of Forrest (2000: 48; see above), however, that tribunal was wrong to contend that 'A doctor does not usually assess the credibility of an applicant'.

appreciation of the nature of expert evidence; yet while it was acknowledged earlier (§6.5) that many experts have only a very superficial awareness of the legal standards applying to expert witnesses, some examples in this book demonstrate a reciprocal ignorance on the part of the Home Office, and even the judiciary, regarding the assessment of expert opinions, and the very nature of expertise. Just as the courts are entitled to expect that experts understand their legal obligations and work within them, so experts deserve a more sophisticated appreciation and treatment of their evidence than the crude empiricism all too often displayed (see also Jasanoff 1995: 68).

A rapprochement would certainly be desirable, but this is not merely a matter of both sides making themselves better informed. It is not my contention that legal treatments of expert evidence result from pig-headed judicial failures to defer to 'some putative, extra-legal "golden standard" of science (or expertise)' (Edmond 2004b: 137). Rather, tensions inevitably arise between law's 'institutional commitment to notions of unambiguous facticity and truth', and the anthropological view that all knowledge is 'value-laden, political, and contested' (Jasanoff 1996: 111; see Good 2004b). Such problems are, moreover, exacerbated by the centuries-old power struggle between experts and judiciary (§6.2), a struggle alive and well in contemporary asylum courts. Thus, when tribunal chairman Mr John Freeman asserts that expert witnesses –

> should not seek to be treated as seers, whose vatic pronouncements are to be brought down from the mountain on tablets of stone, and treated with all reverence as the last word on the subject in question. . . . While . . . their views ought to be taken with due seriousness, that does not mean they must necessarily be accepted. That would be to substitute trial by expert . . . for trial by adjudicator, which is what Parliament has provided (*Zarour*)

– his final sentence is almost certainly a conscious paraphrase of the Court of Appeal's rejection, in *R* v. *Turner*, of psychiatric evidence as to the likely behaviour of the accused (§6.4). The court was concerned that, otherwise, 'trial by psychiatrists would be likely to take the place of trial by jury and magistrates. We do not find that prospect attractive and the law does not at present provide for it'.

Thus, whatever experts may think about the carping to which their evidence is often subject, while in court they are forced to submit to the hegemony of the judiciary. Given their long-running struggle for professional supremacy (§6.2), and the basic epistemological gulf described elsewhere in this book (§2.2; Chapter 11), small wonder that judges and experts fall out over issues like credibility, and differ regularly as regards the weight and status of expert evidence. It is to this issue of evidential weight that we now turn.

Chapter 9

Weighing expert evidence

We were unable to place very much weight on Dr Good's report
(*Thiyagarajah*; dismissed; heard 20/5/2002)

We are bound to say that we are impressed by Dr Good's report
(*Somasundram*; allowed; heard 8/5/2002)

How did two tribunals, sitting at almost the same time and hearing submissions by the same barrister, come to such divergent conclusions about reports which, though not identical because they addressed the particular circumstances of each appellant, offered very similar analyses of the prevailing situation in Sri Lanka? What does this tell us about how the asylum courts weigh expert and objective evidence, and what are its implications for the rendering of justice?

9.1 THE NOTION OF EVIDENTIAL WEIGHT

The weighing of evidence, once found credible and reliable, is the process of estimating the degree to which it affects the probability of a fact in issue. It is a process of assessment through 'appeal to common experience' (Heydon and Ockelton 1996: 7) and 'application of common sense' (IRB 1999b: ¶4.1). Weight is a question of fact rather than law, although in this context the two cannot be wholly segregated (Murphy 2003: 36).

According to the Canadian Immigration and Refugee Board (IRB), which yet again provides an apposite discussion of general principles, to weigh evidence means to assess the reliability and probative value of evidence that has already been determined to be relevant (IRB 1999b: ¶4.1). 'The probative value of evidence,' the same passage goes on to explain, 'is its value in assisting in determining the matters in issue.' As for 'reliability', it should be determined in the round, in light of all the circumstances of the case. Factors to be considered in weighing evidence of all kinds include: the identity, qualifications, knowledge, attitude, and demeanour of the witness or maker of the statement; whether the information is known first-hand; whether it is simply speculative; whether it is credible and consistent with other evidence; whether it is self-serving, interested, or biased; and whether the witness has been subjected to cross-examination (IRB 1999b: ¶5.1.1).

'Weight' can be understood in relation to the familiar notion of the 'scales of justice' (Nathalia Berkowitz, pers. comm.). The orations of legal representatives in asylum hearings make more sense once one realises that they are not necessarily constructing intellectually and narratively coherent arguments, although it presumably helps if they can, but are also striving to drop as many little chunks of evidence as possible, like so many lead shot, into the pan on their own side of the scales, in the hope that their cumulative weight will tilt the decision their way. Hence, for example, the interminable cataloguing, during final submissions, of topics for the adjudicator to take into account, of which the following is entirely typical:

> *Counsel*:   In the respondent's bundle, I refer you to para 5.1.4 of the *Country Assessment*, Amnesty International's concerns about the new Emergency Regulations; para 5.1.8, the LTTE responsible for human rights violations; 5.2.6, thousands of Tamils arrested; 5.2.11, risk factors for further investigation, including relatives known to be LTTE members, and physical scars; 5.2.12, again scars; 5.2.14, concerning detention without charge or trial, some detained without charge for five years; 5.2.18, grounds for arrest; and 5.2.47, reports of torture all over Sri Lanka; 5.2.48, people suspected of links with LTTE will be subject to torture. So, given the factors pertaining to this appellant and the objective evidence, I submit he has a well-founded fear of persecution and ask you to allow the appeal (HX/06456/2001).

9.2 HOME OFFICE *COUNTRY ASSESSMENTS*

In most asylum appeals, as the above extract illustrates, both sides derive country-specific 'objective evidence' from the six-monthly *Country Assessments* (now renamed *Country Reports*) produced by the Home Office's Country Information and Policy Unit (CIPU) for the main asylum-producing countries. These are generally the only sources of country evidence used by HOPOs, whereas applicants' representatives usually cast their nets wider, covering generic reports by bodies such as Amnesty International, Human Rights Watch, and the US State Department, as well as, in a minority of cases, specially commissioned reports by country experts.

Some early *Assessments* were roundly criticised for elementary factual errors and questionable interpretations, though for Sri Lanka it was more a matter of 'distancing from reputable sources, where they detail abuses' (Asylum Aid 1999: 47). For example, the definitive assertion that 'The Sri Lankan government generally respects the human rights of its citizens in areas not affected by the conflict with the LTTE' was followed immediately by 'However, *according to the US State Department* . . . the ongoing war continued to be accompanied by serious human rights abuses committed by the security forces' (IND 1999: ¶5.1.1; my emphasis) – this despite the fact that the source of both statements was the same.

No doubt in response to such criticisms, the italicised phrase was pointedly transferred to the initial sentence in a later version (IND 2002c: ¶5.1.1). Even before that, however, the entire *Assessment* had undergone a striking change in tone, making far more explicit references to human rights abuses by the security forces. For example, one key incident in the escalation of the ethnic conflict was the LTTE's killing of 13 soldiers in 1983, which triggered widespread anti-Tamil riots in the south. These events were described as follows in two successive *Country Assessments*:

> After 13 Sinhalese soldiers were killed in an ambush in Jaffna in July 1983, serious disturbances broke out at the funeral in Colombo, with Tamil homes and businesses being looted and torched (IND 1998b: ¶3.6).

> In July 1983, 13 Sinhalese soldiers were killed near Jaffna, reportedly by a group of Tamil extremists. Violence directed against the Tamil minority started immediately in Colombo, subsequently spreading throughout the country. Several hundred Tamils were killed by Sinhalese groups. In the following few days there were reports that unarmed members of the Tamil minority were being killed at random by the security forces in the north, apparently in retaliation for the killing of their own men, and that Tamil detainees held under the Prevention of Terrorism Act (PTA) were being killed in a Colombo prison. Later that year, the Sri Lankan Government acknowledged 51 killings (IND 1999: ¶3.6).

Although this meant that Asylum Aid's particular complaints no longer had quite the same force, *Country Reports* continued to attract criticisms. The Immigration Advisory Service (IAS) published a detailed critique of the April 2003 *Reports* for 15 countries and briefer comments on six others. These *Reports* were found to be 'extremely selective in [their] use of information, consistently painting a far more positive picture of country conditions than the sources the Home Office has relied upon'. They contained basic inaccuracies where 'the source material . . . did not in fact contain the information CIPU assigned to it and sometimes did not relate to the subject matter at all', as well as many minor errors over dates or names, which could nonetheless prove crucial to credibility decisions in specific cases. Material provided in the present tense was in fact often several years old, with piece-meal updatings which did not truly convey the current situation. Tendentious changes in wording were made compared to the source, such as the conversion of 'separatist' into 'militant' (Carver 2003, from which the preceding quotations are drawn).

Echoing the Asylum Aid critique, IAS found that *Reports* often omitted passages from quoted material, producing a less equivocal impression than the original source. For example, ¶6.1 of the Sri Lanka *Report* omitted the second half of the following passage from the March 2003 US State Department Report: 'the Sri Lankan Government generally respects the human rights of its citizens; *however there were serious problems in some areas*' (italics added). Failure to assess material critically, no doubt partly because of the lack of country expertise among CIPU staff, often created a falsely positive impression. *Reports* consistently failed to distinguish 'official' versions of events in government statements from the actual situation on the ground according to those with first-hand knowledge. In the Sri Lanka *Report*, for example:

> lack of balance between documentation of human rights abuses and reports of government action to address them leads to an impression that there are few serious problems relating to human rights abuses in the security forces. The most obvious example relates to rape in custody, which is mentioned only in passing, while no less then six paragraphs are devoted to human rights training programmes for the security forces (Carver 2003).

IAS (2003) later examined the corresponding October 2003 *Reports*, and found that while some of its criticisms had been taken into account, others had not. The Sri Lankan instances just mentioned remained substantively unamended.

In any case, CIPU's location within the government department actually responsible for asylum decisions was bound to raise questions as to its objectivity. These cut both ways, for while Asylum Aid and IAS accused *Country Assessments* of over-optimism, several HOPOs complained to me that their task was made harder because *Assessments* were too even-handed; in the words of one, it would be better if they served, in effect, as 'the Home Office brief'. The unpublished *Report of the Consultative Group on Country Information and Documentation Centre* (1998) highlighted the importance of reliable country information for sound decision making, and called for an independent documentation centre to be established, perhaps modelled on Canada's Documentation, Information and Research Branch, which is part of the Immigration and Refugee Board and separate from the Department of Citizenship and Immigration. That did not happen, but IND has since gradually moved towards greater internal separation between its country information and country policy activities.

First of all, following the appearance of that report, and after assessing the uses made of CIPU materials by immigration officers, caseworkers, and HOPOs, the Home Office Research Development and Statistics Department (RDS) recommended the setting up of a user panel and an expert panel of topic and country specialists, to monitor the quality of CIPU's output (RDS 2003a, 2003b). On the day that research was published, IND announced the formation of an Advisory Panel on Country Information (APCI), comprising individual scholars and nominated representatives of relevant organisations. Perhaps surprisingly, the chosen academic members, while very eminent researchers, seem never to have acted as country experts and were certainly not listed in ILPA's *Directory of Experts* (1997). APCI meets regularly and examines a selection of CIPU material. All its proceedings, discussions, received submissions, and reports are in the public domain (www.apci.org.uk). One of APCI's earliest actions was to commission independent analyses of the CIPU *Reports* on Somalia and Sri Lanka, which came to very similar critical conclusions to those reached by IAS. In September 2004, in response to one of APCI's suggestions, IND announced the reorganisation of CIPU, and the setting up of a dedicated Country of Origin Information (COI) Service (www.homeoffice.gov.uk/rds/country_reports.html).

Throughout all this, and despite continuing criticisms, *Country Reports* and *Assessments* have continued to be accepted almost unquestioningly by the courts. They *were* criticised by tribunals in the past for not being sourced, but that no longer applies, and while it is common for reports by experts with a lifetime of relevant experience to be savaged by adjudicators and tribunals – on grounds of bias, for example (§9.4) – judicial criticisms of *Country Reports* are now almost unheard of, even though they are mere compilations by UK-based civil servants with no expertise whatever on the countries concerned. For example, the official whom I take to have been responsible for the improvements in recent Sri Lanka *Reports* had never even visited the country until July 2001. One can only assume that they acquire weight in the eyes of the court merely because they bear the imprimatur of the Secretary of State; it seems true of law generally that 'concerns about the reliability of . . . expert evidence . . . are not extended, even in criminal proceedings, to expert evidence produced by the State' (Edmond and Mercer 2004b: 209).

Several countries receiving significant numbers of asylum applicants, such as Canada, the Netherlands, and Denmark, conduct occasional official field visits to key countries of origin. The UK was astonishingly slow in following suit, and the first IND visit to Sri Lanka (only the second such visit anywhere) did not occur until July 2001 (IND 2001), though there was another in March 2002 (IND 2002b). Such visits have obvious benefits and more insidious dangers, depending on the strategy adopted and the choice of personnel. UK visits tend to involve only IND staff, for whom this may be their first experience of the country. The danger that such brief, stage-managed visits will foster delusions of expertise is obvious, especially after factoring in the Home Office's chronic naive empiricism, though it can be minimised if team members confine themselves to reporting and attributing interviewees' opinions, and do not get seduced into amateur ethnography or analysis.

9.3 WEIGHING EXPERT EVIDENCE

The weight to be given to expert evidence depends upon the expert's 'expertise or experience or opportunity to investigate' (Murphy 2003: 36). The IRB Guidelines (1999b: ¶6.7) state that the weight given to expert opinions in asylum appeals should depend on the expert's qualifications, and their relevance to 'the domain asserted'. Unless there are specific reasons to the contrary, '[t]he greater the expertise, the greater the weight'.

However, while it is an error of law to *ignore* relevant expert evidence from a reliable source, such evidence is not necessarily decisive. It may be set aside after 'due consideration', provided 'particular care' is taken to explain why. There are many factors involved in this consideration. Does the testimony fall within the expert's area of expertise and experience, and how were these acquired? Is the expert's opinion based on a full knowledge of all established and relevant facts, using reliable and culturally sensitive methods? To what extent does the expert rely on hearsay material, and is that of a kind normally relied upon by experts in this field? Are the expert's opinions shared by others in the field, or do they display bias or radical views (IRB 1999b: ¶6.7.1)?

Similar principles should apply to the weighing of expert reports in British asylum courts (Symes and Jorro 2003: 735), yet outcomes as different as those presented at the start of the chapter are by no means unusual. There are often perfectly valid reasons why that should be so. A report must always be weighed in the unique context of a particular appeal, so it is entirely proper for two tribunals to read almost identical opinions from an expert, but to give differing weights to the expert's conclusions because of the different circumstances of the two appellants, or to see those conclusions as outweighed in one instance by other evidence submitted:

> A competent expert's report is always entitled to respect and due consideration; but from the point of view of the judicial decision maker such reports will often amount in the end to just one among many other items of evidence which have to be weighed in the balance (*Gomez*).

First and foremost is the matter of credibility. Experts cannot comment on this without risking the IAT's wrath, as we saw (§8.4), and in any case country experts are generally in no position to attempt to do so by the standards of their own professions, let alone in terms of the particular sense of 'credibility' operating in law courts. Instead, provided nothing seems unusual or implausible – in which case they are duty bound to point this out – experts give their opinions on the basis that appellants' accounts are true.[1] If an adjudicator or tribunal decides that the account is *not* true or credible in certain respects, then the expert's premise falls away, and the weight of his or her opinion on those matters is much diminished. Even when two appellants are both judged wholly credible, however, the weight accorded to an expert opinion will depend on its relevance to their particular circumstances. Suppose, for example, that an expert concludes, in each of two reports, that the ceasefire in Sri Lanka enhanced the LTTE's ability to assassinate those in government-controlled areas whom it regards as traitors. Suppose, too, that A is a low-level LTTE sympathiser whose fear relates largely to the government authorities, whereas B was an army informer and fears the LTTE. The probative value of the expert's opinion is potentially far greater in relation to B's claim than A's, so if B's account is accepted it will carry greater weight.

With such matters in mind, it is worth looking in detail at the contrasting tribunal assessments quoted at the start of this chapter. They offer a particularly apt comparison because the instructing solicitors (Van-Arkadie & Co) and the appellants' barrister (Mr Ian Lewis) were the same in both appeals, and because my reports were written only one week apart; the *Somasundram* report, containing 106 paragraphs, was dated 25 April 2002 and the *Thiyagarajah* report (115 paragraphs) was completed on 2 May. There was therefore considerable overlap in their treatment of general political and human rights issues, such that 70 paragraphs appeared in substantively the same form in both reports. Their differences reflected the different circumstances of the appellants. For example, *Thiyagarajah*'s appeal involved questions about Sri Lankan passports, not at issue in *Somasundram*.

Mr Thiyagarajah Sivakumar was a Hindu Tamil from Jaffna District, born in 1973. After leaving school he worked in a shop, and from 1990 onwards began assisting the LTTE in minor ways. While displaced along with the rest of his family during the army's recapture of Jaffna in 1995, he helped the LTTE by tending the wounded, and was himself wounded. When his family returned home, he went to the Vanni with the LTTE. He returned to Jaffna in October 1999, to avoid having to take up arms. In December 1999 he was picked out by a masked informer, and detained. He confessed under torture to having helped the LTTE. He too was then forced to act as a masked informer, and those he pointed out were detained and tortured. He was released under cover of the 2001 New Year celebrations, following payment

---

1 That is different from stating that the account *is* true, a matter beyond an expert's competence. It is therefore remarkable to read the then IAT President, Judge Pearl, approvingly citing an assertion from Dr Phillip Baker of SOAS, that 'he is only prepared to *support* an appellant . . . *when he has assessed for himself whether the person is telling the truth*' (*Zheng*; my italics).

of a bribe by his father. An agent took him to Colombo. He passed through checkpoints on the way using a passport with his own photograph but a false name. He left by air in March 2001, using his false passport.

In his appeal, according to the tribunal, Mr Lewis 'relied almost exclusively' on my report, whereas the HOPO asserted that some of my arguments were 'simply supposition' and 'sheer speculation', which 'approached the appellant's account as though it were entirely credible. That was not what the adjudicator found.'[2] The tribunal decided as follows:

(25) In relation to the report prepared by Dr Good, the Tribunal considered what weight could be attached to its contentions. Dr Good is a Senior Lecturer at the University of Edinburgh and until three years ago was head of the Department of Social Anthropology there. He lived in Sri Lanka from 1970–1972, and was last in the country in September 1996. He has been a member of the Advisory Panel of the OISC since 2001.

(26) Dr Good has never met the appellant. His opinion is based on documents submitted to him by the appellant's solicitors. Given that this appeal turns on the present situation in Sri Lanka since December 24 2001, and in particular since the ceasefire on 24 February 2002, the information upon which the Tribunal works needs to be first-hand and current.

(27) We were taken specifically to passages at paragraphs 27–29, 31–33 and 36 of Dr Good's report. In paragraphs 27–29, Dr Good says in effect that the peace process could fail. That is true of any peace process: but the signs at present are in the other direction. A final ceasefire has been signed, and the relaxation of internal controls continues alongside internationally brokered peace negotiations.

(28) Paragraphs 31–33 deal with an extract from a report by the University Teachers for Human Rights in Jaffna. Reference is made to that organisation's website. The Tribunal has examined the website. The organisation exists solely to record LTTE violations of human rights.

---

2   Nor, indeed, is it what I said in my report, which read as follows: 'I am aware that Mr Sivakumar's credibility, and the truth of his account, are matters for the court, not for me, and I note from the determination that the adjudicator found parts of Mr Sivakumar's evidence to be not credible. However, I can confirm that in every respect bar one, his account is consistent with objective evidence of which I am aware, including sources not cited here. The one unusual feature is his journey from Mannar and the suggestion that the agent had already supplied him with a passport; as far as my experience goes, this normally happens in Colombo.'

This report is not necessarily objective. The language quoted is intemperate. The report pre-dates the final ceasefire and the peace negotiations.[3]

(29) We were also taken to paragraphs 56–59. Dr Good acknowledged there that he had no information as to whether Sri Lankan passports nowadays contained identity card numbers, and his conclusions were based upon the websites of Sri Lankan consulates, as he had not visited Sri Lanka for a number of years. He had no information as to whether a passport was an acceptable substitute for an identity card as recently as 2001. There are similar problems with the observations to which we were taken in paragraphs 98–100. The commentary on an early version of the Wilkie report at paragraphs 102–115 is similarly derivative and adds nothing to the information already before the Tribunal.

(30) For these reasons, we were unable to place very much weight on Dr Good's report.

Mr Somasundram was also a Hindu Tamil, born in Jaffna District in 1975. He was required to help the LTTE while still at school. He was wounded while fleeing with his family during the army's recapture of Jaffna in 1996. After the family returned home they received visits from LTTE members demanding cash contributions. When they declared themselves unable to pay, his brother was forcibly taken by the LTTE; his subsequent whereabouts are unknown. In October 1999, following an LTTE attack, the army came to the house and ill-treated the family. Mr Somasundram was detained, interrogated and beaten. One of those held with him died from his ill-treatment, and the others were forced to dig his grave. Mr Somasundram was tortured and held in solitary confinement. In April 2000 the LTTE overran the camp and freed him, but when he got home all his family had fled apart from his father, with whom he travelled to the Vanni. It took him several months to recover from his injuries. To escape LTTE enrolment, Mr Somasundram travelled to Colombo in early 2001. His father left him with a friend and returned north to try and find the family. Mr Somasundram had lost all contact with him. His father's friend helped him make travel arrangements through an agent. There was a medical report, listing his various scars.

Here my report was less central to Mr Lewis's submissions, and the tribunal does not mention any attempt at direct rebuttal by the HOPO:

(21) We have to reach conclusions as to the view we take of the present position in Colombo in this respect we have the report of the March

3   In subsequent reports, I guarded pre-emptively against such ill-informed dismissal of UTHR's standing by including a laudatory assessment of their work by a Harvard human rights lawyer.

delegation. Against this we have the UNHCR letter of 15 April 2002 which we have set out in full above. It follows that we have a degree of inconsistency we have [sic] the robust views of Dr Anthony Good. We did not have the opportunity of seeing this expert giving evidence before us. There seems to be little doubt that Dr Good is eminently qualified to express opinions in relation to these matters although we note that he was last in Sri Lanka in September of 1996. It is right to say that the March delegation report paints a reasonably optimistic view of the present situation. We note that at paragraph 3.2 it is said that many rejected asylum seekers are simply being waved through at Colombo airport but we cannot read that paragraph as indicating that each and every rejected asylum seeker is waved through. Unfortunately we are given no information as to the proportions that are in fact waved through although we appreciate that it would be very difficult to get such specific information. If we were required to deal with this appeal on the basis of the balance of probabilities we would conclude that it was more likely than not this appellant would not be stopped at the airport and of course on that basis he would not be strip-searched. If he was stopped and interrogated we would again on the balance of probabilities reach the conclusion that it was more likely than not that the authorities would ascertain that there was a record of his previous detention. If he was stopped, interrogated and a record of the previous detention came to light then we would take the view that this appellant would be in difficulties. We reached this conclusion having carefully considered the report of the March delegation. We are bound to say that we are impressed by Dr Good's report and we are concerned about the UNHCR letter of 15 April 2002. We think it is very important to remember the standard of proof that has to be applied in these cases. We are not concerned with the balance of probabilities we are concerned with reasonable likelihoods. We cannot conclude on this evidence that it is not reasonably likely that this appellant will be stopped, interrogated or detained. We are delighted to note that there is some evidence of an improving situation in Sri Lanka although we fully appreciate the fact that the report necessarily, in the main, deals with the region of Colombo. Having said that, we have taken the view that in the particular circumstances of this appellant's case the totality of the objective evidence that we have considered does not give us sufficient confidence to conclude that there is a reasonable likelihood that this appellant would not be persecuted or his human rights be infringed. We have in mind the decision of the President, Mr Justice Collins in the case Jeyachandran ([2002] UKIAT 01869) heard on 21 May 2002. In that case, on not dissimilar facts, he allowed a Sri Lankan appeal. We agree when the President said that each case must be considered on its own facts and we consider that the circumstances in this case are such as to cause us to allow this appeal.

My reports were, of course, not the only evidence before these tribunals. The appellants' circumstances were different too, and there were differently reasoned decisions by different adjudicators. Importantly, the adjudicator had found parts of Mr Thiyagarajah's account not to be credible; as the tribunal observed, he 'expressly rejected the appellant's account of his manner of passing through checkpoints'. In *Somasundram*, by contrast, the adjudicator had 'accepted the appellant's credibility in all respects', and the tribunal had 'little doubt' that before leaving Sri Lanka 'this appellant was persecuted and his human rights were infringed'.

Both tribunals noted the time gap since I had last been in Sri Lanka (see §9.5). The *Thiyagarajah* tribunal added for good measure that I had never met the appellant. Although no explicit point was taken from that, it reads like a comment designed to diminish weight, yet this seems more a strength of such a report than a weakness. It lessens the temptation to pronounce on whether the appellant's story is true, and makes it less likely that the expert can be convincingly accused by the HOPO of naively believing that story. Only once was I asked to interview an asylum applicant in advance, and I refused, partly for that reason and partly because I apprehended, without then fully understanding, the problems inherent in being both an out-of-court advisor to the solicitors, and an expert witness whose primary duty was to the court (Edmond 2004a: 216). Some country experts are, however, regularly asked by solicitors to interview prospective clients whose nationality is at issue, to confirm that this 'Somali' is not really a Kenyan, or that 'Kosovan' not actually an Albanian.

The tribunal in *Thiyagarajah* set out my qualifications in detail, whereas that in *Somasundram* merely noted that I was 'eminently qualified'. In explaining its reasons for not according much weight to the report as a whole, the tribunal in *Thiyagarajah* picked out specific paragraphs with which it took issue, and stressed matters on which I had acknowledged a lack of expertise, such as whether Sri Lankan passports contain National Identity numbers.[4] The tribunal in *Somasundram*, by contrast, assessed my opinion in the round, without singling out particular details; its determination hinted that not all my opinions had been fully accepted, but did so almost admiringly, by describing my views as 'robust'. The reason for this broad contrast seems clear. The *Thiyagarajah* determination was more detailed precisely because it was aiming to discount my report, so as to forestall any appeal on the grounds that it had not been considered seriously. The tribunal in *Somasundram*, having accepted my assessment, had no need to protect itself in that way.

What is harder to decide, however, is the direction of the link between acceptance or rejection of a given report, and the overall decision on the

---

4   In retrospect, I should probably not have responded at all to this question.

appeal. In principle, the weighing of evidence comes before the reaching of decisions, and the reasoning generally presented in determinations certainly follows that sequence. But is that logic sometimes imposed only retro-spectively? Having taken the entire body of evidence into account and decided that an appellant has not made out his case to the required standard, a tribunal clearly needs to justify going against an expert opinion weighing in that appellant's favour, especially when, as in *Thiyagarajah*, counsel has 'relied almost exclusively' on it (see also §9.6).

9.4 BIAS AND OBJECTIVITY

Country experts are less often accused of being credulous than are doctors (§8.5). The issues they address are mostly general ones, because few asylum applicants are high-profile enough for there to be independent corroboration of their stories. Moreover, because they do not usually meet applicants, their opinions appear less dependent on what they have been told. On the other hand, they are far more likely than doctors to be accused of political bias. In *Slimani*, an Algerian appeal featuring an expert report by George Joffé, Mr Justice Collins noted that adjudicators and tribunals:

> regularly have placed before them opinions of individuals about the situ-ation in the country from which the appellant has come and, more importantly, about what is likely to happen to the appellant should he or she be returned. . . . Some such experts are highly respected (and we are happy to place Mr Joffé in this category) and at the very least their evidence can be said to have been given in good faith and to be based on reliable sources. Others range from the generally reasonable to the unacceptable and even venal. But all suffer from the difficulty that very rarely are they entirely objective in their approach . . . Many have fixed opinions about the regime in a particular country . . . This means that more often than not the expert in question, even if he has the credentials which qualify him in that role, will be acting more as an advocate than an expert witness.

Despite the disclaimer, this determination entered adjudicators' folklore as 'the one where Collins has a go at Joffé', illustrating how vulnerable an expert's reputation may be. One of the strongest attacks on a country expert, also by Mr Justice Collins, concerned David McDowall, an expert on Turkish Kurds:

> (8) Each appellant has in support of his claim relied on reports by vari-ous individuals who purport to be experts . . . One such is Mr David McDowell [sic] . . . whose reports are a familiar feature in many cases

involving Kurds from Turkey. His reports suffer from undue prolixity and an acceptance of what an appellant has stated as the truth . . .

(9) We note Mr McDowell's qualifications as a specialist on Middle East affairs. We do not doubt he has contacts with Kurdish organisations and has undertaken a deep study of the historical sufferings of the Kurds in Turkey. But his statement really does no more than argue a Kurdish case relying on historical and anecdotal material . . . Mr McDowell's reports are not objective and seek to determine . . . the issue that is entrusted to us. We find them singularly unhelpful and hope that we shall cease to see them paraded before us (*Isik and Bingol*).

There are two major criticisms here. The first is that McDowall accepts appellants' statements as being true. It is not clear which particular report was before Mr Justice Collins on this occasion; it may have been a 'recycled' one written for another case (David McDowall, pers. comm.). However, the criticism is made in general terms and in a report written at almost the same time, which does mention the above appellant, McDowall says the following:[5]

In short, I accept the plausibility of [G]'s account. I have tried to check the veracity of what he has stated, and the only discrepancy I have found [concerns] the precise number of casualties in Perpa Shopping Centre in August 1993, but I think it equally possible that Amnesty was mistaken regarding the actual number of casualties . . .

That reads to me as merely a conditional acceptance of G's account for purposes of argument. However, such niceties seemed insufficient to satisfy the court, perhaps because McDowall's reports often also contain statements such as, in this instance, 'I find your client's account of torture *credible*' (italics added). Despite his wide experience, McDowall (pers. comm.) was in fact unaware of the special status of 'credibility' assessments, a typical case of an expert receiving inadequate guidance from solicitors.

Second, his reports are described as 'not objective'. His response, in a letter (15 March 2001) to a committee of refugee lawyers, was typically combative; he has been known to write to the IAT complaining about assertions that he is not independent, which no doubt helps explain the strength of the subsequent criticism!

On three occasions I have been accused of lack of objectivity. . . . I do not want to go on about it, but there is no such thing as objectivity. . . . This is not a silly quibble, as it first might seem. It is very important

---

5   I am grateful to David McDowall for generously supplying reports and other correspondence.

indeed to the whole nature of evidence and I must confess to some aston-ishment at the accusation. . . . When giving evidence about the situation in a country, there can be a whole range of opinions, each honestly and carefully held. [W]e all, High Court judges included, are selective about the facts we think are relevant to any case. Selection of evidence is made according to the issue in hand, our values, and the life experiences that have moulded those values. . . . It is on this kind of basis that an attempt is made to say where we think truth lies, and why. To that I plead wholly guilty. I am sorry to be spelling out such a painfully obvious point, but I am aghast that those responsible for determining cases seem unaware of it. Was not that one of the basic realities learnt during History at school?

Although few social scientists would dissent from that *cri de coeur*, courts rarely take such matters into account. No doubt the constant references to 'objective evidence' in asylum hearings and determinations should not be taken too seriously as indicative of an explicit philosophical stance adopted by the courts (§6.1), yet its positivistic overtones do reflect a general reluctance on the part of the appellate authorities, legal representatives, and, above all, the Home Office, to acknowledge the contextualisation to which all knowledge is subject (see also Thuen 2004: 275).

To begin with, experts work within parameters set by others. They receive only certain kinds of information, and are steered towards certain questions, and prevented from addressing others, by virtue of the instructions they receive (see §6.6). Both Jones (1994) and Redmayne (2001) devote particular attention to experts in forensic science, whose chequered history has some general lessons regarding the vulnerability of experts, and their scapegoating when things go wrong. For example, following the moral panic surrounding the findings of Home Office forensic scientist Dr Alan Clift, the internal review of his cases:

> began with the assumption that any miscarriage of justice must be due to the shortcomings of Dr Clift as an individual. It proceeded to look for examples of his prosecution-mindedness and, where selections were found, these were taken as proof positive of his bias. There is a long list of very eminent expert witnesses who have suffered a similar fate (Jones 1994: 248).

'Selections' here refers to the selective presentation of evidence supporting one's conclusions; this happens in all scientific endeavours, but when a foren-sic expert is found to have presented evidence selectively to a court, this raises the possibility of legal challenge. Yet although Clift was made to carry the can, things proved far less straightforward than initially assumed. Because the processes of case construction led the police 'to interpret events in par-ticular ways, to neglect certain lines of enquiry, and to suppress specific items of information' (Redmayne 2001: 13), many selections were not of his own choosing; he was always working within 'terms of reference . . . supplied by the prosecution' (Jones 1994: 246). After 16 cases had been reviewed by the Court of Appeal, the Home Secretary reported that most convictions had proved perfectly safe. None was quashed purely because of doubts about Dr Clift's evidence (1994: 246).

Peterson and Conley (2001: 232) illustrate how posing a question in terms of one deliberately chosen set of parameters can lead an expert, in all innocence, to produce the answer desired by the instructing party. Even if this were not so, bias is almost certainly 'a universal tendency in forensic science' (Redmayne 2001: 13). It may, however, take different forms. Popular conceptions involve *motivational bias*; that is, forensic scientists are seen as biased because they want one side to win, perhaps because their occupational identity leads them to see their role as one of helping the police. *Cognitive biases* are far subtler, reflecting unconscious reasoning strategies or a tendency to prefer evidence favouring hypotheses to evidence casting doubt on them (2001: 15).

There are also overriding principles of profession ethics which might appear as *ethical biases* in the eyes of the law. According to the guidelines produced by the National Association for the Practice of Anthropology in the US, an anthropologist's 'primary responsibility [is] to respect and consider the welfare and human rights of all categories of people affected by decisions, programs or research in which we take part' (NAPA 1988: 8). A court might easily take this to mean that anthropological witnesses are necessarily biased towards the appellants on which they claim expertise, although in fact, as the word 'all' makes clear, their ethical responsibilities extend to legal decision makers every bit as much as to informants (cf. Good, no date; Cynthia Mahmood, pers. comm.).

The popular notion that forensic scientists can approach their investigations with an absolute objectivity, wholly independent of interpretations already placed upon the evidence by the police in constructing their case, is of course hopelessly naive.[6] Quite apart from the fact that they work with evidence preselected by the police, their own disciplinary canons predispose them to view matters in particular ways. It is a commonplace that established scientific paradigms affect interpretation and even perception; it is not just a matter of scientists clinging doggedly to old theories, but of them actually seeing the world through the spectacles those paradigms provide (Polanyi 1958; Kuhn 1962: Bloor 1976). Science expresses the world view of a professional community of scientists, an explanatory paradigm which comes into being through the intuitions of, and is corroborated or falsified on the basis

6   If the courts themselves sometimes act in ways that seem to give credence to that notion, it is generally because of the pre-emptive need for justice to seem objective, rather than out of any naive judicial belief in the infallibility of science (see also §9.8).

of the judgments of, human beings trained in specific ways (§2.2), with histories, statuses, reputations, and differential access to power and resources. We cannot ignore the professional organisation of the scientific community when assessing the theories it collectively approves or rejects. This applies equally, of course, to the disciplines from which 'country experts' are drawn — and to judges (§2.2).

9.5 ORAL EXPERT EVIDENCE

HOPOs often seek to discredit experts' reports by noting that they have not been cross-examined on them. In fact, expert opinions cannot be wholly rejected solely for this reason; rather, the court must weigh them against other objective evidence before it (*Tarlochan Singh*). Even so, given that many of the kinds of issues considered in this chapter might be resolvable in that way, it is surprising how rarely experts are called to give oral evidence at asylum hearings.

Most country and medical experts are understandably reluctant to appear, given the time commitment involved, yet it may sometimes be in their own interests to do so, because if they limit themselves to written testimony they increase their vulnerability to criticism. In any case, they are well advised to observe what I term the 'Freeman test', after the tribunal chairman who observed *à propos* a report by Patrick Gilkes, a well-thought-of expert, that:

> Reputable and conscientious though he is compared to many practitioners in his field, we regret that the lack of the constant discipline of giving oral evidence, subject to effective cross-examination, which provides the best check on the reliability of forensic experts in any other court, may have led to his resorting to assertion, rather than demonstration (*Misrak*).

Whether or not these particular strictures were justified, the general principle is hard to question. The 'Freeman test', then, involves experts asking themselves about every assertion in their reports: do they have the evidence to defend this position to their own professional satisfaction when cross-examined before the tribunal? If not, the assertion should not be in the report.

HOPOs sometimes seek to discredit absent experts on the grounds that they have not been in the country recently (see also §9.3). In one appeal where a report of mine was before the court, the determination records the following exchange:

> Mr Trent [the HOPO] said that Dr Good was last in Sri Lanka in September 1996 and whatever information he had about the situation in

that country must be second-hand. . . . In reply, Mr Ramzam [counsel] submitted that Dr Good's report was based on his knowledge of Sri Lanka and he asked the tribunal to take the report as a whole (*Vijiharan*; glosses added).

Although its determination took me mildly to task for not addressing one issue, the tribunal did not accept the HOPO's general argument. Indeed, it specifically noted that in reaching its decision it had:

> looked at the appellant's situation at today's date which, of course, is the relevant date for consideration of this appeal. It is for this reason that the most recent CIPU report and Dr Good's report have been referred to and relied upon.

There are of course circumstances where having recently conducted *field research* would make a crucial difference, but having merely visited a country recently is of very limited significance in relation to most matters with which country experts are asked to deal. In general, if an expert's CV demonstrates prolonged study of and broad knowledge about a country, it should hardly matter where they happen to be when reading a particular document or news report.

HOPOs may get more than they bargained for if they adopt this line while actually cross-examining experts, as in the following exchange (CC/28161/2001):

> *HOPO*: Can you tell me, when was the last time you were in Burma?
> *Expert(Mr Win Soe)*: I left Burma in 1977.
> *HOPO*: 1977!!?
> *Expert*: Yes.
> *HOPO*: Then can you tell me, how do you *know* about the activities of the government, such as tapping telephones?
> *Expert*: Well, I belong to a political family. My grandfather, my late grandfather, was the Prime Minister of Burma, overthrown in 1972 and imprisoned.

As this illustrates, when experts *do* appear HOPOs often find themselves in difficulty, as they lack the training and background knowledge to cope. On one occasion, I was cross-examined on the difficulties a single Tamil girl would face in making a respectable marriage when her parents were both overseas as refugees. This inevitably required me to explain the intricacies of cross-cousin marriage, at which point the HOPO abruptly ended the cross-examination, quite forgetting to quiz me on my political assessment (which meant, as counsel subsequently whispered to me, that he could not challenge it later in his concluding submissions).

In one well known instance, an absent expert was roundly criticised on grounds that subsequent oral examination suggested were unfair. The expert in question was Dr Jasdev Singh Rai, Director of the Sikh Human Rights Group, whose reports were much used in Sikh asylum cases. He was heavily criticised in a determination written by the then President of the IAT, Judge David Pearl:

> Dr Rai's evidence . . . is not sourced, and appears to lack the requirement of objectivity. It appears to be based on reading and on discussions with others. Much of it would appear therefore to be hearsay evidence (*Chinder Singh*).

That last criticism is surprising, not only because Judge Pearl has impeccable academic credentials as co-author of a standard text on Islamic law (Pearl and Menski 1998), but also because to limit experts to evidence based on direct observation would restrict their role far more than normal (see also Hall and Smith 2001: 59–60). Be that as it may, the tribunal went on:

> we do not believe that Dr Rai's evidence should be given much weight at all. It totally fails to meet the requirements which would normally be expected of an objective and sourced account of events . . . in a particular country . . .

The tribunal gave three specific grounds for this critique. First, Dr Rai had supplied no CV; here the tribunal contrasted him unfavourably with another expert whose report was in evidence, Dr Cynthia Mahmood:

> We have a detailed curriculum vitae for Dr Mahmood. . . . Although primarily an anthropologist, her academic qualifications make it clear that she is well used to weighing information received, and making objective assessments . . . in contrast with Dr Rai, her views should be given weight.

One might take umbrage at the word 'although' in this passage, but the general point is otherwise very clear. Second, Dr Rai's reports were being widely used in appeals other than those for which they had been written. Such 'recycling' was widespread at that time, though this was generally wholly unknown to the experts concerned, as I discovered to my own cost at the start of my research. Third, Dr Rai was not there in person to be cross-examined and justify his opinions.

After that determination appeared in August 1998, Dr Rai's reports were repeatedly criticised by other tribunals, so in March 1999, lawyers in another Sikh case being heard by Judge Pearl called Dr Rai to give oral evidence (*Kuldip Singh*). He was cross-examined on his qualifications and experience, his opinion of the current case, and his attitude towards that previous case, *Chinder Singh*. After criticising the recycling of expert reports, which Dr Rai had explicitly disavowed, the tribunal stated:

> In *Chinder Singh*, the tribunal was faced with [an] unsatisfactory scenario. The representatives knew little about Dr Rai, and it is unfortunate that the tribunal was not told that Dr Rai had been interviewed by the Research Directorate of the IRB in Canada in September 1997, covering aspects of the human rights situation in Punjab. . . . We now have an up-to-date cv from Dr Rai, and of course he gave evidence before us over two days. . . . We do not wish to rehearse the arguments which we addressed in *Chinder Singh*. . . . We concede however that if the tribunal had known that Dr Rai had been asked by the Research Directorate of the IRB to give evidence to it . . . then the tribunal's assessment of Dr Rai's evidence may have been different.

This effort to rehabilitate his reputation thus proved highly successful, underlining the importance of oral testimony in safeguarding an expert's reputation.

9.6 MULTIPLE EXPERTS: THE *KARUNAKARAN* APPEAL

The Home Office twice experimented briefly with using its own medical experts. The first attempt, according to my informant, concerned a series of appeals by Sikhs involving reports by a single Medical Foundation doctor, but was abandoned when the Home Office expert consistently agreed with the MF doctor's assessment. Subsequently, IND produced a generic report entitled *Notes for Assessing Psychiatric Injury in Asylum Seekers* by a Dr Neal, but this was not based on any research whatever among refugees, and tribunals were unimpressed by HOPOs' claims that it should be given greater weight than reports by medical experts who had actually examined the appellants (*Harunaj*; Henderson 2003: 260).

Usually, though, expert evidence comes only from the appellant's side. Consequently, although they must weigh expert evidence against other objective material, adjudicators and tribunals almost never need to balance the opinion of one expert against that of another. Such balancing was, however, carried out in unusual and striking fashion in *Karanakaran*. Mr Karanakaran's[7] first appeal was unsuccessful because, according to the Court of Appeal, the adjudicator found:

---

7 Note that the courts used different spellings of the appellant's name. For lawyers the principal interest of *Karanakaran* concerns the Court of Appeal's comments on risk assessment (§10.4).

no evidence that he or his family were ever singled out for retaliatory oppression. . . . The appellant had therefore failed to make out a well-founded fear of persecution for a Convention reason. . . . He found that the appellant would not face undue hardship if he were to return to Colombo.

In other words, even if Mr Karanakaran *did* have a well-founded fear of persecution in parts of Sri Lanka, 'internal flight' (§4.2.2) to Colombo was still open to him.

For the IAT appeal, his representatives, the Refugee Legal Centre, submitted no fewer than four expert reports by Dr Piers Vitebsky, a Cambridge anthropologist; Dr Mick Moore from the Institute of Development Studies, Sussex; Dr Richard Slater from the International Development Department at Birmingham; and Dr Jonathan Spencer, an anthropologist from Edinburgh. Even so, the tribunal dismissed the appeal. It summarised key points made by the experts, then concluded:

But, when one examines these experts' opinions, most of it is pure speculation . . . The experts say that, in their opinion, it would be unduly harsh for him to return to Colombo. . . . However, their opinions must be looked at in the light of . . . the evidence in this case weighed up accordingly.

However, this assessment was strongly criticised by the Court of Appeal. In Lord Justice Brooke's judgment, 'it was completely wrong for the tribunal . . . to dismiss considerations put forward by experts of the quality who wrote opinions on this case as "pure speculation" ', while Lord Justice Sedley concluded that 'this case must go back for determination by a differently constituted appeal tribunal, if only because of the way in which highly relevant evidence of in-country conditions from experts with respectable credentials was dismissed . . . as mere speculation'.

The case was remitted, and the second tribunal was chaired by the Deputy President. Its determination made clear that it had taken special note of 'the Court of Appeal's castigation of the tribunal's dismissal of letters from Dr Jonathan Spencer [*et al.*] as "purely speculative" ', and had therefore 'read them with care'. However, it drew attention to Lord Justice Brooke's comment about the desirability of the new tribunal having access to 'up-to-date evidence about the situation relating to young male Tamils in Colombo'. The Refugee Legal Centre was again representing Mr Karanakaran, yet as the tribunal pointed out:

Despite that clearly-expressed view . . . none of them has been updated. . . . We do not know whether the writers of the original letters have been approached or not. What is clear is that there is no material before us from which we could draw any conclusion on the views of these four gentlemen about the situation at the present time.

This criticism was clearly justified. Asylum appeals must consider conditions at the date of the hearing, and circumstances in Sri Lanka had changed significantly over the intervening three-year period. A court is entitled to regard absence of evidence as significant when it could reasonably be expected to be there; for example, if there has been plenty of time to produce a medical report, its absence without convincing explanation may suggest that a report *was* obtained but its findings did not assist the appellant (Mr Justice Collins, Mr Mark Ockelton, pers. comm.). Given the clear hint from the Court of Appeal, it was quite reasonable for the tribunal to assume that the experts had been asked to update their reports, but were no longer prepared to stand by their opinions or had replied in ways which the RLC found unhelpful (in fact, at least one of them was never asked for an updated opinion).

These were not the only criticisms levelled at the expert evidence, however. Slater and Vitebsky were said to have overstepped the mark, in that their letters:

> express the view that it would (or could) indeed be unduly harsh for him to be returned there [Colombo]. No doubt those views are entitled to respect, but they are profoundly unhelpful to a tribunal that has to make its own evaluation and judgment on this issue ... It would be quite wrong for us to conclude that it is unduly harsh for the appellant to be returned to Colombo simply because Dr Slater and Dr Vitebsky think it is. It would be equally wrong for us to conclude that it would not be unduly harsh because Dr Spencer and Dr Moore do not specifically say that it would be. Where a balancing of issues, an evaluation and a judgment have to be made by the tribunal, all relevant facts are helpful, but an opinion of a person who purports to have made the judgment himself is likely to be prejudicial rather than persuasive (my gloss in square brackets).

It was not the experts' role to decide whether it would be 'unduly harsh' to return Karanakaran to Colombo, and while this did not allow the tribunal to reject their remaining evidence, it did, clearly, allow it to lessen its overall weight. One cannot blame the experts; they should have been given more precise instructions, or have been asked by the legal representatives to remove such comments.

That same passage also illustrates the tribunal's other strategy for reducing the weight of the experts' opinions: playing off one report against another. The determination drew attention to several other instances where issues had been raised by one or two experts but not the others. For example:

> Dr Vitebsky and Dr Moore consider that the appellant will be at risk
> from the LTTE, but Dr Spencer and Dr Slater do not mention that. Dr
> Spencer regards the risk of round-ups as very real, but records an order
> by the Attorney-General that a major series of arrests should cease.
> None of the other gentlemen mentions that.

After several paragraphs in this vein, the tribunal concluded:

> Despite the expertise of the writers . . . and the identical nature of the
> issues on which they were asked to comment, there is a great deal of
> divergence between their opinions about what the appellant may suffer.

The same general issue, drawing conclusions from the absence of evidence,
arises here in more complex form. It is one thing, if experts explicitly contra-
dict one another, to prefer one of those conflicting views, quite another to
infer 'divergence' from silences in their reports. If the tribunal was indeed
correct in assuming that all the experts were asked similar questions, it may
arguably be the case that some silences suggest a rejection of the relevance of
particular factors. However, they are at least as likely to reflect the different
competencies or interests of the experts, who were bound to be more up-to-
date and better informed on some issues than on others. In any case, the
tribunal was able to pursue this particular strategy only because such an
unusually large number of experts had been instructed, thereby 'over-egging
the pudding', as one adjudicator remarked.

Whenever there are different pieces of evidence with similar claims to
authority, such as contrary findings by experts of equal standing, or generic
reports which do not entirely support an expert's conclusions, it is obviously
essential for courts to weigh one against the other. In asylum appeals, however, the Home Office generally contents itself with producing the current
CIPU *Country Report*. It rarely provides country evidence directly addressing
the particular issues at stake, and almost never produces medical evidence of
any kind. Adjudicators and tribunals are therefore forced to decide what
weight to attach to uncontested expert evidence. This no doubt helps explain
the frequency with which they have recourse to an expert's alleged political
bias, use of inappropriate language ('credibility' being the most obvious
example), or drawing conclusions which go further than is thought proper
(*Sutharshan*; §8.5).

In *Karanakaran*, the situation was intriguingly different. Rather than 'rival'
expert evidence from the two parties to the appeal, the tribunal was faced
with several expert opinions on behalf of the appellant, which it proceeded to
treat 'as if' they were conflicting opinions by weighing one against another.
One can only guess how far the tribunal's lengthy demonstration of
'divergence' between the various expert opinions was an opportunistic strategy for diminishing their weight, en route to justifying its decision to dismiss

the appeal for other reasons. It was, of course, necessary for the tribunal to cut that kind of swathe through the expert reports in order to justify its decision to dismiss the appeal, especially so in view of the Court of Appeal's criticisms of how the expert evidence had been handled previously.

9.7 TRIBUNALS AS EXPERTS

Tribunals often assert that they themselves possess particular expertise of comparable weight to expert evidence (*Zarour*; §8.4). The claim is made most succinctly by Vice-President John Barnes, who asserts that the IAT possesses:

> expertise as a specialist tribunal, not only in the legal issues for its determination, but *also in its knowledge of country situations and, to a lesser extent perhaps, in consideration and evaluation of medical reports* (2004: 349; italics added).

While it is true that higher courts sometimes recognise such expertise on the IAT's part (Barnes 2004: 350), they just as frequently emphasise the reverse, namely, that tribunals are 'bound to place heavy reliance on the views of experts and specialists' (*'S' and Others*). The strength of IAT feelings on the matter are, however, evident in its President's robust rejection of this particular passage:

> We note but respectfully are unable to accept the view of the court . . . The tribunal is accustomed to being served with reports of experts. . . . From them, the tribunal will reach its own conclusions about the situation in the country . . . Further, the tribunal builds up its own expertise in relation to the limited number of countries from which asylum seekers come. Naturally, an expert's report can assist, but *we do not accept that heavy reliance is or should be placed upon such reports* (*SSHD* v. *SK [Croatia]*; italics added).

There is no doubt that experienced adjudicators and tribunal chairs become thoroughly informed at a factual level about, say, the political histories of countries generating asylum claimants. It is in assessing the cultural or political significance of such facts that expertise comes into play, however, and my research suggests that here adjudicators are on far shakier ground. For example, one told me that she had judged it implausible that a Hindu Tamil from Sri Lanka would have been helped by a Muslim as he claimed, because she felt that Muslims would have more in common with Buddhists than with Hindus. I know of no evidence for such a generalisation, which faces two major difficulties even in principle: Buddhists and Hindus worship the same deities, so there is no obvious reason why Muslims should feel greater affinity to one religion rather than the other; moreover, Sri Lankan Hindus and Muslims speak the same language, whereas Buddhists speak a language from a completely different language family.

The issue of tribunal expertise arises particularly in Country Guidelines (CG) cases. There were nearly 300 of these by early 2005, some having acquired this status retrospectively. Like 'starred' and 'reported' decisions (§5.3), they are intended to enhance the IAT's ability to standardise decision making by adjudicators. But whereas 'starred' cases are 'binding on points of law' (*NM and Others*, ¶140), CG cases are meant to establish authoritative assessments of objective or (as the IAT is increasingly saying) 'background' evidence about countries of origin, in relation to issues which recur in numerous appeals (Yeo 2005b: 9). The Court of Appeal thought that this strategy, though 'exotic', could, in principle, be both 'benign and practical' (*S and Others*), but that view presupposes that tribunals are indeed able to carry out comprehensive, effective analyses of all available objective material. In fact, some early CG decisions departed so far from that ideal as to be based entirely upon CIPU *Reports*, with all the deficiencies that entails (§9.2). Over time, however, tribunals became more punctilious about basing CG decisions upon more, and more varied, background evidence.

In *NM and Others* (a legal tribunal including Dr Storey and His Honour Judge Risius, and chaired by the outgoing President Mr Justice Ouseley), the IAT's final CG decision before being replaced under the 2004 Act explicitly set out the reasoning behind the CG system. The starting premise was not merely the direct injustice created by 'variable or haphazard' decision making at second instance level, but the compounding of that injustice by the creation of further uncertainty and inconsistency among first instance decision makers. Beyond a certain threshold, indeed, 'a pattern of inconsistent decision making could involve an error of law' (¶136).

The tribunal was concerned, however, that the Court of Appeal in *S and Others* seemed to have mistakenly understood CG decisions to be intended as precedents, in the same way as 'starred' cases are. It therefore spelled out that CG cases 'are not accurately understood or described as *"factual precedents"* [because] it is always possible for further evidence to show that the original decision was wrong or to expose other issues which require examination' (*NM and Others*, ¶141; original italics). Rather, it is intended that findings in CG cases:

> should be applied except where they do not apply to the particular facts
> ... and can properly be held inapplicable for legally adequate reasons ...
> It may be that the passage of time itself or substantial new evidence itself
> warrants a re-examination of the position, even though the outcome may
> be unchanged. ... The system does not have the rigidity of the legally
> binding precedent but has instead the flexibility to accommodate indi-

vidual cases, changes, fresh evidence and the other circumstances which we have set out (¶140).

While that certainly clarifies the legal status of CG decisions, it takes for granted the ability of the asylum judiciary alone, bereft of independent expert advice, to assess for itself bodies of evidence, however voluminous and complete, regarding countries for which it lacks first-hand knowledge or experience, and contexts whose cultural nuances call for specialised hermeneutic elucidation.

Just as tribunals increasingly claim expertise regarding objective evidence, so too, reciprocally, do they seem to expect experts themselves to display mastery of case law. Although there is no longer any absolute prohibition on them addressing the 'ultimate issue' (§6.2), experts have risked treading on the Court's toes if they sail too close to that particular wind. They must avoid expressing opinions on whether appellants are in fact refugees, and while they may assess how appellants might be treated if returned, they cannot opine whether that treatment would amount to 'persecution' or 'inhuman and degrading treatment' in Convention terms.[8] Recently, however, the 'failure' of experts to address current case law notions of 'risk' has repeatedly been used by tribunals to justify diminishing the weight of their reports.

In *GH [Iraq]*, the tribunal considered reports by Dr K Rashidian and Mr George Joffé, but concluded that 'neither . . . should be treated as expert witnesses for the purposes of this appeal'. The core criticism[9] was that 'neither witness demonstrated . . . an understanding of the legal concepts to be applied in evaluating risk. Both clearly wrote on the assumption that we are concerned with whether safety can be guaranteed. We are not.'

Rashidian's comments that 'There is a serious risk that [*GH*] would be targeted and his life can be in danger', that 'Neither the KDP nor the PUK can provide full protection', and that 'the life of no Kurd in the Iraqi Arabs regime can be guaranteed', were taken to illustrate his 'misplaced approach'. Joffé was criticised for stating that 'conditions in Iraq are not such that individual security and safety can be assured' and that PUK security systems could not provide 'blanket control to allow guarantee of security'. In the tribunal's judgment, these comments showed that:

> neither witness can be regarded as expressing opinions as to risk based on the concept of real risk which it is the duty of adjudicators and this tribunal to apply and to that extent such expressed views must be

---

8   My own hedge against mistakes is to add a disclaimer: 'My comments represent my professional assessment of the situation in Sri Lanka; I do not purport to assess the legal basis of X's claim.'

9   The tribunal also questioned their impartiality and objectivity; easy allegations to make, and virtually impossible to rebut (see also §9.4).

approached with considerable caution as to the evidential weight to be given to them.

One of my own reports was subsequently treated in similar fashion (*SSHD* v. *PS [Sri Lanka]*). The tribunal attributed to me the view that 'sufficiency of protection must guarantee the safety of each individual citizen from the risk which he fears'. This was striking for two reasons. First, a similar 'misconception' was attributed to Human Rights Watch, Amnesty International, and even to UNHCR, the actual custodians of the 1951 Convention. Second, this was not a position taken in either my report or my oral evidence, nor was it actually put to me to give me an opportunity to disavow it. I do in fact agree with the proposition that no State can offer anyone – even, in Sri Lanka, its own President – absolute guarantees of protection. My position is, however, that the key factor in assessing the risks faced by appellants such as PS is not the State's ability to protect them, but rather the 'strength of will', as Professor Casson of the IAT put it at the hearing, on the part of the LTTE to target them. The LTTE can, if it wishes, target virtually anyone; the question was, therefore, whether PS's background suggested that it might indeed single him out.

The IAT itself has subsequently resiled from the position asserted in *GH* and *PS*. The legal tribunal in *NM & Others* reported at length the written, and in one case also oral, evidence of two well thought-of experts, Professor Ioan Lewis and Dr Virginia Luling. It then began its assessment as follows:

> (95) Neither Professor Lewis nor Dr Luling sought to equate their own vocabulary of risk and danger with the words contained in the legal tests that have to be applied by the courts and the tribunal in asylum and asylum related appeals. That in our view is entirely proper. It is not the function of country experts to seek to assess what does or does not breach the Refugee or the Human Rights Convention. Irrespective of the vocabulary in which country experts express their opinion, it remains for judicial decision whether their opinion evidences the existence of a real risk of persecution or of ill-treatment within the meaning of the Refugee Convention and Article 3.

A few weeks before the hearing in *PS*, I had raised my concerns on this very matter in public debate with Dr Storey, at the Immigration Advisory Service's annual conference, with reference to the decision in *GH*, where both experts had made clear what they meant by 'risk'. I found it remarkable, and worrying, that the tribunal sought to discount their expertise purely because they used an ordinary English word, risk, in a perfectly acceptable everyday way. In my own work as an expert I had always assumed that any attempt on my part to express views on 'the concept of real risk' as defined in asylum case law, or to tailor my responses towards it, would be an improper extension of my role, and that it was for the tribunal to perform its own analysis of whether, in light of the evidence in my report, any such 'real risk' existed. The tribunal in *NM & Others* seems to confirm that view. Indeed, it is precisely here, and no further in my view, that tribunals can truly claim to possess expertise.

There are two reasons why this issue seems especially important. From a legal perspective, 'risk' is even more crucial than 'credibility' to deciding asylum claims, in that decisions on credibility are merely precursors to assessing risk (§10.4). More broadly, 'risk' is a central trope of modern society (Chapter 11). Risks and their assessment figure in the news media on a daily basis; there are many professional journals devoted to the topic; it is studied by researchers in disciplines from engineering and physical sciences right through to cultural studies and philosophy; and every large institution has its risk management committee. Any requirement that experts abandon their own disciplinary approaches to risk in favour of the highly specialised, perhaps counter-intuitive, stance taken in asylum case law, would carry with it the danger of turning judicial discussions of risk into an hermetically sealed discourse which took no account of these broader intellectual and social currents.

9.8 JUDICIAL PRAGMATISM

The appeal of stratagems such as those described in the two preceding sections of this chapter is obvious; they allow judicial decision makers to evade the difficulties posed when pesky expert findings stand in the way of conclusions reached on other grounds. Any potential restriction on judicial freedom created by the need to defer to uncontroverted medical or country expertise can thus be emasculated by recourse to the notion of 'weight'. It is important to remind ourselves, however, that such behaviour, like other instances of legal positivism exposed in this chapter, is more a pragmatic response to professional imperatives than an expression of philosophical naivety. Academic scholars can always evade responsibility by stressing the provisionality of their conclusions, but judges have no such luxury. They are ultimately required to decide one way or the other, so there always comes a point where the epistemological pussy-footing has to stop.

Chapter 10

Reaching decisions

> The verdict remains, however, a curious and problematic outcome. We can only speculate on . . . the obscure chemistry of unanimity. What was done with the pile of historical documents . . . [D]id they conscientiously search the record for evidence . . .?
>
> (Clifford 1988: 335)

10.1 JUDICIAL REASONING

While there are no juries in asylum appeals, however far they progress up the legal ladder, here too Clifford's questions cannot be other than matters of fascination. Even in jury trials judges are far more than passive 'referees' (Engeström 1998: 201), and when judges themselves are decision makers their role is greater still. In reaching decisions, says Edmond, they are 'simultaneously interested in resolving a public dispute plausibly and expeditiously, advancing their career, cultivating the law, establishing a personal reputation, resisting or encouraging review and maintaining the social legitimacy of their institution' (2004b: 138).

The question posed here is more limited, however. After deciding on the relevance and credibility of the evidence, after assessing its weight, how do adjudicators and tribunals achieve the final step in the process, that of determining whether the standard of proof has been met? The reasoning in determinations is, of course, fully open to analysis, and indeed generally to appeal. The problem is that this reasoning is, to an unknown and variable extent, constructed post facto in order to justify conclusions reached on more intuitive, less formally logical, grounds. The wide scope afforded to the judiciary in this regard is well recognised by MacCormick:

> A judge knows the proposition of law with which he has to work in a given case. Assume it to be of the form 'If p then q'. He therefore knows that if he 'finds' as facts propositions which entail 'p', he will be committed to the proposition q by way of conclusion. Suppose that q is for some

reason a conclusion disagreeable to him in the context of a particular case. . . . He can simply say that he does not find certain facts proven, and therefore *p* is not the case. Equally, if he is desirous of reaching the conclusion *q*, he need only say that he finds *p* true in the instant case. So, logical though his argument will be on the face of it, it is no more than rationalization, since he determined its course by the way in which he chose to 'find' the facts (1994: 36).

This chapter deals mainly with such 'rationalisations', in the form of the written determinations which convey the courts' decisions and give reasons for them. While this is a limitation, it is an unavoidable one. There is no way for outsiders to know how decisions were in fact reached, and even decision makers themselves may not be fully able to reconstruct that process, because it is not necessarily (or even usually) a matter of the kinds of *conscious* manipulation described by MacCormick. With the best will in the world – and not surprisingly to anyone with experience of similar activities, even something as humdrum as marking student essays – these aspects of judicial decision making are almost impossible to verbalise. My attempts to get adjudicators to describe how they reach decisions yielded little of substance. This does not impugn the honesty of their response, but simply reflects the ineffability of the processes of cognition whereby experienced practitioners assimilate and evaluate complex information.

10.2 THE STANDARD AND BURDEN OF PROOF

In asylum appeals the courts must decide, above all, how applicants are likely to be treated if returned to their countries of origin. The burden of proving entitlement to refugee status rests upon applicants themselves, but how likely must persecution be before their fear is regarded as well founded?

The standard of proof in civil cases is 'the balance of probabilities'; that is, the outcome must be more probable than not. In *Sivakumaran* the House of Lords decided that a lesser standard was appropriate in asylum cases, for two main reasons. First, they involve assessments of future risk, rather than merely claims about the past. Second, the rights at stake are matters of life and death. Lord Keith's view was that there need only be a 'reasonable degree of likelihood' of persecution on return; Lord Templeman thought there should be a 'real and substantial danger'; and Lord Goff referred to 'a real and substantial risk'. Some felt that Lord Goff's phrase implied a higher standard (Harvey 2000: 241), but the general view has been that all three are 'equivalent expressions' (*Horvath*, per Lord Clyde). It is often said that a one in ten chance that an applicant will suffer the feared consequences is enough to establish their case, but unlike in the US (*INS* v. *Cardoza-Fonseca*; Einolf 2001: 117) this is a practical rule-of-thumb, not a legally endorsed principle.

Though the legal focus is on what may happen to refugees in future, their prior experience is an important consideration. *Sivakumaran* made clear that the lower standard of proof applied to assessments of future events, but should this lower standard apply to past persecution too? The IAT was divided on this issue, and matters came to a head with an outcome which over the years has been very rare (§10.3), a split decision. The appeal in question, *Kaja*, was heard by a senior legal tribunal. One member, Mr RE Maddison, thought historical facts should be assessed to the usual civil 'balance of probabilities' standard, and only when assessing future risk should the 'reasonable likelihood' standard apply. The majority – Professor DC Jackson and Mr GW Farmer – argued, however, that adopting different standards for different parts of the assessment was artificial because 'an assessment of future likelihood cannot sensibly be separated from an assessment of the past and present'; furthermore, it would 'remove much of the benefit of uncertainty conferred on the applicant through *Sivakumaran*'. Many asylum cases involve 'greater than normal uncertainty' as to the facts, because the evidence is limited to the applicant's own story and generic 'objective evidence'. They felt there should be a 'positive role for uncertainty' in asylum determinations (Harvey 2000: 242; Symes 2001: 12, 14).

This was resisted by some tribunal chairs and the Home Office challenged it in the Court of Appeal (*Horvath*), where Lady Justice Hale and Lord Justice Stuart-Smith seemed about to decide that appellants had to satisfy the higher standard of 'the balance of probabilities'. A Tamil asylum appeal (*Karanakaran*; see §9.6; §10.4) was being heard in another court, and its judges, including Lord Justices Brooke and Sedley, pre-emptively rejected that view. They emphasised the correctness of *Kaja*, and reasserted that rules of evidence were less strict than in ordinary courts.

The standard of proof issue arose again in October 2000, when the *Human Rights Act 1998* became applicable to asylum cases. HOPOs were instructed to argue that human rights violations had to be proved 'beyond reasonable doubt', but the tribunal decided that the standard of proof for breaches of Article 3 of the ECHR (inhuman or degrading treatment or punishment) was the same lower standard as in asylum appeals (*Kacaj*). As they pointed out, persecution normally involves human rights violations too 'and a finding that there is real risk of persecution would be likely to involve a finding that there is a real risk of a breach of the European Convention on Human Rights'. It would therefore be 'strange if different standards of proof applied'. This decision confirmed the existence of a small 'window' whereby a human rights claim may succeed even if an asylum claim based on the same facts has failed, because the ECHR is not restricted to the five 'Convention reasons'.

Kacaj also considered whether the ECHR had 'extra-territorial' effect; was the UK responsible for any human rights violations suffered by asylum applicants whom it returned? The European Court had decided that the UK authorities might indeed be liable for any violations of core ECHR values – such as those enshrined in Articles 3 and 4 – occurring as the result of expulsion (*Soering; Chahal*; Blake and Husain 2003: 27). The Secretary of State argued, however, that this should not apply to any Article other than Article 3. The IAT found 'extra-territorial effect' a misnomer; the issue was the lawfulness of a decision to expel someone to a place where their human rights might be at risk. It decided that *all* Articles had 'extra-territorial effect' in this sense, but that for most of them any possible violation of ECHR rights would be trumped by the interests of legitimate immigration control, making it 'virtually impossible for an applicant to establish that control on immigration was disproportionate to any breach'. The Court of Appeal later decided that only Article 3 could be engaged by acts of expulsion (*Ullah*; Blake and Husain 2003: 10), but the Lords disagreed, although Lord Bingham cautioned in his leading speech that while it would be consistent with general human rights principles for Articles 2 and 4 to be engaged 'if the facts are strong enough', only a 'flagrant denial' of ECHR rights under Articles 5, 6, 8, and 9 would be likely to engage the UK's Convention obligations.

It is also important to bear in mind which party has the burden of meeting the appropriate standard of proof. Thus, while criminal cases must be proved to a high level of probability ('beyond reasonable doubt'), the burden of attaining that standard rests with the prosecution. Although the standard of proof in asylum hearings is far lower, the burden of proof generally rests upon claimants. In UNHCR's view, however, this burden should sometimes be partly lifted because of the understandable difficulties faced by many claimants in producing corrobative evidence. The UNHCR *Handbook* specifies that 'the examiner', here an Immigration Officer or IND caseworker, should 'use all the means at his disposal to produce the necessary evidence in support of the application' (1992: ¶196). Even if no such evidence is forthcoming, 'if the applicant's account appears credible, he should, unless there are good reasons to the contrary, be given the benefit of the doubt' (1992: ¶196; see §8.1). The *APIs* do indeed mention 'additional evidence . . . gathered specifically to check the applicant's account' (IND 2002a: ¶1.2.10), but make no reference to any duty to obtain evidence *supporting* an application. IND does consult UK missions overseas, but there are no published guidelines on how this should be done, and it is alleged that replies enhancing credibility may be suppressed; that missions sometimes advise against asylum irrespective of circumstances for fear of setting precedents; and that they sometimes approach national security authorities in respect of named applicants, potentially endangering them (Asylum Aid 1999).

Where it is claimed that an applicant's documents are forgeries, the burden of proof is on the Secretary of State to show that they are not authentic, rather than on the appellant to prove that they are, and insofar as decision makers have reasonable doubts over the authenticity of documentary evidence, these should be exercised in favour of applicants (*A, B, C and D*). On the other hand, applicants cannot transfer the overall burden of proof from themselves to the Secretary of State simply by producing documents, and tribunals have argued that it cannot be right that *all* documents be presumed genuine unless the contrary is shown, particularly when they have characteristics which seem to limit their persuasive effect (*Kongo-Kongo*). The burden of proof is also on the Secretary of State if he wishes to invoke Art 1F(b) so as to deny Convention protection to 'terrorists' (*Jothinath*).

10.3 THE 'CHEMISTRY OF UNANIMITY'

First tier asylum appeals to the IAA are heard and decided by adjudicators sitting alone. For tribunals an extra dynamic is introduced by the multiplicity of decision makers, so here Clifford's 'chemistry of unanimity' comes directly into play. The decision-making process, one suspects, must be significantly changed by the need to carry other tribunal members along; it no longer suffices to reach decisions by introspection and justify them post facto by the kinds of 'rationalisation' described by MacCormick (1994; §10.1).

When I showed a draft of one article (Good 2004a) to the Deputy President, Mr Ockelton, he objected to me naming the chair when citing tribunal cases, on the grounds that – unlike the Court of Appeal, where each judge writes an individual opinion even if it is only a single sentence expressing support for the leading judgment – tribunal decisions are collective in the sense that only a single determination is promulgated. I defer of course to his legal authority, but as explained earlier, I write not as a lawyer but as an anthropologist. Tribunal determinations are signed only by the legal member and are very evidently written by them; indeed, several have writing styles so distinctive that one could easily identify them in a 'blindfold test' (§10.5). As my concern is with the forms of reasoning and rhetoric employed in their legal discourse rather than the precise status of their legal authority, I often retain their names in discussions throughout this book.

Moreover, published split decisions have in fact occurred in the past, albeit rarely. The most famous example is *Kaja*, where the majority in a legal tribunal decided that historical facts should be assessed to the same lower standard as future risk (§10.2). There are even a few cases of lay members overruling legal chairs. In *Sadegh*, for example, the chair thought homosexuals could constitute a social group if they were 'clearly identifiable as such in the country of the alleged persecution', but the lay members argued that the practice of homosexuality was voluntary.

A particularly odd situation arose in *Jelusic*, where the appellant was a Croatian citizen with a Serbian mother and a Bosnian Croat father. The adjudicator believed her story, but concluded that she had exaggerated the difficulties she would face if returned. Her initial tribunal hearing took place before Mr Shrimpton, as legal member, and Messrs Edinboro and Kumar, two long-serving lay members. The provisional majority view, seemingly, was that the appellant's fears might be well founded, but the appeal was adjourned part-heard when the HOPO indicated that the Secretary of State was going to review the case. In due course the appeal was relisted, and Ms Jelusic's counsel successfully argued that the same panel should continue to hear it. Counsel had to cry off on the morning of the reconvened hearing, however, owing to family illness, and for some reason Mr Kumar was not present. To complicate matters further, there continued to be differing opinions on the tribunal, as the determination explains:

> in the opinion of the legal member the developments since the application for asylum was made have removed the objective basis for the appellant's undoubtedly genuine fear of persecution. . . . The second member of the tribunal is clearly of the view that the background evidence does go so far as to justify the appellant's subjective fear.

The determination noted that, as it was a two-member tribunal, the case would have had to be adjourned yet again until a three-member panel could be constituted, unless this difference could be resolved. But rather than adjourning, which would also have had the advantage that counsel could be present, the chair gave way, as he explained in his characteristic flowery style:

> This is a question of fact . . . and the legal member accepts that there is room for different views. Although the non-legally qualified members of the tribunal are referred to [as] 'lay members' the Act does not use that expression and it is right to say that the non-legal bring to the tribunal a vast experience and in many cases, including that of Mr Edinboro with respect, judicial experience in other fields of the law. . . . There is no reason at all why a Chairman of the Tribunal should not defer to his lay colleagues on questions of fact [just as] on questions of law it is not infrequently the case that the lay members will defer to the view of the legally qualified chairman.[1]

One can well imagine that decisions in such terms – especially those going against asylum applicants – will almost certainly result in appeals to higher courts. That may be why the mere indication in a determination that there has been such a disagreement is now ruled out. *Practice Direction 9*, issued by the President on 17 January 2002, states (Symes and Jorro 2003: 822):

> (2) The tribunal's determination is that reached by the majority of those on the panel. It is therefore inappropriate that a dissenting view should

---

1 It is unclear why Mr Edinboro's own judicial experience should have allowed his view to prevail on matters of fact concerning the Balkans.

be expressed or that the determination should indicate that it is that of a majority.

Consequently, it is now even less possible than before to gauge the extent to which the opinions of lay members prevail over those of legally qualified chairs.

10.4 RISK ASSESSMENT IN ASYLUM DECISION MAKING

Above all else asylum decisions are assessments of risk, since it is the perceived degree of possibility that asylum applicants will suffer harm if returned home that determines whether their fear of persecution is 'well founded'. Indeed, risk is so central that even an applicant whose account is found to lack credibility may gain refugee status if the risk on return is judged sufficient (Symes and Jorro 2003: 61). Risk assessment in asylum claims is particularly difficult because it depends largely upon individual circumstances rather than precedent decisions. That being so, the degree of past persecution suffered by an individual serves as a key 'proxy indicator' for the risk they may face in future (cf. Hathaway 1991: 88). Both points were made by Lord Clyde in *Horvath*:

> matters particularly relating to [the applicant] will be important. For example his prominence in society . . . or anything else which might make him a particular target of persecution may be relevant. The history of past violations . . . will be among the circumstances to be taken into account.

In assessing risk on return, adjudicators are expected to avoid conjecture, which is essentially 'a mere guess', in favour of inference, defined as a 'reasonable deduction' from the evidence (*Jones* v. *Great Western Railway*). However, because of the evidential difficulties and low standard of proof in asylum cases, adjudicators may legitimately indulge in 'rational speculation', which is seemingly 'not the same as pure speculation . . . in the sense of being conjecture or surmise' (Symes and Jorro 2003: 64). To a non-lawyer such distinctions seem a frighteningly imprecise basis on which to reach life-and-death decisions. As elsewhere in the decision-making process, however, law has recourse to notions of objectivity – in this case, calculations of 'objective risk' – in order to cloak this process in an aura of greater certainty.

'Objectively', then, risk must be assessed relative to circumstances and standards in the appellant's home country, not those in the UK; for example, the risk inherent in threatening phone calls in a totalitarian State should not be diminished by equating them with nuisance calls received in Britain

(*Lucreteanu*; Symes and Jorro 2003: 66). Nor should it be assumed that the authorities in such States will behave logically and predictably (2003: 68–9). For example, a common feature of Sri Lankan appeals is that applicants claim to have been detained and then released without charge, often several times. Even if they accept that ill-treatment or torture occurred during such detentions, the Home Office and many adjudicators and tribunals are prone to conclude that an applicant's release shows they are no longer of interest to the authorities, and so not at risk. This assumes that the most recent detention would also have been the final one, yet as Lee J pointed out in the Federal Court of Australia:

> If a person, detained and interrogated in the cause of counter-terrorism, is released without being charged with an offence, it does not follow that the interest of the authorities in that person ceased with the release from custody (*Thevendran*; Symes and Jorro 2003: 69).

The leading UK authority on asylum decision making and assessment of future risk, is the Court of Appeal's decision in *Karanakaran* (see also §9.6). This, in turn, largely followed the majority decision of the High Court of Australia in *MIEA* v. *Wu Shan Liang*, which stated that it was wrong to equate administrative decision making such as that in asylum appeals with decision making in civil litigation:

> under common law procedures, the court has to decide where, on the balance of probabilities, the truth lies as between the evidence the parties to the litigation have thought it in their respective interests to adduce at the trial. Administrative decision making is of a different nature. A whole range of possible approaches to decision making in the particular circumstances of the case may be correct in the sense that their adoption ... would not be an error of law. The term ... 'evidence' as used to describe the material before the [decision maker] seems to be borrowed from the universe of discourse which has civil litigation as its subject. The present context of administrative decision making is very different and the use of such terms provides little assistance.

In similar vein, Lord Justice Brooke concluded in *Karanakaran* that when applying the Refugee Convention, adjudicators are 'not constrained by the rules of evidence that have been adopted in civil litigation', but should rather 'take into account all material considerations' when assessing future risk. Lord Justice Sedley added that whereas civil litigation involves choosing between two conflicting accounts, asylum decisions entail 'an evaluation of the intrinsic and extrinsic credibility, and ultimately the significance, of the applicant's case'. Appeal hearings before adjudicators and tribunals, he noted:

are not courts of law. Their role is best regarded as an extension of the initial decision-making process ... Such decision makers, on classic principles of public law, are required to take everything material into account. Their sources of information will frequently go well beyond the testimony of the applicant and include in-country reports, [and] expert testimony ... No probabilistic cut-off operates here: everything capable of having a bearing has to be given the weight, great or little, due to it. ... Finally, and importantly, the Convention issues from first to last are evaluative, not factual. The facts, so far as they can be established, are signposts on the road to a conclusion ... they are not themselves conclusions.

Suppose, for example, an adjudicator concludes that certain aspects of the appellant's account have not been established to the 'reasonable likelihood' standard. In civil litigation such matters would thereafter be disregarded entirely in reaching the final decision, but here adjudicators should continue to give them appropriate weight in the final balancing process. Whereas only those nuggets of evidence whose 'facticity-ratings' exceed 50 per cent may be placed on the scales of civil justice, in asylum courts even pieces of evidence judged only 5 per cent probable, say, must still be taken into account and, as Lord Drummond Young put it in the Court of Session (*Islam*), 'given such weight as the decision maker thinks they deserve'. Lord Drummond Young explained that the need to take into account 'evidence of matters that the decision maker thinks are unlikely to have happened' arises because the adjudicator is assessing the likelihood of future events; moreover, 'the question is not whether those future events are probable, but whether there is a reasonable degree of likelihood that they will occur, which is a substantially lesser test'.

Though the Court of Appeal's judgment should serve as a clear precedent, it cannot in fact be assumed that adjudicators always adhere rigidly to the *Karanakaran* framework. First, as Lord Drummond Young noted, the principles themselves are necessarily quite flexible:

> the court should not demand adherence to a precise method or formula, but should rather look at the substance of the decision to discover whether the underlying approach is in accordance with the proper legal principles. The precise wording used by the decision maker does not matter; it is the substance of his decision that counts.

Second, by pursuing the logic of *MIEA* v. *Wu Shan Liang*, the Court treated adjudicator and tribunal hearings as administrative rather than judicial processes; indeed, its main premise was that the procedure was fundamentally different from that followed in civil courts. This slight to their *amour propre* may help account for the reluctance of some adjudicators and

IAT Vice-Presidents – who had been agitating for years to get themselves retitled 'Immigration Judges' – to put the *Karanakaran* principles fully into effect (Care 2004). In reality, though, as Robert Thomas has argued (pers. comm.), it is precisely this blend of administrative process with judicial procedure which gives asylum appeals their unique character.

10.5 DETERMINATIONS AND DECISIONS

The legal end product of an asylum appeal hearing is the written 'determination' produced by the adjudicator or tribunal. Beyond stating whether the appeal is allowed or dismissed, all determinations must fulfil certain minimum requirements. Like all judges (and the following is a comment on law generally, despite the fortuitously apt wording): 'Adjudicators must decide between . . . competing positions, and give some account of their decisions so as to justify them in the framework of the presupposed legal order' (MacCormick 1994: *x*). The IAT has laid down (*Errebai*) the basic requirements in adjudicators' determinations (Deans 2000: 130). They should:

> identify the issues involved, make all relevant findings of fact and reach conclusions giving adequate reasons so that it is clear why the determination has been reached. The oral and documentary evidence must be identified and summarised. Relevant findings of fact must be made giving sufficient reasons to indicate why a witness has been found to be credible or not credible. The risk to the appellant on which he bases his fear of persecution must be identified and assessed in the light of all relevant factors. By setting out these various matters as concisely and succinctly as possible, the determination should make clear that the appellant has had a fair hearing and that his claim has been given the anxious scrutiny that all asylum claims must receive.

Summarising evidence is considered less important than its analysis, which should be sufficient to allow readers to understand how and why decisions were reached. As Schiemann J (*Amin*) put it, adjudicators should indicate clearly:

> (i) what evidence they accept; (ii) what evidence they reject; (iii) whether there is any evidence as to which they cannot make up their mind whether or not they accept it; and (iv) what, if any, evidence they regard as irrelevant.

Determinations must also show that adjudicators have correctly identified the issues to be decided, and properly directed themselves regarding relevant legal provisions. They must therefore refer, however briefly, to the specific decision under appeal, the relevant provisions in law or in the Immigration Rules, and the appropriate standard and burden of proof (Deans 2000: ¶5.01, ¶5.07–08). Matters on which the adjudicator disbelieves the appellant should be spelled out, but otherwise Schiemann J's observations do not require adjudicators to deal in detail with every single point (*Chugtai*). 'Brevity is by no means necessarily a fault' (*Rai*), and 'nothing could be more destructive of the efficient disposal of immigration appeals than the notion that the adjudicator [is] under an obligation to carry through a mechanical process of narration of the evidence' (*Asif*).

According to Conley and O'Barr (1990b: 106): 'Judges who theoretically apply the same law – and sometimes sit in adjacent courtrooms – dispense justice in radically different ways.' By this they mean partly that they come to different decisions on similar matters (see below), but also that they conduct hearings differently and arrive at decisions in different ways. It is certainly true that adjudicators and tribunal chairs have their own distinctive ways of conducting hearings, and although Conley and O'Barr (1990b: 83) imply that written judgments generally display less idiosyncratic variation than oral ones, asylum determinations also vary widely in form and style.

Tribunal decisions, too, bear the hallmark of the chair over whose name they are written, even though the decision itself is regarded as collective (§10.3).[2] For example, some Vice-Presidents affect the style of the Court of Appeal in writing up their determinations (Robert Thomas, pers. comm.). One can identify several prolific tribunal chairs without even reading the determination, from such basic matters as the use of very long paragraphs (Mr Drabu) or very short ones (Mr Fox). They also differ in how their determinations are structured; for example, while most chairs give their decisions in the very last paragraph, a few (Dr Storey, Mr Care) announce their decisions at the start. During my field research, the only tribunal chair who regularly delivered oral determinations (tape-recorded for later transcription) was Mr Justice Collins himself. This too manifested itself in the written form, through frequent 'throat-clearing' phrases like 'and as we say' and – irritatingly for researchers – a propensity not to mention the names of HOPOs and legal representatives. In fact, this exemplifies a broader difference between chairs who structure determinations dialectically – Mr A for the appellant argued this, Mr B for the respondent argued that, then we identified these key issues, and reached this decision – and those who merely present the reasoning process they themselves supposedly went through, suppressing the agencies and sometimes even the identities of the representatives.

Finally, there is the controversial matter of variations in actual decision making between one court and another. There are tens of thousands of

2 Readers 'quickly learn to discern the stamp of individual tribunal chairs in the determinations promulgated' (Harvey *et al.* 1997: 167).

adjudicators' determinations, and I had no access to any archive which would have allowed me to study them systematically, let alone in a statistically valid way. However, there is no doubt that – rightly or wrongly – some have reputations among counsel as 'hanging judges', while others are deemed fair, humane, or even generous. There is, for example:

> a high degree of consensus among RLC caseworkers as to the extent to which a given [adjudicator] will engage with complex issues of law; the chances of him/her finding an appellant credible and the view s/he takes of the situation in countries [producing] significant numbers of applicants (Harvey *et al.* 1997: 133).

It is hardly surprising that outcomes differ from adjudicator to adjudicator, however, because their approaches diverge markedly as regards the importance of particular factors in assessing credibility. By their own admission some take into consideration matters which should not be considered at all, such as the absence of corroborative evidence. This seems particularly true in relation to oral evidence, where a significant minority of adjudicators admit to attaching considerable weight to appellants' demeanour and attractiveness (Jarvis 2000: 39–45; see §8.1).

Alison Harvey's (1996) study of adjudicators' decision making analysed over 600 determinations, both statistically and qualitatively. She reported manifest errors in decision making among adjudicators with regard to definitions of 'persecution' and 'agents of persecution', and in their approaches to victims of civil war (Harvey 1998: 178–80). Other evidence was suggestive of error, such as inconsistent assessments of situations in particular countries.[3]

The fact that there were indeed such errors, inconsistencies and biases among adjudicators only served to emphasise the importance of the IAT's role – not only the obvious one of correcting ad hoc legal errors in adjudicators' determinations, and ensuring that justice is done in particular cases by remitting appeals to be heard *de novo*, but also the more general one of supervising and guiding adjudicators (Harvey *et al.* 1997: 168), thereby fostering greater uniformity in decision making. Yet Harvey *et al.* discerned a 'rough and ready' (1997: 161) approach by the IAT at that time to the question of whether even to grant leave to appeal, and they reported, yet again, a general consensus among representatives that particular tribunal chairs were likely to decide particular points of law in different, idiosyncratic ways (1997: 169).

---

3   For instance, there was in 1997 a 'marked divergence of views' among adjudicators as to whether Sri Lankan Tamils would be free from persecution in Colombo (Harvey 1998: 180). *Plus ça change!*

At that time, moreover, the IAT's supervisory and guidance roles were largely vitiated by the fact that so few of its decisions were actually reported. Things had improved by 2000, when most tribunal determinations were available via the Electronic Immigration Network's subscription database, but there was an unfortunate step backwards in 2003, when the IAT introduced a new category of 'reported' determinations and placed almost insurmountable restrictions on the citing of unreported determinations by legal representatives. From then on, far fewer decisions were publicly available, and those few were selected largely by the IAT itself.[4] Although a desire to provide clear guidance was stated as one motivating factor for this change, as it was for the introduction of starred and Country Guideline cases (§5.3; §9.7), the fact is that it is now less possible than ever before for outsiders to investigate the degree of consistency in IAT decision making.

4   A few unreported decisions are available on the EIN website.

Chapter 11

Risk, authority and expertise

> Judgments of risk and safety must be selected as much on the basis of what is valued as on the basis of what is known.
>
> (Douglas and Wildavsky 1982: 80–1)

11.1 THE SOCIAL CONSTRUCTION OF RISK

This concluding chapter assesses asylum decision making and the role of experts in light of the growing body of literature which portrays risk and its expert assessment as defining features of contemporary society. It examines both judicial and expert assessments from the perspective of reflexivity, not in its self-*centred* navel-gazing guise, but in the structural, self-*confrontational* sense identified by Beck (1994: 6).

A primary feature of such self-confrontational reflexivity is that holders of knowledge question both the social conditions of that knowledge's existence and production, and themselves, through self-monitoring (Lash 1994: 115–16). Self-monitoring also characterises techniques of modern government, so arguments about expertise necessarily bring in notions of 'governmentality' too – a term chosen to indicate the combination of governing and mode of thought, of technologies of power and political rationalities (Lemke 2002). Indeed, Foucault (1993: 203–4) defines government in terms of the 'contact points' where:

> technologies of domination of individuals over one another have recourse to processes by which the individual acts upon himself [and] the points where the techniques of the self are integrated into structures of coercion and domination.

Writers on these topics differ in basic terminology, and to import all these terminological variations would confuse an already complex set of issues without adding value to an argument which can afford to remain agnostic on such matters. For present purposes, therefore, I consistently use 'modern' to refer to the non-reflexive, optimistic, deferential attitudes towards expertise which characterised industrial society until the mid-twentieth century, and 'postmodern' for the reflexive, apprehensive, and sceptical attitudes which have since become predominant. In places this requires a rephrasing of the original arguments, but I hope I have retained their intended meaning.

This venture into rarefied realms of social theory will pave the way for a more pragmatic attempt to draw general lessons from the contrasts between legal and anthropological reasoning identified in earlier chapters. The primary focus is upon 'country experts', but the arguments also apply, *mutatis mutandis*, to medical experts and those from other disciplinary backgrounds.

Despite their difficulty and importance, risk assessments by adjudicators and tribunals (§10.4) are invariably solipsistic. They do not even make explicit reference to risk assessment in other areas of law, despite the burgeoning case law and academic literature on that topic. It has been argued that risk assessment is central to modern criminal justice policy and practice – as regards forms of punishment and the risk of reoffending, for example (Kemshall 2003: 24) – and it also figures largely in many areas of civil justice. Risks posed to entire populations by toxic emissions cannot be viewed in the same way as risks to individuals returned to repressive regimes – they correspond, respectively, to 'epidemiological risks' concerning 'rates of morbidity and mortality among populations' (Dean 1999: 142), and 'case-management risks' posed by or to individuals, which are assessed so that appropriate remedial or coercive measures can be taken (Lupton 1999a: 98) – but they are sufficiently similar for it to seem worthwhile for adjudicators to seek to draw parallels with how other courts deal with risk assessment in environmental and public health contexts (see Jasanoff 1995).

While the lack of reference by asylum courts to this broader case law seems surprising, it comes as no surprise at all that the perspectives of social theorists on 'risk society' (Beck 1992) are ignored entirely. These debates do, however, provide useful analytical perspectives from which to appraise judicial (and expert) approaches to risk assessment, not least because they involve issues already familiar from earlier chapters. For example, Jasanoff (1993) identifies two 'risk cultures' which are at least analytically distinct. 'Artefact risk' assumes that risks are 'objectively knowable and amenable to probabilistic calculation' (Kemshall 2003: 49), while 'constructivist risk', as its name suggests, sees risks as socially constructed. We are led back, in other words, to the same dichotomy as arose in Chapter 6 in connection with expert evidence. In light of that, and the discussion of epistemological differences between law and social science in Chapter 2, one can immediately predict that where risk, too, is concerned, the courts will tend to stand firmly, if implicitly, in the artefactual ('objective') camp, whereas country experts are likely to be constructivists.

In fact, virtually all academic writers on risk are constructivists, at least to the extent that they address the intellectual history of the term itself, showing how and why it came to assume such importance in the globalising world of the late twentieth century (Beck 1992: 19–24; Douglas 1992: 22; Giddens 2002: 21–6; Kemshall 2003: 4–8). Beyond this point, however, opinions diverge. For example, Douglas and Wildavsky (1982: 5) adopted the fairly strong constructivist position that choices between risky alternatives (let us say, the risk that asylum applicants suffer persecution on return, versus the risk of undermining immigration policy by allowing them to remain) are always political, cultural, and indeed moral decisions, because they require a degree of consensus over the relative desirability of possible outcomes. It follows that no absolute or objective risk calculations are possible, since the knowledge of the actuarial sciences, too, is socially constructed.

Those social scientists preferring more limited forms of constructivism criticised what they saw as Douglas and Wildavsky's extreme cultural relativism, and denial of individual agency (see references in Caplan 2000: 11–14). Beck, too, takes a far weaker constructivist stance (Lupton 1999b: 5), but despite their differences, and although they had environmental examples principally in mind, both Beck's characterisation of 'risk society' as 'a developmental phase of modern society in which the social, political, economic and individual risks increasingly tend to escape the institutions for monitoring and protection' (1994: 5), and Douglas's (1992: 22) account of the need, in 'the new global culture', for a 'common forensic vocabulary with which to hold persons accountable', shed light on the question of why the Refugee Convention, and indeed the whole international apparatus of universal human rights, appeared just when they did.

To confirmed artefactualists, moreover, the differences between their positions seem mere hair-splitting. For them, the principal failing of the Douglas–Wildavsky approach is its social reductionism, and consequent failure to recognise that some risks are 'real'.[1] Broadly speaking, such objections echo taken-for-granted views on risk held by many scientists, technologists, and engineers (as well as, ironically, their environmentalist opponents), namely, that there are quantifiable risks out there which ordinary people, because of their reliance on unscientific, subjective intuitions, may fail to recognise (Royal Society 1992: 94). They are also implicit in legal exhortations for adjudicators to make 'objective' assessments of risks of persecution.[2]

Beck (1992: 21) and – especially – Giddens (1994; 2002: 43) draw a clear dichotomy between 'a non-reflexive premodernity beset by dangers and a risk-processing reflexive modernity' (Crook 1999: 168), whereas Douglas

---

1   Douglas herself later denied this: 'The dangers are only too horribly real . . . This argument is not about the reality of the dangers, but about how they are politicized' (1992: 29).
2   Medical views of risk, too, tend to be 'artefactual', which may help explain why doctors seem more ready than country experts to attempt to privilege their own credibility assessments above those of the court with regard, for example, to the assessment of torture scars (§8.5).

(1992) argues that *all* societies are concerned with risk, but in different ways reflecting their own cultural and historical contexts. Beck sees modernity as marking an end to the association of risk with 'otherness' – risk being now so globalised and 'democratic' that it is no longer possible to imagine that one can protect oneself by associating it with dangerous 'others' who can then be distanced – whereas it is precisely their assumed continuing association that links Douglas's writings on cultures and moralities of risk in industrial societies to her celebrated earlier work (1966) on impurity and danger in societies from the opposite pole of the supposed premodern/modern dichotomy. Most commentators agree with Douglas, pointing out the continuing widespread propensity to project 'anxieties and fears about risk' onto 'marginalized and stigmatized' social groups (Lupton 1999a: 123–4).

In asylum appeals, multiple associations between risk, morality, and otherness are in play. There is (1) the asylum applicant's claimed fear of mistreatment by the dominant 'other' if forced to return; most Sri Lankan Tamils, for instance, fear detention and torture by the security forces of the Sinhalese-dominated State, and/or the forced conscription and violent suppression of political dissent practised by the LTTE. Moreover, applicants themselves risk a more radical, double, 'othering' by those in power, whereby they are stigmatised (2) as 'terrorists' or 'deviants' by their State of origin, and (3) as 'bogus welfare scroungers' by certain political, media, and public elements in their would-be country of refuge.

In general, adjudicators' decisions are avowedly concerned only with risk in the first two contexts: information on the first helps them identify the nature of the appellant's fear, while expert evidence on the second helps them assess whether that fear is 'well-founded'. The third type of risk, the stigmatisation of applicants as dangerous outsiders to British society, ostensibly plays no part in their decisions except in those rare cases where such dangers are deemed 'objective' and severe enough to bring applicants within the purview of Article 1F(b), the Convention's 'exclusion clause' (§4.2.7). Yet British government policy displays both of the responses to outsiders identified by Bauman (1995: 2). 'Anthropophagy' – 'devouring' strangers and 'metaphorically transforming them into a tissue indistinguishable from one's own' – is clearly evident in recent Home Office requirements that would-be citizens should first display mastery of British culture and language. At the same time 'anthropoemy', 'vomiting' out strangers and 'banishing them from the limits of the orderly world', is exemplified by suggestions that all asylum applicants be detained in secure 'reception centres', or marooned on remote islands. When government policy tends to such extremes in an escalating dialectic with public opinion, it is impossible to imagine that adjudicators are not influenced, however subliminally, by the prevailing hostility towards the multiply liminal, and hence multiply threatening, outsiders who appear before them.

Lastly, well-educated, wealthy, conservative white men consistently appraise risks as less serious than do other sections of the population (Flynn *et al.* 1994; Graham and Clemente 1996; Lupton 1999a: 23–4). As this is, of course, precisely the group from which most adjudicators and judges are drawn, this too may reduce applicants' chances of gaining recognition for the well-foundedness of their fear.

11.2 THE COMPLICITY OF THE EXPERT

Just as law in general appears quintessentially modern and unreflexive, so asylum courts seem prime examples of that particular form of 'governmentality' which characterises modern, especially neoliberal, States. Although Foucault himself wrote little directly on risk, his ideas on governmentality have been extended into that area by others, who see risk assessment as the very epitome of a Foucauldian moral technology, since 'To calculate a risk is to master time, to discipline the future' (Ewald 1991: 207). Thus:

> The logic of risk shares with Foucault's notion of governmentality a preoccupation to develop control strategies that are technical, efficient, and politically neutral, designed to render crimes impossible or at least without disturbing consequences ... [S]trategies of risk 'make up' people, not as legal–political subjects, but as statistical parameters in an equation based on objective knowledge of past and present conditions (Deflem 1997; citations omitted).

One important institutional mechanism whereby 'risk' became a defining trope of modern governmentality was the development of insurance in the mid-nineteenth century. This 'epoch-making mutation of metaphysical ideas' gave rise to 'a statistically grounded conception of social causality, a philosophy of civil law as the redistribution of *social risk*' (Gordon 1991: 39; original italics), making it possible for:

> insurance technologies to be applied to social problems in a way which can be presented as creative simultaneously of social justice and social solidarity. One of the important strengths of the insurance technique is its use of *expertise* as the technical basis of a form of security which can dispense with recourse to continuous surveillance (1991: 40; original italics).

In this context, risk may be defined as 'the actual value of a possible damage in a determined unit of time' (Ewald: 1991: 205). Strictly speaking, in insurance at least, 'there is no such thing as an individual risk ... Risk only becomes something calculable when it is spread over a population' (1991: 203). Furthermore, risk:

does not arise from the presence of particular precise danger embodied in a concrete individual or group. It is the effect of a combination of abstract *factors* which render more or less probable the occurrence of undesirable modes of behaviour. . . . One does not *start from* a conflictual situation observable in experience, rather one *deduces* it from a general definition of the dangers one wishes to prevent' (Castel 1991: 287–8; original italics).

This has also formed the basis for new strategies of social administration which 'dissolve the notion of a *subject* or a concrete individual, and put in its place a combinatory of *factors*, the factors of risk' (Castel 1991: 281). This refers to the increasing tendency in public health administration to identify persons as being 'at risk' because they embody a particular combination of statistically identified demographic, genetic and social characteristics, rather than because they have been found, as individuals, to be vulnerable; yet they might equally have been written as a commentary on Home Office RFRLs, with their interminable, standardised catalogues of legislative improvements and good intentions on the part of the most repressive of regimes. Indeed, I have had to respond to Refusal Letters which dealt exclusively in generalities and failed to address applicants' personal histories at all. That strategy seemed bewildering when, for example, the applicant was an MP who was widely reported in the media as having fled after voting against his own party whip on a key matter of principle, but can now be understood as the *reductio ad absurdum* of the 'case-management' approach to risk.

Diagnosis, notes Castel, is no longer the product of a concrete relationship between physician and patient, but 'a relationship constituted among the different expert assessments which make up the patient's dossier' (1991: 282). To a degree, this characterises what an adjudicator has to do in deciding asylum claims, but it seems even more applicable to country experts, who see only the dossiers! Castel adds that 'Already here there is the shift from presence to memory, from the gaze to the objective accumulation of facts.' Here perhaps lies yet another locus of conflict between the medical profession and the judiciary, but phrased in a diachronic way which implies that doctors are almost bound to lose out because they represent an historically earlier form of surveillance and expertise. In such contexts, the kinds of clinical training observed by Atkinson (1977; §2.2) seem increasingly anachronistic relics of a yet earlier form of non-reflexive modernity, and indeed Foucault himself (1973: 62) cites 'the Edinburgh clinic' in its original eighteenth-century form as a prime example of a kind of knowing which had not yet developed a truly scientific discourse in which to express itself.

One aspect of what Castel calls the 'total subordination of technicians to administrators' (1991: 291) is that the 'management of problem populations . . . no longer poses problems of *principle*; it is inscribed in a coherent scheme of administration constituting what is termed a policy' (1991: 292; original italics). Again this comment seems directly transferable from the public health to the asylum context, for what better way could there be of describing the increasingly restrictive, opportunistic approaches of successive governments towards interpreting and applying the Refugee Convention?

My research confirmed, moreover, that most asylum lawyers and expert witnesses display precisely that sense of professional disillusionment which Castel identifies as the inevitable consequence of such moves towards administrative (and in this case, also political) expediency. There are, just as he predicts, widespread 'cries of betrayal, charges that their humanist intentions have been distorted for the sake of bureaucratic or even repressive criteria' (1991: 292). These professionals are, however, naive to imagine that legislation comes into existence in order to address matters of principle: rather, its 'essential function' is 'the coherent management of a thorny problem' within the constraints of the 'administrative, juridical, institutional and financial levels of provision' that prevail (1991: 292).

Moreover, these complaining professionals 'also forget that, even if they have been let down and their intentions distorted, their practice has furnished an essential element in the construction of the system' (Castel 1991: 292). In other words, when experts complain about the ways in which their evidence is treated by the courts, they lose sight of their own complicity in such distortions. By agreeing to work within legal conventions and restrictions, they themselves contribute to the 'de-reflexification' of their expert knowledge which inevitably results. But while this leaves them wide open to methodological criticism, morally it is quite a different matter. They have chosen (quite reasonably, as it seems to me who has made that same choice) to view involvement as the lesser evil, and have decided that the troubling of their own professional consciences is a price worth paying if victims of persecution are thereby occasionally saved from the bleakness of refoulement.

But why only 'occasionally'? Why is the expert's risk assessment often not enough to secure such a desirable outcome?

One is initially tempted to explain this, too, in terms of theories of reflexive postmodernity because, as if things were not already complex enough, there is one further aspect of those arguments which still remains to be considered. Whereas a tacit reliance on expertise is widely seen as having been fundamental to the procedures of the modern State, under postmodernity the authority and knowledge of experts no longer remains unquestioned. Citizens are no longer content to defer to their authority, to allow them to shape decision making behind closed doors, far from public scrutiny. One striking feature of postmodernity is that expertise has undergone a radical 'demonopolization' (Beck 1994: 29), becoming increasingly subject to contestation and challenge through public inquiries, campaigns by special interest groups, and so forth. Nor are experts themselves immune to such notions, since one consequence of reflexivity has been to call into question the modernist presumption that they could resolve their differences of opinion and arrive at some kind of ultimate factual truth if they were only given the time and resources to conduct sufficient research. Under postmodernity, experts themselves increasingly came to realise that:

> Research that enquires further and into more difficult questions, taking up all the objections and making them its own, this kind of reflexive research breaks up its own claims to clarity and monopoly; it simultaneously elevates . . . the uncertainty of all arguments (Beck 1994: 49).

In part, no doubt, the opening up of expert assessments of risk to greater scrutiny by lay institutions and the general public represents a 'ritualisation' of risk management strategies (Crook 1999: 173), and there is certainly widespread public cynicism as to the degree of impartiality to be expected in the findings of public enquiries. Yet in the present context, whether or not such procedures genuinely influence final decisions is only part of the question. The point is that such consultation processes, however tokenistic, are now deemed essential, even though speed and bureaucratic convenience would both be furthered by simple deference to the authority of recognised experts.

The temptation, therefore, is to explain the frequent failure of expert evidence to exert a decisive influence over the decision-making processes of the asylum judiciary in terms of this growing postmodern scepticism, from which, the argument might go, judges themselves cannot possibly be immune. No doubt this is indeed the case among adjudicators, or any other citizens, in their non-professional lives, but there is little evidence of any such sceptical reflexivity in their handling of evidence or in the determinations and judgments that they write. Quite the reverse, they display a strong professional resistance to any attempt to expose the contingency and uncertainty of the 'facts' which they 'find' to be 'true'.[3] None of this is particularly surprising when one remembers that they are compelled in the end to reach a definite decision, or when one recalls the earlier discussion concerning legal pedagogy (§2.2), but it does render highly implausible any notion that the courts are fertile ground for postmodern forms of reflexivity.

The treatment of expert evidence in the asylum courts remains, I suggest, firmly within those paradigms of modernity which characterise legal processes generally, and any tendency to minimise the weight of that evidence is more plausibly explicable in terms of the inter-professional struggles for hegemony discussed earlier (§6.2). It is not scepticism regarding expert knowledge and

---

3   At a seminar of judges and adjudicators, the phrase of mine attracting most consternation was a version of that which concludes §2.2 above: 'for anthropologists "facts" are always products of a particular theoretical approach, and "truth" is at best provisional and contested' (Good 2004b: 377).

opinion which is the motivating factor, but fear of its potentially greater authority.

11.3 *ONE-WAY TICKETS* v. *THE SWORD OF DAMOCLES*

So the principles underlying judicial assessments of risk are quintessentially modern, like law in general, whereas experts in the social sciences have become increasingly reflexive regarding the conditions of production of their expert knowledge – and, of course, the acknowledged inter-subjectivity of much of that knowledge particularly fosters such a postmodern critique. Finally, therefore, we must examine the implications for 'country experts' of this fundamental difference and revisit, in light of that, the differences between legal and social scientific discursive practices and styles of reasoning which have already been identified.

With reference to the deductive–inductive contrast explored earlier (§2.2), the French *Code Civil* emphasises deductive reasoning even more than common law systems (MacCormick 1994: 68), which may explain why Latour's characterisation of the French court of last instance, the *Conseil d'État*, evokes so many of the forms of reasoning encountered above. He notes, for example, that its judicial members consistently avoid fundamental questions of meaning in their debates and decisions, while introducing equally Byzantine distinctions of their own, driven by practical imperatives rather than any urge towards philosophical hair-splitting. Such legal practices, he concludes, are built upon 'une *subtilité sans exigence de fondements* – même doctrinaux' (Latour 2002: 26; original italics). Even the subtlest legal reasoning is unconstrained by any concern for philosophical, theoretical, or doctrinal consistency; all that matters is the internal consistency of the body of law itself. Armed with this insight, it becomes clearer how the courts came to arrive at some of the positions assessed critically in Chapter 4.

This, then, is another difference between legal and anthropological thought to add to those discussed earlier, namely, that legal thinking is far more prone to the creation of orthodoxies because it feeds off itself wherever possible, grounding arguments on the pragmatic reasoning of earlier judges (Dworkin 1986: 410) rather than the writings of philosophers or social scientists. Adjudicators and asylum judges do refer to textbooks – principally Hathaway (1991) and Goodwin-Gill (1996) – but this is the exception rather than the rule, and anyway these too are largely based on statute and case law, so their use remains within the solipsistic legal loop. It is common enough for judges to turn to dictionaries too, on the principle that words in statutes are to be understood as having their everyday meanings – for example, *Horvath* reconfirmed this as the correct approach to the key notion of 'persecution' (citing Nolan J in *Jonah*) – but what they rarely, if ever, do is consult basic theoretical texts not explicitly oriented towards the law. This stress upon internal consistency is yet another sign of law's modernist, non-reflexive nature.

With regard to how this consistency is attained, MacCormick (1994: 214) distinguishes two main types of legal interpretation, interpreting statutes and following precedents, which differ in degree rather than kind. In both instances, competing arguments relate to matters of relevancy, interpretation or classification. In reaching decisions, courts must generally 'choose between two rival versions of [a] rule, both more specific than the rule as enacted . . . but each incompatible with the other' (1994: 79). As far as the meanings of the words making up those rules are concerned, it is widely but not universally agreed among legal scholars that general words like those in Article 1A(2) have a core of agreed, unproblematic meaning surrounded by a 'penumbra of uncertainty' where judges are entitled to exercise interpretive discretion (Hart 1961: 119–20; Maley 1994: 29).

However, problems of legal interpretation are often treated in practice as problems of classification. For example, the question 'should "social group" in Article 1A(2) be interpreted as including Pakistani women (or El Salvadorean taxi-drivers, or homosexuals)?' very easily transmutes into 'do Mrs Islam and Mrs Shah belong to a particular social group within the meaning of Article 1A(2)?' Though these two questions are no different in terms of pure logic, they differ in practical significance – the first is more clearly a matter of law, whereas the latter appears more a matter of fact, and hence less susceptible of appeal to a higher court (MacCormick 1994: 95). This kind of transmutation frequently happens in asylum appeals. For example, Lord Steyn's reasoning in *Islam and Shah* seems to move back and forth between these two kinds of question, or involves both simultaneously. Thus, a jump from interpretation to classification occurs in the very first paragraph after his summary of the facts of the two cases:

> the principal issue before the House is the meaning and application of the words 'membership of a particular social group'. . . . Except for the requirements inherent in the words 'persecution for reasons of . . . membership of a particular social group' in Article 1A(2) all the conditions of that provision are satisfied. Two issues remain: (1) Do the women satisfy the requirement of 'membership of a particular social group?'

Because law itself slides so easily from interpretation to classification, it becomes even easier to see how expert witnesses blunder into doing the opposite. But whereas both modes of reasoning are open to judges, the former – since it addresses matters of law – is out of bounds to experts. Hence, for example, the trenchant criticism of experts who 'purport to decide cases for me' (§8.5).

We earlier considered some important implications of the fact that lawyers and social scientists are trained to think and write in radically different ways

(§2.2). One of those differences merits further consideration here, namely, their quite distinct notions of 'subjectivity' and 'objectivity' – a point of particular importance, obviously, given that the courts classify expert reports as 'objective evidence'. What precisely do they mean by so doing? Kandel (1992: 3) gives the most straightforward answer, as we saw (§6.1), namely, that for anthropologists, 'objective' and 'subjective' mean external and internal to the observer, respectively, whereas in legal usage 'objective' refers to the subjectivity of the Reasonable Man.

Writing from a more avowedly legal but still critical perspective, Dworkin identifies two different kinds of scepticism regarding legal claims to be objective – that is, to arrive at the best possible, even the *true*, interpretation of the case at hand. The first he calls 'internal' scepticism (1986: 78–9), because it accepts the possibility of true interpretations but rejects some of those on offer as unsatisfactory (much as Lord Steyn did with *Sanchez-Trujillo* in *Islam and Shah*; §2.2). If one takes what he calls an 'objective belief' – his example, 'slavery is wrong', may helpfully be replaced here by 'persecuted persons should be given refuge' – this is not a metaphysical assertion to be understood on a par with, and tested in the same way as, a fundamental law of physics. Rather, it is a moral assertion – a claim, in Latour and Woolgar's typology of scientific statements (1986: 78–9) – or an asserted generalisation (Dworkin 1986: 81).

Adjudicators do not feel in need of moral instruction from experts, however, and would react badly to any such proselytisation. It is Dworkin's second alternative – external scepticism, a metaphysical theory as to the general impossibility of *any* such claims being true (1986: 79) – which is relevant here. This arises when lawyers 'use the language of objectivity to distinguish between claims meant to hold only for persons with particular beliefs or connections or needs or interests (perhaps only for the speaker) and those meant to hold impersonally for everyone' (1986: 81).

In these terms, when adjudicators describe an expert report as 'objective evidence', they mean that it purports to provide evidence of a general nature as to the situation faced in the past, and/or likely to be faced in future, by persons of this appellant's claimed background. True to what was said earlier, such reports depend upon assumed classifications of the persons in question – 'people wanted by the authorities', for example – which may or may not be accepted by the adjudicator in any given case. Hence the significance of the expert's enforced assumption that the appellant's story will be found by the court to be true (§9.3).

Latour's approach is broadly compatible with Kandel's, though far more complex, and although he contrasts law with laboratory-based science, I wish to extend his insights, *mutatis mutandis*, to anthropology also. He differentiates scientific and legal statements as return and one-way tickets, respectively (2002: 248), by which he means that scientists move to and fro between theories and external observations in a dynamic, dialectical fashion which admits of lacunae, courts controversy, and seeks to extend knowledge or transform understanding; whereas law strives for 'legal safety' through homeostasis, by making sure that all loopholes are closed, any tears in the legal fabric are immediately patched, and all outstanding issues are resolved by assimilation into what is already known and decided (2002: 258–9). The paradox is, therefore, that so-called 'scholarly objectivity' as commonly understood – emotional distance, cool judgment, indifference as to the outcome – is actually far more characteristic of judges than of scholars, whose writings are in fact disguised but passionate pleas in support of their own current points of view (2002: 222). What distinguishes scientific research is thus not *objectivity* as defined above, which is actually – as Dworkin argues too – a special form of subjectivity, but rather what Latour christens *objectity*, 'the ordeal whereby a scholar links his destiny . . . to the experimental testing of phenomena'. This can in turn be seen as 'a very specific form of subjectivisation in which researchers make themselves dependent upon experimental objects' (2002: 250; my translations, here and below; cf. 2004: 106–7).

These differences arise in part from the further paradox that whereas 'scholars discuss precise matters loosely; judges discuss vague matters precisely' (Latour 2002: 251; cf. 2004: 107). This is because scientists must always submit their findings to the 'higher court' of third party judgment through intersubjective testing by the scientific community at large, a threat which hangs above them like the sword of Damocles, curbing their wilder enthusiasms and relieving them personally of the need to sustain any appearance of objectivity; whereas judges in a court of last instance can appeal to no authority other than themselves to overturn or repair their decisions, and hence can only hope to attain objectivity by meticulously cultivating attitudes of dispassion and indifference. Legal 'objectivity' therefore entails no 'object' in any literal sense, but consists rather of a particular state of mind and an associated dependence upon formalistic, disciplined styles of speech and clothing. The irony is, therefore, that those very features of law most commonly ridiculed by outsiders as meaningless irrelevancies actually form the principal bases of legal claims to objectivity (2002: 251; 2004: 107).

Latour's analysis, complex though it may be, was worth introducing even at this late stage because he supplements his contrast between scholarly research and legal judgment by simultaneously drawing a further distinction between scholarship and expertise.[4] Experts, he says, seem to combine the two personae we have just been opposing; scientists apparently become temporary judges of last instance, whose opinions carry a particular authority derived from their assumed ability to assess objective facts. This is an illusion,

---

4   The points summarised here are those which seem generalisable; some of Latour's other comments reflect the different statuses of experts in the French and British legal systems.

however. In the first place, the stances of experts and researchers are really complete opposites; from the former, lawyers seek indisputable matters of fact, but for the latter nothing is ever finally decided, no black boxes ever remain unopened, and no facts are wholly beyond dispute. If this is true even of laboratory-based science, how much more so for the constantly self-reflexive approaches to factuality and truth that permeate research in the social sciences? And in the second place, the facts relayed by experts always relate to some event or circumstance 'out there', whereas judges 'ask for no more transcendent conclusion than a simple ending of the discussion' (Latour 2002: 253). Appeal dismissed.

As we saw (§6.2), experts and judges have battled down the centuries over who is to enjoy 'the last word' (Latour 2002: 252), but whereas Jones (1994: 5) criticises the ways in which legal processes distort science into forms of crude scientism, thereby at least implying the possibility of introducing a more truly scientific spirit into such proceedings, Latour's analysis suggests that given the goals, attitudes to knowledge, and discursive practices of law, things could hardly be otherwise. In any case, we must take the world as we find it.

All this may seem a far cry from the pornographic vignettes with which the book began, yet it is not, I hope, merely self-indulgent. If we anthropologists are to perform adequately when assuming the temporary mantle of expert in asylum matters – in terms of conforming to the requirements of what is after all, for better or worse, the law of the land; of conveying to the court our views on the matters we have been instructed to discuss; and, of course, of helping ensure that no-one at risk of such appalling mistreatment is returned to the hands of their torturers – it is vital for us to be clear about what we are doing. For experts' reports to be effective in these three senses, yet still true to the ethical demands of their own disciplines, they must at the very least reflect an informed understanding of what it means to appear in a court of law as a purveyor of 'objective evidence'. This book has attempted to explore precisely that.

I did not simply set out to chart externally and dispassionately – as dispassionate as social science research can ever, in light of the above, be said to be! – how an expert's role differs from that of a scholarly researcher. Nor is it merely a question of the kinds of genre-hopping required routinely of many professionals, which at least allocates their contrasting discursive practices to distinct times and places (Good 2006b). Rather, this research has involved acting out both roles simultaneously, experiencing directly their differences and the problems to which these give rise. Modifying Latour's aphorism slightly, one might say that whereas scholars discuss precise matters loosely, experts are expected to discuss vague matters precisely. I leave it to the reader to judge whether the preceding discussion, amalgamating those two roles, has produced greater vagueness or enhanced precision.

Postscript

With a topic like asylum – politically controversial and in one's own country – the customary academic stance of neutrality towards the data themselves while reserving partisanship for debates with fellow anthropologists is hard to maintain and justify. Some readers may feel disappointed that the preceding analyses rarely display overt political engagement, unlike the admirable recent book by Louise Pirouet (2001), who draws upon a far longer and broader history of personal activism than I am able to claim. This difference arises partly from a personal sense that scholarship is often more effective in the long run than polemic,[1] but also from explicit methodological choice, if that is not too grand a term for pragmatic relativism – the insistence that one should not criticise without first seeking to understand. Here at last, however, it seems appropriate to make some brief moral judgments, held in suspense during the writing of the book, about the administrative and legal processes it describes.

The growing scale of international migration undoubtedly creates practical problems for governments and civil societies in the principal countries of destination. Yet even as they pander to the anti-immigrant prejudices of the far right for perceived electoral advantage, Western governments are acutely aware that large-scale immigration is the most feasible means of maintaining their economies and social welfare systems in the face of ageing populations. Such general issues raised by migration are, however, only tangential to the theme of this book. For all that the media wilfully confuse the two, and recognising that most decisions to move to another country involve complex, multiple motives, the focus here is not on 'economic migrants', but upon people for whom the 'push' factors of appalling ill-treatment and persecution

---

1 Culhane's fascinating account of uses of anthropological evidence in First Nation land claims in Canadian courts illustrates the danger of polemics. Her analysis is weakened by what can only be termed the character assassination of the Crown's expert, who is made scapegoat for the court's decision even though she is only mentioned once in a judgment hundreds of pages long (1998: 270).

at home far outweigh the 'pull' factors of expected better lives elsewhere; victims of racial, political, religious or gender discrimination, of failed civil societies and unresolved civil wars; individual human beings who have suffered almost unimaginable rapes and tortures, and have been physically and psychologically damaged as a result.

From that perspective, the UK's political response over the past two decades has been a deepening scandal, a growing outrage against decency and civility. Whether responsibility for this lies with political cowardice in anticipation of public hostility, or whether that hostility has itself created the abject attitudes of politicians – and it is probably a bit of both, a spiral of self-fulfilling, increasingly strident, and ever more overtly xenophobic rhetoric – the outcome can only make one deeply ashamed of the behaviour of one's government and many fellow citizens.

But where do judicial processes stand in all this? Are such strictures also applicable to the adjudicators of Taylor House and the Eagle Building, or the tribunals in Bream's Buildings? There is no simple answer. Before my research began I pictured the entire apparatus – Home Office, Immigration Appellate Authority, the higher courts – as one gigantic, oppressive monolith. That naive view did not survive two minutes into my first interview with a senior adjudicator, which revealed that our respective assessments of Home Office incompetence were not at all dissimilar. Later still, it became apparent that 'the Home Office' too was a category demanding further disaggregation. Presenting Officers, for example, spoke disparagingly of the Refusal Letters produced by caseworkers, and criticised the documentary output of their own Country Information and Policy Unit.

Repressive administrative and judicial systems may, of course, be operated by individuals whose personal views are far more enlightened but who feel obliged to 'do their duty', and are 'only following orders'. The prime targets for censure by those who feel outraged by the scapegoating – and worse – of 'asylum seekers' (a term now invested with such negative connotations that I have generally avoided it above) must be the legal and bureaucratic systems set up to grant or withhold asylum, and the government policies which shape or maintain those discourses and procedures, rather than the persons compelled to implement them. And yet, while it may be Parliament which passes laws, Home Office caseworkers and asylum adjudicators have powers to interpret them in ways that have life-changing implications for individual applicants and may set precedents for future decisions too. Even the most hegemonic discourse can be successfully resisted, especially by powerful persons such as judges. Individual Home Office officials and judges can be, and should be, held responsible for the consequences, for good or ill, flowing from the exercise of what is in practice a considerable degree of discretion.

It would be absurd to maintain that all asylum claims are genuine, and hugely unjust to level blanket accusations of racism or xenophobia against adjudicators or Home Office staff. In Spijkerboer's Pythonesque but nonetheless apposite words, an assumption of bad faith – that the decision maker must be 'a bad or silly person' – is 'an overly simple way out' (2000: 10). In my research, I came across many adjudicators and tribunal chairs who do indeed apply the level of 'anxious scrutiny' enjoined by Lord Bridge (*Bugdaycay*). Nonetheless, the final question posed – but not, I fear, fully answered – is this. How are we to separate the systemic injustices of legislated asylum procedures from the individual prejudices of the 'woolly liberals' and 'hanging judges', selected at random to deal with the actual appeals of particular asylum applicants?

Bibliography

Adler, Z (1987) *Rape on Trial*, London: Routledge & Kegan Paul

Akram, SM (2000) 'Orientalism revisited in asylum and refugee claims', *International Journal of Refugee Law* 12: 7–40

Aleinikoff, TA (2003) 'Protected characteristics and social perceptions: an analysis of the meaning of "membership in a particular social group" ', pp 263–311 in E Feller, V Türk and F Nicholson (eds), *Refugee Protection in International Law: UNHCR's Global Consultations on International Protection*, Cambridge: University Press

Alvarez, L and Loucky, J (1992) 'Inquiry and advocacy: attorney–expert collaboration in the political asylum process', pp 43–52 in RF Kandel (ed.), *Double Vision: Anthropologists at Law*, (NAPA Bulletin, No 11), Washington DC: American Anthropological Association

Anderson, B (1991) *Imagined Communities: Reflections on the Origin and Spread of Nationalism*, London: Verso

Arendt, H (1958) *The Human Condition*, Chicago: University Press

Astuti, R (2000) 'Kindreds and descent groups: new perspectives from Madagascar', pp 90–103 in J Carsten (ed.), *Cultures of Relatedness: New Approaches to the Study of Kinship*, Cambridge: University Press

Asylum Aid (1999) *Still No Reason at All: Home Office Decisions on Asylum Claims*, London: Asylum Aid

Atkinson, JM and Drew, P (1979) *Order in Court: the Organisation of Verbal Interaction in Court Settings*, London: Macmillan

Atkinson, P (1977) 'The reproduction of medical knowledge', pp 85–106 in R Dingwall, C Heath, M Reid and M Stacey (eds), *Health Care and Health Knowledge*, London: Croom Helm

Barnes, J (2004) 'Expert evidence – the judicial perception in asylum and human rights appeals', *International Journal of Refugee Law* 16: 349–57

Barsky, RF (1994) *Constructing a Productive Other: Discourse Theory and the Convention Refugee Hearing*, Philadelphia: John Benjamin Publishing Co

—— (1996) 'The interpreter as intercultural agent in Convention refugee hearings', *The Translator* 2(1): 45–63

—— (2000) *Arguing and Justifying: Assessing the Convention Refugees' Choice of Moment, Motive and Host Country*, Aldershot: Ashgate

Bauman, R (1984) *Verbal Art as Performance*, Prospect Heights IL: Waveland Press

Bauman, Z (1995) 'Making and unmaking of strangers', *Thesis Eleven* 43: 1–16

Beck, U (1992) *Risk Society: Towards a New Modernity*, London: Sage

—— (1994) 'The reinvention of politics: towards a theory of reflexive modernization', pp 1–55 in U Beck, A Giddens and S Lash, *Reflexive Modernization: Politics, Tradition and Aesthetics in the Modern Social Order*, Stanford: University Press

Berk-Seligson, S (1990) 'Bilingual court proceedings: the role of the court interpreter', pp 155–201 in JN Levi and AG Walker (eds), *Language in the Judicial Process*, New York: Plenum Press

—— (2002) *The Bilingual Courtroom: Court Interpreters in the Judicial Process*, Chicago: University Press

Berkowitz, N and Jarvis, C (2000) *Immigration Appellate Authority: Asylum Gender Guidelines*, London: Immigration Appellate Authority

Bijleveld, C and Taselaar, AP (2000) *Motieven van Asielzoekers om naar Nederland te Komen; Verslag van een Expert Meting*, Den Haag: Ministry of Justice

Billings, PW (2000) 'A comparative analysis of administrative and adjudicative systems for determining asylum claims', *Administrative Law Review* (Winter): 254–303

—— (2002) 'Alienating asylum seekers: welfare support in the Immigration and Asylum Act 1999', *Journal of Social Security Law* 9: 115–44

Bingham, T (1985) 'The judge as juror: the judicial determination of factual issues', pp 1–27 in P Rideout and J Jowell (eds), *Current Legal Problems*, London: Stevens & Sons

Black, R (2001) 'Fifty years of Refugee Studies', *International Migration Review* 35(1): 7–32

Blake, N and Husain, R (2003) *Immigration, Asylum and Human Rights*, Oxford: University Press

Blommaert, J (2001) 'Investigating narrative inequality: African asylum seekers' stories in Belgium', *Discourse and Society* 12(4): 413–49

Bloor, D (1976) *Knowledge and Social Imagery*, London: Routledge & Kegan Paul

Böcker, A and Havinga, T (1999) 'Country of asylum by choice or by chance: asylum seekers in Belgium, the Netherlands and the UK', *Journal of Ethnic and Migration Studies* 25 (1), 43–61

Bohannan, P (1957) *Justice and Judgment Among the Tiv*, London: Oxford University Press

—— (1964) 'Anthropology and the law', pp 191–9 in S Tax (ed.), *Horizons in Anthropology*, Chicago: Aldine

Bourdieu, P (1977) *Outline of a Theory of Practice*, Cambridge: University Press

Boyle, J (1985) 'The politics of reason: critical legal theory and local social thought', *University of Pennsylvania Law Review* 133: 685–780

Briggs, CL (1988) 'Disorderly dialogues in ritual impositions of order: the role of metapragmatics in Warao dispute mediation', *Anthropological Linguistics* 30: 448–91

Brown, B, Burman, M and Jamieson, L (1993) *Sex Crimes on Trial: the Use of Sexual Evidence in Scottish Courts*, Edinburgh: University Press

Burgess, AW and Holmstrom, LL (1974) 'Rape trauma syndrome', *American Journal of Psychiatry* 131: 981–6

Burgess, D (1997) 'Legal representation can kill', *New Law Journal*, 21 March

Campisi, J (1991) *The Mashpee Indians: Tribe on Trial*, Syracuse NY: Syracuse University Press

Caplan, P (2000) 'Introduction: risk revisited', pp 1–28 in P Caplan (ed.), *Risk Revisited*, London: Pluto Press

Care, G (2004) 'Review of Symes and Jorro, *Asylum Law and Practice*', www.iarlj.nl/content/latestnews/word/, consulted 29 May 2004

Carver, N (ed.) (2003) *Home Office Country Assessments: an Analysis*, London: Immigration Advisory Service

Carver, N (2005) 'An "effectively comprehensive" analysis?', pp 31–73 in C Yeo (ed.), *Country Guideline Cases: Benign and Practical?*, London: Immigration Advisory Service

Castel, R (1991) 'From dangerousness to risk', pp 281–98 in B Burchell, C Gordon and P Miller (eds), *The Foucault Effect: Studies in Governmentality*, Chicago: University Press

Chambers, R (1983) *Rural Development: Putting the Last First*, London: Longman

Cicchino, P (2001) 'Love and the Socratic method', *American University Law Review* 50: 533–50

Clifford, J (1988) *The Predicament of Culture*, Cambridge MA: Harvard University Press

Cohen, AP (1996) 'Anthropology is a generalising science or it is nothing', pp 26–30 in T Ingold (ed.), *Key Debates in Anthropology*, London: Routledge

Cohen, J (2001) 'Errors of recall and credibility: Can omissions and discrepancies in successive statements reasonably be said to undermine credibility of testimony?', *Medico-legal Journal* 69(1): 25–34

Cohen, S (1995) *Still Resisting After All These Years: a Century of International Struggles Against Immigration Controls 1895–1995*, Manchester: Greater Manchester Immigration Aid Unit

Colin, J and Morris, R (1996) *Interpreters and the Legal Process*, Winchester: Waterside Press

Comaroff, JL and Comaroff, J (1987) 'The madman and the migrant: work and labor in the historical consciousness of a South African people', *American Ethnologist* 14: 191–210

Conley, JM and O'Barr, WM (1988) 'Fundamentals of jurisprudence: an ethnography of judicial decision making in informal courts', *North Carolina Law Review* 66: 467–507

—— (1990a) 'Rules versus relationships in small claims disputes', in AD Grimshaw (ed.), *Conflict Talk*, Cambridge: University Press

—— (1990b) *Rules versus Relationships: the Ethnography of Legal Discourse*, Chicago: University Press

—— (1998) *Just Words: Law, Language and Power*, Chicago: University Press

—— and EA Lind (1978) 'The power of language: presentational style in the courtroom', *Duke Law Journal* 78: 1375–99

Coussey, M (2003) *Independent Race Monitor: Annual Report April 2002–March 2003*, London: Home Office

—— (2005) *Annual Report 2004–5, Independent Race Monitor*. London: Home Office

Crawley, H (1999) *Breaking down the Barriers: a Report on the Conduct of Asylum Interviews at Ports*, London: ILPA

—— (2001) *Refugees and Gender: Law and Process*, Bristol: Jordans

Crook, S (1999) 'Ordering risks', pp 160–85 in D Lupton (ed.), *Risk and Sociocultural Theory: New Directions and Perspectives*, Cambridge: University Press

Culhane, D (1998) *The Pleasure of the Crown: Anthropology, Law and First Nations*, Burnaby, BC: Talon Books

Danet, B (1980) 'Language in the legal process', *Law and Society Review* 14: 445–564

Daniel, EV (1996) *Charred Lullabies: Chapters in an Anthropography of Violence*, Princeton NJ: Princeton University Press

—— and Thangaraj, Y (1995) 'Forms, formations and transformations of the Tamil refugee', pp 225–56 in EV Daniel and JC Knudsen (eds), *Mistrusting Refugees*, Berkeley: University of California Press

Dean, M (1999) 'Risks, calculable and incalculable', pp 131–59 in D Lupton (ed.), *Risk and Sociocultural Theory: New Directions and Perspectives*, Cambridge: University Press

Deans, M (2000) *Notes for Adjudicators*, Immigration Appellate Authority

Decourcelle, A and Julinet, S (2000) *Que reste-t-il du droit d'asile?* Paris: L'Esprit Frappeur

Deflem, M (1997) 'Surveillance and criminal statistics: historical foundations of governmentality', pp 149–184 in A Sarat and S Silbey (eds), *Studies in Law, Politics and Society, Volume 17*, Greenwich CT: JAI Press, www.cla.sc.edu/socy/faculty/deflem/ZCRIST.htm, consulted 23 March 2004

DIMA (Dept of Immigration and Multicultural Affairs) (1997) 'Guidelines on gender issues for decision makers', *International Journal of Refugee Law* 7: 195–212

Dobbin, SA and Gatowski, SI (1998) 'The social production of Rape Trauma Syndrome as science and as evidence', pp 125–45 in M Freeman and H Reece (eds), *Science in Court*, Aldershot: Ashgate

Donovan, JM and Anderson, HE III (2003) *Anthropology and Law*, New York–Oxford: Berghahn

Douglas, M (1966) *Purity and Danger: an Analysis of the Concepts of Pollution and Taboo*, London: Routledge & Kegan Paul

—— (1992) *Risk and Blame: Essays in Cultural Theory*, London: Routledge

—— and Wildavsky, A (1982) *Risk and Culture*, Berkeley: University of California Press

Driessen, PA (1983) 'The wedding of social science and the courts: is the marriage working?', *Social Science Quarterly* 64: 476–93

Durkheim, E (1915) *The Elementary Forms of the Religious Life*, London: George Allen & Unwin

—— (1933 [1893]) *The Division of Labor in Society*, New York: Free Press

Dutton, J (2003) 'What to believe? A critique of the assessment of plausibility in asylum applications', *The Electronic Immigration Network Bibliotech*, www.ein.org.uk/resources/full.shtml?x=163847, consulted 9 March 2004

Dworkin, R (1986) *Law's Empire*, Cambridge MA: Harvard University Press

Edmond, G (2000) 'Judicial representations of scientific evidence', *Modern Law Review* 63: 216–51

—— (2004a) 'Thick decisions: expertise, advocacy and reasonableness in the Federal Court of Australia', *Oceania* 74: 190–230

—— (2004b) 'Judging facts: managing expert knowledges in legal decision making', pp 136–65 in G Edmond (ed.), *Expertise in Regulation and Law*, Aldershot: Ashgate

—— and Mercer, D (2004a) 'Experts and expertise in legal and regulatory settings', pp 1–31 in G Edmond (ed.), *Expertise in Regulation and Law*, Aldershot: Ashgate

—— and Mercer, D (2004b) 'The invisible branch: the authority of Science Studies in expert evidence jurisprudence', pp 197–241 in G Edmond (ed.), *Expertise in Regulation and Law*, Aldershot: Ashgate

Einolf, CJ (2001) *The Mercy Factory: Refugees and the American Asylum System*, Chicago: Ivan R Dee

ELENA (European Legal Network on Asylum) (2000) *The Application of the Concept of Internal Protection Alternative*, www.ecre.org/research/ipa.doc, consulted 10 January 2001

Engeström, Y (1998) 'The tensions of judging: handling cases of driving under the influence of alcohol in Finland and California', pp 199–232 in Y Engeström and D Middleton (eds), *Cognition and Communication at Work*, Cambridge: University Press

Evans-Pritchard, EE (1937) *Witchcraft, Oracles and Magic Among the Azande*, Oxford: Clarendon

—— (1951) *Kinship and Marriage Among the Nuer*, Oxford: Clarendon

Ewald, F (1991) 'Insurance and risks', pp 197–210 in G Burchell, C Gordon and P Miller (eds), *The Foucault Effect: Studies in Governmentality*. Chicago: University Press

Faigman, DL (1999) *Legal Alchemy: the Use and Misuse of Science in the Law*, New York: WH Freeman & Co

Fenton, S (no date) 'Expressing a well-founded fear: interpreting in Convention refugee hearings', www.refugee.org.nz/welcome.html, consulted 14 November 2002

Fienberg, SE (ed.) (1989) *The Evolving Role of Statistical Assessments as Evidence in the Courts*, New York: Springer-Verlag

Finnegan, R (1992) *Oral Traditions and the Verbal Arts: a Guide to Research Practices*, London: Routledge

Flynn, J, Slovic, C and Mertz, C (1994) 'Gender, race, and perception of environmental health risks', *Risk Analysis* 14(6): 1101–8

Forrest, D (2000) 'Guide to writing medical reports on survivors of torture', pp 35–53 in *Guidelines for the Examination of Survivors of Torture*, London: Medical Foundation

Fortes, M (1970) *Time and Social Structure, and Other Essays*, London: Athlone Press

Foucault, M (1973) *The Birth of the Clinic: an Archaeology of Medical Perception*, London: Tavistock

—— (1993) 'About the beginning of the hermeneutics of the self', *Political Theory* 21(2): 198–227

Fox, A (2001) 'An interpreter's perspective', *Context* 54: 19–20

Frey, B (2002) 'Documenting a well-founded fear: how medical caregivers can assist survivors in the asylum process?', pp 45–61 in M Peel and V Iacopino (eds), *The Medical Documentation of Torture*, London, San Francisco: Greenwich Medical Media Ltd

Fuglerud, Ø (1999) *Life on the Outside: the Tamil Diaspora and Long Distance Nationalism*, London: Pluto Press

Fuller, CJ (1994) 'Legal anthropology', *Anthropology Today* 10(3): 9–12

Geertz, C (1966) 'Religion as a cultural system', pp 1–46 in M Banton (ed.), *Anthropological Approaches to the Study of Religion*, (ASA Monographs, 3) London: Tavistock

—— (1973) *The Interpretation of Cultures*, New York: Basic Books

—— (1983) *Local Knowledge*, New York: Basic Books

Giannelli, PC (1980) 'The admissibility of novel scientific evidence: *Frye* v. *United States*, a half-century later', 80 *Columbia Law Review* 1197–250.

Gibney, MJ (2004) *The Ethics and Politics of Asylum: Liberal Democracy and the Response to Refugees*, Cambridge: University Press

Giddens, A (1994) 'Living in a post-traditional society', pp 56–109 in U Beck, A Giddens and S Lash, *Reflexive Modernization: Politics, Tradition and Aesthetics in the Modern Social Order*, Stanford: University Press

—— (2002) *Runaway World: How Globalisation is Shaping Our Lives*, (new edition) London: Profile Books

Giffard, C (2000) *The Torture Reporting Handbook*, Colchester: Human Rights Centre, University of Essex

Gluckman, M (1955) *The Judicial Process Among the Barotse of Northern Rhodesia*, Manchester: University Press

—— (1965) *The Ideas in Barotse Jurisprudence*, New Haven CT and London: Yale University Press

Goldman, LR (1986) 'A case of "questions" and questions of "case" ', *Text* 6: 345–92

Gombrich, R (1971) *Precept and Practice: Traditional Buddhism in the Rural Highlands of Ceylon*, Oxford: Clarendon

Good, A (1996) 'Anthropology is a generalising science or it is nothing', pp 30–6 in T Ingold (ed.), *Key Debates in Anthropology*, London: Routledge

—— (2003a) 'Anthropologists as expert witnesses: political asylum cases involving Sri Lankan Tamils', pp 93–117 in RA Wilson and J Mitchell (eds), *Human Rights in Global Perspective: Anthropological Studies of Rights, Claims and Entitlements*, (ASA Monographs, 49) London: Routledge

—— (2003b) 'Acting as an expert: anthropologists in asylum appeals', *Anthropology Today* 19(5): 3–7

—— (2004a) ' "Undoubtedly an expert"? Country experts in the UK asylum courts', *Journal of the Royal Anthropological Institute* (N.S.) 10: 113–33

—— (2004b) 'Expert evidence in asylum and human rights appeals: an expert's view', *International Journal of Refugee Law* 16: 358–80

—— (2006a) 'Gender-based persecution: the case of South Asian asylum applicants in the UK', pp 274–99 in NC Behera (ed.), *Gender, Conflict and Migration*, Delhi: Sage

—— (2006b) 'Writing as a kind of anthropology: alternative professional genres', pp 91–115 in G De Neve and M Unnithan (eds), *Critical Journeys: the Making of Anthropologists*, Aldershot: Ashgate Press

—— (in press) 'Are women a "particular social group"? Gender blindness in the 1951 Refugee Convention', in F von Benda-Beckmann, K von Benda-Beckmann and A Griffiths (eds), *Law, Power and Control*, Oxford: Berghahn

—— (no date) 'Role confusion in the asylum courts: some instantaneous ethical dilemmas', seminar paper, Manchester University, 28 November 2005

Goodwin-Gill, G (1996) *The Refugee in International Law* (2nd edn), Oxford: Clarendon

Gordon, C (1991) 'Governmental rationality: an introduction', pp 1–51 in G Burchell, C Gordon and P Miller (eds), *The Foucault Effect: Studies in Governmentality*, Chicago: University Press

Graham, J and Clemente, K (1996) 'Hazards in the news: who believes what?', *Risk in Perspective* 4(4): 1–4

Grahl-Madsen, A (1966) *The Status of Refugees in International Law*, Leyden: Sijthoff

Gramsci, A (1971) *Selections from the Prison Notebooks*, London: Lawrence & Wishart

Gulliver, PH (1963) *Social Control in an African Society*, London: Routledge & Kegan Paul

Gunn, TJ (2003) 'The complexity of religion and the definition of "religion" in international law', *Harvard Human Rights Journal* 16: 189–215

Hacking, I (1999) *The Social Construction of What?*, Cambridge MA: Harvard University Press

Haines, R (1998) 'Membership of a Particular Social Group', *Interim Reports of Inter-Conference Working Parties, International Association of Refugee Law Judges*, www.iarlj.nl/wp/wp2.htm, consulted 23 December 2003

Hall, JG and Smith, GD (2001) *The Expert Witness* (3rd edn), Chichester: Barry Rose Law Publishers Ltd

Hart, HLA (1961) *The Concept of Law*, Oxford: University Press

Harvey, A (1996) *The Risks of Getting it Wrong: the Asylum and Immigration Bill Session 1995/96 and the Determinations of Special Adjudicators*, London: Asylum Rights Campaign

—— (1998) 'Researching *The Risks of Getting it Wrong*', pp 176–98 in F Nicholson and P Twomey (eds), *Current Issues of UK Asylum Law and Policy*, Aldershot: Ashgate

——, Haywood, P and Storey, E (1997) *Reviewing the Asylum Determination Procedure: a Casework Study*, London: Refugee Legal Centre

Harvey, C (2000) *Seeking Asylum in the UK: Problems and Prospects*, London: Butterworths

Hastrup, K (2003) 'Violence, suffering and human rights: anthropological reflections', *Anthropological Theory* 3(3): 309–23

Hathaway, J (1991) *The Law of Refugee Status*, London: Butterworths

Henderson, M (1997) *Best Practice Guide to Asylum Appeals*, London: ILPA

—— (2003) *Best Practice Guide to Asylum and Human Rights Appeals*, London: ILPA/Refugee Legal Group

Hepner, TR (2003) 'Expert witnessing: anthropology and Eritrean asylum seekers in the United States' (Paper at American Anthropological Association meeting, Chicago, November 2003)

Herlihy, J, Scragg, P and Turner, S (2002) 'Discrepancies in autobiographical memories: implications for the assessment of asylum seekers: repeated interviews study', *British Medical Journal* 324 (7333): 324–7

Heydon, JD and Ockelton, M (1996) *Evidence: Cases and Materials* (4th edn), London: Butterworths

Hodgkinson, T (1990) *Expert Evidence: Law and Practice*, London: Sweet & Maxwell

Home Office (1998) *Fairer, Faster and Firmer: a Modern Approach to Immigration and Asylum* (Government White Paper CM4018), London: The Stationery Office

—— (2001) *Asylum Statistics: United Kingdom 2000*, (HOSB 17/01) www.homeoffice.gov.uk/rds/pdfs/hosb1701.pdf

—— (2002) *Asylum Statistics: United Kingdom 2001*, (HOSB 09/02) www.home
office.gov.uk/rds/pdfs2/hosb902.pdf

—— (2003) *Asylum Statistics: United Kingdom 2002*, (HOSB 08/03) www.home
office.gov.uk/rds/pdfs2/hosb803.pdf

—— (2005) *Asylum Statistics: United Kingdom 2004*, (HOSB 13/05) www.home
office.gov.uk/rds/pdfs2/hosb803.pdf

Humphreys, S (1985) 'Law as discourse', *History and Anthropology* 1: 241–64

Huxley, J and Haddon, AC (1936) *We Europeans: a Survey of 'Racial' Problems*,
London: Jonathan Cape

Hymes, D (1981) *'In Vain I Tried to Tell You': Essays in Native American Poetics*,
Philadelphia: University of Pennsylvania Press

IAA (Immigration Appellate Authority) (2002) *The Role of the Interpreter in an IAA
Hearing*, www.iaa.gov.uk/Interpreters/IAA-Int-Role.htm, consulted 20 August
2002

—— (2003) *Handbook for Self-Employed Interpreters*, London: Court Service

Iacopino, V (2002) 'History taking', pp 101–15 in M Peel and V Iacopino (eds), *The
Medical Documentation of Torture*, London, San Francisco: Greenwich Medical
Media Ltd

IAS (Immigration Advisory Service) (2003) *Home Office Country Assessments: an
Analysis. December 2003 Addendum*, London: Immigration Advisory Service

ICMPD (International Centre for Migration Policy Development) (2002) *Practical
Guide to the Effective Gathering and Usage of Country of Origin Information*,
Vienna: ICMPD

ILPA (Immigration Law Practitioner's Association) (1993; 2nd edn 1997) *Directory of
Expertise on Conditions in Countries of Origin and Transit*, London: ILPA

IND (Immigration and Nationality Directorate) (1998a) *Asylum Directorate Instructions, July 1998*, www.homeoffice.gov.uk/ind/adint.htm, consulted October 1999

—— (1998b) *Country Assessment: Sri Lanka, November 1998*, London: Home Office

—— (1999) *Country Assessment: Sri Lanka, March 1999*, London: Home Office

—— (2001) *Report of CIPU Fact-Finding Mission to Sri Lanka, 9–13 July 2001*,
London: Home Office

—— (2002a) *Asylum Policy Instructions*, London: Home Office, www.ind.home
office.gov.uk/default.asp?PageId=711, consulted 15 April 2002

—— (2002b) *Report on Visit to Sri Lanka, 14–23 March 2002*, London: Home Office

—— (2002c) *Country Assessment: Sri Lanka, April 2002*, London: Home Office

—— (2002d) *Country Assessment: Nigeria, October 2002*, London: Home Office

INS (Immigration and Naturalization Service) (1995) 'Gender guidelines: considerations for Asylum Officers adjudicating asylum claims from women', *International
Journal of Refugee Law* 7: 700–19

IRB (Immigration and Refugee Board) (1993) 'Guidelines on women refugee claimants fearing gender-related persecution', *International Journal of Refugee Law* 5:
278–97

—— (1998) *Assessment of Credibility in the Context of CRDD Hearings*, Ottawa: IRB
Legal Services

—— (1999a) *Convention Refugee Determination Division Handbook*, Ottawa: IRB

—— (1999b) *Weighing Evidence*, Ottawa: IRB Legal Services

—— (2000) *Nigeria: State Protection Available to Potential Victims of Ritual Violence
or Individuals Threatened by Cult Members since the Change of Government in late*

May 1999, IRB Research Directorate, www.cisr.gc.ca/en/researchpub/research/publications/index_e.htm?id=24&cid=161, consulted 27 March 2003

Jackson, D (1999) *Immigration Law and Practice* (2nd edn), London: Sweet & Maxwell

Jackson, M (2002) *The Politics of Storytelling: Violence, Transgression and Intersubjectivity*, Copenhagen: Museum Tusculanum Press

Jarvis, C (2000) 'For these or any other reasons: an examination of judicial assessment of the credibility of asylum seekers in the United Kingdom with particular reference to the role of the immigration adjudicator', unpublished LLM dissertation, London

Jasanoff, S (1990) *The Fifth Branch: Science Advisors as Policymakers*, Cambridge MA: Harvard University Press

—— (1993) 'Bridging the two cultures of risk analysis', *Risk Analysis* 13(2): 123–9

—— (1995) *Science at the Bar: Law, Science and Technology in America*, Cambridge MA: Harvard University Press

—— (1996) 'Research subpoenas and the sociology of knowledge', *Law and Contemporary Problems* 59(3): 95–118

Jones, CAG (1994) *Expert Witnesses: Science, Medicine and the Practice of Law*, Oxford: Clarendon

Justice, ILPA, and Asylum Rights Campaign (1997) *Providing Protection: Towards Fair and Effective Asylum Procedures*, London: Justice

Kagan, M (2003) 'Is truth in the eye of the beholder? Objective credibility assessment in refugee status determinations', 17 *Georgetown Law Journal* 367

Kalin, W (1986) 'Troubled communication: cross-cultural misunderstandings in the asylum hearing', *International Migration Review* 20: 230–41

Kandel, RF (1992) 'How lawyers and anthropologists think differently', pp 1–4 in RF Kandel (ed.), *Double Vision: Anthropologists at Law*, (NAPA Bulletin, No 11) Washington: American Anthropological Association

Katz, P (1981) 'Ritual in the operating room', *Ethnology* 20: 335–50

Kemshall, H (2003) *Understanding Risk in Criminal Justice*, Maidenhead: Open University Press

Kennedy, D (1976) 'Form and substance in private law adjudication', *Harvard Law Review* 89: 1685–778

Kirsch, S (2001) 'Lost worlds: environmental disaster, "culture loss", and the law', *Current Anthropology* 42: 167–98

Koser, K and Pinkerton, C (2002) *The Social Networks of Asylum Seekers and the Dissemination of Information about Countries of Asylum*, (Home Office Research Study, 243) London: Home Office Research, Development and Statistics Directorate

Kuhn, TS (1962) *The Structure of Scientific Revolutions* (2nd edn), Chicago: University Press

Kuper, A (2001) *Culture: the Anthropologists' Account*, Cambridge MA: Harvard University Press

Kuper, L and Smith, MG (eds) (1969) *Pluralism in Africa*, Berkeley and London: University of California Press

Lal, V (1997) *From Reporter to Refugee*, Oxford: WorldView Publishing

Lambert, H (2001) 'The conceptualisation of "persecution" by the House of Lords:

Horvath v. *Secretary of State for the Home Department*', *International Journal of Refugee Law* 13: 16–31

Langness, LL and Frank, G (1981) *Lives: an Anthropological Approach to Bibliography*, Novato CA: Chandler & Sharp

Lash, S (1994) 'Reflexivity and its doubles: structure, aesthetics, community', pp 110–73 in U Beck, A Giddens and S Lash, *Reflexive Modernization: Politics, Tradition and Aesthetics in the Modern Social Order*, Stanford: University Press

Latour, B (2002) *La Fabrique du Droit: une Ethnographie du Conseil d'État*, Paris: Éditions la Découverte

—— (2004) 'Scientific objects and legal objectivity', pp 73–114 in A Pottage and M Mundy (eds), *Law, Anthropology, and the Constitution of the Social: Making Persons and Things*, Cambridge: University Press

—— and Woolgar, S (1986) *Laboratory Life: the Construction of Scientific Facts* (2nd edn), Princeton: University Press

Law Society (no date) *Guide to Instructing Experts*, www.sweetandmaxwell.co.uk/online/ew/guide.doc, consulted 15 April 2002

Leach, ER (1961) *Rethinking Anthropology*, London: Athlone Press

Leggatt, A (2001) *Tribunals for Users: One System, One Service*, London: Stationery Office

Lemke, T (2002) 'Foucault, governmentality, and critique', *Rethinking Marxism* 14(3): 49–64

Linde, C (1993) *Life Stories: the Creation of Coherence*, New York: Oxford University Press

Llewellen, K and Hoebbel, EA (1941) *The Cheyenne Way*, Norman: University of Oklahoma Press

Lord Chancellor's Department (1998) *Review of Appeals: a Consultation Paper*, www.homeoffice.gov.uk/ind/consult.htm, consulted 22 November 1999

—— (no date) *Civil Procedure Rules, Part 35: Experts and Assessors*, www.lcd.gov.uk/civil/procrules_fin/contents/parts/part35.htm, consulted 13 November 2002

Lupton, D (1999a) *Risk*, London: Routledge

—— (1999b) 'Introduction: risk and socio-cultural theory', pp 1–11 in D Lupton (ed.), *Risk and Sociocultural Theory: New Directions and Perspectives*, Cambridge: University Press

MacCormick, N (1994) *Legal Reasoning and Legal Theory*, (revised edn) Oxford: University Press

MacCrimmon, MT (1998) 'Fact determination: common sense knowledge, judicial notice, and social science evidence', *International Commentary on Evidence*, www.law.qub.ac.uk/ice/papers/judicial1.html, consulted 26 February 2002

Mahmood, CK (1996a) 'Asylum, violence, and the limits of advocacy', *Human Organization* 55: 493–8

—— (1996b) *Fighting for Faith and Nation: Dialogues with Sikh Militants*, Philadelphia: University of Pennsylvania Press

Maine, HS (1861) *Ancient Law*, London: John Murray

Maley, Y (1994) 'The language of the law', pp 11–50 in J Gibbons (ed.), *Language and the Law*, London: Longman

Malinowski, B (1926) *Crime and Custom in Savage Society*, New York: Harcourt Brace

Malkki, LH (1995) 'Refugees and exile: from "refugee studies" to the national order of things', *Annual Review of Anthropology* 24: 495–523

Mason, E (2001a) *Guide to Country Research for Refugee Status Information*, www.llrx.com/features/rsd.htm, consulted 1 August 2001

—— (2001b) *Annex: Human Rights, Country and Legal Information Resources on the Internet*, www.llrx.com/features/rsd_bib.htm, consulted 1 August 2001

McBarnet, D (1981) *Conviction: Law, the State and the Construction of Justice*, Oxford: Macmillan

McDowell, C (1996) *A Tamil Asylum Diaspora: Sri Lankan Migration, Settlement and Politics in Switzerland*, Oxford: Berghahn

McGhee, D (2001) 'Persecution and social group status: homosexual refugees in the 1990s', *Journal of Refugee Studies* 14(1): 20–43

McKinley, M (1997) 'Life stories, disclosure and the law', *Polar: Political and Legal Anthropology Review*. 20(2): 70–82

Medical Foundation (1999a) *Lives Under Threat: a Study of Sikhs Coming to the UK from the Punjab*, London: Medical Foundation

—— (1999b) *Staying Alive by Accident: Torture Survivors from Turkey in the UK*, London: Medical Foundation

—— (2000) *Caught in the Middle: a Study of Tamil Torture Survivors coming to the UK from Sri Lanka*, London: Medical Foundation

Mellinkoff, D (1963) *The Language of the Law*, Boston: Little, Brown & Co

Merry, SE (1988) 'Legal pluralism', *Law and Society Review* 22: 869–96

—— (1990) *Getting Justice and Getting Even: Legal Consciousness Among Working-class Americans*, Chicago: University Press

Mertz, E (2002) 'Performing epistemology: notes on language, law school, and Yovel's legal-linguistic culture', *Stanford Agora* 3, www.law.stanford.edu/agora/volume2/mertz.shtml, consulted 29 December 2002

Messer, E (1993) 'Anthropology and human rights', *Annual Reviews of Anthropology* 22: 221–49

Michigan Guidelines (1999) *The Michigan Guidelines on the Internal Protection Alternative*, University of Michigan Law School, www.refugee.org.nz/Guidelines.htm, consulted 11 January 2005

Mikkelson, H (1998) 'Towards a redefinition of the role of the court interpreter', *Interpreting* 3(1): 21–45

—— (no date, a) 'Verbatim interpretation: an oxymoron', www.acebo.com/papers/verbatim.htm, consulted 1 February 2004

—— (no date, b) 'Court interpreting at a crossroads', www.acebo.com/papers/crossr~1.htm, consulted 14 November 2002

Moore, SF (1973) 'Law and social change: the semi-autonomous social field as an appropriate subject of study', *Law and Society Review* Summer 1973: 719–46 [also in Moore (1978): 54–81 (q.v.)]

—— (1978) *Law as Process: an Anthropological Approach*. Oxford: University Press

Morison, J and Leith, P (1992) *The Barrister's World and the Nature of Law*, Buckingham: Open University Press

Morris, R (1995) 'The moral dilemmas of court interpreting', *The Translator* 1(1): 25–46

Morrison, J (1998) *The Cost of Survival: the Trafficking of Refugees to the UK*, London: Refugee Council

Morton Williams, P (1960) 'The Yoruba Ogboni cult in Oyo', *Africa* 30(4): 362–74

Moser, C (1993) *Gender Planning and Development: Theory, Practice and Training*, London: Routledge

Muller-Hoff, C (2001) 'Representations of refugee women: legal discourse in Europe', *Law, Social Justice and Global Development Journal* 2001(1), http://elj.warwick. ac.uk/global/issue/2001–1/mullerhoff1.html, consulted 30 January 2004

Murphy, KM and Cuccias, MJ (1997) 'The application of Daubert or Frye analysis to expert testimony in the "soft sciences" ', *Federation of Defense and Corporate Counsel Quarterly* 47(3), Spring, www.thefederation.org/Public/Quarterly/ Spring97/MURPHY.html, consulted 26 December 2002

Murphy, P (2003) *Murphy on Evidence* (8th edn), Oxford: University Press

Musalo, K (2002) *Claims for Protection Based on Religion or Belief: Analysis and Proposed Conclusions*, (Legal and Protection Policy Research Series: doc. PPLA/ 2002/01) Geneva: UNHCR

—— and Knight, S (2001) 'Steps forward and steps back: uneven progress in the law of social group and gender-based claims in the United States', *International Journal of Refugee Law* 13(1/2): 51–70

NAPA (National Association for the Practice of Anthropology) (1988) 'Ethical Guidelines for Practitioners', *Anthropology Newsletter*, November 1988: 8–9, www.aaanet.org/napa/code.htm, consulted 27 November 2005

National Audit Office (2004) *Improving the Speed and Quality of Asylum Decisions* (HC535), London: Stationery Office.

Needham, R (1975) 'Polythetic classification: convergence and consequences', *Man* (N.S.) 10: 349–69

O'Barr, WM (1982) *Linguistic Evidence: Language, Power and Strategy in the Courtroom*, New York: Academic Press

—— (2001) 'Culture and causality: non-western systems of explanation', *Law and Contemporary Problems* 64(4): 317–23

O'Nions, H (1999) 'Bonafide or bogus? Roma asylum seekers from the Czech Republic', *Web Journal of Current Legal Issues* 1999(3), http://webjcli.ncl.ac.uk/ 1999/issue3/onions3.html, consulted 3 January 2003

Paine, R (ed.) (1985) *Advocacy and Anthropology: First Encounters*, St John's: Memorial University of Newfoundland

Parmentier, RJ (1986) 'The political function of reported speech: a Beluan example', unpublished manuscript cited in Conley and O'Barr 1990b: 196n

Pearl, D and Menski, W (1998) *Muslim Family Law*, London: Sweet & Maxwell

Peel, M (1998) 'Problems in medical report writing for asylum seekers', pp 152–7 in F Nicholson and P Twomey (eds), *Current Issues of UK Asylum Law and Policy*, Aldershot: Ashgate

—— (2002) 'Male sexual abuse in detention', pp 179–90 in M Peel and V Iacopino (eds), *The Medical Documentation of Torture*, London and San Francisco: Greenwich Medical Media Ltd

——, Mahtani, A, Hinshelwood, G and Forrest, D (2000) 'The sexual abuse of men in detention in Sri Lanka', *The Lancet* 355 (9220): 2068–9

Peterson, DW and Conley, JM (2001) 'Of cherries, fudge, and onions: science and its courtroom perversion', *Law and Contemporary Problems* 64(4): 213–40

Phelan, M (2001) *Immigration Law Handbook* (2nd edn), London: Blackstone Press

Pirouet, L (2001) *Whatever Happened to Asylum in Britain? A Tale of Two Walls*, Oxford: Berghahn

Polanyi, M (1958) *Personal Knowledge*, Chicago: University Press

Popper, K (1989) *Conjectures and Refutations: the Growth of Scientific Knowledge* (4th edn), London: Routledge & Kegan Paul

Porter, T (1995) *Trust in Numbers: the Pursuit of Objectivity in Science and Public Life*, Princeton: University Press

Pospisil, LJ (1971) *The Anthropology of Law: a Comparative Theory*, New York: Harper & Row

Radcliffe-Brown, AR (1935) 'Patrilineal and matrilineal succession', *The Iowa Law Review* 20: 286–303

—— (1945) 'Religion and society', *Journal of the Royal Anthropological Institute* 75: 33–43

—— (1950) 'Introduction', pp 1–85 in AR Radcliffe-Brown and D Forde (eds), *African Systems of Kinship and Marriage*, London: Oxford University Press

—— (1952) *Structure and Function in Primitive Society*, London: Cohen & West

RDS (Research Development and Statistics Directorate) (2003a) *Country of Origin Information: a User and Content Evaluation*, (Home Office Research Study, 271) London: Home Office

—— (2003b) *Information on Asylum Seekers' Country of Origin: an Evaluation of its Content and Usefulness*, (Findings, 211) London: Home Office

Redfield, R (1947) 'Testimony in *Sweatt* v. *Painter*', www.law.du.edu/russell/lh/sweatt/docs/svptr2.htm#redfield, consulted 19 September 2002

Redmayne, M (2001) *Expert Evidence and Criminal Justice*, Oxford: University Press

RWLG (Refugee Women's Legal Group) (1998) *Gender Guidelines for the Determination of Asylum Claims in the UK*, London: RWLG

Renaker, TS (1996) 'Evidentiary legerdemain: deciding when Daubert should apply to social science evidence', 84 *Calif. L. Rev.* 1657

Rigby, P and Sevareid, P (1992) 'Lawyers, anthropologists, and the knowledge of fact', pp 5–21 in RF Kandel (ed.), *Double Vision: Anthropologists at Law*, (NAPA Bulletin, No 11) Washington DC: American Anthropological Association

Roberts, P (1999) 'Tyres with a "Y": an English perspective on Kumho Tire and its implications for the admissibility of expert evidence', *International Commentary on Evidence*, www.law.qub.ac.uk/ice/papers/expert1.html, consulted 26 February 2002

Robinson, V and Segrott, J (2002) *Understanding the Decision Making of Asylum Seekers*, (Home Office Research Study, 243) London: Home Office Research, Development and Statistics Directorate

Robinson, V, Anderson, R and Musterd, S (2003) *Spreading the 'Burden'? A Review of Policies to Disperse Asylum Seekers and Refugees*, Bristol: Policy Press

Rock, P (1993) *The Social World of an English Crown Court*, Oxford: Clarendon

Rosaldo, R (1976) 'The story of Tukbaw: "they listen as he orates" ', pp 121–51 in F Reynolds and D Capps (eds), *The Biographical Process: Studies in the History and Psychology of Religion*, Paris/The Hague: Mouton

Rosen, L (1977) 'The anthropologist as expert witness', *American Anthropologist* 79: 555–78

—— (1989) *The Anthropology of Justice: Law as Culture in Islamic Society*, Cambridge: University Press

Rouland, N (1994) *Legal Anthropology*, Stanford: University of California Press

Rousseau, C, Crépeau, F, Foxen, P and Houle, F (2002) 'The complexity of determining refugeehood: a multidisciplinary analysis of the decision-making process of
the Canadian Immigration and Refugee Board', *Journal of Refugee Studies* 15(1):
43–70

Royal Society (1992) *Risk: Analysis, Perception and Management*, London: The Royal
Society

Ruppel, J (1991) 'The need for a benefit of the doubt standard in credibility evaluation
of asylum applicants', *Columbia Human Rights Law Review* 23: 1ff

Rycroft, R (2005) 'Multi-authorship of asylum accounts: an interpreter's perspective',
paper presented at '*Breaking down the barriers: a team effort*', conference on public
service interpreting, Heriot-Watt University, Edinburgh

Sahlins, MD (1965) 'On the ideology and composition of descent groups', *Man* 1965,
104–7

Said, E (1991) *Orientalism*, Harmondsworth: Penguin Books

Sanjek, R (1996) 'Race', pp 462–5 in A Barnard and J Spencer (eds), *Encyclopedia of
Social and Cultural Anthropology*, London: Routledge

Sarat, A and Felstiner, WL (1990) 'Legal realism in lawyer–client communication',
pp 133–51 in JN Levi and AG Walker (eds), *Language in the Judicial Process*,
New York: Plenum Press

Scannell, R (1999) 'Asylum and people at risk', pp 73–91 in N Blake and L Fransman
(eds), *Immigration, Nationality and Asylum under the Human Rights Act 1998*,
London: Butterworths

Scarry, E (1985) *The Body in Pain*, Oxford: University Press

Scheffler, HW (1966) 'Ancestor worship in anthropology: or, observations on descent
and descent groups', *Current Anthropology* 7: 541–51

Schuster, L (2003) *The Use and Abuse of Political Asylum in Britain and Germany*,
London: Frank Cass

—— and Solomos, J (1999) 'The politics of refugee and asylum policies in Britain:
historical patterns and contemporary realities', pp 51–75 in A Bloch and C Levy
(eds), *Refugees, Citizenship and Social Policy in Europe*, London: Macmillan

Schwandner-Sievers, S (2005) ' "Culture" in court: Albanian migrants and the
anthropologist as expert witness', pp 209–28 in S Pink (ed.), *Applications of
Anthropology: Professional Anthropology in the Twenty-First Century*, Oxford:
Berghahn

Skultans, V (1974) *Intimacy and Ritual: a Study of Spiritualism, Mediums and Groups*,
London: Routledge & Kegan Paul

Sokolovskii, S and Tishkov, V (1996) 'Ethnicity', pp 190–2 in A Barnard and J Spencer
(eds), *Encyclopedia of Social and Cultural Anthropology*, London: Routledge

Solan, LM (1993) *The Language of Judges*, Chicago: University Press

Southwold, M (1978) 'Buddhism and the definition of religion', *Man* (N.S.) 13:
362–79

Speaight, A (1996) 'Seven essentials', *New Law Journal* 146: 1100–2

Spijkerboer, T (2000) *Gender and Refugee Status*, Aldershot: Ashgate

Stevens, D (2004) *UK Asylum Law and Policy: Historical and Contemporary
Perspectives*, London: Sweet & Maxwell

Storey, H (1998) 'The "internal flight alternative" (IFA) test and the concept of
protection', pp 100–32 in F Nicholson and P Twomey (eds), *Current Issues of UK
Asylum Law and Policy*, Aldershot: Ashgate

Symes, M (2001) *Caselaw on the Refugee Convention: the United Kingdom's Interpretation in the Light of the International Authorities*, London: Refugee Legal Centre

—— and Jorro, PA (2003) *Asylum Law and Practice*, London: LexisNexis

Tambiah, SJ (1973) 'Form and meaning of magical acts: a point of view', pp 199–230 in R Horton and R Finnegan (eds), *Modes of Thought: Essays on Thinking in Western and Non-Western Societies*, London: Faber & Faber

Thayer, JB (1969) *Treatise on Evidence at Common Law*, New York: Rothman Reprints

Thomas, R (2003) 'The impact of judicial review on asylum', *Public Law* Autumn: 479–510

—— (forthcoming) 'Assessing the credibility of asylum claims: EU and UK approaches examined', *European Journal of Migration and Law*

Thuen, T (2004) 'Anthropological knowledge in the courtroom: conflicting paradigms', *Social Anthropology* 12(3): 265–87

Travers, M (1999) *The British Immigration Courts: a Study of Law and Politics*, Bristol: Policy Press

Trost, R and Billings, P (1998) 'The designation of "safe" countries and individual assessment of asylum claims', pp 73–99 in F Nicholson and P Twomey (eds), *Current Issues of UK Asylum Law and Policy*, Aldershot: Ashgate

Turner, S (1995) 'Torture, refuge, and trust', pp 56–72 in EV Daniel and JC Knudsen (eds), *Mistrusting Refugees*, Berkeley: University of California Press

Turner, T (1997) 'Human rights, human difference: anthropology's contribution to an emancipatory cultural politics', *Journal of Anthropological Research* 53: 273–91

Tylor, EB (1871) *Primitive Culture* (2 vols), London: John Murray

UNHCR (1992) *Handbook on Procedures and Criteria for Determining Refugee Status*, Geneva: UNHCR

—— (2002a) *Statistical Yearbook 2001: Refugees, Asylum-seekers and Other Persons of Concern: Trends in Displacement, Protection and Solutions*, Geneva: UNHCR

—— (2002b) *Gender-related Persecution*, (Guidelines on International Protection, 1. Doc. HCR/GIP/02/01.) Geneva: UNHCR

—— (2002c) *Membership of a Particular Social Group*, (Guidelines on International Protection, 2. Doc. HCR/GIP/02/02.) Geneva: UNHCR

—— (2004) *Refugees by Numbers, 2004*, www.unhcr.ch, consulted 20 November 2005

von Benda-Beckmann, K and Strijbosch, F (eds) (1986) *Anthropology of Law in the Netherlands: Essays on Legal Pluralism*, Dordrecht: Foris

Wade, P (ed.) (1995) *Advocacy in Anthropology*, Manchester: Group for Debates in Anthropological Theory

Walker, AG (1990) 'Language at work in the law: the customs, conventions, and appellate consequences of court reporting', pp 203–44 in JN Levi and AG Walker (eds), *Language in the Judicial Process*, New York: Plenum Press

Weber, M (1963) *The Sociology of Religion*, Boston: Beacon Press

Weiner, JF (1999) 'Culture in a sealed envelope: the concealment of Australian Aboriginal heritage and tradition in the Hindmarsh Island bridge affair', *Journal of the Royal Anthropological Institute (N.S.)* 5: 193–210

West, R (1988) 'Jurisprudence and gender', *University of Chicago Law Review* 55: 1–72

Weston, A (1998) ' "A witness of truth": credibility findings in asylum appeals', *Immigration and Nationality Law and Practice* 12(3): 87

Wilson, AJ with Chandrakanthan, AJ (1998) 'Tamil identities and aspirations', in *Demanding Sacrifice: War and Negotiation in Sri Lanka. (Accord: International Review Of Peace Initiatives*, 4) www.c-r.org/accord/sri/accord4/tamil_identity.shtml, consulted 29 May 2004

Wilson, RA (ed.) (1997) *Human Rights, Culture and Context: Anthropological Perspectives*, London: Pluto Press

—— and Mitchell, J (eds) (2003) *Human Rights in Global Perspective: Anthropological Studies of Rights, Claims and Entitlements*, (ASA Monographs, 49) London: Routledge

Winslow, M (1981[1862]) *A Comprehensive Tamil and English Dictionary*, New Delhi: Asian Educational Services

Woolf, Lord (1996) *Access to Justice: Final Report to the Lord Chancellor on the Civil Justice System in England and Wales*, London: Stationary Office

Wynne, B (1996) 'May the sheep safely graze? A reflexive view of the expert–lay knowledge divide', pp 44–83 in S Lash, B Szerszynski and B Wynne (eds), *Risk, Environment and Modernity: Towards a New Ecology*, London: Sage

Yanagisako, SJ and Collier, JF (1987) 'Toward a unified analysis of gender and kinship', pp 1–34 in JF Collier and SJ Yanagisako (eds), *Gender and Kinship: Essays towards a Unified Analysis*, Stanford: University Press

Yeo, C (2005a) 'Introduction', pp 7–8 in C Yeo (ed.), *Country Guideline Cases: Benign and Practical?*, London: Immigration Advisory Service

Yeo, C (2005b) 'Certainty, consistency and justice', pp 9–29 in C Yeo (ed.), *Country Guideline Cases: Benign and Practical?*, London: Immigration Advisory Service

Index